The KPT Bryce™ Book

Susan A. Kitchens

Addison-Wesley Publishing Company

Reading, Massachusetts • Menlo Park, California • New York
Don Mills, Ontario • Wokingham, England • Amsterdam
Bonn • Sydney • Singapore • Tokyo • Madrid • San Juan
Paris • Seoul • Milan • Mexico City • Taipei

Library of Congress Cataloging-in-Publication Data

Kitchens, Susan A.
    The KPT Bryce book / Susan A. Kitchens.
        p.   cm.
    Includes index.
    ISBN 0-201-48355-6
    1. Computer graphics. 2. KPT Bryce. 3. Title.
T385.K493   1995
006.6'869--dc20   95-20206
                                    CIP

Sponsoring Editor: Martha Steffen
Project Manager: Sarah Weaver
Production Coordinator: Erin Sweeney
Cover design: Jean Seal
Cover illustration: Susan A. Kitchens
Text design: Greg Johnson, Art Directions
Set in 11.5 point Minion by Greg Johnson, Art Directions

2 3 4 5 6 7 8 9 10–MA–9998979695
Second printing, October 1995

Addison-Wesley books are available for bulk purchases by corporations, institutions, and other organizations. For more information please contact the Corporate, Government, and Special Sales Department at (800) 238-9682.

In memory of Jeffry Michael Kessinger,

. . . fellow explorer of virtual worlds,

. . . one who sought to make *this* world a better one.

Requiescat en pacem.

Contents

Acknowledgments

Before writing this book (my first), I've heard others compare book writing to having a baby. I cannot testify to the latter from personal experience, but I am convinced that the analogy fits. The one difference is that during the months of a book's gestation, one is both genetic engineer as well as expectant parent. In the case of humans, as the offspring changes from zygote to fetus to infant, the leg bone somehow gets connected to the thigh bone without conscious thought on the part of the expectant mother. Not so the expectant author. The skeleton, muscles, and which-gets-connected-where are all the result of exacting conscious thought. Book gestation is the most consuming time, filled with sleepless nights. But when it's done, there are no late-night feedings, nor does the book need to be potty trained!

Although book-creation occurs in seclusion with a computer, the software, keyboard, and word-processor, there are untold contributions by others without which this book would never have seen the light of day.

Special thanks to Kai Krause, for his response to an overly detailed email query I first sent him about one of his Photoshop tips uploaded on America Online, and for everything that followed. This book is, in a sense, the logical progression of that initial correspondence.

Thanks also go to Eric Wenger, for the vision of creating natural landscape scenery, without which none of this—the software or this book—would have happened. Eric made it possible to have an extended dialog about the software and working methods, and especially to dissect the Deep Texture Editor.

Thanks go to those at HSC Software who assisted in numerous ways, especially Phil Clevenger, Rob Sonner, Paul Fritz, Sarah Elder, and John Wilczak. In addition, Ben Weiss was my math tutor, answering math-o-phobe questions and checking certain technical passages for accuracy. Scott Fegette helped me tidy up some structural elements of the book. Julie Sigwart read major portions of the manuscript and offered valuable suggestions.

There were those who shared their expertise in other areas. I sat under the tutelage of Mike McDowell for the Geology 101 section. Jim Potter shared his insights on 68K and Power PC processor differences, and math coprocessors in particular.

Ken Badertscher contributed enormously to my understanding of what DEMs are and how they work. Moreover, he wrote the software DEMview—especially created to make Bryce terrains from USGS digital elevation models. Thanks go to the individuals and companies who also contributed software for the book's CD: Sean Barger, Dave Theurer, and Cara Ucci at Equilibrium for Debabelizer Lite; Lisa Cleary at Adobe Systems for Photoshop and Illustrator tryout versions; Peter Lee for Peter's Player; and to Craig Clevenger and Greg Ogarrio at HSC Software for the Kai's Power Tools sample plug-in collection.

Thanks to Jan Sanford at Pixar, and to Mike Murdock, who contributed a tutorial with techniques for using Bryce with Pixar products.

Thanks to Mark Jaress, for some computer equipment loans that saved my… well, that helped me out when I was in dire need; to Ron Kinsey for the use of a DAT drive; and to Liz Delgado, whose color printer came in handy for proofing during the manuscript stage.

The community of people who participate in the Bryce dialog on AOL contributed to this book with their comments, questions, frustrations, and discoveries about Bryce. There were many who shared generously from their experiences. In particular, the contributions of Rodney Kieth and Victor von Salza, both in the area of animation, have added greatly to the wealth of information here. In addition, there are many whose work is featured in the gallery on the CD. Thanks also to those whose work is featured in these pages.

Barbara Garrett, Lester Eisel, Mary Janss Forrest, Joyce Gruman, Jackson Ting, and Robert Bailey read manuscript portions for clarity. Major thanks go to Karen Schoeni, who input manuscript changes, and major major thanks go to Chris Casady, who also input changes and prepared all those images for the Bryce gallery on the CD.

Thanks to those at Addison-Wesley, especially Martha Steffen, Kaethin Prizer, and Sarah (Mistress of the Schedule) Weaver; to Laura (make it consistent) Michaels of Montview Publications; and to Greg Johnson of Art Directions. They've been a pleasure to work with.

Thanks to friends and family for support and encouragement, and to Haley and Andrew, who graciously allowed their Auntie Susan to be consumed by her other persona, AuntiAlias, during the course of this project.

Susan Aimée Kitchens
auntialias@aol.com

Foreword

Once upon a time, there was a man in Paris with a vision: He would make a software program that could generate landscapes! Subtle ones, real ones, terrains with erosion, fog and mist and refracted waves and complex surfaces, reflecting textures, tinted atmosphere, the *works*. At first it was a whimsy that he—Eric Wenger— created for his own fun alone.

Once upon five years later, as the program was spitting out beauty at the rate of one image every other day, there was a man with another vision: He would make this software available to actual humans out there! Subtle ones, real ones, reflecting Texans and Californians and waves of others, would surface, lured by the erosionous zones and the general fun atmosphere. And he—Kai Krause—designed an interface for his own fun alone.

The program was called Bryce, after the really surreal real canyon out in Utah.

Within weeks it became the cult hit out in the Mac software scene. It entered the top ten list of all graphics software in the #4 spot (measured by dollar volume) and lingered there for months. We set the intro price at $99, and we included a pretty deep manual and even a CD ROM, with hundreds of scenes to get the user started.

That ease of entry, the pricing strategy by HSC CEO John Wilczak, and the philosophy to let even total non-3D beginners to get into the game let Bryce quickly penetrate whole new circles of users: Not only the "I-need-3D" architects, CAD users, and designers, but even whole classes of school children and laymen and -women got into the act! Several hundred Beta users were in on the secret forum room for Bryce and made nearly 800 images before the software was ever even released.... In short: it really really worked, more so than anyone would have thought, including the author himself, Eric.

Twice upon that saga, there was a woman who entered the picture.

First she joined me as an employee at HSC Software in the very early KPT days. She saw our first baby, Kai's Power Tools, come to life back in 1992. Within a mere 15 months we rocketed through a series of whirlwind transitions. (As of this writing in the spring of '95 HSC went from a handful to over 100 souls running the ship.)

She has more mileage on KPT from the inside out than almost anyone else, being product manager, then art director and co-lecturer, designer, and writer. She co-authored and designed the KPT manual and, when Bryce came out, she designed and illustrated its manual.

Then she put on a new hat: Realizing just how much more was hidden inside the software and how much beauty and subtlety was attainable, she pursued her love of learning new things and then sharing those with others. So here she is now in her newest role. No longer an employee but on her own, sailing a ship of one through these new waters, she—Susan Kitchens—wrote a book to explore the extreme depths of the software for her own fun alone.

Bryce is the kind of program that benefits more than most from having deeper information available. Rarely is the spectrum of possible outcome so vast and at the same time so linked to understanding what is going on underneath the hood. Many tens of thousands of users are reaching certain levels of expertise all on their own, and most will be delighted by getting a booster stage on that rocket: This book has a wealth of information on how to make those killer images that—until now—only Eric Wenger, as Bryce's author, has been capable of. (Eric was helping out here, too, of course.)

The special aspect to consider here is that aside from all the easily controlled options on the top layers (it wasn't really easy to make it that easy, thank you very much), there are a wealth of additional subtle controls that, in the end, make all the difference in the world to go from "nice" to "spectacular" imagery. This is a key to the great benefit that Susan's book can bring: She *will* be able to transfer these new lofty heights of imagery to each reader!

Bryce has one unique advantage here: In a paint program, and indeed in most applications, the skill of the user cannot be transferred easily. There is no shortcut to experience. You cannot just "copy" your friend's ability to paint. In a completely algorithmic program like

Bryce, however, the benefits of one person's persistence and ingenuity can become everyone's benefit that very same day :). When one Beta person made a chocolate Hershey's Mountain texture, suddenly everyone was able to pick that as one more choice to be applied to any object from then on....

Not only has Susan taken you through those layers of subtlety to lofty new heights of imagery, but she's found a long list of such special overachievers venturing into new areas of Brycean excellence. The inclusion of the CD ROM chock full with material will make it not only easy and fast but downright pleasurable to upgrade yourself.

Many of the deeper parts of the book describe parts of Bryce that have not really been publicly exposed before. Some are the results of Eric Wenger's explaining some of the inner workings in a way that maybe even he himself had not heard before (hey, that's a good one ;)). The reader is invited to peek into the deepest recesses under the hood and, empowered with that extra level of understanding, one can really get to a new level of *aha!* for all parts of the program.

If you are using the program even just once in a while, it can multiply your pleasure factor. If you are doing *any* kind of real art or professional commercial projects (such as the numerous CD ROMs, backgrounds, advertising, game mattes, etc.) it can *seriously* enhance your results.

This is the best way to think of this book:

It is really a very inexpensive upgrade to Bryce, a kind of Bryce 1.2!

Kai Krause
Executive Vice President, HSC Software

1

Introduction

When you get the thing dead right and know it's dead right, there's no excitement like it. It's marvelous. It makes you feel like God on the Seventh Day—for a bit, anyhow.

Dorothy L. Sayers, *Gaudy Night*

The History of KPT Bryce

KPT Bryce (Bryce, for short) is the brainchild of Eric Wenger, a talented artist, musician, and programmer from France. The son of a geologist, Eric grew up with a sensitivity to Earth's form and environs. That kind of sensitivity was combined with an artist's careful, observing eye. I saw a landscape triptych of the American southwest desert painted by Eric. To put down all those details on canvas requires that one *see* them. The exacting scrutiny required in the art of drawing and painting led to the creation of software that makes such realistic images.

Eric wrote this software on the side, while working at other tasks. (Notable among those was the creation of the software application ArtMixer.) It was a personal pursuit, a digital form of grinding his own pigments and mixing with binder to make paint so that landscape pictures could be painted onscreen. Instead of cadmium, cobalt, and oxide of chromium, Eric worked with new discoveries of fractal geometry for generating rugged mountainous terrains. Adapting the sound synthesizer model to synthesize visual noise, he developed an intricate means of putting realistic surfaces on those rugged terrains. He built an entire world in which to place those surfaces and other objects, with lightsource and atmospheric effects of clouds, haze, and fog. He culminated the process by using the ray-tracing renderer as the binder to adhere mathematical "pigment" to the computer monitor's "canvas."

Although Eric was by no means a "Sunday painter," this was nevertheless a private pursuit. Eric wrote the software for himself—the result of, and for the sake of, his artistic, observing eye.

He showed his software to his friend Pierre Bretagnolle, who, in turn, brought it to the attention of Andreas Pfeiffer, the editor of France's largest Macintosh magazine, *SVM Mac*. Pfeiffer was instrumental in introducing Eric and his landscape application to John Wilczak and Kai Krause of HSC Software. From this introduction grew the partnership that brought Eric's personal creation into a form for the general public.

Kai had a vision and an observer's eye no less exacting than Eric's. He, however, concentrated in a different area—creating user interfaces that put a friendly face on top of powerful features without bogging down the user in the complex details. Kai had through his Kai's Power Tools pioneered the precedent-setting new standards for user interfaces that provide tons of functionality while hiding the underlying mathematical complexity. So, continuing in this vein, he worked with Eric to make Bryce an application that is easy to use. As a result of the shell he created for Bryce, a beginner can get a quick start from the preset combination palettes and in only a matter of minutes be on the way to creating a new Brycean world.

Kai made the interface three dimensional so that a user can instinctively reach for this control or that knob to do this technique or that manipulation. The five main palettes divide the flow of work according to their logical sequence. The Master Palette holds the keys to the other palettes and the most important controls for viewing your scene. It also brings preset skies, grounds, and terrains into the scene. The other four palettes divide the flow of Bryce into the four steps of the Bryce process:

1. Creating objects in the Create Palette
2. Editing those objects in the Edit Palette
3. Designing the environment in the Sky & Fog Palette
4. Rendering the scene in the Render Palette

The other hidden part of this equation is the computing power. Although Bryce is easy to use, this doesn't mean the technology behind it is simple, trivial stuff. The mathematics that underlie it are staggering. So staggering, in fact, that the program would not run on computers that only a few years ago were state of the art. Today, with the faster 030 and 040 Macintoshes, and now especially with the Power Macintosh, the means to create one's own worlds is available to a wide population.

Yet, the 1.0 version of the software was not the culmination of the dynamic creative process by Eric and Kai (aided by Phil Clevenger and others at HSC Software). More was yet to come. More features, especially animation and the ability to import three-dimensional models created by other applications. And more ease of use, such as additional work on the interface design to make the Bryce technology even easier to use. Rather, release of version 1.0 signaled that it was a time to call a halt to the development process, to draw a line in the sand and say, "This is it. Let's introduce it to the public. Let's put Bryce out there."

Why "Bryce"?

Why is this software called Bryce? In the southern part of Utah is a national park called Bryce Canyon (see Fig. 1–1C in the color section). The park is a place of fantastic geological columnar formations, called hoodoos, that were created by millennia of erosion. The formations look like fanciful images, and many are named for the myths and legends and images that are evoked by their shapes.

Bryce Canyon is not really a canyon; it is a rim, with a drop-off into a deep valley. The high elevation (over 8,000 feet) and high level of precipitation result in snow and freezing temperatures for more than half the year. Because of the daily cycle of freeze and thaw, water works its way into the rock formations and expands as it freezes in the rock crevasses. In the daytime, with each thaw, the water runs off, taking with it a tiny bit of rock. This process produces the crevasses and formations of the hoodoo. The play of light on these formations in the early morning and late afternoon creates dramatic vistas. You can hike down from the rim in and among the tall hoodoos deep into a wonderland filled with discovery that stirs the imagination.

Wandering into a natural place of mystery—this is Bryce the place. KPT Bryce the software, which enables you to create your own fantastic creations, is named for that park. It is software that allows you to make your own landscapes—personal visions of mystery and wonder.

An Emotional Experience

Those visions of mystery and wonder are integral to the experience of working in Bryce. One time when I had the opportunity to work side-by-side with Eric, we talked about the software and its success. He asked me why I thought it is so popular. I answered without hesitation, "It's the emotional experience that comes from working with it." And there *is* an excitement to working in Bryce. From the first click on the Terrain icon on the Create Palette, to watching the erosion process unfold in front of you in the Terrain Editor, to adjusting the clouds and haze to be *just so,* to the satisfaction at getting the surface appearance just right, to solving a problem or discovering a new way to do something, to being mesmerized while watching each successive render pass as more and more detail emerges—there is something inherently satisfying about the creative process of working in Bryce.

What This Book Covers

This book covers KPT Bryce 1.0.1, the "fat binary" version that runs on 68K Macintoshes and Power Macintoshes. It is the product of my own keen observer's eye as I've sought to answer the questions, "What does it do?" and "What can I do with it?" I observe its behavior and tell you what it does.

While I apply my behaviorist eye to the software, I am assuming a couple of things. I assume you know how to use your Macintosh computer. If you don't, please refer to the documentation that came with it.

I also assume that you have looked through the *KPT Bryce Explorer's Guide* (the manual) and have at least done the "Whirlwind Tour" at the beginning. Although there is sufficient overlap with the manual to get you oriented, this book takes up where the manual leaves off. If you're new to Bryce, you'll get the background on some key concepts, but this book will push you onto the "Bryce Power User" track.

Bryce lets you get into a complex world—not as complex as our own, but complex nonetheless. In Bryce, everything is related to everything else. There's a risk of making oversimplifications while looking at the big picture or getting mired in the detail while exploring all the possibilities. I take an approach that cruises between these two risks, giving a look at the big picture while examining plenty of detail. Because everything is related to everything else, however, there are some cross-references that take you back to that chapter over there and to this chapter over here.

Here's a basic rundown of what you'll find in each chapter:

Chapter 2—System Requirements for Using Bryce: Here I do an initial bit of housekeeping. I discuss the details of hardware requirements, what you can do to make Bryce run smoothly on your machine, and what you need to get to make Bryce run on your Mac if you find that you cannot run it.

Chapter 3—Camera and Scene: In this chapter, I delve into the concept of camera and scene, discussing ray tracing, and, since we're talking about cameras, how to use the camera controls.

Chapter 4—Streamline Bryce Working: Here I present a global perspective of the work process in Bryce, all the while sounding the refrain, "Make it efficient." That is, set up your work so as to reduce unnecessary render time. I also discuss some Bryce application behavior that's consistent throughout the software.

Chapter 5—Selecting and Editing Controls: In this chapter, I take you to the Edit Palette, where you explore the unseen grid structure of Bryce and all of the controls. Here's where you'll find everything you need to know in order to manipulate your objects within Bryce Space.

Chapter 6—Skies and Light: Here I dissect a complex set of colors and sky conditions, exploring each in detail so that you know what it does and how it works to give you your atmosphere and mood lighting.

Chapter 7—Terrains, Terrains, Terrains: In this chapter, I show you how to edit terrains in the Terrain Editor, from the most straight-forward mountains to the innovative grayscale-to-height creations.

Chapter 8—Material World: Here, in the deepest chapter of the bunch, I delve into all those things that go into defining the surface of your objects. For the first time, I reveal the secrets of the Deep Texture Editor.

Chapter 9—Superlative Nature Imagery: In this chapter, I examine scenes and draw conclusions about the best way to make scenery that imitates nature.

Chapter 10—Multiple Object Construction: Here I cover nonscenery images, that is, tricks for creating more complex objects from Bryce primitives.

Chapter 11—Brycing Out of This World: In this chapter, I cover space scenes and a few other assorted odds and ends.

Chapter 12—Render unto Bryce: Here I give some background on how render works, tips for rendering, and some ideas for using the other render options.

Chapter 13—Printing Bryce Images: No, there's no print command in Bryce. But you'll want to get your images off your monitor screen and onto paper. In this chapter, I introduce the concept and hazards of transferring an image from the screen to a color print.

Chapter 14—What's Wrong with This Picture?: Here I offer a diagnosis of the most common problems in creating Bryce images and tell you how to fix them.

And finally, the CD. Tucked into the back cover of this tome is a little plastic disc. Take it out and look at what's on it; there's so much more to be seen. Many of the scenes used in the illustrations are included on the CD so that you can go in and poke around yourself to see what's what. There's also a host of other goodies on it. Some animations and tips, list files, some sample tryout software, resources such as presets, scenes by others using Bryce, more in-depth resource files of things seen in this book, and more. If you don't have a CD ROM drive, then beg, borrow . . . well, see if you can get your hands on something that will enable you to take a look at the CD's contents.

A Final Word . . .

As a final word, please be an observer. Let what you are doing in Bryce aid your observing our world out there and let the world out there aid in your observing what you're doing in Bryce.

And let this book hang out and be your companion while you work. I trust you will find my observations and explanations to be of value.

Most important, please play. You probably are reading this book because you're already having fun with the software. I certainly have had fun with Bryce while writing this book, and I recorded my observations in a spirit of the playfulness that is a part of the software, and, indeed, a part of the creative process in general. So have fun with the software and take joy in your own creations!

2

System Requirements for Using Bryce

Resistor, transistor, condensers in pairs,
Battery, platter, record me some airs;
Squeaker and squawker and woofer times pi,
And Baby shall have his own private Hi-Fi.

Frederick Winsor, *The Space Child's Mother Goose*

In This Chapter . . .

- The types of computers that can run Bryce
- How you can modify your computer so that it will run Bryce
- Bryce file formats and why there are two files for each Bryce scene

Hardware Requirements

To run Bryce, you need enough RAM and either a Power Macintosh or a Macintosh computer that has a math coprocessor.

RAM

What Bryce is undertaking—ray-tracing—is not trivial. There are two factors that determine how much RAM a scene needs: the amount and complexity of objects and the final render size.

RAM is required in order to render a scene. You can create default size scenes on a machine that has 8 MB RAM. However, for smooth operation of Bryce or for rendering large images, you need more.

Bryce holds all information for the scene in RAM at one time, so you need enough RAM to hold it all. If your scene has a lot of terrains and if some or all of those have resolutions larger than the default of 128 (256, 512, 1024), then more RAM is required.

Also affected by the amount of RAM allocated to Bryce is the image resolution size of a scene. The larger the render size, and therefore the greater number of ray-traced computations involved, the more RAM required. A 640 × 480 scene requires more RAM than a 320 × 240 scene.

If your scene is too large for the amount of RAM available, Bryce alerts you with the message: "Not enough memory to build internal structures. Delete some terrains or reduce the resolution." So, if you want to render those big scenes the likes of which measure one or both dimensions, you will need more RAM.

You can successfully extend RAM life by using a utility called RAM Doubler (by Connectix). RAM Doubler will not increase the physical amount of your RAM, but it will allow you to allocate close to the full amount of RAM to several applications, as well as to your system software. This means you can allocate almost 8 MB RAM to Bryce, assuming you have at least that much on your system. There have been cases of RAM Doubler being used to keep Bryce and Photoshop open simultaneously, each assigned 7.9 MB RAM, on a machine that has 8 MB of physical RAM. So RAM Doubler lets you go back and forth between two applications without having to quit either one.

Math Coprocessor

Bryce will run on any Macintosh in the 68K processor family (Motorola chips with these numbers: 68000, 68020, 68030, 68040) that has a math coprocessor, also called an FPU (floating point unit).

In the 68020 and 68030 families, the math coprocessor is a separate processing chip that handles mathematical calculations. The chip is also referred to as 68882 (68881 in the oldest Macintosh model).

The 68040 processor family comes in two flavors: the standard 68040 processor chip, which includes the math coprocessor, and the 68LC040 chip, which doesn't.

The Power Macintosh family of computers approaches math co-processors differently. I'll discuss them a bit later in this chapter.

Table 2–1 lists all Macintosh models and shows which come equipped with a math coprocessor and, for those that don't, what options are available.

The computers for which Optional is checked will accept a math coprocessor as an option. In some cases, the coprocessor is a separate card that installs in the Nubus Slot. In others, it is something that installs in the processor direct slot. These run usually under $100. And yes, I've heard of cases where people have spent more on that little chip than they have on the software that has inspired them to buy the chip. And not a complaint from anyone that they had to do so, either!

TABLE 2–1 Math Coprocessor Availability on Macintosh

	Has a Math Coprocessor?			
	Yes	No	Optional	Options
MACINTOSH FAMILY				
Macintosh Classic II*		■		Third party boards/Daystar
Macintosh Color Classic*			■	Third party
Macintosh SE/30*	■			
MACINTOSH II FAMILY (68030 FAMILY)				
Macintosh II (68020)*	■			
Macintosh IIx*	■			
Macintosh IIcx*	■			
Macintosh IIci*	■			
Macintosh IIfx*	■			
Macintosh IIsi*		■	■	
Macintosh II vi*			■	§
Macintosh IIvx*	■			§

	Has a Math Coprocessor?			
	Yes	No	Optional	Options
MACINTOSH QUADRA/CENTRIS FAMILY				
Macintosh Quadra 700*	■			§
Macintosh Quadra 800*	■			§
Macintosh Quadra 900*	■			§
Macintosh Centris 610*	■			§
Macintosh Centris 650*	■			§
Macintosh Quadra 605		■		§
Macintosh Quadra 610			■	§
Macintosh Quadra 650		■		§
Macintosh Quadra 630		■		§
Macintosh Quadra 660AV	■			§
Macintosh Quadra 840AV	■			§
Macintosh Quadra 950	■			§
MACINTOSH LC FAMILY				
Macintosh LC*		■		
Macintosh LC II*		■		
Macintosh LC III			■	
Macintosh LC 475		■		§
Macintosh LC 520*			■	§
Macintosh LC 550			■	§
Macintosh LC 575 (68LC040)		■		§
POWER MACINTOSH FAMILY⁺				
APPLE PERFORMA FAMILY				
Performa 200*		■		
Performa 400/405/430*		■		
Performa 410		■		
Performa 450*			■	
Performa 460*			■	
Performa 600/600CD*			■	
Performa 466/467			■	
Performa 475		■		
Performa 550			■	

| | **Has a Math Coprocessor?** | | | |
	Yes	**No**	**Optional**	**Options**
Performa 560			■	
Performa 575		■		
Performa 577		■		
Performa 578		■		
Performa 6100 (PowerPC)+		■		
MACINTOSH POWERBOOK				
PowerBook 100*		■		
PowerBook 140*		■		Third party
PowerBook 145*		■		Third party
PowerBook 160*	■			‡
PowerBook 165c*	■			‡
PowerBook 180*	■			
PowerBook 180c*	■			
PowerBook Duo 210*		■		
PowerBook Duo 250*		■		
PowerBook Duo 270c*	■			
PowerBook 145B		■		
PowerBook 165			■	Third party
PowerBook 170		■		‡
PowerBook Duo 230			■	
PowerBook Duo 280			■	§ (pending)
PowerBook Duo 280c			■	§ (pending)
PowerBook 520			■	§ (pending)
PowerBook 520c			■	§ (pending)
PowerBook 540			■	§ (pending)
PowerBook 540c			■	§ (pending)

* Discontinued.

§ Can be upgraded to Power Macintosh.

+ All Power Macintoshes (Power PC) have the ability to run Bryce 1.0.1 (Fat Binary, Native Power Macintosh software).

‡ Third-party upgrade can change to a PowerBook 180 level CPU, including a math coprocessor.

ACCELERATOR BOARDS

Aside from the optional math coprocessors that are available from Apple, there are third-party developers that have math coprocessor and accelerator products that include an FPU. Companies such as Daystar, Newer Technology, and Radius carry one or both types of products.

Daystar Digital Boards

Daystar has a Universal Power Cache board that will fit into all 68020/68030 machines, thereby bringing them up to a clock speed of either 33MHz or 50MHz, depending on the cache card model. There are cache cards with a math coprocessor, as well as without. With these, you can speed up your older machine as well as give it that ray-tracing FPU oomph! Adapter boards are available for those machines requiring special fittings.

Daystar also used to carry strictly FPU Cards. While they're no longer manufacturing them, the cards likely can be found on the used market.

PowerBook Accelerators

Apple offers a math coprocessor chip for its PowerBook. Also, Digital Eclipse offers a logic board swap for models in the PowerBook 100 series whose numbers are higher than 100 and lower than 180. The swap gives the models speeds equivalent to that of a PowerBook 180 and also includes a math coprocessor.

THE POWER MACINTOSH

The Power Macintosh family of computers integrate math coprocessing functions as a part of the 601 chip for applications that are written in "Power Macintosh Native" code. If the code is not native, the Power Mac will emulate a 68LC040 chip. This means if you are using software that is written for the 680X0 family of processors, you have no math coprocessor on a Power Macintosh.

To run Bryce on a Power Macintosh, you need the Native Power PC version of Bryce, also known as fat binary, where the same application code will run native on both Power Macintosh and 68K machines. The release version of KPT Bryce 1.0.1 is fat binary. (KPT Bryce 1.0 is an application for 68K machines only.)

A shareware application called Software FPU, by John Neil, emulates a coprocessor. Although you can run Bryce with it, Software FPU does not provide enough oomph to run Bryce at a creditable speed.

The Power Macintosh central processor includes the ability to perform math coprocessor functions. This is but one of the reasons the Power Macintosh version of Bryce operation and rendering is so much zippier. If you have a Power Macintosh and version 1.0.1 of KPT Bryce, you'll be fine.

24-Bit Color—It Looks Better That Way; It Really Does!

The Bryce interface is full color, which makes sense, as there's a full-color environment in Bryce. Optimally, your video display will have full 24-bit color (millions of colors). In Bryce, you are making adjustments to atmospheric conditions and multiple lighting colors, so the more color information you have, the better. However, many of the newer Mac models come with only 16-bit color (thousands of colors), and some older ones have only 8-bit (256 colors). If your system has only 8-bit or 16-bit, rest assured that Bryce internally operates at full 24-bit color, although you may not see all the colors on your screen. If you render an image on a machine (say, a PowerBook Duo) that has a 16-bit display and then transfer the image to a computer that has a 24-bit display, you'll see all the colors.

The current Macintosh models can accept Video RAM (VRAM) upgrades for increased color resolution. VRAM is usually the least expensive means of achieving higher video output. You can also buy video accelerator cards to get millions of colors on your Macintosh. Either way, enhanced video is money well spent.

Bryce's Document Formats

Scene and PICT Document Formats

Bryce creates a three-dimensional world and renders a two-dimensional image of it. The three-dimensional world information—including objects, terrains, materials, and sky settings for the scene—are saved in a Scene document. The rendered scene is saved in a PICT image document. Figure 2–1 depicts Finder icons for both documents.

A PICT document format has four channels (or 32 bits). The first three—red, green, and blue—contain the image itself. The fourth contains the information about the render's progress. Figure 2–2 shows the fourth channel of an image being rendered. The black areas are parts of the image that have not been rendered. With each successive pass, there is more white, until with a full render, the entire image is white. When the image anti-aliases, Bryce turns just the anti-aliased area black.

Auxiliary Files

There are three types of auxiliary files that can be modified or created in Bryce during the working process. These files contain information about materials, PICT documents, or presets used in the scene.

While creating material settings (the textures and illumination settings for any object), Bryce works with several different file formats. One of these is the shader file—the first type of auxiliary

Scene File   Scene File .p

(a)   (b)

FIGURE 2-1 (a) Scene document icon; (b) PICT document icon.

FIGURE 2–2 The fourth channel of an image in progressive stages of render.

file I discuss here—which has a .SHD suffix. Shader files contain material presets that create textures and surfaces like water, rock, and sand. To access other shader files from the Materials Editor, click Open List… ; to create a new shader file, click the New List… button (both buttons are located just to the right of the preset preview windows). Shader files usually reside in the Bryce Application folder. Any time you add a materials preset in the Materials Editor, you are altering that file. Therefore it is important that you back up shader files when you back up your other files. Otherwise, if you experience some data catastrophe and need to re-install Bryce, the basic shader file that's installed would replace your precious shader file with your other shader presets.

The second type of auxiliary file is a list file. When you add or paste 2D PICT textures in Bryce and use more than one image for any given scene, Bryce keeps them all together in a list in a file. I suggest you call this file FILE.LIST (also as recommended by the Bryce software documentation), where *file* is a placeholder for whatever name you want to assign. Just be sure to keep the suffix .LIST so that you can find your list files easily. Bryce needs the data in a scene's list file when it renders the scene. So don't lose your lists! Back up your files!

The third type of auxiliary file is the Preset file. Whenever you create new presets in the Preset Thumbnail controls in the Master Palette, you are adding to the KPT BRYCE PRESET file.

Conclusion

In this chapter, I told you everything you need to know about the hardware requirements for using Bryce, and probably far more than you ever wanted to know about which Macintosh models have math coprocessors and which do not. Have coprocessor, RAM, and 24-bit color, will travel in Bryce. As you travel in Bryce, you will be creating two types of files: Scene and PICT. In addition, there are a few minor auxiliary file types you should watch out for and back up with the rest of your files.

CHAPTER 3

Camera and Scene

"Remarkable view," announced the Humbug, bouncing from the car as if he were responsible for the whole thing.

"Isn't it beautiful?" gasped Milo.

"Oh, I don't know," answered a strange voice. "It's all in the way you look at things."

. . . Milo turned around and found himself staring at two very neatly polished brown shoes, for standing directly in front of him . . . was another boy just about his age, whose feet were easily three feet off the ground.

. . . "How do you manage to stand up there?" asked Milo, for this was the subject which most interested him.

. . . "Well, in my family everyone is born in the air, with his head at exactly the height it's going to be when he's an adult, and then we all grow toward the ground. When we're fully grown up, or, as you can see, grown down, our feet finally touch. . . . You certainly must be very old to have reached the ground already."

"Oh no," said Milo seriously. "In my family we all start on the ground and grow up and we never know how far until we actually get there."

"What a silly system." The boy laughed. "Then your head keeps changing its height and you always see things in a different way? Why, when you're fifteen things won't look at all the way they did when you were ten, and at twenty everything will change again."

Norton Juster, *The Phantom Tollbooth*

In This Chapter . . .

- A brief introduction to all of the working pieces of Bryce
- The concepts of three-dimensional space, the virtual world, and the two-dimensional camera

- The Camera controls on Bryce's Master Palette
- How to better work with the Bryce camera

In Bryce, you make scenes and then take pictures of them with your Render "camera." Working in Bryce is analogous to taking pictures of our own three-dimensional world. The world itself is three-dimensional, and the camera captures a two-dimensional representation of one place and time of that world. Similarly, when you're working in Bryce, you are balancing between manipulating the three-dimensional world and moving your camera around to take a two-dimensional snapshot of a particular place and time in that three-dimensional world.

Your World and Welcome to It

Bryce is a virtual world of three dimensions. The world itself, and all objects in it, have width, height, and depth. Each of the three dimensions is referred to as an axis: Width is the x axis, height is the y axis, and depth is the z axis. All objects in Bryce's world have width, height, and depth. Each object has an independent existence in the larger space within Bryce. Therefore you can manipulate each, placing it anywhere in the width, height, and depth of the virtual world.

Brycean Objects

Objects in Bryce can be any of 10 types, as listed in the Create Palette (see Fig. 3–1). From left to right, they are ground, terrain, sphere, disc, cone, pyramid, cylinder, plane (or square), cube, and infinite plane. These objects have the following characteristics:

- *Position.* Each object occupies its own position in the three-dimensional space.
- *Size.* Each has its own size (size is controlled in the Edit Palette).
- *Orientation.* Each is oriented in the three-dimensional space. It can be rotated on any of the three axes: x, y, and z (orientation is controlled in the Edit Palette).

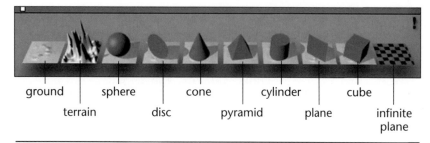

ground | sphere | cone | cylinder | cube
terrain | disc | pyramid | plane | infinite plane

FIGURE 3–1 The Create Palette with the 10 different types of objects that can be created in Bryce 1.0.

- *Material Attributes.* Each object's surface properties are a combination of texture, color, surface perturbances, and the manner in which the object absorbs or reflects light. The combination of all of these factors is the Materials setting and is controlled in the Materials Editor (⌘-M or click on the Materials Editor control on the Edit Palette).

The Brycean Environment

Brycean objects exist in space. Using the atmospheric controls, you can make it outer space or a home world or an alien world. These settings are manipulated in the Sky & Fog Palette, with some master settings in the Render Palette. In Bryce you can make the following transformations to your environment:

- *Lighting.* The virtual Brycean world has a light source. It can be day or night. The color and direction of the sun or moon can be adjusted to any place in the sky.
- *Atmospherics.* You can give your virtual world some clouds. Set their type, amount, and color. Or take them all away.
- *Moisture: Fog and Haze.* Your world can be influenced by the presence of water moisture in the air, whether fog or haze. Brycean fogs and hazes can be any color. Set their amounts as you please.

Take away atmosphere and moisture to put yourself in outer space and create new worlds to colonize!

These factors can make for an extremely complex world with an infinite number of possible combinations. It *is* your world. Create it with reckless abandon and then take as many computer snapshots of it as you please!

Brycean Kodak Moments

Remember your world in pictures. Bryce creates PICT images of the wireframe scenes by rendering them. The particular process involved is called 3D ray-tracing.

"Take a Picture"—How 3D Ray-Tracing Works

To best help you understand how ray-tracing works, I'll follow our real world/virtual world model and take a moment to discuss how the eye and the camera register visual information.

HOW THE EYE SEES AND HOW A CAMERA SEES

Light emanates from a source (sun, moon, electric lights) and bounces off of Earth's surfaces. Depending on the color of those surfaces, different rays of light are absorbed and what is not absorbed bounces. Those bounced light rays that reach the eye are focused through the eye's lens onto the retina. The light information is then transmitted to nerve impulses that travel through the optic nerve to the visual portion of the cerebral cortex of the brain.

The camera "sees" in the same way (see Fig. 3–2). Light from the external world passes through the camera's lens and then exposes film. The film is processed, and prints or slides are created that show the image. The film or transparency and printed photographic paper are all two-dimensional surfaces. (Okay, okay, all do have just a touch of thickness, making them three-dimensional. But a millimeter's thickness notwithstanding, they are "flat" surfaces.) The process of seeing with a camera involves a dimension shift from a three-dimensional world to a two-dimensional image.

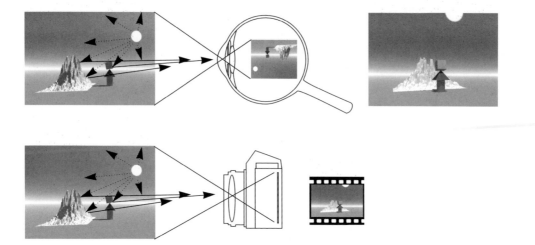

FIGURE 3–2 The eye and the camera both register visual information. Light emanates from a source, bounces off objects, and is registered on the eye's retina or a camera's film.

HOW BRYCE "SEES"

In the real world, there are real objects and real atmosphere and real light sources. When seeing with your eyes, you are continuously registering moments in time. When making photographs, you capture a particular moment in time.

In a corresponding way, Bryce has a virtual world with virtual objects and virtual illumination. Bryce renders a two-dimensional PICT image to capture a moment in its virtual space and time. How does Bryce do this? By ray-tracing. When Bryce renders, it shoots virtual rays into the world to determine the colors of the image. It's not a process of photochemically registering *what is already there,* where the results are seen instantaneously (with the eyes) or with a reasonable delay (film processing). Rather, Bryce's virtual world requires mathematical calculations to follow those rays as they bounce through the world and to record the color of the ray's final destination. Therefore, instead of my talking about an entire image or what can be seen on a piece of film, I'll narrow it down to seeing pixel by pixel.

For each pixel in the scene, Bryce shoots out a virtual ray into the image. Where does it go? For one pixel, the ray's path may take it to one side of a terrain. Ah! This particular portion of the terrain has a basic texture color of sienna brown. But the ambient light is a light Naples yellow, so the sienna brown is altered based on the ambient light. Further, the surface is very matte, so it doesn't create any direct reflections but rather reflects the light everywhere. Also, the sun is close to the horizon and is a reddish color at that. So the color of that portion of terrain is reddened by the sun's color.

Now, for a different pixel in the same scene, as the ray bounces out into the world to find the ultimate color and light source, the color may be different where the terrain is in shadow. But the scene also has a few reflective spheres. A ray of light that shoots out toward one of the spheres bounces off the sphere into the world surrounding it. Reflective surfaces increase the ray's journey time. Or, in the case of multiple reflective objects nearby, the ray may bounce from this sphere here to that other sphere to the terrain way over there. All atmospheric conditions complicate the situation, adding more variables into the calculation that answers the question, "What color will this pixel ultimately become?" If there are transparent objects, then there are further diversions of that ray. And what if the transparent object bends the light as it passes through the object? The ray will go off into a slightly different direction as it seeks out its final color resting place.

As Bryce ray-traces, it uses a progressive method. It goes through six passes as it renders. The first pass takes the image in chunks of 1024 pixels (32 × 32) and shoots one ray into the scene for each chunk to determine that pixel's color (see Fig. 3–3). When it completes that pass, it divides those pixels in half, shooting one ray out for each 256 pixels (16 × 16 pixels) During the second pass, four more calculations are performed than during the previous pass. Each successive pass makes four times the number of calculations as the previous pass did, resulting in a more detailed image. Finally, at the sixth pass, one ray is shot out to determine the color for one pixel.

Bryce makes that ray-traced calculation for every pixel in the scene. It follows the light to its source to determine what color it is. For a

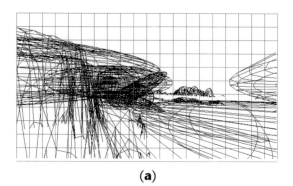

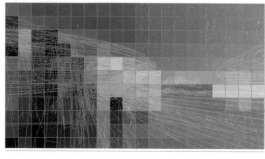

(a)   **(b)**

FIGURE 3–3 **(a)** The wireframe view with a 32 x 32 pixel grid (the first rendering pass) super-imposed. For each square, Bryce shoots a ray into the scene to determine the final color. **(b)** The result after the first rendering pass. (Wireframe view is barely visible for reference.)

scene that's 640 × 480 pixels, that's 307,200 rays that go out into the world, bouncing here and there to determine the final color for each pixel! (And we haven't even talked about what happens at the anti-aliasing pass!) That's a *lot* of calculations! When you first started using Bryce, perhaps you thought a math coprocessor with Bryce wasn't really that necessary. Do you think differently now?

A FLEXIBLE APPROACH

So, you have a virtual three-dimensional world that is rendered into a two-dimensional image. This gives you flexibility as you approach worldmaking and rendering.

■ *You Can Change Your Mind.* The progressive render process al-lows you to experiment and then change your mind. After a couple of rendering passes, you can determine if you like what you see so far and then decide whether to let the render progress further. You don't have to wait until the entire image is rendered single pixel by single pixel (whew!). You can stop after a bit and alter the entire scene. Or you can hone in on one section by drawing a marquee around the critical section and then letting that render out more fully. Or you can scrap the scene altogether and take a different approach to get your Brycean Kodak moment.

- *You Can Have Multiple Views of One Scene.* You don't have to necessarily have a one Scene document/one view for your scene. All the information is there for that world. You can save several different views of it, and it will all be in the one file. (More on this later in the chapter.)

- *You Can Select Different Times of Day.* You can save a series of skies for your scene (time of day and so on) in the Skies Preset Thumbnails in order to keep track of your different times of day for any particular scene.

(However, if you will be rendering your scenes using the drag-and-drop feature, you will need to create individual Scene documents for each view of the scene. Create your series of scenes and then drag the Scene document icons onto the Bryce Application icon, turn off your monitor, and leave the office or go to bed. Bryce renders each one in turn so that when you come back, you'll have one or more scenes completely rendered.)

Obviously, you can spend a good deal of time perfecting the one world. Then once it's in satisfactory condition, take rendered pictures of it to your heart's content! Look at it from the south in the morning and then saunter over for an east view in time for Brycean noon. Spend Bryce's late afternoon focused on one detail area and then at sunset take a panoramic view to the northwest. Don't forget to slip out at night to take it all in once more under Bryce's perpetual full moon. It's all the same world, shown at different times of day focusing on different sections.

Bryce's Document Structure

Bryce makes worlds and then takes rendered pictures of them. Bryce's entire file structure is based on these two processes: working in the three-dimensional world and then taking a two-dimensional snapshot of that world. In doing these two processes, Bryce creates two documents, one for each mode of operation. The Scene document contains all the information about the three-dimensional world, including the placement of the camera for looking at that world. The rendered scene is saved in a PICT image document.

Although I went over file structures and working with Bryce in Chapter 2, I mention it again here in the two-process context.

View and Camera Controls

As with any real-world camera, you must consider certain factors when working with Bryce's camera. What is the camera's position? Where is the camera in the scene? Is the camera upright? Is it rotated this way or that? Then there's the matter of the kind of lens that's on the camera. How much of the surrounding world enters the lens? A long telephoto lens shows only what's ahead; a wide angle lens shows more of the panorama.

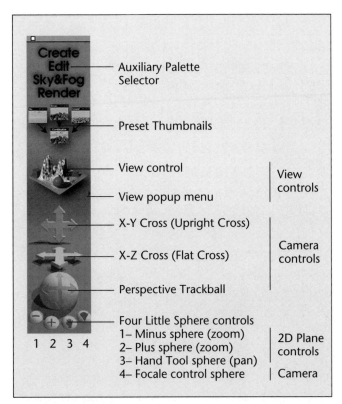

But there's more to working with Bryce's camera than just determining its position. There are three different dynamics at work. The View and Camera Controls on the Master Palette are divided roughly into three areas that correspond to the three dynamics of camera and scene. Taken in their natural groupings, these controls are the View controls, the Camera controls, and the Four Little Sphere controls (see Fig. 3–4).

The first dynamic is the general orientation to your scene. When looking at your scene in your monitor, you may be looking at the Main View (through the camera) or at your scene from Top, Side, or Front View. The View controls on the Master Palette allow you to select the general view of your scene.

FIGURE 3–4 The View, Camera, and Four Little Sphere controls on the Master Palette.

The second dynamic is the Camera controls themselves—where the camera is positioned and the "lens" depth is set. The Camera controls on the Master Palette affect the camera's position in your scene.

The third dynamic is the position of the 2D Projection plane—the virtual plane on which the three-dimensional scene is projected. Your camera can be oriented in BryceSpace in any position and facing any direction. Wherever the "film" is, the 2D plane extends outwards on all sides. The "film" of that camera is measured in pixels. (The size of the "film" is set in the Render Palette when you choose your scene's resolution.) It is the active "photosensitive" area of the 2D plane that captures light. I refer to this photosensitive area of the plane as the "active image area." The plane can be slid up or down, left or right, to make any portion the active area. Three of the Four Little Sphere controls on the Master Palette allow you to adjust the 2D Projection plane. Figure 3–5 shows the Views part of the Master Palette that control camera position and the 2D Projection plane.

Next, I take a more detailed look at each of the View and Camera controls.

(a)   **(b)**

FIGURE 3–5
The View part of the Master Palette showing (a) controls for the camera position and (b) controls for the 2D Projection plane.

The View Control

The View Diorama control allows you to look at your Bryce scene in different ways. Available views are Main, Top, Side, and Front Views.

Dragging the View Diorama changes the preview on the Master Palette. Release the mouse button, and your view of your scene changes to match the Diorama view. If you wanted, say, to put your scene in Top view, drag the View Diorama until you see the Top view preview.

In the Diorama preview, the light source comes from above and to the left. So when you're looking at the Front View of the Diorama, the Diorama seems darker than when you are looking at the Side View of the Diorama. You may find this confusing at first.

tip

Here is a speed tip for when you're in another view and you want to go back to Main View: You can drag all the way to the left to go there directly. This tip is helpful if your machine is slow or if the scene is so complex that Bryce pauses before drawing the wireframe view of the scene. It's also helpful if you happen to land yourself in the wrong view ("Oh, no, I didn't want to look at this in Front View. Hurry up, Bryce!") while on your way back to the Main View of the scene.

tip

Now, here is a *major* speed tip. The absolute best way to navigate quickly is to use the number keys to shift between views. Starting with 1 as the Main View, the numbers correspond to the positions in the Views menu list. Use either the numbers at the top of your keyboard or, on extended keyboards, the numeric keypad.

Main View	1
Top View	2
Side View	3
Front View	4
Saved Views	5–9

Alternatively you can navigate to other views via the View popup menu, where you can select—with no possibility of ambiguity—the different views.

View Popup Menu Items

In addition to allowing you to switch among the four general views of your scene—Main, Top, Side, and Front—the View menu gives you options for collecting and saving different camera angles and for getting your camera back to square one. These options are the following:

- *Add View As....* Here's where you can collect and save your different camera angles—16 in all. I have more to say on this in the "Saving Camera Views" section of this chapter.

  The first two View Menu options following the four basic view positions offer you the means to return to the default camera position and start over:

- *Reset Views (Camera).* This option takes you back to the default Bryce camera position and puts you at the default Zoom setting of 100%.

- *Center Image (2D Projection plane).* This option centers the 2D Projection plane, taking it back to its default position. So if you have scrolled out to some far region in BryceSpace and are now lost—whether you are in Main, Top, Side, or Front View—then selecting Center Image will bring you back home. All views will be brought back to the center point of their respective two-dimensional planes. Selecting Center Image will not change the Zoom value back to its default, however. Reset Views resets the Zoom.

These next two options allow for quick changes in perspective:

- *Ground Camera.* This option moves the camera to just above ground height.

- *Zoom to Selection.* Although this option is in the View menu, I will discuss it later in the chapter when I talk about the Zoom control of the Four Little Sphere controls.

Cross Controls

The Cross controls move the camera's position inside of Bryce. Since the camera is placed in the width, height, and depth of the Bryce environment, the camera position is referred to in x, y, and z terms. The X-Y Cross works along the x- and y-axes and so moves the camera left/right and up/down. I find that "Upright" is a more descriptive term than X-Y, so I refer to this Cross control as the "Upright Cross."

The X-Z Cross (see Fig. 3–6b), which I call the "Flat Cross," works along the z-axis and so moves the camera left/right and forward/backward. The images in Figure 3–6 show the camera and the respective planes of motion that are brought about by each of the Cross controls. The vertical plane represents the range of camera movement using the Upright Cross control, and the horizontal plane represents the range of motion using the Flat Cross control.

You can constrain all of the camera movements. The Cross controls will change to show you when they are constraining camera movement in one direction. You can also use the modifier keys to constrain in one direction: Control key for the x-axis, Option key for the y-axis, and Command-key for the z-axis.

The Trackball Control

The Trackball control changes the camera position in relation to the entire world. Movement is not restricted to horizontal or verti-

FIGURE 3–6 The virtual camera with two planes emanating from it:
(**a**) The camera in a starting position; (**b**) in response to dragging down on the Flat Cross control, the camera moves deeper into the scene.

FIGURE 3–7 (**a**) A world inside a globe; (**b**) the camera's position changed with the Trackball control.

cal, but is an integrated rotation around Bryce's world center. Here's a way to think of it. Suppose your Bryce world is inside a globe (see Fig. 3–7a). When you rotate the camera, its distance from the globe's center stays the same, even though it moves up or down, left or right to change position (see Fig. 3–7b).

Since the camera moves relative to world center, then the position of individual objects in BryceSpace will affect apparent camera movements. If you are, for example, trying to rotate the camera around a particular object and you happen to have your object placed way off center, your rotation actions will not be pleasing; the world will seem to rotate on an ellipse. To obtain better rotation around a particular object, place your desired objects at world center.

You can use the constrain keys in conjunction with the Trackball for precise movements. To rotate around the *x*-axis (horizontally), hold down the Control key. This is a very helpful constraining motion to keep the camera from wobbling. To pan up or down from one spot, press the Option key to constrain movement along the *y*-axis.

TRACKBALL'S EASTER EGG CONTROL

The Trackball has a cool Easter Egg feature. Press the Command key while dragging on the Trackball control and up pops a scene in a small window with an animation! Drag to the left and right to view the animation. It's a little fly-in on a terrain in the water, starting from low and flat and spiraling higher until the view is from

tip

To find world center, if you don't know where it is (there is no "X marks the spot"), create an object. It comes into being at world center (think of it as Bryce's Eden!). You must have the View Linked option UNchecked (Bryce's default option) in the "!" dialog box in the Create Palette.

FIGURE 3–8
Pressing the Command key while dragging the Trackball to see an Easter Egg spiraling animation.

directly overhead. All the time the camera is focused on the center of the tiny lagoon (see Fig. 3–8).

When you let go of the mouse button, your view is adjusted to be the same as the camera angle from that particular frame of the animation. If you want to try a quick series of other views on the subject, try using this technique.

However, be aware that once you Command-drag the Trackball, you're committed. When you let go, you will have a new view of your scene. You can't get out of this move even by trying to drag back to your place of origin (this works with the Trackball when dragged in its usual, non-Easter Egg mode). So if you have the slightest doubt about whether you'll later be starting a new view from scratch, save your view before you Command-drag the Trackball.

Focale—A Camera with Different-Sized "Lenses"

The Focale control is analogous to switching lenses on a camera. A wide-angle lens takes in more area than a telephoto lens. For the numerical measurements, though, don't think of Focale as the equivalent of camera lens focal length. Bryce uses degrees, not millimeters. (The numerical degree measurements are in the Camera dialog box, accessed by double-clicking the Cross or Trackball controls.) The degree number corresponds to the angle that is seen. The largest, 170°, is close to your seeing half the world before you, whereas 10° is a tightly focused, narrow view.

Drag to the right to increase the Focale setting or to widen your perspective. The scene seems to move farther away, but actually, the scene "decreases," since the camera is letting in more image area to the left and right of the scene. Drag left to decrease the Focale setting. Figure 3–9 shows a scene at different Focale settings.

2D Projection Controls

There are two "moving parts" to the camera view equation: the camera position and the 2D Projection plane. The camera can be

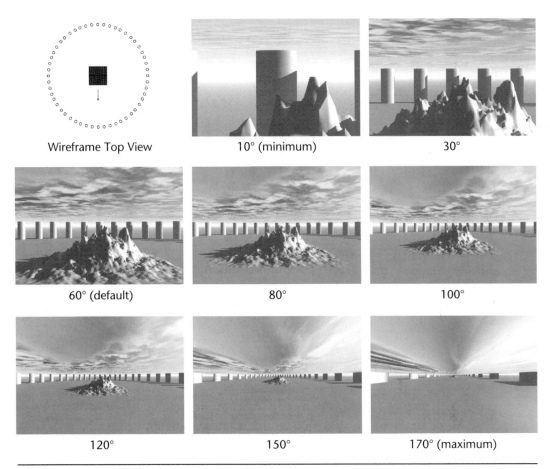

Wireframe Top View · **10° (minimum)** · **30°**

60° (default) · **80°** · **100°**

120° · **150°** · **170° (maximum)**

FIGURE 3–9 A scene with different Focale settings.

located anywhere. Wherever the camera is located, the 2D Projection plane travels with it. You can move the plane up and down, left and right, in order to put a certain segment in the active image area to take the picture. You can also zoom in or out from that spot. Three of the Four Little Sphere controls enable you to do that.

To scroll along the plane, use the Hand Tool. This infinite plane extends out in all directions (in Fig. 3–10, it is represented as finite with projection arrows, if only to indicate its presence). The camera position itself does not change, but the plane may be slid over to determine a new active image area. Think for a moment of the

(a)

(b)

FIGURE 3–10
(**a**) A virtual Bryce scene on a virtual monitor with a virtual infinite plane represented by projecting arrows. (**b**) After scrolling up and to the left, the active image area changes.

finite infinite plane and ask, "Is the active image area in the upper left-hand corner? The lower right-hand corner? How about along the bottom edge in the center?"

There are differences between moving a camera up and moving the 2D plane up to "frame" the image just so. In the scene in Figure 3–11a, the horizon line is right smack dab in the middle. There's too much sky and not enough of the foreground terrain. If you drag up on the Upright Cross to move the camera, you'll change the relationship between objects (see Fig. 3–11b). Instead, scroll up with the Hand Tool to maintain the relationship between objects (see Fig. 3–11c). The camera angle does not change.

Clicking the Plus Sphere (+) zooms you into the image. This action is not the same as moving the camera closer to the image. Instead, you are focusing on a smaller area and making that area fill the entire active camera view.

ZOOMBIGUITY

There's a problem with the word "zoom." In camera terms, you can alter the focal length of a zoom lens on the fly. It's a smoother way of changing lenses, say, from 50 mm to 80 mm to 200 mm. You

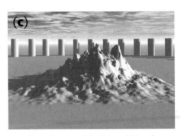

| (a) 60° (default) | (b) Drag up on Camera Cross | (c) Scroll up with Hand Tool |

FIGURE 3–11 The difference between moving the camera and scrolling the 2D plane: (**a**) Original image; (**b**) dragging up on the Upright Cross; (**c**) scrolling up with the Hand Tool.

zoom in and out, all the while being positioned in one place. Standing right here, zoom from 60 mm to 130 mm. This will bring you closer to your subject. This is, in some ways, related to the action of the Focale control.

However, I'm talking about using zoom in the Macintosh sense. In other Macintosh applications, you change the view of the document by zooming. You can look at something in actual size, you can magnify it, or you can reduce it so that the entire page fits in the document window. This is a two-dimensional zoom process. In some applications, such as Photoshop, you can hold down a tricky modifier key combination, drag a marquee around the area you want to focus on, and presto chango! Next thing you see, your monitor is filled with just that area that was inside the marquee.

When Bryce uses the Plus and Minus Sphere keys and the Zoom to Selection option in the popup menu, it is acting like the more classic Macintosh zoom-to-magnify. It is a two-dimensional zoom. The fact that you're in a three-dimensional application that uses something called a camera may make zoom confusing.

When you click the Plus and Minus Spheres, you are selectively choosing smaller or larger areas of the "scene" to project onto the 2D Projection plane. You're magnifying that particular area when you zoom in and you're reducing it when you zoom out.

ZOOM TO SELECTION

The Zoom to Selection option is a new way to define a view. It's Bryce's version of the tricky modifier key combination used while marqueeing an area. "Hey, I'd like to do a closeup on that," you say. Suppose you have a finished render and there is one area of the image that interests you. When the scene is in the PICT mode, drag a marquee around it (see Fig. 3–12a). Then select Zoom to Selection from the Views popup menu. That area then fills the window (see Fig. 3–12b). Render again (see Fig. 3–12c) and select File > Save As... to save your detail image as a separate scene.

You can create several snapshots of the same scene in this way. Consider it your "Postcards from the Bryce Edge."

Camera Dialog Box

To get a little more control over the camera position, double click either the Crosses or the Trackball to open the Camera dialog box (similar to the "!" dialog boxes). This dialog box allows you to use numerical settings to alter the camera's angle and position, as well as to change where you are on the flat 2D Projection plane from where you view Bryce. Each item in it is labeled according to its corresponding controls on the Master Palette (see Fig. 3–13). The Camera controls are in the top part of the box and the 2D Projection controls are in the bottom.

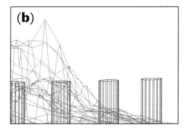

FIGURE 3–12 Bryce close-ups: (**a**) Drag the marquee then Zoom to Selection; (**b**) the marqueed area fills the screen; (**c**) the rendered image.

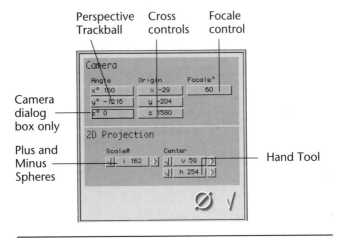

FIGURE 3–13 The Camera dialog box, labeled according to corresponding Master Palette controls.

Next I take you through each part of the Camera dialog box.

CAMERA: ANGLE

The angle part of the Camera dialog box describes the camera's orientation in space. The orientation is indicated in degree increments. There are ten units for every degree: a complete circle has 3600 degrees, not 360. So, you have a ton of precision for setting up your camera if you need to do so numerically. (This comes in handy if, for example, you're doing animations by hand.)

The Trackball changes the settings of the camera angle. However, you cannot change the *z* setting except by numbers. Remember that. If you change only the numbers on *z*, for instance, it rotates around the *z*-axis. The camera will do a roll.

Try this: Create a scene that includes something on the ground. Double-click one of the Crosses to access the Camera dialog box. Type 450 in the *z* box in the lower left-hand corner (that figure is equal to 45°). Now your scene is pitched at an angle. Next, use the Trackball to try to reorient yourself back to level. Don't get dizzy! You can't get yourself back there! You can't do it by dragging the camera around, either. The only way to do so is numerically.

So anytime you want to roll the camera angle, remember this dialog box.

CAMERA: ORIGIN

The Origin part of the Camera dialog box is for changing the camera's offset, that is, its location. To change these settings, use the Cross controls, since you are moving the actual camera location.

The offset concerns the position of the camera in BryceSpace. "Offset" means the camera's offset from world center.

CAMERA: FOCALE

I discussed Focale earlier in the chapter when I talked about the four little spheres. In the Focale part of the dialog box is the number that controls the camera's focal length. If you've created a new scene after having some other scene open and discovered that your new scene looks a little strange or warped, then check out the number here. It may be that it is close to 100 or more. In some cases, you may want it that way; in others, you may not.

2D PROJECTION: SCALE%

Scale% refers to the zoom factor. Here are the numbers for the Plus (+) or Minus (–) Sphere controls. Think of it as the enlargement or reduction of the scene on the active viewing rectangle. The default is 100%. Zoom up or down. When you click the + or –, Bryce will enlarge the image by double factors. After you click the + eight times, it won't go any further. At that point, the readout says 2500%. However, you can type in numbers to get a higher zoom factor, if you need it.

Likewise, when you zoom out, you can click the – nine times before zooming stops. The readout at that point is 2%.

The zoom works in factors of 1.5. So from 100%, it multiplies that figure by one and a half to get 150. It then multiplies that figure by one and a half to get 225 and so on up to 2500%. On the – Sphere side, the zoom takes 100 and divides that by 1.5 to get 66, then 44, and so on down to 2%.

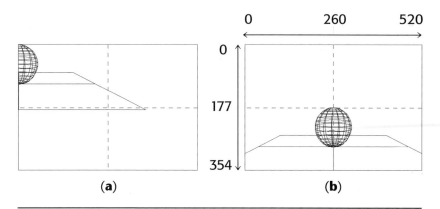

FIGURE 3–14 (**a**) The image at offset value 0,0; (**b**) the image at Center Image 177,260.

If you don't like those particular numbers and want to see something in between, say, at 135% or 89%, all you need to do is type your own numbers in the Scale% portion of the dialog box.

Changing the number from a positive value to a negative value (press the – key) turns the scene upside down. Who knows what that's useful for, but someday it may come in handy.

2D PROJECTION: CENTER

Center has two numerical values: v and h (for vertical and horizontal). These refer to the amount of offset from world center. A default center image does not have the values of 0,0 (see Fig. 3–14a). Rather, it is half the size of your scene. If you have set up your scene in default view, 520 × 354, then half of that is 260 × 177 (see Fig. 3–14b); 0,0 will place world center and the horizon in the upper left-hand corner of your scene image. The default, Center Image, aligns world center with the center of the active image area. The numerical setting for that will always be half of the Render Image size.

When you change scene sizes, Bryce gives its best guess, putting the old scene in the new active image area. Both the Center and the Scale% are adjusted. You may need to tweak either setting. Go to the Camera dialog box to set the Scale% back to 100.

How-to: Camera Placement That's Just So

Now that I've talked about the theory of the camera controls, I offer in this section some more-practical, working knowledge for setting up your camera positions. You don't always need to adjust your camera by using the controls on the Master Palette. You can also directly manipulate it while working in the Top, Side, or Front View of your scene.

The Little Blue Box

When looking at your scene in Top, Side, or Front View, the camera is represented on the screen as a blue box with a line extending from it. It can be moved directly by dragging it. You can move the camera around and aim it. Drag the box to move the entire camera (see Fig. 3–15).

tip

If your camera is positioned over another object, say, a terrain, you need to ensure the object is UNselected before you attempt to move the camera. Otherwise Bryce interprets the dragging motion as your intention to move the terrain.

For precise aiming, move the tip in the direction you want to point your camera. To aim the camera at a particular object, drag the tip until it touches the object (see Fig. 3–16a). When you release the mouse button, the camera retracts to its original size, but is aimed directly at the object (see Fig. 3–16b). When you go back to Main View, the object will be placed in the center of your view (see Fig. 3–16c).

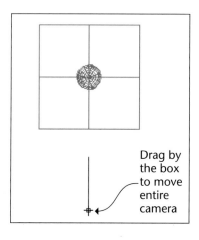

Drag by
the box
to move
entire
camera

FIGURE 3–15 Repositioning the camera by dragging the camera by the box (Top View)

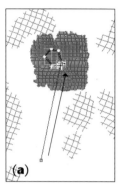  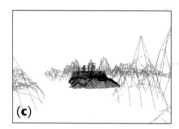

FIGURE 3–16 Changing the camera view: (**a**) Dragging the tip of the camera to the object (Top View); (**b**) after releasing the camera (Top View); (**c**) the castle tower in the precise center of the scene (Main View).

When you do a test render in Top, Front, or Side View, you can still see the camera on top of the rendered image. Some beta testers back in Bryce's early days thought this was a software bug. Not so! It's a very powerful feature. It enables you to precisely place the camera in your scene. Say you have a terrain that has deep ravines. You need to get the placement just right or else the camera will be hidden inside the ground. Not a great view. If you use the Cross controls to navigate yourself to that ravine, you will probably put your computer in danger of ruin (or worse!) from your frustrated outburst after many tries to place your camera just so. Don't sweat it. There's an easier way.

Render the scene a little from the Top, Side, or Front View. When you click to stop the render, the camera should reappear. (If it doesn't, then toggle to wireframe view and back with the Escape (Esc) key. The camera should reappear.) Now you can place your camera while you look at the accurately rendered scene. Figure 3–17 shows an example of how this works. The terrain has lots of dips and peaks, thereby making it hard for you to navigate deep within the narrow places using the Camera controls on the Master Palette.

Look at all of the scenes called Top View wireframe and so forth for aiming up canyons.

FIGURE 3–17 A terrain with dips and peaks that make camera navigation difficult.

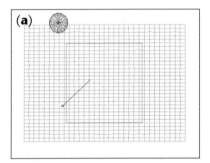 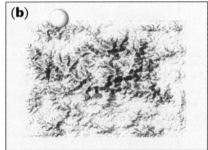

FIGURE 3–18 (**a**) Wireframe view of a terrain; (**b**) rendered view of the same terrain.

CASE STUDY: PRECISE CAMERA PLACEMENT FROM TOP VIEW

Figure 3–18a shows the terrain in Fig. 3–17 in Top View. There's quite a bit of dramatic viewing, if only you can get your camera in there. However, placing the camera from the wireframe view of the same terrain is problematical. You cannot tell from the crosshatching of the wireframe where to put the camera. To get your camera precisely placed, first render the scene in Top View (see Fig. 3–18b). After a few render passes, the situation will become obvious. You will see where to place the camera.

Here are a few general Bryce tips to help you while you do this:

■ Make sure you have the View Linked check box in the Sky & Fog "!" dialog box unchecked. Otherwise you'll get something generally very dark, as overhead sun is actually shining from your horizon.

- Placing the sun not exactly overhead will show the heights and depths of the terrain by casting slight shadows where the canyon is deep.

- You can work faster if your terrain doesn't have a three-dimensional texture applied to it. The default white plastic texture you get when Bryce first opens is ideal for this kind of treatment.

From here, follow these steps:

1. Drag the camera (box end) and then adjust the angle (needle end) (see Fig. 3–19a).

2. You'll probably have to make another adjustment to the camera to ensure it's pointing up or down properly. Do that in the Side View (see Fig. 3–19b).

3. Check out the scene in Main View (see Fig. 3–20). You have navigated yourself into the midst of the wireframe morass. Do a little test render. If it ends up being solid gray, your camera is probably under the terrain. Go back to Main View and render the scene for a few passes.

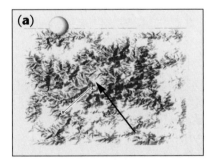

(a)

(b)

FIGURE 3–19 Camera Placement, first in (**a**) Top View; (**b**) then in Side View.

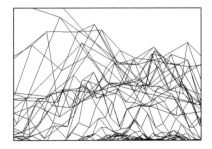

FIGURE 3–20 The resulting wireframe in Main View.

FIGURE 3–21 Three renders of the same terrain: (**a**) The rendered terrain from the steps described in the text; (**b**) looking down the same canyon from above; (**c**) looking up a different canyon on the other side of the mountain.

4. Use the Cross controls for fine-tuning. Don't be surprised if a little move to the left or right results in a completely gray render. You've precisely navigated yourself into the narrow ravine and won't have a lot of room to maneuver inside there. Figure 3–21 shows three renders of the ravine.

UPSIDE-DOWN CAMERA—NOT!

Moving the camera around in Top, Side, or Front View is an extremely efficient way to navigate through your scene. However, when moving the camera around in Side and Front Views you need to keep in mind the following: When you move the camera tip from one side (see Fig. 3–22a) to face the other way (see Fig. 3–22b), the result will be an upside-down view (see Fig. 3–22c). Although that little blue box with the protruding needle doesn't have anything to indicate up or down, the view is still upside-down. Beware.

Instead of dragging the camera in Side or Front View to change orientation, you can try one of two alternatives: Go to Top View to change the general direction (since you're viewing from the top, you'll never be able to turn the camera upside-down) and then flip back to Side or Front View to fine-tune placement.

OR you can use the Trackball. Hold down the Control key when using the Trackball to constrain the rotation upon the x-axis. You'll rotate around to the other side of your world. If your terrain is off

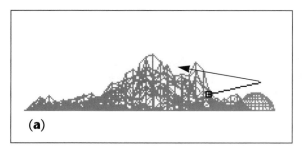

(a)

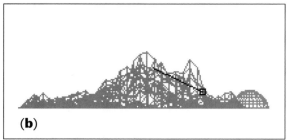

(b)

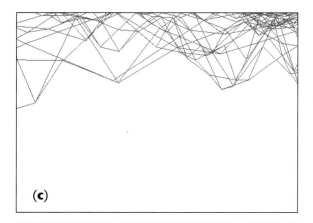

(c)

FIGURE 3–22 Camera adjustment surprises in Side or Front View: (**a**) camera position before; (**b**) camera position after; (**c**) upside-down result.

"center" (where new things appear in your world), then your Trackball camera rotation may take you into unexpected territory. Should that happen, simply move the camera from Top View.

Of course, this upside-down camera may be exactly what you intend in some cases. However, it is more likely the case that you want to avoid turning your camera upside down!

Saving Camera Views

The way cool thing about the camera is that you can save your different views. In the View menu, the Add view as... menu item takes you to a dialog box where you can add your view.

To delete a view, hold down the Option key as you access that menu. All of your options will be listed as "Delete view such 'n such."

You can have a maximum of 16 views of each scene. If you already have 16 views in the menu when you go to add a new view, then Bryce will throw away one— the second from the bottom one—in order to make room for your new one. Chances are the second view from the bottom is one you just put in there, so you'll probably be sorry to see it go. If I were you, I wouldn't trust Bryce with that decision, since Bryce's reasons for choosing the view are far more arbitrary than yours. You want a minimum of weeping and gnashing of teeth. Better to choose yourself which ones to delete. Throw away some of the earlier ones.

Where do those camera views come from, anyhow? Over time, as you open different Bryce scenes, you'll see the preset list grow and shrink. Why? Bryce saves the list of views with each Scene document. Also, when it creates a new document it remembers the last set of views.

Let's say you open a scene that has a north, south, east, and west view. Then you finish with that document and want to create a new one. When Bryce creates a new document, it asks, "What are my current saved view settings? Ah, that's right. There's north, south, east, and west from that last scene."

This is how your list of views can be amassed. You start with some basic directions of the compass, add a couple of your own. Close. A new document will have all of those, then you might add some more.

Every once in a while, when you open up a new scene in Bryce, check the Add view as... list and purge any views that have just been hanging around for the ride.

Think Like a Photographer!

A final note. Think like a photographer! You are both creating a world and then making a picture of it, so when you set up your camera position you will be doing the same things that all photographers do when they make pictures: composing the shot.

If you've taken any photography classes, you'll recall that the discussion on composition relates to what you're doing in Bryce. Here are a few compositional pointers.

VARY THE HORIZON LINE

Bryce's default position for the horizon line is smack dab in the middle. It cuts your image right in half. It's more interesting and pleasing to have the horizon be lower or higher than exact center. Try the upper third or lower third as an alternative. Figure 3–23a–c shows different horizon lines. Part a shows an image that is a mere half and half. See how boring it is? Parts b and c divide up the space asymmetrically. The results are more pleasing and balanced. In both cases, one side is dominant and the other is secondary. As a result, your eye is led to look at one side or the other.

FEATURE A DOMINANT ELEMENT

Your image will have some elements that are dominant and others that are secondary. If all are dominant or all are secondary, the image will not be as interesting.

Look at your image. Are there lines or elements that lead your eye toward the one dominant element?

Figure 3–23d–f shows various placements of a single terrain in an image. Part d shows the standard Bryce default: center terrain on a centered horizon. Boring. In Part e, things are more interesting. The terrain is not centered. Combine that with a high horizon, and there is a focus on the terrain in the lower left, with a dominant diagonal line, all of which is balanced by the open space to the right. Part f takes things further. A gradual series of diagonals level out as the terrain becomes more distant.

Parts g, h, and i show more complex compositions. Part g has flowing s-shaped lines. Your eye is led from the front to the back. Part h has a contrast between vertical lines on the left and horizontal lines on the right. Part i has foreground elements, which frame the distant terrain.

If all this composition stuff is new to you, try this. On a blank piece of paper, use a pencil to draw a series of rectangular boxes, similar to those shown in the figure. They don't have to be big. Make them about the size of large postage stamps. Then fill them in with different strokes. Round, angular, squiggly, whatever. Make a few strokes in one, then go on to the next. Don't consciously try to make landscape thumbnails. (If you are making landscape thumbnails, fine; don't fight it.) Just play and go for interesting shapes. When you have a half a dozen to a dozen, stop and look back over them. Are there any that you prefer? Why? When you can think of why, even if it's not necessarily a left-brain verbalized understand-

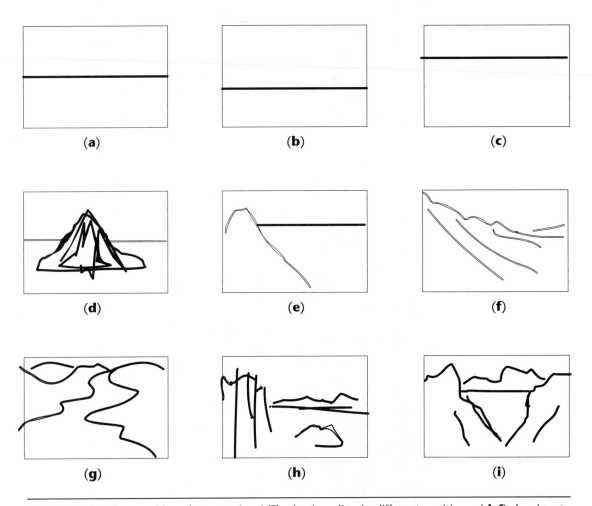

FIGURE 3–23 Composition elements: (**a–c**) The horizon line in different positions; (**d–f**) dominant element in different positions; (**g–i**) more-complex compositions.

ing, you're on your way to developing a sense of what makes a good composition.

Another composition idea: Look at some published material that has landscape or nature photography, such as *National Geographic, Arizona Highways,* and *Audubon,* coffee table books, and Sierra Club calendars. Analyze the images you find appealing. What is it about this or that one that makes it nice?

For a fun book that is not about composition but that deals a lot with how to compose line drawings, pick up *The Dot and the Line,* by Norton Juster. (It's a fun read, too!)

So, as you are composing your picture, keep in mind the following:

■ Include some kind of dominant line in the image.

■ Sticking with the horizontal format isn't necessary. For a more dynamic, striking image, try vertical.

■ Add lines in the image. For example, diagonal and serpentine shapes draw your eye into and through the image.

■ Place something close for interest and something far away for scale.

Other things you can do as a "photographer" of your Bryce image:

■ Adjust the camera position. What was dull seen from one perspective becomes downright visually engaging when seen from another. Photographers do it all the time.

■ Change the focal length of the lens. Use the Focale control to adjust the angle of the lens. Skies are wonderful when you open the angle of vision way up wide.

■ Adjust the time of day. Photographers are notorious for going to places at certain times of day, looking for the most dramatic light. The best time of day is just after sunrise and just before sunset. Midday lighting tends to be harsh. When working in Bryce, though, you don't need to go out at sunrise in order to capture the delicate light of dawn. All you need to do is adjust the light in your Bryce scene.

Warning notes: Two warnings to keep in mind. First, say you have a scene that is in Side, Front, or Top View. You then save it in a different view and close the document. When you open it again, the saved view will be the new Main View. You may not like it when this first happens to you. Remember to close your scenes when they're in Main View.

Second, beware! Camera settings have no Undo function. As I discuss more deeply in Chapter 4, only actions that actually edit the *objects* are undoable. Changes to *views* cannot be undone using ⌘-Z.

Conclusion

In this chapter, I discussed how ray-tracing works, using the eye and camera as analogies. Bryce creates a three-dimensional world and takes a two-dimensional picture of it. Its own file structure follows from this three-dimensional/two-dimensional structure. From theory, I launched into the practical, discussing all of the View and Camera controls. The Camera controls are broken down into two categories: moving the actual camera in three-dimensional BryceSpace and moving it closer to or farther from the objects—up, down, left, right. The 2D Projection plane on which the image falls, the ray-tracing "film," has its own set of adjustment controls. Finally, I concluded with suggestions about how to create good composition and how to think like a photographer as you approach creating and rendering an image of your three-dimensional Bryce world.

CHAPTER 4

Streamline Bryce Working

"Well," said Rabbit, ... "We'd better get on, I suppose. Which way shall we try?"

"How would it be," said Pooh slowly, "if, as soon as we're out of sight of this Pit, we try to find it again?"

"What's the good of that?" said Rabbit.

"Well," said Pooh, "we keep looking for Home and not finding it, so I thought that if we looked for this Pit, we'd be sure not to find it, which would be a Good Thing, because then we might find something that we *weren't* looking for, which might be just what we *were* looking for, really."

"I don't see much sense in that," said Rabbit.

"No," said Pooh humbly, "there isn't. But there was going to be when I began it. It's just that something happened to it on the way."

A. A. Milne, *The House at Pooh Corner*

In This Chapter . . .

- The best ways to set up scenes
- Efficient ways of working with objects and material settings
- Effective rendering and batch rendering
- Tips on working with Bryce dialog boxes
- How to deal with Bryce anomalies
- Preferences setup
- Other general things about Bryce that are good to know in the interests of speed and efficiency

In this chapter, I tell you how to optimize your Bryce working method and answer the question, "Given the time it takes to render scenes, what is the most efficient way to work in Bryce?" Different activities in Bryce will cost more in processing time. It's best when working in Bryce to postpone introducing the effects that cost the most for as long as possible. There are many steps in creating a scene; ensure you are getting the most out of the early stages. Then when you do test renders to ensure your image is going as planned, you won't be waiting for unnecessary things to be rendering.

Setting Up Your Scene: Start Small

The first part of efficient working in Bryce is to set up your scene and your working conditions in the program.

When setting up your scene, keep in mind that you're working in a three-dimensional world that you will eventually render to a two-dimensional PICT. When choosing your file resolution, don't think along the lines of, "Well, my final resolution has to be 1500 × 800 pixels," and then create a scene with that render size. You have an entire three-dimensional world there inside your scene, no matter the render size. So take liberties! Take *small* liberties. Start out small by using Bryce's default setting or one of the settings listed in the Render Size popup menu of the Render Palette (see Fig. 4–1a). Once you've got your scene where you want it, then you can make the size bigger. Postpone the long rendering time until after you have set up everything the way you like it.

If you know ahead of time that the scene you're working on will eventually become extremely wide or extremely tall, don't go to the Custom Format dialog box just yet (see Fig. 4–1b). While you are still creating objects and setting them up in relation to one another, look at your scene from Top, Side, or Front View. An extremely wide scene will not allow you to see as much from Top View. Set up the objects in your scene in default and then go back later—when you are establishing your camera angle—and narrow the dimensions.

If you know that your scene will be at one of the extremes of height or width, then you can use the custom settings to dial in your numbers. To start, use small numbers. Rather than increase one of the

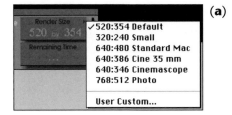 (a)
 (b)

FIGURE 4–1 (**a**) The Render Size popup menu on the Render Palette; (**b**) Custom Format dialog box.

numbers, make the other one smaller. Don't exceed your monitor dimensions. You can always change it later when you are ready for your final render.

When you change an image from a basic size ratio to one that is extreme, you may have to change the camera angle some. Bryce gives the new scene size its best shot for camera angle and so on, but invariably, you'll have to adjust a little bit to get things just so.

Wireframe Workings

Working in wireframe view is the fastest way to view your scene, right? Well, yes and no. Viewing in wireframe is certainly faster than completely rendering the scene, especially while the scene is still evolving. But there are things you can do to make your computer draw the wireframe on-screen as quickly as possible. You also can reduce the clutter of wireframe objects when you have many of them placed in your scene.

Drawing the Wireframe Quickly

In the Preferences… dialog box (Edit > Preferences… or ⌘-P), you can set the Wireframe Resolution to different levels of detail. There are two popup menus for setting numbers of the wireframes (see Fig. 4–2).

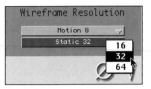

FIGURE 4–2 Wireframe Resolution popup menus.

One is for wireframes in motion, and the other is for wireframes at rest (static). The higher the number, the more detail. The more detail, the longer it takes for Bryce to draw the scene on the screen. This is why the motion wireframe numbers are lower than the static ones; Bryce has to draw them while you are dragging the terrain from point A to point B—with every step in between. Find a happy medium between the amount of detail you need to see and the amount of speed you can live with. Set the numbers lower for general working purposes. If you need higher detail in order to check something, you can always increase the setting in the dialog box. Be aware, however, that the settings there are global and will affect every object in your scene. You cannot choose one setting for one object and another for a different object.

Reducing the Clutter of Wireframe Objects

Once you have finished placing an object and you're ready to move on to another part of your scene, you can reduce the overall clutter of the wireframe objects in the scene by changing the object's wireframe to a simple one: a box (Objects > Show as Box, or ⌘-B). To change it back to the full wireframe mode, or lattice, select it and type ⌘-L (or Objects > Show as Mesh).

Changing the object's wireframe gives Bryce a "shortcut" for rendering the wireframe. You can have the highest detail wireframe resolution for those objects you're currently working with, since it's much simpler to draw a wireframe for a box than it is for a mountain shape. This render speed increase will be noticeable when you have multiple objects in your scene. So change into boxes the

tip
Changing many objects to Show as Box is the one workaround to having your entire scene set to a higher resolution of 64 in static mode. You can hone in on only those objects you want to see in detail, and the rest can be boxes.

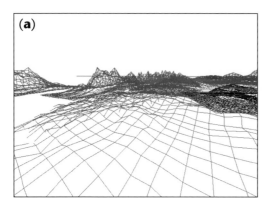 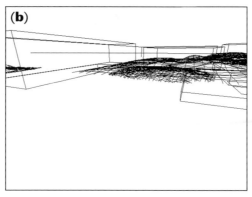

FIGURE 4–3 (**a**) Scene with many wireframe terrains; (**b**) the same scene with several terrains showing as boxes

objects that you can ignore for now. You can always change them back later. In the meantime, Bryce is operating faster. Figure 4–3 shows a scene with lattice (a) and with boxes (b).

Finally, you may do the same lattice-to-box action to a set of grouped objects. (More on grouping in Chapter 5.) The group will be changed to a box.

Trim Out the Render Fat

The settings in the Render Palette, not surprisingly, control different aspects of your scene that will cause the render time to increase or decrease. I've already mentioned the scene's resolution in pixel size. The left column of controls in the palette switch on different render options (see Fig. 4–4). Click the check boxes so that Auto Update, Use Shadows, Atmosphere, and Fog & Haze are all turned off. Bryce will not need to make calculations for any of those atmospheric conditions, so rendering time will be reduced. You will, of course, switch them all back on when you do your final render. But for now you'll save time on intermediate renders while you're still setting up the scene.

FIGURE 4–4 Render Palette with Render Options highlighted.

Putting Objects in Your Scene

Now that you've optimized your settings for the overall way Bryce works, it's time to focus on ways to optimize the scene creation process. In this section, I take you through some steps to build a scene, postponing the time-consuming renders until last.

Creation and Composition Always Come before Material Goods

The single most important thing you can do to save time while working in Bryce is to refrain from assigning any material settings to your objects until the end of your scene creation process. When you first launch Bryce, all objects take on a smooth white "plastic" surface. For your initial setup, this is fine. Work first on the overall shape of your world and what goes where before you begin tinkering with the intricacies of materials for each object. And if you have a scene with any complexity at all (more than one object), you *will* have to do a bit of tinkering.

In the scene creation process, you need to do many intermediate renders. For each of those intermediate renders, there's a potential for efficiency or sluggishness. I keep score on the number of renders for this hypothetical scene-building process. As the number of renders adds up, consider how much more time would be spent if each one were bogged down by having to render unnecessary detail.

As you work on your scene, you will probably ask and answer questions about your scene in this general order:

What objects are in the scene?

Where are they placed in relation to one another?

Where is the camera?

What are the atmospheric conditions?

What does each element look like (that is, what are its material settings)?

To answer these questions, especially the first two, you will probably need to look at your scene from the Top, Side, and Front Views. Seeing your scene in wireframe from alternate views may suffice. However, you may need to render in one of the other views in order to completely check that all of your elements are placed in proper relation to one another. While you're in Render mode (with the rendered image on screen), drag a marquee around only that portion of the image, then select Clear and Render (⌘-H). A few render passes will help you check for placement and other compositional details.

Score: Speedy Little Renders: 1 or *more;* Inefficient Renders: 0.

If you need to provide contrast between one object and another while setting up the scene, change one object's color. In the Materials Editor, assign it a different Diffuse color. You'll be able to distinguish the new object from the others, but you haven't traversed into the territory that makes rendering take a long time.

Score: Speedy Little Renders: 2 or *even more;* Inefficient Renders: 0.

Once you have your elements in place, compose your scene for the camera. For this, you will probably do at least a test render or two.

Score: Speedy Little Renders: 3 or *lots more;* Inefficient Renders: 0.

Now Blue Sky It

When you return to fine-tune your sky and fog, go to the Render Palette and switch on the Atmosphere controls. Now you'll use them. The top option, "Auto Update," is useful if you set things up a certain way, as I explain next. Otherwise, it can be a nuisance.

1. Select an initial sky setting. You'll get an automatic render across your whole image. Stop it after one or two passes.

Score: Speedy Little Renders: 4 or *tons more;* (this *is* a cumulative process!); Inefficient Renders: 0

2. With the rendered image on screen, drag a marquee around a vertical strip of the image. This is the only place Bryce will render, thereby giving you faster rendered responses to your atmospheric choices.

3. Change the sun's position, Fog & Haze settings, colors, clouds, shadows—all to your heart's content. With each change, your little strip renders away, thereby giving you the basic idea within two or three passes.

Score: Speedy Little Renders: 5 and probably *scads more;* Inefficient Renders: 0.

Zip-zip-zip-zip-zip! You've accomplished so much so far in setting up your scene. How much longer would these renders take if you'd included the sluggish parts? Now that you've got everything else out of the way, it's time to bring on that time-consuming stuff!

Cost of Materials

What is the time-consuming stuff? The surface attributes of objects, primarily three-dimensional, texture-based materials, cause the rendering process to take longer. Even so, some parts that make up the material setting are costlier than others. What are the "costly" parts of the materials? Reflectivity, transmitivity, bump gain, and high-contrast detail.

Reflectivity costs. As the ray is traced to find the color for that pixel, the material bounces the ray from here to there to some other place in order to get the final color. Higher physics notwithstanding, the shortest distance between two places is a straight line. If you introduce bouncing lines, the distance is greater and the render time increases.

Transmitivity costs. Bryce needs to calculate how much of the ray stays here with the object and how much goes through the object to whatever lies beyond. Transmitivity is a variation on the not-so-short distance between two places, since part of the ray travels beyond the normal stopping place.

Bump gain costs. Each individual bump needs to be calculated, and because there's a change in the surface, the new element—height—is added to the width and depth equations. Also, the introduction of indentation in the surface structure results in tiny shadows and light shifts, thereby giving Bryce more to do when it comes time to anti-alias the image. A bumpy, mottled surface takes longer to render than a smooth surface does.

Related to bump-induced anti-aliasing is the last costly material trait: *high-contrast detail.* When there is a lot of color contrast in a close space, much calculation will take place, especially during the anti-aliasing pass of the render cycle. Bryce will look to the surrounding 8 pixels to determine the final color of the one in the center. If there's high color contrast in those pixels, then Bryce needs to look more "carefully" in order to determine the final color.

What Kind of Time Difference Will Materials Make?

The seashore scene in Fig. 4–5, at default size, was rendered under different conditions. In Table 4–1, the time estimates of Bryce's second render pass are noted for each set of conditions. These times are on a Quadra-level computer.

As you can see, materials add four times the render time to your image, far more than introducing any atmospheric rendering condition does! The lesson is very clear: Get rid of those materials that are going to slow you down. Put them in later after you've set up everything else.

Can't Go Back?

"Okay, Kitchens," you may be saying right now, "I already assigned a three-dimensional, texture-based material to objects in my scene. It's slowing me down. What can I do now?"

FIGURE 4–5 In all cases, the ground surface had reflectivity set: (**a**) Completely blank scene; (**b**) atmospheric conditions added; (**c**) material settings applied plus atmospheric conditions.

TABLE 4–1 Scene rendered under different conditions to show how cost of materials affects render time

Materials	Shadows	Fog & Haze	Atmosphere	Time (minutes)
No	No	No	No	10
No	Yes	Yes	Yes	21
Yes	Yes	Yes	Yes	43

Piece o' cake! There's *always* a workaround. If you need to temporarily deactivate a material setting, here's how to do it. In the Materials Editor, change the mode from 3D Solid Texture to None. You'll keep your illumination and effects and color settings, but the main time consumer—the 3D Solid Texture—will go away. When you are ready to bring it all back, scroll through the mode options until you get back to it. Bryce remembers your 3D Solid Texture, so all should return to as before. If your material setting has reflectivity and transmitivity, then you can always let the setting render in the preset window and then save it. Change the mode to None and take away the costly illumination settings. Then when you're ready to go back, grab that preset and run.

The Need for Speed

Some of the previous speed-up-the-process cautions may not seem so necessary to you if you are running Bryce on a Power Mac. In fact, all three test situations for Table 4–1 resulted in a time estimate of five minutes on a Power Mac. However, I've run Bryce on a Macintosh IIcx (not fast), on that same IIcx with a Radius Rocket in it (Quadra level, and much quicker), on a Quadra 800, and on a Power Mac (downright zippy). I know what it's like to wait for a slower computer. Even if the computer is fast, though, it's a good idea to shave off as much time as possible up front.

DISTANCE RENDER

If you're running Bryce on a top-of-the-line Power Mac, then this section is not for you. Perhaps you're using one of the other non-top-of-the-line Macintosh models. As you are carefully placing all of your scene's elements, your test renders are taking too much time. So you'll want to do everything you can to make Bryce run faster. Try distance render as an alternative. You can see the general shape of things, and Bryce isn't forced to slow down for details.

Batch Management

Dragging and dropping the Bryce Scene icons (or aliases) onto the Bryce Application icon (or alias) allows you to render a series of images. Suppose you created several scenes and set them all to render overnight. In the morning, you return to your computer . . . and the renders aren't finished. Here's a way to remember which ones still need rendering:

1. Before doing your first batch render and while you're in the Finder, change the label of all of the scenes that are on your To Render list to "Essential." Then select View > By Label. All of your Scene document icons are now grouped together. (See Fig. 4–6.)
2. Drag the Scene icons to your Bryce Application icon, shut off your monitor, and go to sleep (or leave the office).
3. When you return to your computer, Bryce will have rendered half of the six scenes. The fourth is halfway through the anti-aliasing pass. Save the scene in progress and go to the Finder. All

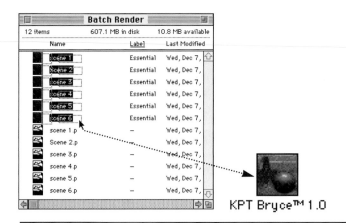

FIGURE 4–6 Batch render list—before rendering.

of your scene icons are still labeled "Essential" except for scene four; its label changed back to None when you saved it. Change it back to "Essential," since you know you have some more rendering to do. See Figure 4–7.

4. Unlabel the scenes that were completed so that you don't drag those to the Bryce Application icon the next time you do a batch render session. Select View > By Date. A series of PICT icons appears near the top of the folder (along with the Scene icon for the fourth scene you just saved). You can see from this list those scenes whose labels you want to change back to None. The scene names shown in Figure 4–7 are for a medium- to small-sized list. When you get a scene backlog of some two dozen images, this technique comes in extremely handy.

As a result, you have kept your icon labels up to date. The next time you want to do a batch render, all you need to do is simply view by label, select the labeled Scene document icons, and drag them to your Bryce Application icon (or its alias).

Variation on this theme: If you are working on several Scenes whose documents reside in different folders on your hard drive, create a To Be Rendered folder. Make aliases of your scenes in progress and put them in that folder. The originals stay in their own folders, and you get your batch rendering done.

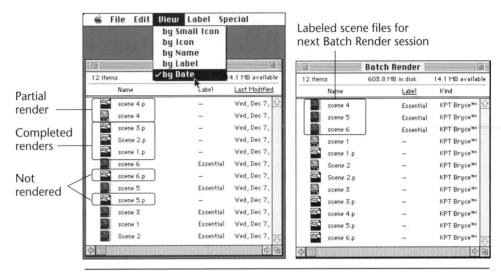

FIGURE 4–7 Batch render list—after rendering three and a half scenes.

Variation for System 7.5: System 7.5 has a folder called Recent Documents. The system creates aliases for the 10 most recent documents you have had open. Access Recent Documents from the Apple menu. Select the entire folder. There you will find your recent Scene document aliases, all ready to be dragged to your To Be Rendered folder for later batch processing.

General Brycean Behavior and Other Technical Considerations

This last section of the chapter turns the focus away from making you a "Bryce efficiency expert" to simply being a Bryce expert. Here I discuss general things about the way Bryce behaves.

Anomalies in Bryce

Of course, when talking about behavior, everyone likes to focus on the unexpected and the quirks. When things work as expected, there usually isn't much reason for comment. It's when events are contrary to expectations that discussion gets revved up. Here I talk about anomalies, discussing the particulars while indicating the bigger picture.

LIMITED UNDO FEATURE

Bryce's Undo (⌘-Z) is not your typical "Make a move—any move—and immediately undo it" type of Undo feature. Bryce's undos are limited to actions in the Edit menu and on the Edit Palette. Also, when you undo actions from the Edit category, you cannot redo them with another ⌘-Z.

The reason for this Undo in one category only stems from the developers of Bryce wanting to make the underlying technology available to as wide an audience as possible. There is a lot of serious calculation taking place behind the scenes (no pun intended). It requires a hefty amount of computing power to keep track of all of those actions. To allow for Undos for everything would swell Bryce's memory requirements so much that Bryce could not be an application for widespread use. Aaah, doesn't it make you look back fondly at the days when 8 MB of RAM was the be-all and end-all? In order to create a product that packs a lot of punch into a box for just over a hundred bucks and that is accessible to as wide an audience as possible, the developers made some sacrifices in the interest of seeing Bryce run on lowly machines with a "mere" 8 MB of RAM.

Therefore only the Edit functions are undoable. This does have its distinct advantages when working in the Edit functions, however, as I explain in Chapter 5, which covers Edit controls.

But it can also be a pain sometimes. Here are some workarounds. "Revert to saved" is an option I've used in times of desperation. If I've worked on a particular object, I may copy that to the Macintosh clipboard before reverting, then paste it back into the scene. Also, two good compromise measures to keep intermediate benchmarks of the scene in progress are to save camera views in the Add View As... menu and to save Sky presets.

NO PROMPT WHEN SAVING FILES

For the same reason Bryce doesn't recognize some of the actions you perform as being undoable, it will allow you to close a document without giving you a prompt asking if you want to save changes. You may be surprised at how abruptly the work you have done with the camera or skies and fog or even a render can all go away without Bryce's stopping and saying, "Wait, you haven't saved this!" In this sense, Bryce is not as forgiving of user actions as are most other Macintosh applications.

However, there are circumstances when Bryce will ask you if you want to save changes, such as when you close the document. In Bryce this happens when you quit the application, as well as when you open or create a new document. Only one scene can be open at a time, so creating or opening a new document forces the current one to close. (Bryce has no File > Close option. Nor does it have a close box in the document window.)

For Bryce to ask you if you want to save changes, you need to do one of the following:

- Create a new object or set of objects.
- Do something that's worthy of undoing, that is, an edit function.

A variation on this happens when you change the scene's image resolution in the Render Palette and then save the document. Bryce will present you with the Save As… dialog box, at which time you may rename the differently sized document or save it over the old one. (Use this technique when you make high-resolution scenes based on smaller originals. The first one could be called something like SCENE NAME and the new one, when you are given the chance to rename it, could be called SCENE NAME.HIREZ.)

The only time the "Revert to saved" function is grayed out in Bryce is when you have created a new scene and have not yet saved it. When you change from one resolution to another, Bryce treats the situation the same as if you had just created a new document.

TABLE 4–2 Preferences and other settings that carry over from one scene to another.

and Expert Mode is...	When Bryce Is Open		When Relaunching Bryce	
	ON	OFF	ON	OFF
Sky Setting	R	R	R	F
Camera Placement	R	F	R	F
Saved Camera Views	R	R	R	R
Materials Setting	R	R	F	F
Wireframe Color	R	R	R	F
Wireframe Resolution	R	R	R	F
See Underground	R	R	R	R

R = Remembers   F = Forgets

Preferences: Expert Mode

In the Preferences dialog box (Edit > Preferences...), you have the option of choosing different states under which Bryce will run.

Preferences are saved with each document. So, what happens when you close a document for which the preferences were something other than the default? In other words, how are the preferences saved from scene to scene or transferred from scene to scene? Well, when you type ⌘-N to create a new scene, Bryce remembers preference settings from the previous scene.

Table 4–2 lists the different preference settings that carry over from scene to scene. Some Bryce will remember from the previous scene; others it will forget and so will revert to the default settings. In the table, "When Bryce Is Open" refers to what happens when you create a *new* scene after a previous scene has been open. "When Re-launching Bryce" refers to what is remembered from the previous time Bryce was up and running.

Bryce remembers camera and sky settings from the previous scene when you create a new scene. Also, when the Expert Mode is switched on, Bryce remembers the camera and sky settings from one work session to the next. Whatever state the sky was in when you last quit Bryce is the same state the sky will be the next time you relaunch the application.

Not Enough Memory and Default Settings

If you open up a scene that requires more memory (RAM) than you have allocated to Bryce, Bryce will alert you that it doesn't have enough memory and is reverting to default format. What you will then immediately notice is that the resolution of the scene changes. But what you may not notice until later is that all of your settings went back to default. This means, for example, that if you were in Expert Mode when you ran up against Bryce's memory limit, you are no longer in Expert Mode. If you had set Bryce so that it opens a new document when you launch the application, you will be forced back to the Combinations dialog box the next time you open Bryce.

Monitors: What to Do with Screen Savers, Clocks, and Other Details

You will probably have Bryce render during the time you are away from your computer, for example when you are asleep or on your lunch hour. So, you will inevitably run into the question of what to do with your monitor. Should you keep it on and let your screen saver run?

Some screen savers interfere with the rendering process. Super-Clock and System 7.5's Clock, too, have been known to throw a wrench in the render machinery. Screen savers and on-screen clocks tend to interfere with the rendering process because they are continuously asking for the computer's attention. Bryce, however, wants as much of the processor as it can get while rendering. It "concentrates" on the task at hand and does not constantly monitor for keystrokes and mouse clicks (which is why you may wait a few seconds when it is stopping a render). Having to be on constant lookout for events on a system level slows down Bryce's rendering time. Clocks are continuously updating a portion of your screen.

Screen savers are also watching to see how long it has been since the mouse was last moved or a key was pressed.

Who's going to get the upper hand in this situation: Bryce, which wants to ignore all outside stimuli, or the screen saver and/or clock, which prefer to stay aware of the outside stimuli? I'd rather give Bryce the upper hand. After all, when I come back to my computer, I get pretty images. Besides, the clock on the wall works just fine. I have, however, successfully rendered images on a machine that had both SuperClock! and AfterDark running, so I know it can be done. That is just not my chosen setup.

My recommendation here is to disable the screen saver and then shut the monitor off while you're away so that there will be nothing on a system level that interferes with the render process. And, if you're the one that pays the utility bills you'll save some nickels.

Keyboard Shortcuts

Part of any tally of behaviors includes a section on keyboard short-cuts. This is not *the* definitive list; see Appendix A for that. Rather, it's a discussion of some general behavior on Bryce's part where there is a common keyboard shortcut theme. In this section I discuss Palette behavior, Bryce's Full Screen Mode, and Bryce's dialog boxes.

PALETTES AND THEIR GENERAL BEHAVIOR

When you are in non-Expert Mode, you can only have two palettes show at one time—the Master Palette and one of the Create, Edit, Sky & Fog, or Render Palettes. Changing from one palette to another is relatively easy. If you have a small monitor, non-Expert Mode is a good way to work.

If you're a key shortcut aficionado, you can call up the palettes by their keyboard equivalents:

⌘-1 = Master Palette

⌘-2 = Create Palette

⌘-3 = Edit Palette

⌘-4 = Sky & Fog Palette

⌘-5 = Render Palette

⌘-F = Full Palette

In Expert Mode you can have as many palettes showing as you like. If all your palettes are on-screen, you can use the pertinent keyboard equivalent command to bring the desired palette to the front.

The Master Palette is always active, even if it is positioned behind one of the other palettes. The only place on the Master Palette where you can control its movement is the bar at its top. So it can be behind another palette, yet you are unable to move it. Use the keyboard equivalent (⌘-1) to make it pop out in front again. That's quicker than closing or moving all the other palettes that obscure the Master Palette.

FULL SCREEN COMMAND (⌘-F)

Bryce's default method of displaying on-screen is to black out everything but the scene and the palettes. If you have a cluttered desktop or other applications and windows open, this enables you to concentrate solely on Bryce. But there may be times when you want to have your scene be in a regular window. When you are in Expert Mode, ⌘-F will toggle you back and forth between Full Screen Mode and Window Mode.

Why would you want Bryce to be in Window Mode? There are two possible reasons. First, if you are working on several versions of a scene and discover that you've lost your place ("Wait a second, which scene was this?"), then by having Bryce in Window Mode, you can see the file name on the window's Title Bar. (You can do the same by selecting Save As... from the File menu. Bryce automatically puts the current file name in the Save dialog box. Once you've found out the name, click Cancel.)

Second, you may want to toggle between two applications. Say you are carefully working on a terrain and need to change it in Photoshop. You can toggle between Bryce and Photoshop with a mouse click on any of the background application's open windows. You can see the other application beneath the current one when you are in Window Mode.

DIALOG BOXES

Bryce's dialog boxes, especially those that are in the "!" dialog boxes, Camera controls, Terrain Editor, and Materials Editor (Illumination controls, Mapping control, Deep Texture Editor) have numerical settings. You can type the numbers in directly. Any horizontal bar that turns blue when you click it will accept numerical typing. The following conventions apply:

- To change any positive number to a negative and a negative to a positive, type a minus sign (–).
- To move from one box to the next, press the Tab key.

However, if you make a mistake when entering numbers, you cannot press the Delete key to change the number just entered. Instead, you must click or tab to another area and then come back to change the number.

Conclusion

In this chapter, I discussed ways to optimize your working situation so that you get the most processing bang for the time buck. The most important thing to remember is not to set up your material settings until last, as they will make your intermediate renders take longer.

I also discussed the various idiosyncrasies of Bryce: the vagaries of Bryce's Undo feature, what preferences are carried over from Expert Mode and from one scene to the next, whether to turn off your monitor during render, keyboard shortcuts, and numerical entry.

CHAPTER 5

Selecting and Editing Controls

"The Caterpillar was the first to speak. "What size do you want to be?" it asked.

"Oh, I'm not particular as to size," Alice hastily replied; "only one doesn't like changing so often, you know."

"I *don't* know," said the Caterpillar.

Alice said nothing; she had never been so much contradicted in all her life before, and she felt that she was losing her temper.

"Are you content now?" said the Caterpillar.

"Well, I should like to be a *little* larger, sir, if you wouldn't mind," said Alice: "three inches is such a wretched height to be."

"It is a very good height indeed!" said the Caterpillar angrily, rearing itself upright as it spoke (it was exactly three inches high).

"But I'm not used to it!" pleaded poor Alice in a piteous tone. And she thought to herself, "I wish the creatures wouldn't be so easily offended!"

"You'll get used to it in time," said the Caterpillar; and it put the hookah into its mouth and began smoking again.

. . . Then it got down off the mushroom and crawled away into the grass, merely remarking as it went, "One side will make you grow taller, and the other side will make you grow shorter."

"One side of *what*? The other side of *what*?" thought Alice to herself.

"Of the mushroom," said the Caterpillar, just as if she had asked it aloud; and in another moment it was out of sight.

Lewis Carroll, *Alice in Wonderland*

■ All the different ways to select objects
■ What it takes to resize, rotate, move, group, flip, align, and ground Brycean objects
■ Bryce's internal grid
■ Grouping and ungrouping objects

In this chapter, I discuss some of the deeper whys and hows of editing and selecting and provide you with a more integrated concept of working with the Edit controls and how they work together. I talk about what you can and can't do and the most efficient way to work. There also are some hidden gems for smooth working in Bryce tucked here and there along the way, so keep a lookout for them!

Natural Selection

There are several ways to select Bryce wireframe objects in order to perform an action. When you have a scene with several objects in it, it's helpful to know all of the different ways by which you can select and deselect the different objects in your scene. Here are your selection choices:

■ Click the object directly.
■ Drag the marquee over one or more objects to select it (or them).
■ Use the Tab key to cycle through different objects in a scene.

You also can use the Edit Palette (see Fig. 5–1) as follows to select objects:

■ Click the arrows (this action is similar to using the Tab key). There are two sets of arrows, upper and lower. Click the upper set to cycle forward and backward. The right arrow cycles you forward from one object to the next, and the left one cycles you backwards. In the lower set, click the left arrow to select the first

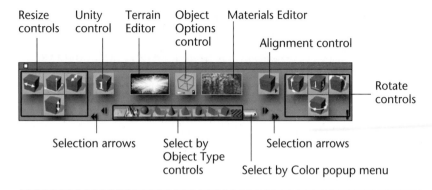

Resize controls | Unity control | Terrain Editor | Object Options control | Materials Editor | Alignment control | Rotate controls

Selection arrows | Select by Object Type controls | Selection arrows | Select by Color popup menu

FIGURE 5–1 The Edit Palette.

object created and the right arrow to select the last object created.

Note: The Edit Palette is unlike the Tab key in this one respect: When you're in the Edit Palette, you can cycle in either direction. Click to the left or the right to go in either direction. When you use the Tab key, however, you cycle forward through from one object to the next to the next. You cannot reverse direction.

■ Use the Object Selection icons, which are the same as the Create Object icons. Click the Sphere Object Selection icon to select all spheres.
■ Use the "select by color" popup menu. This method of selecting objects works in conjunction with the Object Options control. You can assign different colors to different objects and then select all objects of that color.

Shift Key and Selections/Deselections

Get more control with selecting by using the Shift key. Use it to select more than one object or as a toggle to deselect/select an object. This is most intuitive in the direct "click-object-to-select-it" process.

Sometimes when clicking an object, you'll inadvertently select two objects. In the image in Figure 5–2, this happens easily in Top View when a portion of the terrain is "hidden underground." You may

FIGURE 5–2 Both objects are selected when you click, even if one is hidden from view underground (Top View).

not be able to see it, but it's still there, and it will be selected when you click it. So if both objects are selected but you want to select only the one, hold down the Shift key and click on the terrain (or whatever you don't want selected) to deselect it.

Sometimes you will have several objects that are perfectly aligned with the camera. That is, there are several objects there, but it looks as if there is only one. In this case, clicking on the visible object usually selects the first object and not all the other objects underneath. If you want to select all of the objects, hold down the Shift key and click. Bryce will select everything under the cursor.

You could easily find yourself in a situation where you have several terrains and other objects, all of which overlap one another as you view them from the camera's perspective. With that complex a scene, if you click something directly, you'll select a whole host of objects. It's at that point that you should consider the other options for selecting.

Shift Key and the Select Control Icons

You can use the Shift key in conjunction with the select control icons.

Say, for example, you have two terrains and a sphere selected and you want to deselect the sphere. Hold down the Shift key and then click on the Sphere Selection icon. Voila!

Now, let's say that you have all of those objects selected and you want to add the pyramid to your selection. Hold down the Shift key and click the pyramid. The pyramid will be added to your selection.

SHIFT KEY AND THE SELECT BY COLOR POPUP MENU

If you want to select all of the objects whose wireframes are white, simply use the "select by color" popup menu (see Fig. 5–3b). Then, if you want to add an object(s) of another color, hold down the Shift key while selecting that color. To change the colors of your

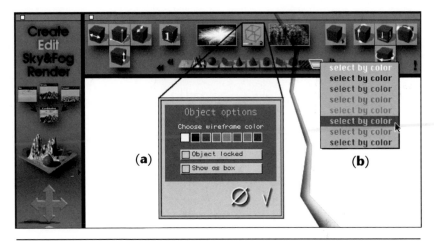

FIGURE 5–3 (**a**) The Object Options dialog box for setting the color of the wireframe object; (**b**) the "select by color" popup menu for selecting all objects of a certain color.

wireframes, click the Object Options control to change the selected object's wireframe color (see Fig. 5–3a).

SHIFT KEY AND ALL OPTIONS

You can get even more sophisticated than that. You can combine all of these selection processes in order to hone in on your desired object.

Say you have a scene with four terrains, a ground, a pyramid, and a sphere. Two of the terrains, the ground and the sphere, are colored black. The other two terrains and the pyramid share a different color (see Fig. 5–4a). If you want to select only the two terrains that are colored black, you cannot do so by clicking the Terrain Select control. Nor can you do so by selecting the color: "select by color: (black)." You first have to eliminate the other black objects or eliminate the other terrains, as follows:

1. Select "select by color" (see Fig. 5–4b).
2. Deselect the objects you do not want.
3. Shift-click the Sphere Select control. This deselects the black sphere (see Fig. 5–4c).

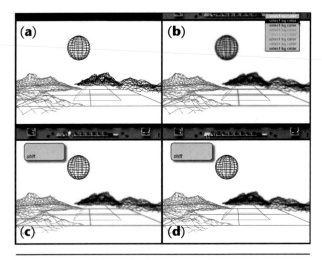

FIGURE 5–4 Selected objects are shown as fuzzy or glowing: (**a**) Wireframe view of scene; (**b**) "select by color" to select objects; (**c**) deselecting the sphere; (**d**) deselecting the ground.

4. Shift-click the Ground Select control. Doing this deselects the black ground (see Fig. 5–4d).

The Underlying Structure of the Brycean Universe

Now that your object is selected, you can do something to it. Change its size. Change its position. Change its attributes. Or change its orientation in the world. This is what the other controls in the Edit Palette are for. I'll take a look at them in turn, but first, I want to discuss the Brycean universe, the *xyz* space, and the underlying grid.

XYZ Axes

Most of the adjustments in the Edit Palette work in *xyz* space. Although the *x, y,* and *z* of the Camera controls are always oriented with the camera, the *xyz* controls under the Edit Palette are absolute. It would be as easy to capriciously change them as it

FIGURE 5–5 *x-, y-,* and *z*-axes in Bryce as seen from default view.

would be to shift the direction of north by 28° or so. No can do! In Bryce's virtual space, they're fixed. You expand an object, say, in one direction, rotate it in another, and move it in the third.

Think of the different axes this way. Assuming you are in default view, you are facing "north" (see Fig. 5–5). The *x*-axis is east/west. The *z*-axis is north/south. The *y*-axis is altitude (height—up and down). You can also think of the *x*-axis as defining width, *y*-axis as height, and *z*-axis as depth. However, *width, height,* and *depth* imply the dimensions of an actual object. In Bryce, we're talking about the overall space. As I discuss the different controls, I refer to this space. It is most helpful to remember two things: which dimension is which, and that the *x, y,* and *z* here are dimensions in the overall Brycean universe.

Now that you know that the *x-, y-,* and *z*-axes are absolute, I'll take a little side trip into the grid before talking about how to work with these axes practically.

The Grid

Inside the Brycean universe is an invisible internal grid, which is controlled via a command in the Alignment popup menu, "Snap to grid." Other than that and a cursory mention in the *KPT Bryce Explorer's Guide,* though, not much has been said about the grid. Yet the grid is the underlying unseen structure to the Brycean universe, and many of the Edit controls occur in relation to the grid. You can work more efficiently in Bryce when you are aware of the grid.

The grid has no set of units or measurements that correspond to the real world. No inches, picas, miles, kilometers, or anything like that. Bryce is a world unto itself and the Brycean Units and Measurement Council devised this particular set of units by their own internal logic for our use and pleasure. The grid and units of measurement correspond to the sizes of objects as they come into being in the Brycean universe.

When you create a primitive in Bryce, it comes into a certain defined space. I will call that defined space a *unity unit*. The unity unit is the size and orientation that objects snap to when you click the Unity button. (I discuss the concept of unity more later in this chapter.) When you create a ground, infinite plane, or terrain, the object comes into Bryce at four times the size of a unity unit. I call that a *terrain unit*. (Although terrains pop into the scene covering four times the area of a unity unit, they remain one unity unit high. Also, the ground and infinite plane, although their wireframes are one terrain unit in size, aren't literally at that scale. Both of these planes render on an infinite scale.)

The unity unit is the foundational unit of measurement, though. For each unity unit, there are four *grid units*. Finally, there are 51 *option-nudge units* to one grid unit. ("Option-nudge" is the name for the action of holding down the Option key while nudging objects.) The chart below and Figure 5–6 show you how all of these units fit together.

$$51 \text{ option-nudge units } = 1 \text{ grid unit}$$

$$4 \text{ grid units } = 1 \text{ unity unit}$$

$$4 \text{ unity units } = 1 \text{ terrain unit}$$

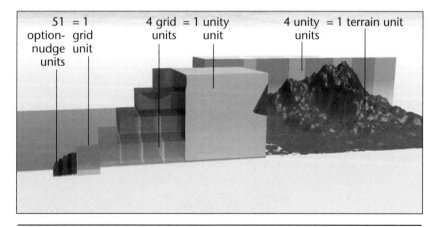

FIGURE 5–6 Bryce's grids and different units of measure and their equivalents.

Don't blame me for the strange numbering. It's like wondering why there are 12 inches in a foot, 36 inches in a yard, and 5,280 feet in a mile. (And how many inches are in a light year, anyhow?) Once you live in this world, it makes sense. Or at least you get used to it.

I will refer back to these standards of measurement in my discussion of other Edit controls in this chapter. Most important to remember are the unity unit and the grid unit. Four grid units to a unity unit. Makes perfect sense, doesn't it?

Moving Objects in Bryce

You can move objects around in your scene either by dragging them or by selecting them and nudging with certain keys. To drag them, select and drag. Drag in the Main View, or, for more precision, in Top, Side, or Front View. Far more precision is obtained by using the nudge keys. The next section explores nudging in detail.

Moving Objects by Nudging

You can use the arrow keys and the page up and page down keys to move objects by one grid unit, as summarized next:

The *arrow keys* move objects horizontally.

The *left* and *right* arrow keys move objects along the *x*-axis.

The *up* and *down* arrow keys move objects along the *z*-axis.

The *page up/page down* keys move objects vertically along the *y*-axis.

MOVING OBJECTS IN TOP VIEW

When you are in Top View, the arrow keys work precisely as you see them: up, down, left, right. Page up moves objects toward you; page down moves objects away from you.

MOVING OBJECTS IN FRONT VIEW

In Front View, the movements of the left and right arrow keys are still obvious, that is, pressing the keys moves objects left and right, respectively. The down arrow key moves objects toward you; the up arrow key moves them away from you. The page up and page down keys move objects up and down, respectively.

MOVING OBJECTS IN SIDE VIEW

Side View is a bit trickier because the arrow keys don't move in the directions indicated on the keyboard labels. In fact, they're switched:

The *down* arrow moves objects *left.*

The *up* arrow moves objects *right.*

The *left* arrow moves objects *away* from you.

The *right* arrow moves objects *toward* you.

The *page up* and *page down* keys move objects up and down, as usual.

MOVING OBJECTS IN MAIN VIEW

In Main View, you can change your camera location, so you cannot predict whether objects will move left, right, up, or down, or toward or away from you when using nudge keys. In the default (Reset Views), however, the nudge key movements are similar to the movements in Front View. The left and right arrow keys move objects left and right, the up and down arrow keys move objects toward and away from you, and the page up and page down keys move objects up and down.

If you haven't already played around with moving an object, do so. With a bit of practice, you'll find that knowing which key moves in which direction in which view becomes completely intuitive, although you may still get a bit tangled up in Side View.

MORE MOVEMENT NOTES

When you press any of the arrow keys to nudge an object, the object will be moved by increments of one grid unit. That doesn't necessarily mean they will move *on the grid,* however; they will move over by that grid amount. Of course, if your object is already aligned to the grid, it will stay on the grid as it moves.

To nudge by even smaller increments, hold down the Option key as you press a nudge key. Pressing a nudge key 51 times equals one regular nudge.

CONSTRAIN KEYS

Although the Macintosh generally uses the Shift key to constrain the movement of the cursor, there are only two directions involved—horizontal and vertical, as you look at your monitor. Because Bryce works in three dimensions, it departs from the limitations of one constraining key. It has three, one for each dimension, as follows:

> The *Control key* constrains along the *x*-axis.
>
> The *Option key* constrains along the *y*-axis.
>
> The *Command key* constrains along the *z*-axis.

Make sure you hold down the constraining key *before* you begin dragging. Bryce will not let you press the constraining key part way through the drag and then pop your object onto that axis. When you hold down the constraining key, the cursor changes to an arrow. Then when you drag, the object will move only on that one axis.

The constrain keys work in any of the views. However, each view has one axis on which a constrain key won't work. That axis is whichever axis you are peering down in order to see the scene, as follows:

> In Top View, the *y*-axis (Option key) does not work.
>
> In Side View, the *x*-axis (Control key) does not work.
>
> In Front View, the *z*-axis (Command key) does not work.

When you are in Main View with the Reset Camera View default, looking straight on at your scene down the *z*-axis, Bryce will operate the same way as in Front View—the Command key for the *z*-axis will not work. Rotate the scene ever so slightly with the Trackball, and the *z*-axis constrain key comes to life. As long as you're peering straight down the *z*-axis, though, nothing will budge on that axis.

Moving Things That Are "Hard to Move"

If you're in Side or Front View and you want to drag something that's flat, such as a square, disk, ground, or infinite plane, you might have a bit of a problem. Those are very difficult objects to select from that angle because Bryce "sees" objects in a ray-traced fashion. In other words, almost all of the rays pass above or below the flat object, so it's hard for Bryce to "see" at that angle (see Fig. 5–7a). But there are times when you must look at your scene from that angle in order to make your adjustments; the other angles simply won't do. Here's how to have complete control over that flat object.

RECIPE FOR THE HARD OF MOVING

Follow these steps to move a flat object:

1. Create a small sphere to use as a "moving partner." Make it a different color from all the other objects in your scene (see Fig. 5–7b).
2. Select the sphere and flat object as follows: First, cycle through with the Tab key until your flat object is selected. Next, hold down the Shift key and select the sphere either by directly clicking it or by selecting by its unique color in the "select by color" popup menu.
3. With both objects selected, drag the sphere. The flat object will go along for the ride! (See Fig. 5–7c.) Place your flat object wherever it needs to go.

Never again will you be eluded by an object that doesn't want to move!

Duplicating Objects

Bryce has a command for duplicating objects (⌘-D). It's under the Edit menu, of course. The Duplicate function creates a copy of the selected object(s) and places that copy one nudge unit back on the z-axis (assuming that you are looking at your scene from the standard default view facing "north.") Like the nudge keys, Duplicate works along the grid.

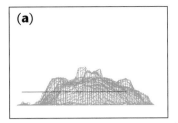

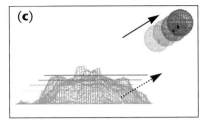

FIGURE 5–7 Moving using a moving partner: (**a**) the flat object; (**b**) create a sphere; (**c**) moving the sphere with the flat object following along.

If you want to override Duplicate's one-direction limitation, you can go through the copying process yourself. By placing a copy of the object exactly on top of the original, you could use any nudge key to move it in any direction. Copy-paste-nudge (⌘-C, ⌘-V, nudge-key) does just that.

The Copy function creates a copy. That much is clear. The Paste function places the copy precisely on top of the original object. (You can, if you'd like, delete the original between the copy and the paste steps. The pasted version comes back into the scene right in the same spot the original occupied.) Now nudge in any direction.

In fact, the Duplicate command seems to be a macro of that copy-paste-nudge process. Try duplicating a few times and then for the heck of it, a paste. (Don't copy first; that's the whole point!) A new copy shows up in the same place as the second-to-last duplicated object.

FIGURE 5–8 Brick wall built by copy-paste-nudge duplication of objects.

The advantage of copy-paste-nudge is that you can, of course, nudge in any direction you like. The newly pasted object is the active selection, so you can work in a continuous stream of copy-paste-nudges to build all sorts of things! Build walls by laying a row of bricks: Copy-paste-nudge right, copy-paste-nudge to the end of the row. Select all the bricks in that row, and copy-paste-nudge to make the wall (see Fig. 5–8). See Chapter 10, where I discuss multiple objects construction, for more about this type of construction.

Rotating and Resizing

Now I take a look at the two sets of controls on either side of the Edit Palette: Resizing and Rotation. Before discussing the specifics of which control does what, a bit of *xyz* general orientation is in order.

Both sets of controls are set up similarly—a row of three controls, with another control centered below. There is no label that says, "This control is *x*." So how do you tell them apart? To follow along in this section, you will need to know this, as all the directions for using the controls will refer to them as *x* or *y* or *z*.

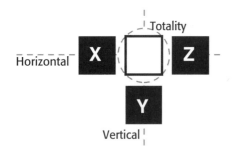

FIGURE 5–9 How to tell your *xyz*'s apart in the Resize and Rotate controls on the Edit Palette.

There are two ways to conceptualize which is which, aside from the arrow markings on the objects (see Fig. 5–9). First, they are set up on two different planes. The *x* and *z* are on the horizontal plane; the *y*-axis is the vertical plane. Where the two planes intersect is a special tool. For Resize, it is the Proportional Resize tool (it resizes in all dimensions—horizontal and vertical). For Rotate, since you can't rotate all axes at once, it is the Ground control, which sets the selected object on ground level. Second, if you account for the special tool and "read" from left to right, the tools are placed in alphabetical order, *xyz*.

Resize Controls

Using the Resize controls, you can take objects that start out symmetrical (a cube or pyramid) and create objects that are far different from their original shape. A cube primitive becomes a flat "board," a square tile, a rectangular brick, or a diamond, and so on. A pyramid makes a flag. Plus, the same basic primitive can take all manner of different shapes. A cylinder can be a column, a teeny tiny tube, almost a piece of string, and a flat coin. This object flexibility is yours with the Resize controls. Figure 5–10 shows several objects created using Resize.

FIGURE 5–10 A ridiculously simple scene in which all objects were created from primitives.

The Resize controls, on the left of the Edit Palette, will make a selected object grow or shrink. Drag from one of the controls and watch the object grow. When you like what you have, let go. Use the Proportional control to reduce or enlarge uniformly or use one of the three Axis controls to change the size in a particular direction.

When you shrink your object (assume for the moment that you're working with the Proportional Resize control), the Resize control reaches a pause point: It stops when the object's size is one fourth what it was. So if you start out with an object at a unity unit and shrink it until it pauses, it's exactly one fourth its original size. And what is one fourth of a unity unit? A grid unit!

If the copy-paste-nudge sequence didn't strike you as particularly wonderful, think about it again. This shrink-to-one-fourth-size capability is extremely handy. Once your object is in grid unit size, you can make copies of it with full assurance that each one copy will neatly stack next to or on top of the others. Here's where you get those brick walls and tiled floors.

This one-fourth grid unit size rule assumes you shrank the object from its native unity unit size. If you enlarge it first prior to shrinking it, the shrunken version will be one fourth whatever size it was enlarged to. It won't necessarily be grid size.

When you enlarge an object, there is no pause point at which the object reaches a certain size. More than likely, while dragging the control, you'll run into the edge of your monitor, thereby reaching an unnatural pause point. If you are working on a Mac with a small (13-inch or 14-inch) monitor, you may find that you need to reposition your Edit Palette lower on your screen in order to get the full range of resize motion in one pass. To make an object shrink to precisely one fourth its size, resizing in one pass is essential.

There is a key combination that will do proportional enlargements and reductions. To enlarge, press the multiply (*) key; the object's size doubles. To reduce, press the divide (/) key; the object's size shrinks to half. Pressing the / key twice is the same as dragging the resize control to reduce the object to one fourth its size. You can use the / and * keys located on either the keypad or the regular keyboard.

The one-fourth pause point doesn't occur only with the Proportional Resize tools. The x-, y-, and z-axes resize tools also stop at one-fourth size when reducing. When you want to make one primitive fit with another, pause points enable you can make objects that fit together very quickly. Let's take a look at how the grid works with both Resize and nudge units to create a composite object.

RESIZE AND NUDGE RECIPE

Follow these steps to create a composite object (see also Fig. 5–11):

1. Create a cube and a pyramid. Select one of them.
2. Use the Resize Z control (top right in the cluster) to bring the depth of the object to one-fourth size. Drag until it stops. It will be precisely one fourth its depth.
3. Select the other object. Do the same thing (reduce it to one fourth). See? It's an exact match! No need to "eyeball" it.
4. To set one object exactly on top of the other, select the one destined for the top (in this case, the pyramid). Press the page up key four times; this will put the pyramid on top of the cube. Was that easy or was that easy?

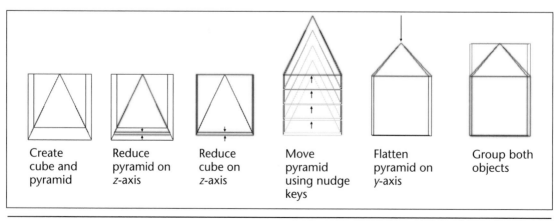

| Create cube and pyramid | Reduce pyramid on z-axis | Reduce cube on z-axis | Move pyramid using nudge keys | Flatten pyramid on y-axis | Group both objects |

FIGURE 5–11 Composite object from a cube and pyramid.

5. Extra credit: Flatten the pyramid by dragging down on the Resize Y control. Then group both objects.

Center Object

The "!" dialog box has an additional option for editing your objects. When you click the "!," this dialog box opens. Here, you can make a choice about how Bryce scales your objects (see Fig. 5–12).

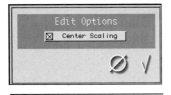

FIGURE 5–12 Edit Options box showing Center Scaling *on.*

When Center Scaling is *on,* all actions performed on objects will originate from the object's center. When Center Scaling is *off,* any action will originate from the object's bottom (in Resize and Rotation) or by the axis in question (in alignment).

When you use the Resize controls, Center Scaling *off* treats all objects as they are from the bottom. This works fine for Proportional Resize and Resize Y (height). But for all intents and purposes, Resize X and Resize Z are the same when Center Scaling is *off* as when it is *on.* (It would be nicer if X enlarged an object to the right and Z enlarged it to the back.)

Turn Center Scaling *off* when you have one object set atop another. However, when you have one object placed *inside* another, such as two spheres where one sphere is a cloud layer over a planet, resize with Center Scaling *on* in order to keep the uniform relationship between the spheres.

I talk about Center Scaling more when I discuss the Rotation and Alignment controls later in this chapter.

Rotation

The cluster of Edit controls on the right side of the Edit Palette alter the orientation of the object. Rotate the object along the *x*-, *y*-, or *z*-axis. As you look at the controls, think of the axis as a skewer piercing the object (see Fig. 5–13). The object rotates around that skewer or axis.

Of all the Edit controls I discuss in this chapter, the Rotation controls are the one set that has no relation to the grid units. However,

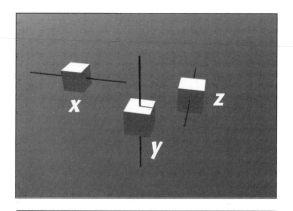

FIGURE 5–13 Each axis depicted as a skewer.

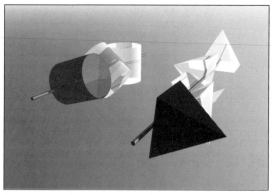

FIGURE 5–14 Rotation with Center Scaling *on* (cylinder) and *off* (pyramid).

Center Scaling has *everything* to do with object rotation. When you rotate an object with Center Scaling *on,* the object will always move around its center. The cylinder in Figure 5–14 has been rotated with Center Scaling *on.* When Center Scaling is *off,* the object will rotate around its bottom. The pyramid in Figure 5–14 has been rotated with Center Scaling *off.*

Note: There are no constrain keys that enable you to rotate by precise (usually 45°) increments. If you want to make a square lie down flat (Bryce creates the square upright), you will have to rotate it. Since there's no constrain key, you must control the degree of precision by hand. Looking at a square from Side View, you can precisely "eyeball" it fairly easily as you rotate. It's flat when it's a solid horizontal line with no jagged breaks.

Rotation and Resizing Together (or Apart)

Once you have rotated any object, you cannot resize it on any one axis and have the object keep its basic shape. Using the Proportional Resize control or the * and / keys are the exception to this. No matter where your object is oriented in space, it will stay consistent to itself when you resize proportionately.

Earlier I discussed *x*-, *y* -,and *z*-axes in the Brycean universe. These axes are fixed in space and unchangeable; this is no lie. Resizing along, say, the *x*-axis takes place in an east/west direction no matter which way the object is facing or where it is rotated. So if you have moved it out of its basic alignment, you will no longer have a cube with planes that are 90° from each other. Your nice even cube will have become a warped polygon. Sure, that's what you may want it to be. But if you thought you were resizing the *object along the object's own x-axis,* you're in for a sad surprise!

Or, say you elongate a cube (see Fig. 5–15a) along the *x*-axis so that it is a "brick" shape and then you rotate it (see Fig. 5–15b). You cannot later say, "Well, I need that brick to be a little longer," and then drag on the Resize X control. Once the object has been rotated, any additional "lengthening" will pull it in such a way that it no longer looks like a brick (see Fig. 5–15c). Figure 5–15 compares two sets of shape distortion. The bottom row has been rotated, whereas the top row has not.

Think of Bryce's Resize controls as a force field. You select the object on which the force field will act and then drag to control the force field until you make the object just so. It's like a room with shrinking walls. Once those walls start squeezing in, it doesn't matter which way the cone or cube is facing (see Fig. 5–16). It's going to get smaller along that one axis.

If you think of Resize as invoking the *z* force or the *x* force or the *y* force to act on your selected object(s), you won't have any nasty surprises when you're adjusting the sizes of your objects. Adjust their size first; rotate them later. And may the Force be with you. Live long and prosper. You get the idea.

However, there may be cases when shape distortion is the desired end. Rotate the

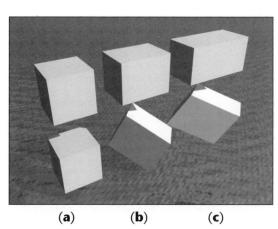

(a)　　**(b)**　　**(c)**

FIGURE 5–15 Top row has no rotation; bottom row has (**a**) objects as they were created; (**b**) objects enlarged along the *x*-axis; bottom object then rotated; (**c**) objects enlarged *again* along the *x*-axis.

FIGURE 5–16 The cone is progressively flattened by resizing on the *y*-axis. The arrows show how the crushing force comes "from the outside," squashing the object with no regard for the object's own orientation.

object and then make it grow or shrink in any of the three directions to make it into that shape you want. A pyramid can be forced into a right angle, and with judicious use of the Rotate controls, you can coax terrains to have overhanging edges. For more on how to create a terrain overhang, see Chapter 9, where I cover superlative nature imagery.

In the default view, when you're looking at objects that have popped into the Brycean universe all aligned with those *x*, *y*, and *z* forces, it would seem that the lengthening/shortening forces come from "within" the object. Once your object has been rotated slightly, the force acts on the object from the same direction; the object is altered differently. This has its advantages because there are situations when this kind of tweaking is a desired occurrence. But if you've been painstakingly altering the position and rotation of an object and then decide it needs to be an eentsy bit wider, you will have to start over. Of course, if you have rotated it only slightly, then all you need to do is rotate it back.

Unity Button: A Way to Start Over

I have told you to resize before you rotate. Sometimes it's not easy to take this advice. A particular scene has you deeply absorbed. All of a sudden you realize, too late, that you warped your beautiful object out of alignment. How do you get it back into alignment?

If you warped it just one action ago, there's always Undo (⌘-Z). But two moves and you're out. It's time to click the Unity button. The Unity button is the "All ye all come free free free!" yell in the

FIGURE 5–17 The fourth set of objects after clicking the Unity button.

hide-n-seek of Bryce. (Regional yells may vary.) It pops the object back into its original size, shape, and alignment. It aligns it with the grid. It brings it back from your old rotation. Of course, if you had made your cube into a brick, you no longer have a brick. It's a cube once again. Start over. This time, however, you're a little wiser. Figure 5–17 is a continuation of Figure 5–15. The fourth set of objects has been brought back to the original size and alignment with the Unity button.

An exception to this are terrains. Terrains do not go back to their original shape when you click the Unity button. Their original shape is four times larger than the unity unit size. When Bryce brings a terrain back to unity it will scrunch the terrain into the unity unit space (see Fig. 5–18).

Getting Out of a Terrain Jam

If your terrain has been hopelessly warped beyond recognition, you can, in three easy steps, make it the exact size it was when it first appeared in your scene. Follow these steps:

1. Click the Unity button.
2. Reduce on the y-axis until you can reduce no more. You've just made it one-fourth height, thereby making the terrain the same proportion it was when first created, only smaller.
3. Press the multiply key (*) twice.

There. Good as new!

The practical lesson from all of this is to make all of your size adjustments *before* you do any rotation of an object. Of course, the *xyz* size adjustment will be proportional, so you can still change the overall size without getting interference from the rotation and positioning.

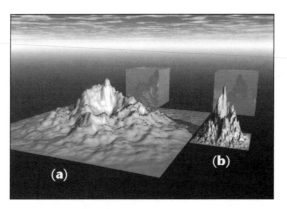

FIGURE 5–18
(**a**) Terrain at its original size;
(**b**) terrain after clicking the Unity button.

The Alignment Controls

In this section, I discuss the controls found in the Alignment popup menu on the Edit Palette. These controls operate on one or more objects and affect their orientation in BryceSpace. The controls are Flip, Alignment, and Randomize.

Flip

Flip does just that—flips your object along the axis described. From Figure 5–19, you can see the effect of flipping along each axis—*x*, *y*, and *z*.

Flip X swaps the object's orientation along the east-west axis—what was facing east is now facing west. However, what faced up still faces up and what faced bottom still faces bottom. But the object is inverted. Notice in the figure that the letters and numbers are wrong-reading as they're flipped.

Flip Z flips the object along the north-south axis. Flip Y flips the object vertically.

Whether the "!" dialog has Center Object checked does not affect flipping. Flipping occurs from the center of the object regardless.

FIGURE 5–19
(**a**) Original image;
(**b**) Flip X; (**c**) Flip Y;
(**d**) Flip Z.

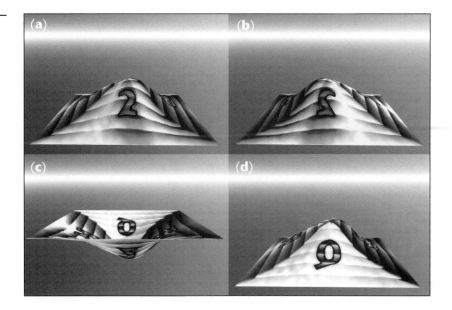

WHEN TO USE FLIP

When positioning objects, Flip works well. You don't like it facing in *this* direction? Flip it so that it's now facing *that* direction. That's fairly self-evident. However, when you're creating more-complex objects from a series of primitives, then Flip is an excellent tool in your toolbox.

This feature comes in handy when you want to create an object symmetrically. Simply create a duplicate and flip it. There are two ways you can duplicate:

1. ⌘-D duplicates the object and offsets it slightly.
2. To flip the object precisely from its current position, here's what you do. Press ⌘-C to copy the object and ⌘-V to paste the copy in the same location as the original's. Then select Flip. The copy will be flipped.

What if you want to flip an object when you are aligning or sizing it carefully? To create the x-, y-, and z-axes arrows in Figure 5–5, I altered a cube primitive object. Then I created a pyramid and positioned it on one end of the rectangle, squashed it, and got it *just right*. When one arrow was finished, it was time for the other one. Stop. Think about this for a moment. Would you want to go through all that positioning and squashing to get yet *another* primitive to be "just so?" No! Neither did I. So I copied the pyramid, pasted it, flipped it, and then moved it to the other end of the flattened cube.

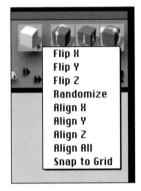

FIGURE 5–20
Alignment popup menu.

Alignment

Alignment precisely lines up two or more objects along the axis or axes specified. Alignment works differently depending on whether you have Center Scaling *on* or *off*. The Alignment popup menu is shown in Figure 5–20.

Figure 5–21 features two objects: a cone and a cylinder. When you first create them, they pop into the world already in alignment (see Fig. 5–21a). Suppose you want to alter their sizes and then align them to create a cylindrical tower with a cone-shaped roof (see Fig. 5–21b). To do this, you need to keep them centered on the x- and z-axes (those are the flat axes) and have each on a different position on the y-axis (the height axis) (see Fig. 5–21c).

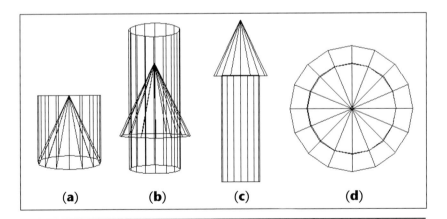

(a)   **(b)**   **(c)**   **(d)**

FIGURE 5–21 Aligning a cone and cylinder: (**a**) Cylinder and cone as created (Main View); (**b**) cylinder and cone after resizing and all aligned (Main View); (**c**) cylinder and cone positioned (Side View); (**d**) cylinder and cone aligned on x- and z-axes and Center Scaling *on*.

Note: When aligning objects in this type of centered fashion, Top View is the easiest view to work in to ensure alignment happens properly.

To align on both the *x*- and *z*-axes, select both objects. Then, in the Edit Palette's Alignment popup menu, select Align X. Next select Align Z. The result is shown in Figure 5–21d.

Just in case you think this center scaling stuff in the "!" dialog box doesn't matter, here's a different scenario for comparison. First select Align X; the objects line up on their left edges, as shown in Figure 5–22.

Remember, you're looking at this from Top View—the *x*-axis's zero point is on the left, and the *z*-axis's zero point is on the bottom. Remember those graphs from algebra? (Or last week's sales meeting!) The *x*-axis is the bottom one. When *x* is zero, it's equivalent to the left edge of the graph.

The second step of this noncenter scaling example is to align *z*. Doing this aligns the "bottom" edge (at least according to our point of view, where we're looking at these objects from Top View).

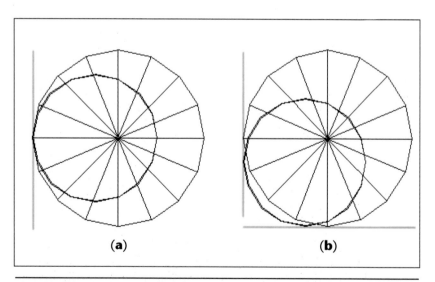

(a)   (b)

FIGURE 5–22 Cone and cylinder aligned first on the (**a**) *x*-axis and then (**b**) *z*-axis with Center Scaling *off*.

ALIGNMENT RECIPE FOR CENTER SCALING OFF

When would you use alignment with Center Scaling *off?* Any time you need to make objects flush with one another on their edges. You'll typically use this with square-shaped objects: cubes, squares, and pyramids (pyramids have square bases).

Here are the steps for aligning a series of smaller cubes along a larger horizontally stretched cube. Begin with a cube, stretched out wide and grown up tall. Think of it as the main part of a fence wall. You need one of those checkerboard turrets at the top of the wall. The turrets will be made by a series of small cubes. Follow these steps:

1. Create one cube. Shrink it to one-fourth size.
2. Here comes the alignment time. Make sure you're in Top View. Select both cube objects and choose Align X and then Align Z from the Alignment menu (see Fig. 5–23a).
3. The top cube is flush with the two outside edges of the wall. Now that you've aligned them, you can easily duplicate the top (small) cube along the top of the wall. Select the small cube and then copy-paste-nudge (right arrow). Keep doing this to finish the wall (see Fig. 5–23b).

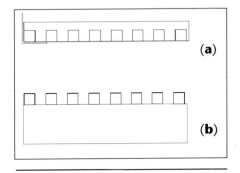

(a)

(b)

FIGURE 5–23 Alignment with Center Scaling *off*: (**a**) Top View; (**b**) Front View.

In this example, I showed you both how Alignment works and a couple of situations you'd use it for.

When you are in the Alignment menu deliberating over which axis to choose, think of it this way: Usually you want everything to align either horizontally or vertically. If you want everything on the same horizontal plane, you'll need to align to one spot on the vertical axis—the *y*-axis. If you want to stack things up vertically, then you'll need to align on the two horizontal axes, *x* and *z*.

Alignment also snaps the object to the invisible grid.

The other Alignment control in the Edit Palette is the Ground button. It aligns your entire object (or its lowest edge) with Bryce's ground in your scene. (Bryce's ground level is distinct from the ground primitive; a ground primitive is creased at ground level but can be moved above or below the ground level.)

Randomize

Now that you've got all your ducks lined up in a row, I'll talk about the opposite process—Randomize. Randomize operates on your selected object and changes its rotation and location. It does not change its size.

For example, to create a flurry of confetti, do this:

1. Create a square and duplicate it about a dozen times.
2. Select all squares by clicking the Object Selection Square control.
3. Choose Randomize from the Alignment menu. Usually the randomize effects get better after three or four applies.

> **tip**
> Remember that *x* and *z* relate to the flat dimensional plane and that *y* is different. The *y*-axis is vertical.

Use Randomize and Align together. For the underwater scene shown in Figure 5–24, I created a number of bubbles (spheres) using the Duplicate command. I then selected them all and chose Randomize from the Alignment menu. Next I lined them up vertically by choosing Align X and Align Z. The bubbles aren't spaced uniformly as they rise toward the surface, but they're aligned vertically, appearing to emanate from one source as they make their way to the water's surface.

CONE CAMPGROUND CASE RECIPE 1—PRIMITIVE OBJECT SYNCHRONIZED BALLET

In this case study, I take the randomize-then-align process one step further. It's all well and good to randomize spheres, since they're uniform in shape. But for nonuniform objects, such as cones, Randomize orients them every which way. If they all need to be

FIGURE 5–24
Air bubbles in this underwater scene oriented using both Randomize and Alignment.

oriented flat side down, then you'll need to go through a couple more steps. The Unity button is part of the process. Figure 5–25 shows the progress of the process.

1. Create a cone. Duplicate it many times. Select all of those objects. (See Fig. 5–25a.)
2. Select Randomize from the Edit Palette's Alignment menu. Randomize one or several times, to taste. (See Fig. 5–25b.)
3. Align all of these objects on one horizontal plane by clicking Align Y. (See Fig. 5–25c.) (Just in case the use of the term *horizontal* and the function Align Y is confusing you: When you choose Align Y—the vertical axis—all your objects move to the same vertical elevation. On *that* elevation, they'll all be on one horizontal plane.)
4. Orient the objects in the same direction by clicking the Unity button. Each object will pop back to its original size and orientation. However, all of the cones will still be randomly scattered about the BryceSpace. (See Fig. 5–25d.)
5. Adjust size and rotation to taste. (See Fig. 5–25e.)

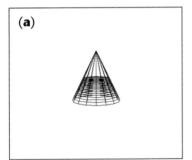

(a)

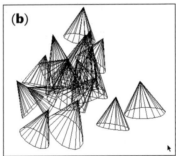

(b)

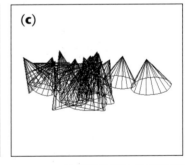

(c)

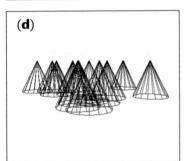

(d)

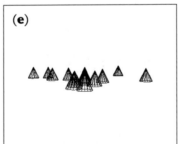

(e)

FIGURE 5–25 (a) A cone duplicated many times; **(b)** Randomize; **(c)** Align Y; **(d)** unity; **(e)** cones reduced proportionately.

FIGURE 5–26
Final randomized
cone scene.

Unity also aligns the objects to a grid. You'll discover that your objects will be in a formation of sorts. You may have to select some individual objects and adjust them manually to get them out of alignment in order to achieve a haphazard look. But barring that last little bit of touch up, this process is the quickest way to use the Edit tools to create a host of cones camped out along the horizon. Figure 5–26 shows the results.

Group Grope

The Cone Campground recipe continues in part 2 that follows, but I set it aside momentarily to discuss the Group and Ungroup commands. These commands do not live under the Edit menu; they live under the Objects menu in Bryce. Like most of the other commands there (Edit Terrain, Edit Materials, Object Options, the texture commands), Group and Ungroup are logical extensions of the Edit controls.

How Groups Work

What happens when you group and ungroup a set of objects? When they are grouped, they are no longer a number of selected individual objects; instead they act as *one object.* Any Edit function you can perform on one object can be performed on a group. (The one exception to this is the Terrain Editor. One terrain, one edit. That's it.) You can change the group's size or its orientation. You also can ground the group. All Rotation and Resize operations will work on a group of objects as though the group were one object. This means you can go back and forth between Grouped Object Conglomerate and Ungrouped Selected Plethora and perform different actions as you desire.

CONE CAMPGROUND RECIPE 2—GROUPING

The act of grouping objects is excellent for making intermittent moves to a conglomeration of objects. Let's go back to the cone campground. In the example in Figure 5–26, all the cones were flat on the ground. However, suppose you want to make the cones on one plane, but that entire plane is rotated? To do that, use the Group command (⌘-G under the Objects menu) before rotating. Finish by adding one last bit of polish by rotating all of the individual cones back so that the flat part is facing the ground. Here are the steps for doing this:

1. Switch to Side View for this step. Select the cones and group them (⌘-G) (see Fig. 5–27a). Rotate by dragging down slightly on the Rotate X control (see Fig. 5–27b). Once the rotation is complete, click the Ground button to raise the entire group above ground level (see Fig. 5–27c).

2. Switch to Main View for this step. Figure 5–28a is the same as Figure 5–27c, only it's in Main View. Rotate the plane of cones again. This time swing them around so that they face you as they "descend." Use Rotate Y for this rotation (see Fig. 5–28b). The grouped "plane" is now in position. Now it's time to work with the cones as individual objects.

Now that the whole group of cones is oriented, it's time to adjust their individual orientations.

3. Ungroup (⌘-U). All the cones are still selected (see Fig. 5–29a). In Side View, Rotate X (see Fig. 5–29b). Then move to Front View (see Fig. 5–29c). Front and Side Views provide the necessary perspective to make this and the next rotation adjustments.

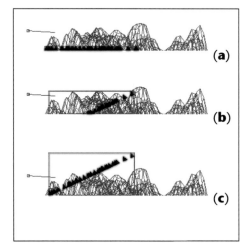

FIGURE 5–27 Side View: (**a**) Select; (**b**) check progress of rotation; (**c**) raise to above ground level.

FIGURE 5–28 Main View: (**a**) Grouped cones after grounding; (**b**) rotating group on *y*-axis.

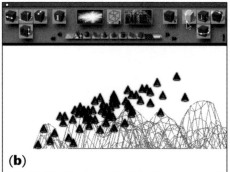

FIGURE 5–29 (**a**) Ungroup (Side View); (**b**) Rotate X (Side View); (**c**) Rotate X (Front View).

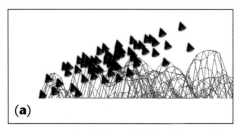

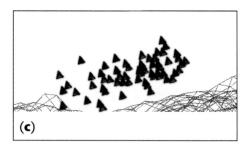

4. So far so good. but you're not quite there yet. Go to Front View. Rotate one last time (Rotate Z). The cones now are facing the ground (see Fig. 5–30a).

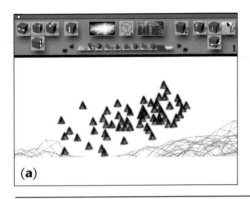

(a) **(b)**

FIGURE 5–30 **(a)** Rotate Z; **(b)** the result from Main View.

FIGURE 5–31
The results of steps 1–5.

5. Go to Main View to admire your scene (see Fig. 5–30b).

6. Render. The result is shown in Figure 5–31.

Disclaimers Regarding Groups

The "when grouped, all objects act as one object" rule does not apply when you use the Alignment controls. The position of individual objects will change *within* the group if you align grouped objects. Also, clicking the Unity button will make the group behave strangely because the group will be forced into that unity unit-sized cube. You may not like the results, so don't be flippant with the Unity button!

Also, when your objects are grouped, you cannot select them with the Object Selection icons. Even though the group comprises several objects, such as those cones, clicking the Cone Selection icon in this case will have no effect. Once those cones are in a group, Bryce does not think of them as individual cones, but as a group.

Complex Composite Objects

The other important use of grouped objects is to control object clutter. In the previous case, you momentarily wanted to make all the cones act as one, so you grouped them. But in cases when you use many primitives to comprise a complex structure, grouping allows you to work with them easily. Figure 5–32 shows two moderately complex sets of objects, towers.

Each tower is composed of a series of primitives and a terrain besides. There are two larger cylinders and a small terrain between them. (The terrain between, shaped like an inverted cone, is not to be confused with the mountain terrain.) The roof is a cone, and a very small cylinder and a pyramid create the banner. (For more information on how this was created, see Chapter 10, which deals with creating multiple objects.) Figure 5–33 shows the tower wireframe.

Once all the individual objects are created and aligned, the obvious thing to do is make all of them function as a unit by grouping them.

FIGURE 5–32 A rendered set of towers.

Another advantage to grouping is that all grouped objects are selected when you click on any one of them. For example, the small cylinder atop the tower roof isn't easily selected. When the selection marquee has been dragged over to select all objects—even the tiny ones—Bryce sometimes doesn't pick up the small things. Putting all of the objects into your group ensures all will be selected. If you resize or change the cluster in any way, you will change the entire group, not the individual elements.

On the other hand, you will need to ungroup any time you want to select and alter any one element. So it's possible to set up a group of primitives for a tower, group the tower, move it into the desired position, adjust the tower's size, and then ungroup it to assign material attributes to each part of it.

There is an additional strategy for working with objects in groups to speed up the render time. I discuss this in Chapter 12, which deals with rendering.

Colors in Groups

I take a two-prong approach to colors and groups. One is to use color as a means of organizing a set of objects (which may or may not be grouped) by giving them the same color. The other relates directly to the discussion about grouped objects.

USE WIREFRAME COLOR TO ORGANIZE A NUMBER OF DIFFERENT OBJECTS

Without using the Group command to make assorted objects into a group, you can roughly categorize different sets of objects by assigning them different colors. There are a couple of good reasons for doing this. First, when you have several different objects that all share the same material attribute, make them all the same wireframe color. In this way, if you change the material setting, you can change them all very easily. By selecting by color prior to making the adjustment, nothing with that particular material setting will be left out. Second, when you are constructing a very complex conglomerate object with many individual parts, assigning different colors to different parts helps in the construction process. You may

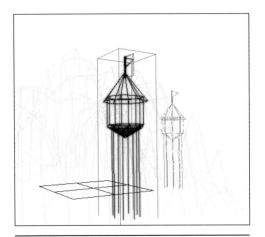

FIGURE **5–33** The tower wireframe.

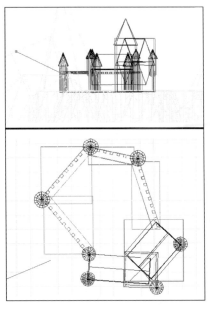

FIGURE 5–34
Wireframe
view of a
castle.

eventually end up grouping the entire object or changing the colors according to material settings later when you're through with the construction phase.

Figure 5–34 shows a wireframe view of a complex conglomerate object, a castle. Different parts are assigned different colors. For example, all of the cylindrical towers at the corners of buildings and walls are the same color. And the cone roofs atop the towers are the same color.

COLOR AND GROUPED OBJECTS

This section is not a discussion of "why to group things that are the same color." It's more a set of warnings about the way object color behaves with grouped objects.

When you create any object, it takes on the color that was assigned the previous object. The default wireframe color is white; when you freshly launch Bryce and create an object, the wireframe color will be white. After you have created a couple of objects, you may decide that you want to make an object a different color. So you open the Object Options dialog box and change the color to black. The next time you create an object, say, a ground, it too will be black.

Watch out for this. You later may want to select all black objects, thinking of the object whose color you switched to black. That ground you recently added will also be selected.

Now, for how this works with groups. When you group an object, the bounding box is a light gray. This does not belie the fact that *Bryce just assigned a wireframe color label to the group from the last Object Option color!* You cannot tell what the color is by looking at the grouped object. Here's an example. Say you have a castle with objects that are primarily blue and pink. You group them together. Just before you created that group, though, you selected your ground and colored it black. Now you select the castle to group it. The bounding box is a light gray. The colors of the objects themselves are blue and pink. *But the group is treated as black.* Select by color and choose black and there it is, all selected (along with your ground). This is an attribute of Bryce that might sneak up from behind and grab you unawares.

The only way to tell the group's color when looking at it in wireframe view is to change the group to a simple shape—a box (Objects > Show as Box, or ⌘-B). The gray wireframe bounding box is the only thing that shows, and it, in turn, shows its wireframe color. This is fine if you want or need to make all the wireframe detail go away for a while. However, if you need to look at the individual objects that are part of the group, then tread lightly when using wireframe color.

If you decide you are going to change the color of the group from black to pink and you select the group to change it, both the group *and all individual elements* will be pink. To change the group's label color without changing individual elements, select or create a different object (something other than your group). Change its wireframe color to the color you want your group to be. Ungroup the group and then regroup it. When you regroup it, Bryce assigns it the color label you just chose.

When you have different colored objects in one group, you will not be able to select individual objects by color. Bryce does not look at the individual objects that are the same color and think "pink" or "blue." Bryce sees a group and thinks "group." But Bryce also sees the group and thinks "black," even though you cannot see that color from looking at the group onscreen, as long as you are viewing the group in lattice mode.

Undo Doings

Recall from Chapter 4 that KPT Bryce's Undo command (the famous ⌘-Z) works with those commands that are under the Edit menu.

Commands on the Edit Palette are undoable. The bi-i-i-ig exception to this rule is the Unity button. Once you click the Unity button, there's no going back. Bryce treats the Unity button as the Ultimate Undo. Once you click it you've gone back as far as you can go. Enjoy the trip!

There is one exception to the not-undoable Unity button: If you do some action and then click the Unity button and then Undo, Bryce will take you back to the state before the action. Suppose you move the object and click the Unity button. Then you repent with a ⌘-Z. Your object returns to the size and place it was before the move.

Also important to remember about Bryce's Undo is that it is not a toggle (undo, redo, undo, redo, *ad boredom*). You have just one undo. That's it. However, since it works only with certain editing functions and not others, it opens up some options. Try something. Render. Don't like it? Undo.

You can make an adjustment in the Materials Editor and then go back to the scene and render a little bit. Draw a marquee over a portion of the image and then render. After a few passes, if you decide you liked the previous setting better, a ⌘-Z will undo the materials edit action and take you back a step to the previous material setting.

In fact, between the time that you make the first materials edit action and the second, you can be in the Materials Editor and render a preset to the .SHD list (by clicking the plus (+) button). If you decide to undo that last change of material to the object (whether or not you render), you still keep the preset. Working with materials presets is a different activity than changing an object. When it comes to undos, Bryce pays attention to whether your action *actually changed the object*. This means you can do anything to change an object and render to try it out, and if you don't like the result, undo. This is great when you want to move an object to precisely align it. Move it. Render a bit. Did you get it right? Well, if it's over the mark, Undo will move it back. If it's not far enough, then keep moving it.

Although Render is under the Edit menu in Bryce, it is a separate function altogether. It may help to think back on the two modes of working in Bryce and the two types of documents that Bryce creates. You create a Scene document of your three-dimensional world. That scene is "what you do to the objects" in your Bryce world. When you render, you are "taking a picture" of what you did. The resulting image is saved to a separate document, a PICT with the .P suffix. Undo affects the three-dimensional world, the scene. More specifically, Undo affects the edit functions that are done to the Scene document. When you render, you're shifting over to another mode to see what you did. This means you can *not* undo a render. Rather, you render to see what you have done to the scene.

Conclusion

In this chapter, I took you deep into the Edit controls and Bryce's internal grid. I showed you how to select, move, resize, rotate, align, and group objects in Bryce and discussed the ways by which all these edit activities coordinate with each other.

CHAPTER

6

Skies and Light

The line of the horizon was clear and hard against the sky, and in one particular quarter it showed black against a silvery climbing phosphorescence that grew and grew. At last, over the rim of the waiting earth the moon lifted with slow majesty till it swung clear of the horizon and rode off, free of mooring; and once more they began to see surfaces—meadows widespread, and quiet gardens, and the river itself from bank to bank, all softly disclosed, all washed clean of mystery and terror, all radiant again as by day, but with a difference that was tremendous. Their old haunts greeted them again in other raiment, as if they had slipped away and put on this pure new apparel and come quietly back, smiling as they shyly waited to see if they would be recognized again under it.

Kenneth Grahame, *The Wind in the Willows*

In This Chapter . . .

- Changing cloud shape and color
- Positioning the sun and moon in your Brycean sky using the Lightsource control
- Fog and haze—controlling water moisture in Bryce
- All about color—how each Color setting for Sky & Fog affects your Bryce scene
- Freestanding clouds and fog
- Making glowing objects using primitives

In Bryceland, you can create an atmosphere to mimic the best day you ever had in your life or any other kind of day you've had. Working with the Sky & Fog Palette to make that atmosphere is a mixture of incredible ease and daunting complexity. The Palette's controls are easy to work with—drag one of the thumbnails and immediately the preview changes. At the same time, there are several interconnecting variables at work in your Brycean atmosphere. How do you know which one is which? When you aimlessly drag here or there and watch the preview to see what comes out, you may get something you like; you may not. The hit-or-miss approach may work fine at the beginning, but it gets old quickly. It's better to go straight to a particular control to change some aspect of your Brycean sky.

That directness comes from a deeper understanding of each Sky & Fog Palette control. In this chapter, I look at each one in turn, isolating each as it influences all the others.

The Sky & Fog Palette

The Sky & Fog Palette has many controls, each with additional options (see Fig. 6–1). There are many variables that you can manipulate in making your Brycean sky. Five swatches for choosing color. Two sets of cloud controls to manipulate one or both of Bryce's two types of clouds. Fog and haze and shadow. Light source direction—both day and night—that influences the rest of the scene. The one setting here will influence the outcome of that other setting over there. Because there are so many interconnected parts, a lot of this chapter's step-by-step directions will simply be exploratory exercises. There's no particular rendered image goal in mind behind these exercises. They help you become fluent with all of the Sky &

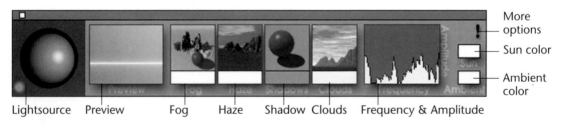

FIGURE 6–1 Sky & Fog Palette.

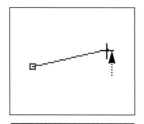

FIGURE 6–2 Side View: Camera dragged up slightly.

Fog parameters. Once you see what each one does to the sky and scene as a whole, you can go on to create more complex sky effects. Toward the end of the chapter, I include some recipes for creating specific effects in Bryce.

Note: For working in this section, ensure your camera is angled a bit higher than the normal default allows. The default splits the horizon exactly in half, but you'll want to see more sky than horizon. Go to Side View and drag the end of the camera up ever so slightly. See Figure 6–2.

Clouds, Clouds, Clouds

In this section, I look at all the different ways to adjust and manipulate clouds in Bryceland. There are so many different factors to manipulate. This section teases them out individually so that you can be aware of which control influences which behavior.

Stratus and Cumulus

Brycean clouds come in two flavors: Stratus (sometimes referred to as Sirrus) and Cumulus. You can set up either or both types of clouds in your scenes.

Here are the main differences between them:

Stratus	Cumulus
Higher, wispier cloud	Lower, more substantive cloud
Color comes from sun color	Color comes from Cloud/ Ambient color
High amplitude, high definition	High amplitude, high definition
Low amplitude, wisps dissolve into high-altitude haze	Low amplitude, low definition

Cloud Shape

There are several ways you can adjust your clouds. In the Sky & Fog Palette, the four means of adjusting clouds are Frequency,

Amplitude, Cloud coverage, and Cloud color. In the "!" dialog box, there are three unique controls for clouds: Altitude, Select Stratus or Cumulus, and Cloud Texture. In addition, you can make numerical adjustments for all of the Cloud controls that are on the external palette, with the exception of color.

This exercise explores the different controls in answer to specific questions about how to make the clouds do this or that. Both stratus and cumulus clouds are included in this study of Brycean cloud shapes.

Exercise: Adjusting Cloud Shape

Start with the basic default sky that ships with Bryce. To get that, select Edit > Preferences and click the "Revert to default settings" button. You now have a blank sky. To place clouds in that sky, go to the "!" dialog box. In the Sky Model section, click the Stratus radio button. Click OK. Now you have your initial cloud setting for this exercise (see Fig. 6–3).

Note: If you have a Power Macintosh, you will have enough speed to view the changes for each step as they render to the entire scene. In the Render Palette, click the Auto Update option. Otherwise, explore and watch the changes render in the Preview window on the Sky & Fog Palette.

Ensure your camera is angled a bit higher than the normal default allows. The default splits the horizon exactly in half, but you'll want

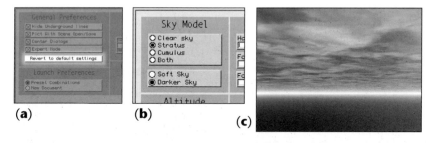

FIGURE 6–3 Creating your initial cloud setting: (**a**) Preferences dialog box; (**b**) Sky & Fog "!" dialog box; (**c**) rendered clouds.

to see more sky than horizon. Go to Side View and drag the end of the camera up ever so slightly.

Next, ask these questions:

1. *Do you want different clouds?*
Change from stratus to cumulus via the "!" dialog box. (Or, as a variation, select both. Try both on your own; this exercise continues by working with cumulus only.) Figure 6–4a shows cumulus clouds after switching in the "!" dialog box.

2. *Do you want more clouds?*
More clouds in the sky, that is, more individual cloud shapes, can be obtained via the Frequency control. Drag the graph to the right to increase frequency and to the left to decrease frequency. Figure 6–4b shows the graph for increasing frequency, and Figure 6–4c shows the rendered result. You can also type in any value from 0 to 1 in the "!" dialog box.

3. *Do you want more cloud cover?*
Drag the Cloud coverage thumbnail. Dragging to the right increases cloud coverage and to the left reduces it. Coverage determines the amount of cloud cover in your sky. You can have the same number of cloud puffs (frequency), but you can change how much they cover the sky (coverage). By adjusting the Cloud coverage thumbnail, the same number of cloud puffs can grow in proportion until they dominate the sky (see Fig. 6–5a) or shrink back to daintily decorate it (see Fig. 6–5b).

FIGURE 6–4 Cumulus clouds: (**a**) Change clouds to cumulus; (**b**) graph to increase frequency; (**c**) more clouds in sky.

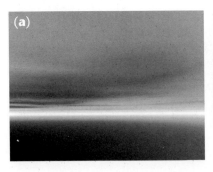
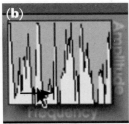

FIGURE 6–5 Adjusting cloud coverage with the (**a**) thumbnail changes cloud amounts so they (**b**) dominate and (**c**) daintily decorate the sky.

4. *Do you want the clouds wispier or more defined?*
Adjust Amplitude to control how wispy or defined the clouds are. When you drag down so that the graph gets spikier, your clouds become more well defined (see Fig 6–6a). When you drag up, the graph becomes more leveled out and the clouds become more diffuse at their edges.

The "!" dialog box includes a section for numerical entry of the amplitude. The numerical range is 0–5. The higher the number, the spikier your graph; the lower the number, the smoother your graph. With an amplitude of 0, you won't be able to see your clouds at all. The cloud graph is repeated in the "!" dialog box so that you can compare graph to numbers.

Note: With stratus clouds, a lower amplitude setting—or wispier clouds—results in a high-altitude haze. The less defined

FIGURE 6–6 More cloud definition by increasing amplitude.

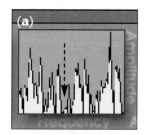  

the stratus clouds are, the greater the high-altitude mist, since the clouds are dispersed. Figure 6–7 shows the default stratus clouds at four ranges of amplitude—higher, default, and low. So if you want a hazy sky when you don't have haze elsewhere, use a lower amplitude setting and stratus clouds.

5. *Do you want the clouds to be placed differently in the sky?* Would you rather your clouds changed places with the sky? You can swap your "cloud" and "sky" areas by setting Amplitude to be positive (see Fig. 6–8a) or negative (see Fig. 6–8b). The default is usually positive. Compare the images in the figure. The basic cloud shape is the same. But a positive amplitude setting will put the cloud *here,* whereas a negative setting will put it *there.*

Begin with Bryce's default cloud setting and its underlying texture and you will probably see a cloud dominating the upper left-hand corner of your preview window. To place that cloud elsewhere, invert the amplitude in order to swap placement of clouds with sky.

Looking at the graph, you can tell that it's negative by the flat spots at the top. If it's positive, it has flat spots at the bottom.

tip
You can easily change the amplitude from positive to negative in the "!" dialog box by selecting the number so that it's highlighted and then pressing the minus (–) key. If it's positive, it will change to negative; if it's negative, it will change to positive.

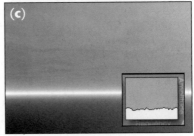

FIGURE 6–7 Stratus clouds at three levels of amplitude: (**a**) high; (**b**) default; (**c**) low.

FIGURE 6–8 (**a**) Image with a positive amplitude; (**b**) image with a negative amplitude.

6. *Do you want your clouds to be at a different altitude?*
Changing the altitude will change the way your clouds look in the sky. Change the Altitude setting in the "!" dialog box. One hundred is Bryce's default altitude setting. Figure 6–9 shows some samples of the same cloud settings, where only the altitude is changed. In some ways, adjusting the altitude is the same as adjusting the frequency of the clouds—the higher the clouds, the higher the frequency. Your eye is able to see more area farther away, so the clouds farther away seem to have a higher frequency. When the altitude is lower, you can see fewer clouds.

Here is the same cloud shown at an altitude of 10, 100, 1000, and 10000. The higher the altitude, the more clouds can be seen. If you want your clouds higher in the sky, adjust the frequency accordingly.

FIGURE 6–9 The same cloud settings but different altitudes.

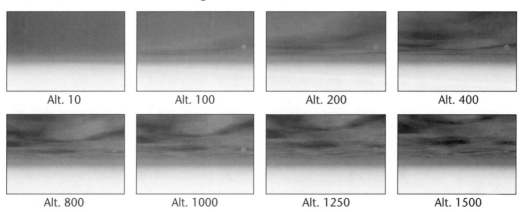

Alt. 10   Alt. 100   Alt. 200   Alt. 400

Alt. 800   Alt. 1000   Alt. 1250   Alt. 1500

FIGURE 6–10
"!" dialog showing
the Set Stratus and
Set Cumulus buttons.

7. *Do you want the clouds to look different?*

To make your clouds depart completely from their current shape, adjust the underlying texture via the "!" dialog box by clicking the Set Stratus or Set Cumulus button (see Fig. 6–10). Doing this will take you to the Shallow Texture Editor, your friend from the Materials Editor. (If the Materials Editor is just an acquaintance, I'll have to introduce you so you can get to know one another better.) If you hold down the Option key when you click the Set Stratus or Set Cumulus button, you will access the Deep Texture Editor.

When you click OK to leave either of these two editors and go back to your scene, you will have changed one of the textures from the 3D Solid Texture list in the Materials Editor. At the top of the list are two textures, Sirrus (Stratus) and Cumulus. You just changed one of those when you changed the texture via the "!" dialog box. You can essentially make the same type of changes to your clouds by accessing the Texture Editors from the Materials Editor. (See Chapter 8, "Material World," for more information about the Materials Editor and Texture Editors.)

When you change the texture, you change it at Bryce's base level. However, do not fear that by changing the base cloud texture you can't get back to the ole standard. There are a couple of ways you can keep your experimental clouds and still come home for a comforting cumulus dinner. Store your strange skies either in their own Scene documents or in the Skies Presets. Then, when you want to start off anew with Bryce's default clouds, go to the Preferences dialog box. There you have two options. You can click the "Revert to default settings" button. Or, switch off Expert mode, quit, and re-launch Bryce.

Clouds and Sunlight

Whatever their size and shape, clouds never obscure the sun's light. You may not be able to directly see the sun, since the cloud cover covers it, but the sun will cast light nonetheless. If you've set a high amount of cloud cover to create dark threatening clouds, pull your shadow setting back to make the direct sunlight less apparent. You'll also need to make some color adjustments to your clouds and to other color settings as well. I take up the topic of clouds and color later in this chapter when I cover all the color controls of the Sky & Fog Palette. The next section, however, will consider the Lightsource control, so that you will know how to set up the sun to hide behind or peek out from behind those Brycean clouds.

Solar and Lunar Direction

At the outer limits of the Brycean world is a sphere. This virtual edge is Bryce's sky dome. On the surface of that sky dome are Bryce's light sources. The sun illumines Bryce during Bryce's daytime, and the moon comes out during Brycean night. In this section, I discuss the Lightsource control in two parts. The first discusses the concept behind the Lightsource control and the Brycean sun and moon. The second delves a bit deeper into the numerical details behind the Illumination control in the "!" dialog box.

Basic Bryce Astronomy

How do you set time of day? With the Lightsource control. Think of the Lightsource control's different locations as different times of day. There is a sunrise position, a high-noon position, late morning and early afternoon positions, and so on. With the "View linked" option checked (in the "!" dialog box), you will stand with your back to the sunrise when the Lightsource control is positioned at the bottom.

A different way to think of the Lightsource control is as the top view representation of the Brycean sky dome. Where you place the light is where the sun is shining in the sky. At the edges of the circle are different points along the horizon, and center is light from the top of the sky. In that case, the top edge is the northern horizon, bottom is south, and east and west are to the left and right sides, respectively (see Fig. 6–11). No, this is not a strict "the sun rises in the east and sets in the west" situation. Remember, Bryce is another world entirely. You can make your sun rise and set wherever you want.

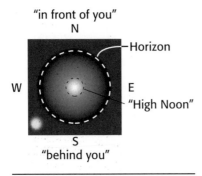

"in front of you"
N

Horizon

W

E

"High Noon"

S

"behind you"

FIGURE 6–11 The Lightsource control with Bryce sky dome positions superimposed.

To change from day to night, simply click the sun at the bottom left of the Lightsource control. It changes to a moon, and it's now nighttime in Bryceland (where a certain king has been heard to croon, "Love me render"). Click again to change back to day.

You may have noticed in your explorations that the sun and moon are on the same continuum. They're in the opposite ends of the sky. If you create a scene that has no ground in it, set the sun at high noon, and then point your camera down into the depths . . . peekaboo! There's the moon! In fact, anywhere you place the sun, the moon will ride along opposite it. Figure 6–12 shows a miniature Bryce sky dome, with sun above and moon below half way around the Brycean world.

That moon, incidentally, will always be full. (It makes sense; after all, it's always opposite the sun.) The opposition of sun and moon explains why you place the sun visibly on the horizon by moving the Lightsource control toward the "top" of the sphere and the moon by placing the control to the "bottom." When you move the Lightsource control to position the moon so that it is visible in your scene, you may find a problem dealing with the moon's counter position to the sun. Things may not seem predictable until you realize the following: *When using the Lightsource control, you are always controlling the sun's position; the moon follows along.* When the Lightsource control is centered, the moon is centered as well. But when the Lightsource control is placed on the left side, the moon appears on the right and vice versa. To place the moon left of

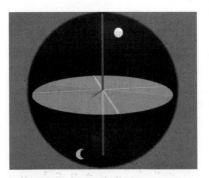

FIGURE 6–12 Bryce sky dome with sun and moon in opposite positions.

center in your scene, you need to move the Lightsource control to the right. You are positioning the sun's position half way around the Bryce sky dome, and the moon follows along (see Fig. 6–13).

Sun and Moon Secrets in the "!" Dialog Box

The Lightsource control on the Sky & Fog Palette was designed for pure intuitive play with your light sources. Drag the sun to the position you want, and there you are. You don't need to deal with numbers to get the sun's position just so.

Deep in the "!" dialog box, however, you can alter the numbers for the Lightsource controls. This is good for precise incremental change for animations or other sequential events.

Here's what happens numerically when you drag the Lightsource control. Like the other controls in Bryce that have x, y, and z, the illumination positions do as well. (What a surprise! Another case of

FIGURE 6–13 Opposite Lightsource behavior with night skies: (**a**) Centered Lightsource; (**b**) Lightsource on right, moon on left; (**c**) Lightsource on left, moon on right.

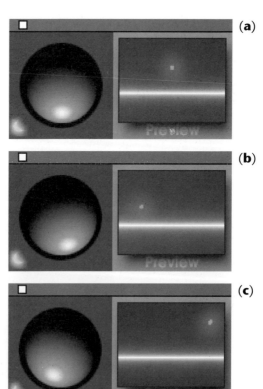

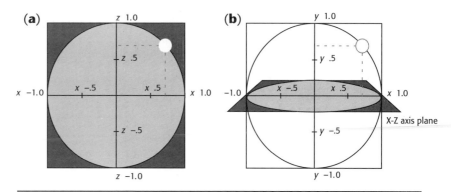

FIGURE 6–14 Lightsource position and corresponding numerical settings: (**a**) Top View representation; (**b**) Side View representation.

those ole x-, y,- and z-axes! Well, for a three-dimensional application, Bryce is surprisingly consistent at assigning x, y, and z attributes to most everything.)

Figure 6–14a shows the sun's position as if you were looking from Top View. The horizontal position of the sun is expressed by the x- and z-axes. Noon is $x = 0$, $z = 0$; northern horizon is $x = 0$, $z = 1$; southern horizon is $x = 0$, $z = 1$; eastern horizon is $x = 1$, $z = 0$; and western horizon is $x = -1$, $z = 0$.

To include the y setting, look at Figure 6–14b. The y setting corresponds to the sun's height in the sky. High noon is $y = 1$ (or a close .9), and at any place that the sun is on the horizon, $y = 0$. If y has a negative value, the sun is below the horizon, thereby making it night and placing the moon above the horizon.

You may enter numbers that would make the light position fall outside the circle. Internally, however, Bryce calculates the numbers and places the light source at a point on that circle.

Fog and Haze

Both fog and haze are manifestations of moisture in the air. Haze is overall moisture, whereas fog is localized, clinging to the ground.

This section discusses the contributions haze and fog make to Brycean atmosphere.

Haze: On a Hazy Day, You Can't See Forever

Haze indicates distance. As you walk to and fro upon the earth, one visual cue indicates that something is far away—there's a lot of haze in the air between you and that object. The farther away an object is, the more its details and color intensity are obscured by the water moisture in the air. Or, to put it differently, the more haze you have to look through, the farther away the object will appear. The Haze control is very simple—drag in the Haze thumbnail control to change haze amount. Select haze color from the haze color swatch.

A little haze goes a long way. With just an infinitesimal haze setting, you will see the haze line on your horizon. If your scene is just a plain blue sky, the presence of the most infinitesimal amount of haze (.000001 in the "!" dialog box) will make all the difference as you look off in the infinite distance.

Once you start adding objects to your scene, however, a higher haze setting will give the appearance of distance. Take a look at the scenes by Eric Wenger on the Bryce CD (and on the book's CD, too). The haze setting is often above 50 for a sense of distance and scale. What was just a dinky-looking terrain swells to massive grandeur once all the haze is there to tell you that the mountain is really quite large.

Fog

Fog, in real life, is a cloud layer that clings close to the ground. Bryce's Fog control allows you to create any color mist that clings to the ground. There are two parameters, aside from fog's color. Determine the overall amount of fog with Fog Amount and the height of the fog with Fog Height. In the Thumbnail control, there are two directions to drag to change either setting. Dragging right and left changes the amount of fog; dragging up and down changes

FIGURE 6–15 The Fog thumbnail and corresponding numerical controls in the "!" dialog box.

its height. Two corresponding sets of numbers tell you what you have. The "!" dialog box allows for precise numerical entry and fractional amounts for either fog parameter. See Figure 6–15.

Bryce fog is heaviest at ground level and dissipates as it goes up. No matter the *amount* of fog, there will always be more at ground level than at the top edge. Under ground level, though, the fog maintains a uniform thickness of that heaviest level (see Fig. 6–16a). Don't let all of that go to waste! By moving all of the elements in your scene (including your ground plane) below ground level, you can create foggy scenes in which you have a thick uniform bank of fog at the bottom that dissipates higher up.

Figure 6–16b shows two identical flat planes with terrains atop them. The one on the left is at ground level; the one on the right is below ground level. The camera angle is near ground angle. Notice the uniform dissipation of the fog on the left terrain, while the right terrain has a thick portion of fog that hugs the ground and then dissipates up from there.

FIGURE 6–16 Fog and ground level: (**a**) Above ground level, fog dissipates but has uniform thickness below; (**b**) two "grounds" and terrains at different levels demonstrate fog's uniform thickness below ground level.

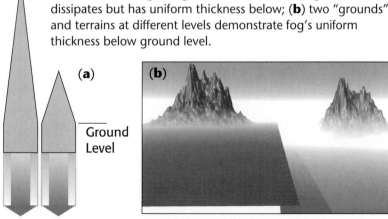

(**a**)

Ground Level

You can also use fog to create a haze effect. This is useful when the objects in your scene are on a smaller scale or are otherwise set up in such a way that a high haze amount does not achieve the desired "distancing" effect.

In situations where you do not want to give haze a universal influence, create localized haze with the Fog controls. Set your camera low enough so that it is within the fog bank. A small amount of fog that extends fairly high will enable you to have some haze-type effects in only the lower portion of your scene.

FREESTANDING FOG

If you want to create freestanding fog that is local to one particular area in your scene, you can use a sphere or cube primitive and give it foggy material attributes. Figure 6–17 shows a localized fog and the material setting used to make it. To adjust the visibility of the edges, increase the Transmitivity setting or change the size of the sphere.

Shadows

Bryce will allow you to control the harshness of the shadows with the Shadow control. There are a couple of things to note about this. Bryce's clouds may block the view of the sun or the moon, but they don't cast shadows on your Brycean world. So you can have clouds

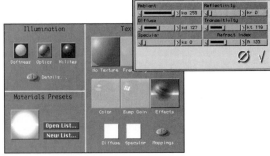

FIGURE 6–17 Localized fog and the material setting used to make it.

that have a coverage amount of 100% and the sun will still be there, bright as can be. This is advantageous for creating those days that have a front of dark storm clouds off in the distance while the sun is shining overhead. Or, if you are completely overtaken by bright sun underneath and you want to have an overcast sky, tone down the harsh light by reducing the shadows. Adjust the depth of shadow in the Sky & Fog Palette. The control is pretty self-explanatory.

The color of the shadow is the ambient color. Also, in a night sky, shadows are less distinct.

"!" Dialog Box and More Precise Control

So far in this chapter, I have talked of things that can be done in the "!" dialog box. But the "!" dialog box has been secondary to the other concepts being discussed. Here I let it parade out in front for a bit while I discuss some of its particulars.

With the exception of shadows, all the controls in the Sky & Fog Palette's thumbnails have corresponding controls in the "!" dialog box. This is true for their amounts; colors are set only in the external palette. You can set Fog Height and Fog Amount more precisely and directly by typing numerical amounts. The same thing is true for haze. In fact, you can set Haze at .001 in the "!" dialog box, whereas in the external Sky & Fog Palette, there are no options between 0 and 1.

If you have entered a very small haze amount (such as .001) in the "!" dialog box and later drag to 0 in the Haze thumbnail, the haze may not go away. The thumbnail's numerical readout is 0, but there is still haze present. Drag to a higher Haze setting, then back to 0 to rid your scene of those last little traces of haze.

"View linked" is an option that can be controlled only in the "!" dialog box. Use "View linked" when you want to change your camera's position or angle in your scene but have already labored to get the atmospheric elements "just so." You don't want to repeat the process. Fine. Make sure you've checked "View linked."

When working in progress on a scene, you may wish to render from Top View. Turn "View linked" off. Otherwise the areas of sun and shadow will be bizarre! Also, if you are creating a series of images for one scene, where you are rendering from different angles, make sure "View linked" is off. The light will come from the same direction even if the camera is not. The same thing holds true for animation.

Color

Until now, I've discussed the controls of the Sky & Fog Palette without introducing color. The type and shape of clouds, the sun and moon, fog and haze, and the extra options in the "!" dialog box have all been examined. Now is the time to focus on color. Bryce's atmospheric controls provide a rich and varied capacity for color to create the subtlety that is so much a part of natural landscapes. There are five different colors to mix and match: the Sun and Ambient color settings, Cloud color, Fog color, and Haze color. In addition, there is the color of the sky dome itself, set by the position of the light source. All of these colors interact with one another, resulting in sophisticated color combinations. In this section, I will discuss each type of color in turn, starting from the bare sky dome color set by the light source position and then coloring the light and shadow with Sun color and Ambient color. To that foundation I will add the colors assigned to the atmospheric moisture element—high-altitude clouds, all-over haze, and low-altitude fog.

Of course, the best way to learn how these colors interact is to play with them to see what happens. This discussion will be a guided play time interspersed with discussion about the significance of each color.

The Bryce Color Pickers

Prior to the explanation of the color of each atmospheric control, I introduce the mechanics of working with Bryce's color pickers.

There are two color pickers. The first is the KPT popup color picker. Press the mouse on any of the color swatch areas on the Sky & Fog Palette and up it pops. Drag to your desired color and release. You can also select a color from anywhere on your screen. The KPT color picker is good as a starting point. Since all the colors there are very saturated, you may want to adjust your chosen color afterwards. Hold down the Option key and click again on the color swatch. Up pops the second color picker. This one adjusts with sliders and gives you a choice of four different color models: Red Green Blue (RGB), Hue Lightness Saturation (HLS), Hue Saturation Value (HSV), and Cyan Magenta Yellow (CMY). For Brycean color subtlety, I like the HLS and HSV pickers, and of those, prefer the HLS (see Fig. 6–18a).

Drag on the Saturation (S) slider to pull the saturation back (see Fig. 6–18b). With dark colors, that's probably all that is needed. With lighter colors, de-saturating the color will make it darker, and you may need to bring up the Lightness (L) to get back in the same general range (see Fig. 6–18c).

You may continue to go color-shopping at this point if you like. Once you find an acceptable level of saturation and brightness, drag around the Hue (H) slider to find a different hue in the same general range.

tip

Here's a color picker tip. When you're picking white, don't drag at the far end of the grayscale part of the menu bar. To get white, you'll be aiming for a small area. There's plenty of white just above in the menu bar, and the color picker samples from anywhere on your screen.

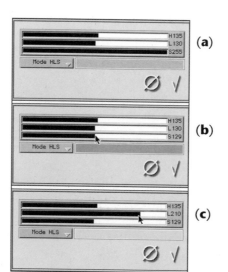

FIGURE 6–18 De-saturating light colors: (**a**) Original saturated color; (**b**) pulling back saturation; (**c**) increasing lightness.

For those who are CMYK oriented, the CMY color picker is not a CMYK picker with a missing K. It is the complementary side of the RGB picker. Red's complement is cyan, green's is magenta, and blue's is yellow. Select a color and look at it with the RGB slider and then the CMY slider. They're opposite. If there's a color that will be outside of the CMYK gamut by the RGB standards, it will also be outside the CMYK gamut in the CMY color picker.

So, now that you're equipped to use both of the color pickers for a full range of color and subtlety, it's time to move on and discuss the atmospheric color controls themselves.

Color and Bryce Atmosphere

The different controls for assigning color are the following:

- *Light Position.* Not a direct color control, but sky dome, cloud, and haze color are affected by it nonetheless.
- *Sun.* The color of the actual sun (when it's visibly positioned in your sky) and the color of direct light as it falls on objects in your scene.
- *Ambient.* The color of indirect light everywhere in your scene, especially in shadow.
- *Clouds.* The color your cumulus clouds take on when in shadow. Also, when Atmosphere in the Render Palette is switched off, the color of your sky dome.
- *Haze.* The color of the general water moisture, dust particles, and all other airborne matter that's suspended in your Brycean sky.
- *Fog.* The color of the localized moisture that clings to the ground level in your scene.

How do the colors affect the Brycean sky and the Brycean world? While discussing the controls that affect the sky dome, light, and shadow, I'll be looking also at how these affect the clouds that are in that sky. By the time I get around to the Cloud color swatch, you'll know that there's a lot more to influencing cloud color than simply using that one swatch.

Exercises

In these exercises, I'll be taking you through alternating explanation and exploration. They are not intended to help you make that killer sky in three easy steps. Rather, they are to help you become fluent at navigating through all the complexities. In preparation for these exercises, get ready to add skies to your Presets. That way, if you come across a splendid sky that you just gotta have, you can save it by using the Preset thumbnail controls.

EXERCISE PREPARATION

You can save any sky in the Sky Preset thumbnails on the Master Palette. Positions, amount, and color of all atmospheric phenomena and conditions will be "remembered" for later use. To save sky settings into the Preset thumbnails, you must have your preferences set to Expert mode. (⌘-P takes you to the Preferences dialog box.) Anytime during the exercises when you see a sky you adore, click the Sky thumbnail in the Master Palette, render it (see Fig. 6–19a), and then click the Add (encircled plus) button (see Fig. 6–19b). (To replace an existing setting, click the Recycle button.) You then can continue with the exercises with the assurance that the wonderful new sky you just encountered is something you can return to.

- In the Sky & Fog "!" dialog box, make sure "View linked" is checked.
- In the Render Palette, make sure Auto Update is checked.
- Use the Escape key to toggle to Render mode and then drag a marquee around a small vertical stripe in your image. When your image updates after each new change, you won't have to wait for the whole thing to render. You'll get the speediest view

FIGURE 6–19
(**a**) Clicking the ball renders a thumbnail image of your sky; (**b**) clicking the Add button saves it.

of the different manipulations. (Disregard this last bit of advice if you're using Bryce on a Power Mac.)

To create your initial sky setting, follow these steps:

1. Start again with Bryce's default clouds. In the Preferences dialog box, click the "Revert to default settings" button. Then go to the Sky & Fog Palette's "!" dialog box to select stratus clouds.

2. Drag down on the graph to increase amplitude slightly for better cloud definition.

3. Create a ground plane and one or two assorted primitives so that you can see how atmospheric color changes affect objects in your scene.

TIME OF DAY

The first color manipulation is time of day. You set time of day with the Lightsource control. This control affects the color of Bryce's sky dome itself, which changes color according to the Lightsource position. It also affects cloud color.

Recall the Lightsource conventions mentioned previously. Bryce's high noon is Lightsource at the center. Place the sun at the top horizon (north) for sunset.

1. Explore stratus clouds and Lightsource position. Drag the Lightsource Preview to the bottom (south). The stratus clouds turn red. Drag up in increments toward the center, letting Bryce render between each little movement. The clouds change from red to yellow to white. Drag the light source up toward the top (to north, sunset, 12 o'clock). The clouds turn reddish again, although the glare of the sun may make it hard to see this. Drag along the horizon's edge off to either side. Change to Night View and look at the different colors again depending on the Lightsource position.

2. Adjust cumulus clouds and color. Change the cloud type to Cumulus in the "!" dialog box. Drag the sun position all around the sky, repeating the movements from the previous step. Does sun position act the same with cumulus as it does with stratus? How about when the sun is shining from behind

the clouds when you drag the Lightsource control toward sunset?

Figure 6–20C (see color section) explores different sun positions as they affect sky dome color and cloud color. The sun is shown at four different basic heights, from three perspectives: behind, to the side, and in front. Side and behind are almost identical. When the sun is on the horizon, the haze and clouds are red. When the sun is near the horizon, the sky is violet and haze and clouds are orange-beige. When the sun is at mid-sky, the sky is a vivid blue and the clouds and haze are white. When the sun is directly overhead, all colors are washed out to a lighter blue. When the sun is facing you, the same is generally true, except the sky color is lighter and is reddened by the sun's presence. (Changing to Darker Sky in the "!" dialog box deepens the sky dome color, especially for the half of the sky where you face into the sun.)

When the sun is closer to the horizon, all sky colors take on a reddish cast. This is similar to the way light works in real life, since the sun's rays have to travel through more atmosphere to reach your eyes. Longer distance draws out the longer red light wavelengths. Conversely, when the sun is positioned directly overhead, the sky is blue because the shorter light waves bounce about. The strongest red is when the light is "behind" you (bottom position).

Go inside the "!" dialog box to numerically manipulate the Lightsource control. Sky color is determined by the y factor. The reddish horizon corresponds with a y value of 0; the sun is on the horizon and the overall color is red.

3. Change from day to night and move the Lightsource control to different places. The sky dome is noticeably darker and the cloud color stays in the same general range as it was during the day.

THE SUN'S COLOR

Now that you've played with the bare bones sky and light source position, it's time to give some color to that light. Sun color affects the scene overall, primarily where light falls directly on objects. However, sun color also has an effect on cloud color.

tip

Fix discrepancies between the sky in your scene and the sky in the Preview window. When the sun is close to the horizon and the preview shows a predominantly red sky, but your actual scene is more drab than that, your camera is aimed up toward the sky. However, the Preview window assumes you are looking straight on at the horizon. If your camera angle is up, the dominant colors in the sky may be blue or gray. Change the camera angle, using the Trackball to move it up or down ever so slightly. If you can't move your camera angle, move the light source. The preview will show the same drab colors that you had in your sky, but your rendered sky will turn a brilliant red.

1. Change the cloud type back to stratus. Then assign a sun color. Switch the Lightsource back to Sun (day). Sun color is transferred to the clouds. Stratus clouds take on the sun color.

2. Drag the Illumination control around. Notice that when the sun gets down toward the horizon, the cloud color is a mixture of oranges and reds.

3. Have an Amplitude adjustment hour. Place the sun closer to the center (close to noon) than to the horizon. Drag up the Amplitude graph to even out the spikes somewhat (that is, lower the amplitude) and notice that stratus clouds become hazier. The overall high haze takes on the sun color.

4. Change the Lightsource control to night, and drag the light source around. Sun color has no effect during Bryce's deep midnight. Only when the light source nears the horizon does sun color creep into the clouds. Change back to daytime.

5. Alter sun color and cumulus clouds. Change the clouds back to cumulus and select a different color for the sun. Compared to the stratus clouds, there's only a subtle change in cloud color. Drag the sun all around to see how the color affects things at different times of day. Try the same thing for night. Set the sun to white again.

The stratus clouds pick up the sun color easily. So to change the color of the stratus clouds, change the color of the sun. To a limited extent, there is an influence on the cumulus cloud color when a different sun color is chosen. But that's more of a little color lacing the edges than it is a pure color.

So far, this exploration has shown that a change in sun color affects the color of other objects in the scene. But it hasn't yet addressed the question of *which color*. Cast an overall tone in your scene by your selection of sun color. Warm up your scene with a warmer sun color. Likewise, cool it down with a wintry chilly cool color. Figure 6–21C (see the color section) shows two sets of warm sun colors and two sets of cool sun colors. When the sun is high in the sky, it's realistic to make the sun colors subtle. For that glowing sunset and the red rays just before dusk, change the sun color to a more intense red-orange and place it low on the horizon. (Of course, if you want to make a fiery red orange sun at high noon, go right ahead. It's your world.) A deep blue sun casts a strong "moonlight." This is an effective color alternative, as long as you don't want to have much sky showing, or—heavens forbid!—the moon itself.

In the images for the figure, the ground, terrain, and sphere all have Bryce's default white plastic material setting. There is a bit of white haze, and the cloud and ambient colors are white. So you can see how much influence the sun color has on the entire scene. Portions of the images have ambient color in them as well. I discuss Ambient momentarily.

The sun color is apparent by the color of its light. When you position the sun so that you can see it directly, it is, well, the sun color! Think about making your sun ultramarine or black or day-glow green for skies that do not resemble our home world. You're not limited to the yellows, oranges, and reds that are associated with our own Earth's sun! The sun, when seen directly, is greatly affected by the amount of haze and fog. With the presence of haze, it will easily lose its strength. So be gentle with it.

Incidentally, there is no corresponding control for the moon's color. It never changes.

AMBIENT COLOR

In the same way that the sun color affects the scene overall, so also does ambient light. Ambient light is the sum total of all light in your scene. The color of ambient light affects the color of objects both in direct sunlight and in shadow, but it is far more pronounced in shadow. For the general color of light in your scene, think of the sun color as the color of direct light and the ambient color as the color of shadow. There are more subtleties to it than that, but that's the gist of the situation.

Figure 6–21C, previously discussed as a part of sun color, uses the same set of warm and cool colors for ambient color. The set of images in the left column has a portion in which there is only ambient color and a white sun color. The presence of *any* ambient color is better than white, since white tends to make the shadows look washed out. When both the sun and ambient settings have color, the result is a richer-looking scene. Bear in mind, of course, that these samples are using the default white plastic. Your mileage may vary with material settings that have different colors. You may not require sun and ambient colors of this intensity to get a rich effect.

The RGB values for the four different colors are provided so that you can try out your own ambient and sun combinations. The top half has the sun in a high position, and the bottom half has the sun placed in a lower position. Compare the different images, especially in the shadow and highlight areas. The middle column compares warm with warm colors and cool with cool colors, whereas the right column compares mixtures of dissimilar colors.

For images with good lighting contrast, use a darker color for ambient light than you do for your sun color.

Bearing these points in mind, try out a bit of ambient color choosing yourself.

1. Try different ambient colors in your scene. Change your cloud type back to Cumulus. Select a lighter ambient color and see how it influences the clouds and your objects. Move the sun into a high position and then a low position.
2. Select a darker ambient color and look for the same things. (Of course, check out these colorings at night, too!) Then change the ambient color back to white.

CLOUD COLOR

This is the first of the moisture-atmospheric color conditions. The following is self-evident: Setting the Cloud color swatch will affect the color of the cloud. But lest you think this is *too* simple, this statement applies only to cumulus clouds. Stratus clouds are influenced only by sun color. Try it yourself.

1. Set cloud color and stratus clouds. Change your cloud type to stratus. For comparison's sake, select a deep color for the cloud control. No change. *Stratus clouds are not affected by cloud color, only by sun color.*
2. Now change to cumulus clouds. Change the cloud color. This time you will see a far most dramatic color influence on the clouds. Cumulus is strongly influenced by ambient color.

HAZE COLOR

Haze color tends to put an overall color cast to a sky (and all objects in it).

When the haze amount is high enough, the haze color will interact with the ambient color. Your haze color will provide a secondary "ambient" color. In some cases, that little bit can be too much.

In most standard day-sky scenes (Atmosphere *on*, sky a blue, sun roughly overhead), a white haze gives the scene a bluish cast. When the sun is close to the horizon, the haze takes on a reddish cast. Earlier I mentioned that our own sun's position was lower in the sky and therefore its rays traveling through more of Earth's atmosphere are more red. Haze is the Brycean element that is most responsive to this trait and therefore most closely approximates the behaviors of Earth's atmosphere.

Figure 6–22C shows different haze settings in a scene that is half sea, half land (see color section). Notice the distance of terrains from the camera and how their details are obscured by haze.

All that I said earlier about the sun's position and sky color also applies to haze. Moving the light source will change the color of haze. In fact, there are two color changes occurring simultaneously: While the sky dome changes from a light blue to deep blue to violet, haze changes from white to light orange to red.

Now try this exercise. First, modify haze color and stratus clouds. Then change the color (and amount) of haze. Increase the haze amount to somewhere in the 30–40 range and assign a color to the haze. Try these settings for a night sky, too.

FOG COLOR

Here's another simple, self-evident statement for you: Set your fog's color with the Fog thumbnail color swatch. (Yawn.) Figure 6–22C also shows some examples of different fog amounts and fog heights.

Fog will also add a tint to the sky, assuming your camera position is low and your fog height is high. Try this exercise. Give your scene some fog and give the fog a color. Drag the Illumination control around and add colors for both sun and ambient. Notice that the fog color is not affected by the lighting colors.

COMBINING HAZE AND FOG COLOR

Combining fog and haze color takes you to an interesting place. You can select a color to be distinct on its own or select one to mix with your haze color. Fog colors can be intriguing, yea, exciting when combined with haze color. Though fog maintains its color when mixed with lighting controls, the combination of haze and fog creates some very subtle and pleasing effects. If your fog is dark and the haze is light, then the resulting combination can be down-right fetching. Try a light yellow haze with any dark color fog. Black fog provides a delightful surprise, as does dark green.

Figure 6–23C shows the same scene with a combination of haze and fog colors. For each color combination, the light source is shown in three different positions—daytime, nighttime, and dusk, with the sun on the horizon. The double combination of haze with sun position and fog with haze colors results in a surprising new color. The result is not a straightforward mix of the fog and haze colors, as there are other factors at work. Sun position, sky color, and ambient color all will enter into this delightfully complex area of atmospheric color.

One of my favorite examples of this combination is on the Bryce application CD. It is a scene in the Landscapes > Kai folder called "Harbor of Thor." The fog is a dark blue-green; haze is light flax. The result is an ethereal blue.

Try this exercise free-for-all. Lay down this book, put *all* the Sky & Fog controls to work with all their colors, and simply play.

But by now this will not be hit-or-miss playing. When you tweak here and adjust there, your playing will have more direction to it. If you find yourself gravitating toward this or that control to move further in a particular direction, then congratulate yourself! You've started building an internal sense for all of Bryce's atmospheric controls. (If not, don't fret. Keep working and exploring. It will come.)

Changing Your Sky in the Render Palette

On the Render Palette is a checklist of Render options. Three of the four options directly affect the appearance of your sky. The one that makes the most drastic difference is Atmosphere.

Atmosphere Off

When you turn *off* Atmosphere, clouds and the sun and moon will no longer be visible in your scene. The sky dome's color is set by the Cloud control color. The cloud color becomes the sky's color. However, you can still see sunlight or moonlight reflections off of a reflective surface.

If you have haze in your scene, the position of the sun will change the color of the sky, the same as when Atmosphere is turned *on*.

Exercise—Is It Midnight or Is It a Red Dusk?

Try this series of exercises to develop your "Atmosphere off" fluency:

1. Open the file "No Atmosphere file" from the CD or create a new Bryce scene. In the Render Palette, make sure that all options but Atmosphere are on. In the Sky & Fog Palette, make sure that fog and haze amounts are all at zero. Set all of the colors (Fog, Haze, Cloud, Sun, Ambient) to white to begin. Create a cone or other simple primitive object in the scene and, in the Materials Editor, give it No Texture and Ambient and Specular colors of white. With this you'll be able to compare sky to object as you change your sky around.
2. Draw a marquee around a portion of your image so that when the image automatically updates, it won't render every-thing. (Ignore this step if you have a Power Mac.)
3. Select a color for your sky in the Clouds thumbnail. (Make it a deep, darker color.) Change the sun's position a few times, just to see how it affects the object but not the sky.
4. Add a bit of haze. You don't need much. A setting of 1 or 2 or so will do just fine. Now adjust the sun's position. Make sure

you get it down toward the horizon, too. Switch from day to night and change the position around some more. You get reddish haze at midnight when the moon is straight up in the sky.

5. Change the color of the haze. Make the haze a lighter color, up toward the top of the popup color picker colors. Now adjust the sun's position again. When the sun is at high noon, switch to night. There's quite a difference in color.

6. Add fog. Make the amount less than 10 and the height more than 50. Make the fog deep blue and the haze white and the scene at night. Change the cloud color to black. You get nice reddish tones. Now change the haze to a light, light yellow. Beautiful! With night coloring and light color haze (the red effect tends to die out when you select greenish colors), you can get soft dusky peach-hued skies that are stunning in their subtlety. See Figure 6–24C (in the color section) for a day and night example.

7. Add color to Sun and Ambient and compare day and night effects. See how the Sun and Ambient color affects the object? The degree of effect differs depending on whether it's night or day.

The trick here when mixing all of these colors is not to be bright and brash and bold. Subtlety is the key. Take a look through the skies in Eric's folder on the Bryce CD or on the scenes on this book's CD. Open each one and look at the sky controls. You have an unseemly combination of colors to create stunning effects. There also is a Preset file on the CD that has dozens of skies.

Try some other combinations. Make the sky black and check out all the different effects. Make the sky deep green. This is the place you can create your out-of-this-world worlds!

Note: If you were to try a similar hazy-day-and-night render sequence with Atmosphere *on* in the Render Palette and later you removed all haze, you might still get a residual hazy effect during the day. To clear your sky, switch to night and back. This anomaly should be fixed in Bryce versions after 1.0.1.

SUNSET WITH MEDIUM-BLUE SKY AND WARM REDDISH MOUNTAIN GLOW

1. Create a new scene. In the Render Palette, turn Atmosphere off (or keep the same settings from the previous recipe).
2. Create a ground and a terrain.
3. Make the terrain a "mountain range in the distance." Widen it and make it taller. Then move it away from you.
4. In the Sky & Fog Palette, select a medium deep blue for Cloud color.
5. Move the sun close to the horizon to the east or the west and change the sun color to a deep orange-red.
6. Put in some haze (1–20) and give it an amber color.
7. Ambient Light: Try dark. Try the same general color as the sun's. Dark green, dark red, dark purple. Just sample any color in the color picker that's close to the bottom.
8. Render. You will have a mountain lit up by a setting sun, with the background sky a deep blue color. See Figure 6–25C in the color section.

If you want to place clouds in this scene, you will need to put them in using an infinite plane. If you do that, make sure that your sun is absolutely on the horizon or else it will cast cloud shadows on the ground and on the mountain. (See Fig. 6–26C—also in the color section.) More information about infinite planes follows later in this chapter.

Fog and Haze Off

Removing fog and haze will take away any indications of atmospheric conditions. This assumes that you also have Atmosphere off. You can always shut off either element or both in the Sky & Fog Palette by setting the amounts to 0. But a lack of both Atmosphere and Fog & Haze takes you into the realm of deep space, a vacuum. Sun and Ambient color will still affect the color of the objects in the scene.

For those views from deep space with a black or deeply colored night sky, this is the option to choose.

Skies and KPT Bryce 1.0, 1.0.1, PPC, and 68K

Version 1.0.1 (the fat binary version of Bryce that runs on both Power Macintosh and 68K platforms) has an added feature: Modulate haze according to altitude. So if your clouds are way up high in the sky, the haze won't be concentrated low on the horizon. Figure 6–27 shows the relationship between altitude and haze.

However, the presets that ship with KPT Bryce were created in version 1.0, which has no special altitude-haze connection.

So, what happens if you have something for which the altitude settings don't make a difference and you put that something in a version where altitude does make a difference? You'll get surprises! So what you see in the little Thumbnail preview is different from what you get when you start to render.

The difference between 1.0 and 1.0.1 on a 68K machine is negligible. (In fact, the modulated altitude does not work on the 68K version.) But when you're on a Power Mac . . . whoa! No, the sky is not broken, but it may need to fall a bit if you're going to get the result you were looking for when you clicked that thumbnail or opened up the Scene document from the KPT Bryce application CD.

There are actually two differences between 1.0 and 1.0.1 on a Power Mac. I just discussed the first one, the difference in the software

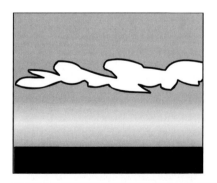 

FIGURE 6–27 The amount of haze is also modulated by altitude of clouds.

between version 1.0 and version 1.0.1. (Version 1.0 does not run on a Power Mac.)

The other difference concerns hardware and explains why the haze discrepancy is more noticeable on a Power Mac.

The Power PC chip in a Power Mac handles the task of numerical calculations differently than does the 68K. You can thank that difference for the speed on a Power Mac.

The 68K math coprocessor chip internally calculates numbers at 96 bit (though it hands those numbers to other parts of the computer at 80 bit). The Power Mac handles numbers at 64 bit. Fine, you say. What does *that* mean? The number of bits is the amount of space the processor sets aside to describe and calculate each number. The higher the number of bits, the more precision. The 68K math coprocessor sets aside more space than does the Power Mac, so the calculations are carried out with a little more exactitude.

It's not that the Power Mac is not precise with its calculations. In fact, 64 bits is plenty; it's an industry standard. But when going back and forth from 68K to Power Mac to calculate the same thing, the Power Mac is, well, a bit hazier.

Charming, you say. You have your Power Mac, and it's downright zippy. You're not going to trade it in for a 68K. I agree with you. So let's talk about how to solve this haze discrepancy.

What are you going to do when you open up a Scene document and re-render it or grab the sky settings from it? Immediately you'll notice that the sky has more or less haze than it did before.

If your scene has more haze, then reduce the altitude in the "!" dialog box. If your scene has less haze than it did before, make the altitude higher. Since altitude and frequency are related to one another, adjust the frequency to compensate for the change in altitude. High clouds brought lower get a higher frequency.

Note: Even if you have turned Atmosphere *off* in the Render options, changing altitude will still affect the haze.

Alternative Clouds

FIGURE 6–28 Sky Preset #2 has an infinite plane cloud layer in it.

Brycean clouds are wonderful inventions of a mathematical nature. However, there are some limitations. They do not cast shadows. "Real" clouds do. In this section, I explore real shadow-casting Brycean clouds in their two forms—infinite planes and freestanding spheres.

Infinite Planes for Cloud Layers

Create an infinite plane and give it the kind of material setting that will make a separate layer of clouds. If you want to grab one that's already created, then look for Sky Preset #2 (see Fig. 6–28).

Now, if you select this and take a look at it in the Materials Editor, the preview that renders looks like nothing! Most successful infinite plane cloud layer looks like mush in the Materials Editor preview. The reason for this is the extremely low frequency of the underlying texture, since an infinite plane is spread out over a large area. Also, there is usually some transmitivity in the Illumination controls. Other material settings are Alpha set to Transparency and Effects set to Regular Fuzzy. The 3D Texture setting Low Smogg is a good basis for building infinite cloud layers. I cover materials more in Chapter 8, "Material World." But this should help you play intelligently with the variables.

Make sure that the Transmitivity setting is very high if you want to see anything else beyond that layer of clouds, especially if you want to look up through one cloud layer to a higher layer of clouds.

"Gaia Evening," an image by Eric Wenger on the KPT Bryce CD, is an example of several Sky & Fog concepts I've discussed here. The scene has a low-lying cloud layer just above ground level. The evening sky is the Atmosphere *off* reddish, hazy dusk I discussed earlier in the "Atmosphere Off" section. When the moon is straight overhead, there are no shadows and objects in the distance are diffused by haze. The light yellow haze gives the impression of dusk, even though the position of the sun is elsewhere.

tip

If you need to create a special sky color that requires Atmosphere *off*, yet you also need clouds, first work in the Sky & Fog Palette to create the cloud look that you want. Then select your infinite plane, go into the Materials Editor, and assign the underlying cloud texture to the infinite plane. The top two textures in the 3D Texture list, Sirrus and Cumulus, are the textures for the sky. You may need to enter the Deep Texture Editor and change the underlying noise from 2D to 3D. (Again, please see Chapter 8, "Material World," for more details.)

For creating layers of clouds that aren't part of the Bryce sky dome, you needn't necessarily use an infinite plane. If your scene encompasses a confined space or if you want your cloud layer effect to be local (as opposed to infinite into the distance), then use a disc or square, or a sphere or cube. (Of course, if you're going to take several views of the same scene or use it for a 360° render, then you may cheerfully pass up this advice.)

 On the KPT CD and on this book's CD, there is at least one scene that shows this. It is called "Cloudscape4."

Freestanding Cloud Structures

You needn't restrict yourself to flat planes with clouds by using spheres. Bryce enables you to create freestanding clouds. An effective freestanding cloud is not created with one sphere, though. Several spheres are needed to create that cotton-puffy, ice-cream-cone cloud shape.

The trick to creating good cloud structures is to use multiple spheres and to enlarge them to a size that gets the right cloud dimension. Don't create clouds and limit their size to the small unity unit size. Enlarge the sphere. Enlarge it again. Brycean clouds work better when enlarged considerably. Figure 6–29 shows a wireframe view of a scene with many clouds. Compare the size of the spheres in this scene to the size of the ground plane. Good freestanding clouds are large.

For more information on this, see Chapter 9, "Superlative Nature Imagery."

Primitive Light Forms

Take any Bryce primitive object and make it glow. While objects in Bryce 1.0/1.0.1 cannot cast light with shadows, they can be made to glow. Create suns and moons and light beams and cones of light this way.

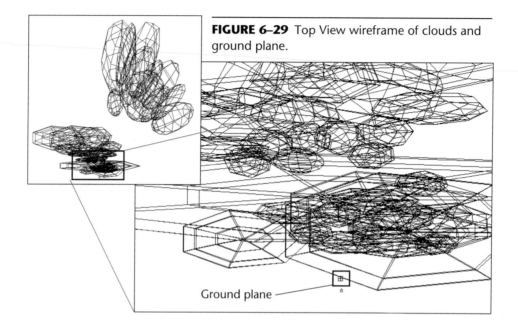

FIGURE 6–29 Top View wireframe of clouds and ground plane.

Ground plane

Objects are made to glow via the Materials Editor. (See Fig. 6–30.) Three options contribute to an object's glow: Effects, Illumination Details, and Diffuse color. First, select Fuzzy Additive in the Effects control. Second, in the Illumination section, hone in on Ambient and Transmitivity (I prefer to do this in the Details dialog box, as it is more precise). Third, the Diffuse color that you select will be the color of your glowing object.

Figure 6–31 shows a series of glowing objects. In all of them, the horizon intersects with the object so that you can see the additive effect at work. As the ray passes through the object, it adds the value of the "glowing" object to the value of whatever lies behind it. Those values, when added together, become brighter, and the object glows as a result.

There are three sets of glowing objects. The top row has different values for Transmitivity. Higher Transmitivity settings result in a fuzzier object. In the case of the spherical objects shown here, the Transmitivity setting causes the spheres to maintain their round shapes.

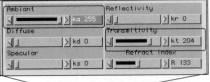

FIGURE 6–30 The controls that make primitives glow are Effects, Illumination Details, and Diffuse color.

The second row has different Ambient settings. As the Ambient setting is decreased, the object doesn't glow as much. But the lesser glows appear flat. And a 0 setting is still barely visible!

The bottom row adjusts both Ambient and Transmitivity in proportion to one another. As the glow decreases with ambient, fuzziness increases with Transmitivity to result in definite spherical shapes. The sphere on the right has now completely disappeared.

Since you can get different levels of glow, put one object inside another for a light-bulb-and-halo effect, that is, a light bulb in a frosted globe.

Figure 6–32C shows a series of light bulbs (see the color section). Different settings and colors account for the variety.

A different light bulb effect was used in the lighthouse shown in Figure 6–33. Two cones "cast" the light.

You can also create your own suns and moons with spheres. Shown are two sunsets in the water. (You can tell that I live on the West Coast. If I lived on the East Coast, these would be called "watery sunrises.")

The first image is the sun sliding below the horizon, shining through a layer of dark smoky haze (see Fig. 6–34C in the color section). (It's my best representation of an eerie sunset seen on the

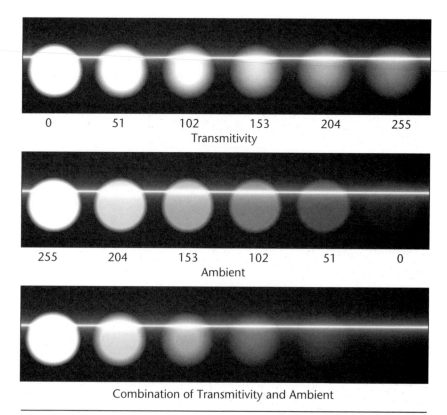

FIGURE 6–31 Top row has different levels of Transmitivity; center row has different levels of Ambient; bottom row combines both Ambient and Transmitivity.

FIGURE 6–33
Lighthouse with glowing cones.

Pacific Ocean during the California firestorm in October, 1993.) Since a high amount of haze overpowers Bryce's sun, I needed to "boost" the sun. I flung a large glowing sphere far out on the horizon and placed some freestanding clouds in front.

The following recipe is a variation on using glowing spheres to create a sunset (or sunrise, for you Right Coasters!) on the water.

Recipe for Sun on Water with Blue Sky

This recipe takes advantage of the fact that when Atmosphere is off, the sun is not visible. However, you can still see the sun reflected on water and other reflective surfaces.

1. Create a new scene. In the Render Palette, turn Atmosphere off.
2. Create a ground and a sphere. Using the Materials Editor, make the ground a water surface. Enlarge the sphere and move it "back" toward the horizon. Make the sphere a glowing light. To do that, in the Materials Editor make the mode No Texture. Change the Illumination controls so that Ambient and Diffuse are set to high and the Effects control is set to the Fuzzy Additive. Select a sun color. It's okay to make it darker, as the Additive Effect will lighten it.
3. Make a medium blue sky. In the Sky & Fog Palette, select a cloud (sky) color of medium blue. Move the Lightsource control so that it is at the top, or back. Change the sun color to a yellow orange color.
4. Create some fog and haze, just the barest amount. The Haze setting is as low as it will go, .005; the fog amount is 1; and the fog height is 4. Assign yellow-orange colors for each. Figure 6–35 shows the Sky & Fog Palette with numerical settings for each control.
5. Render. You'll have sunset on the water, with a blue sky that reaches down toward the horizon. See Figure 6–36C in the color section.

Render Palette options:
No Atmosphere

Light		Fog:		Haze	Shad 0	Altitude		Fog	Haze	Colors Clouds	Sun	Amb
x	0	Amt	1	.005		500	R	228	246	82	239	255
y	0.05647	Ht	3.98				G	231	176	117	158	255
z	0.76						B	150	72	176	12	255

FIGURE 6–35 The Sky & Fog Palette numbers for this recipe.

Conclusion

In this chapter, I told you about Brycean atmosphere and lighting. Cumulus and stratus clouds can be changed by frequency, coverage, amplitude, color, altitude, and underlying texture. Bryce's sky dome houses the sky as well as the sun and moon (which are opposite one another). Fog and Haze are the versatile controls for manipulating the moisture in your Brycean world.

The colors in Bryce are interconnected. Change your scene's color by changing the sun's position with the Lightsource control. Then add Sun for light and Ambient for shadow and mix and match your "moisture" colors to create extremely sophisticated blends.

Atmospheric controls in the Render Palette allow you to make custom-colored skies. Finally, create freestanding clouds with spheres and infinite planes. Create glowing objects using primitives and the Fuzzy-Additive Effects control.

7

Terrains, Terrains, Terrains

"I only wanted to see what the garden was like, your Majesty . . . ."
"That's right," said the Queen, patting her on the head, which
Alice didn't like at all: "though, when you say 'garden,' *I've* seen
gardens, compared with which this would be a wilderness."

Alice didn't dare to argue the point, but went on: ". . . and I
thought I'd try and find my way to the top of that hill . . . ."

"When you say 'hill'," the Queen interrupted, "*I* could show you
hills, on comparison with which you'd call that a valley."

"No, I shouldn't," said Alice, surprised into contradicting her at last:
"a hill *can't* be a valley, you know. That would be nonsense . . . ."

The Red Queen shook her head. "You may call it 'nonsense' if you
like," she said, "but *I've* heard nonsense, compared with which that
would be as sensible as a dictionary!"

Lewis Carroll, *Through the Looking Glass*

In This Chapter . . .

- How to work with the Terrain Editor controls to make terrains
- How to make clipped terrains for waterfalls and special effects
- How to work with Photoshop or other image editing applications and the Terrain Editor
- How to create unusual terrain forms—words and images
- How to create terrains using United States Geological Survey (USGS) Digital Elevation Models (DEMs)

Each time you click the Create Terrain icon in the Create Palette, a terrain is randomly generated from a Fractal Noise map. No two Bryce terrains are alike (unless you duplicate the actual wireframe, of course!). You control the terrain information in the Edit Palette in the Terrain Editor (or, when your terrain is selected, access the Edit Palette by typing ⌘-T).

There is much wealth in the Terrain Editor. In this chapter, I explore all of its richness, from your basic garden-variety mountain to other, more fanciful shapes. I look at ways to edit terrains solely in Bryce's Terrain Editor, as well as in other applications.

Gee Too Aitch

How does Bryce control the shapes of a terrain? It generates them from grayscale image information. Different levels of gray correspond to different heights. The lowest elevation is represented by black and the highest elevation by white. This is called a G2H map (G2H for short).

In the map is a two-dimensional grayscale representation of a three-dimensional entity. As you look at the G2H terrain image in the Terrain Editor, you need to make a mental shift away from looking at a two-dimensional image as a picture of something in which lights and darks are shadow and highlight. Think of light and dark as different heights. If it's darker, it's at a lower altitude; if it's lighter, it's higher.

The grayscale *image* determines the shape of the terrain, so the Terrain Editor is actually a specialized *image editor.* This discussion of the Terrain Editor focuses first on all the controls in Bryce for adjusting and shaping the grayscale image. Later it turns to outside sources for adjusting or creating grayscale imagery that will become mountain shapes within Bryce.

The Terrain Editor Controls

The Terrain Editor's primary controls are the Height controls, located on the left-hand side of the Terrain Editor (see Fig. 7–1). The Height controls enable you to create and modify terrains and set the amount of image detail in those terrains.

Resolution

Buttons for creating terrain forms

Buttons for altering terrain forms

Filter

Smooth/ Polygonal

Clipping

FIGURE 7–1 The Terrain Editor.

The Filtering control, on the right-hand side, is also a Height control. The title of the control on the Terrain Editor is "Filtering." To avoid confusion between the *action* of *filtering* and a *thing* called a *"Filtering" control,* I use the word "Filter" when referring to the control. Filter allows you to change the shape of your terrain.

In this section, I provide a brief description of the Height controls along with helpful pointers about using each.

tip

If your terrain looks too triangulated and you can see "facets" in it, your resolution probably is not high enough. Increase your resolution to the next highest increment. Also, check to see that your Render Style is set for Smooth Surface.

Terrain Resolution

The Resolution popup menu (see Fig. 7–2) allows you to select options for the amount of detail in your terrain. The numbers refer to the number of pixels. Each pixel represents a datum, or point of information. The higher the number for resolution, the more detail you have for transitions from this one point to the next. Bryce's default is 128, but my personal default is 256. However, I don't always start out with 256 but may do some manipulations at one resolution and then "enlarge" the resolution a bit later.

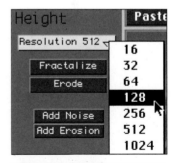

FIGURE 7–2 Resolution popup menu.

Creating Terrain Shapes

There are two ways to create terrains. One is to import them. You can paste an image into the Terrain Editor or open an image via the Merge PICT dialog box. I discuss these options in greater detail later in the chapter.

The other way is to use the Fractalize and Erode controls in the Terrain Editor. Fractalize generates a terrain from fractal noise; Erode generates a terrain with an eroded shape (see Fig. 7–2). Each uses a different procedure to transform the image information in the terrain. The overall shape remains, however. For example, if your terrain has a light diagonal stripe, it stays diagonal. But it's now a fractalized or an eroded diagonal terrain.

Altering Terrain Shapes

The rest of the buttons to the left of the Terrain preview aren't radical transformers. They merely alter the terrain G2H map (but oh, how they alter!).

They are grouped into two sets. The top one consists of Add Noise and Add Erosion, which are mellower versions of the two create controls, Fractalize and Erode. The bottom one is a series of controls that perform additional alterations. They are Gaussianize, Smooth, Sharpen, Darken, Lighten, Invert, Equalize, and Zero Edges.

I consider each set in turn.

ADD NOISE/ADD EROSION

The Add Noise and Add Erosion controls are derivatives of the Fractalize and Erode controls. They modify a terrain.

You can use the Add controls to continue working with an existing terrain rather than using Fractalize or Erode to create a new terrain. To intensify the effect, use the same kind of Add control as create control. Select Add Erosion to continue eroding the already eroded terrain. Select Add Noise for even more irregularities in a fractalized terrain. (See Fig. 7–3.)

FIGURE 7–3 A fractalized terrain is roughened by applying Add Noise.

Conversely, use the other Add control to complement the first effect. If your basic terrain is one type, modify with the other. Eroded terrains are very smooth; use Add Noise to give them some rough spots. In the same way, use Add Erosion to make crevasses in your fractalized terrain.

Add Noise can be used in another way: as an alternative way to smooth a terrain. For instance, if you have added too much erosion, you may end up with crevasses that are too pronounced. You may want to soften them. Smooth (discussed in a bit) is one way to do this; Add Noise is another. Which one you should use depends on whether you want to generally roughen or smooth the terrain in the process of making the crevasses more subtle. For subtler crevasses with a rough touch, click Add Noise.

TIME-LAPSE TERRAIN ALTERING

Two of the terrain-altering controls will continue to act on the terrain for as long as their buttons are pressed:

tip
Use these options together. First erode. Then smooth. Then erode some more. It's good to smooth the erosion a bit at the end so that the terrain has no angular crevasses.

- Add Erosion, which continues to erode the terrain. Little channels will be dug into the darkest portions of the terrain as it is "eaten" away.
- Smooth, which smooths out a mountain shape. The effect is the same as that from applying blur. You will probably use this one a lot.

When you temporarily reduce the terrain's resolution, both adding erosion and smoothing will have more pronounced results.

OTHER ALTERATION OPTIONS

The following options apply only once no matter how long their buttons are depressed. Repeated clicks on the buttons will, of course, reapply the effect.

- *Gaussianize.* Darkens the outside edges of the terrain, treating the terrain as though it were a giant bell curve. The curve is highest in the middle and goes down at the edges. It is a good choice when you have a terrain where the high points are concentrated in the center. Use it to smooth out a plateau into a perfectly curved mound for unworldly, ancient Druid-like artifacts!

- *Sharpen.* Makes a terrain bumpier. Try sharpening the living daylights out of a terrain before a Gaussianize apply. When used with subtlety, it creates bumps. When applied in extremity, you can create trees. Figure 9–31, in Chapter 9, "Superlative Nature Imagery," shows a forest created from a sharpened terrain.

- *Darken.* Darkens a terrain overall, thereby making most of it lower in elevation. It does not change the terrain's extreme light values. So if you have high points in your terrain (white and nearly white), Darken will add contrast by lowering all the dark and mid-gray areas.

- *Lighten.* Lightens the entire terrain (except for the black value), thereby raising the elevation overall. Use it to bring out additional terrain height information from the mid-to-low areas.

- *Invert.* Inverts the information so that the low places are high and vice versa. Use it to create canyons. Also use it as an inverse erosion process. Add erosion to a standard terrain's dark area and then invert and add some more erosion. Because erosion concentrates on "digging deeper" in the lowest (or darkest) areas, adding erosion to an inverted terrain will result in heightened ridges once you invert the terrain back. If you add noise while the terrain is inverted, you will darken what had been the light edge around the terrain's perimeter. If you then re-invert, the edge will be lighter. I say more about this below in the Zero Edges part of this list.

■ *Equalize.* Evens out all the tones in your image so that there is white and black. It won't balance the grays, however. In other words, if you have a terrain that is primarily dark gray, clicking Equalize will lighten it enough so that the lightest portion will be white. The remainder of the image will be adjusted accordingly.

■ *Zero Edges.* Applies a black line around the perimeter of your terrain, thereby ensuring the outside edge is black or low. Sometimes this will be enough to correct a zealous lightening or add an apply of noise while the terrain was temporarily inverted. Zero Edges will change it back.

If Zero Edges does not do the trick, then you have two other options: (1) Use Gaussianize, which will do the same thing (but darken a lot more of the area, or (2) copy the PICT and paste it into Photoshop or another imaging application and then apply additional darkening around the edges by hand.

FILTERING AND SIDE VIEW VISUALIZATION

On the right of the Terrain Preview is the Filter section (see Fig. 7–1). The Filter is a Height control; it enables you to change any height level of your G2H map. Readers familiar with Photoshop's Arbitrary Map dialog box will be familiar with the working mechanics of this.

FIGURE 7–4
Dragging the cursor in the filter to change the Filter's "shape."

Think of the Filter section as a cutaway of your mountain terrain. The terrain's shape will be determined by the shape of the diagonal. In its default (reset) state, the straight diagonal line moves from black to white, smoothly. Change the Filter to other shapes by dragging in the area (see Fig. 7–4). The cutaway follows as you drag.

When you look at a G2H map, you may be fooled into trying to read a three-dimensional illusion in that two-dimensional depiction. The image in Figure 7–5a looks to the eyes to be a sphere. It's not a sphere, however; it's a cone (see Fig. 7–5b). The gray values move evenly from black to white. Your eyes need to undergo a bit of retraining if you are going to work a lot with the grayscale terrain maps (and, if you like this thing called Bryce, you probably will!). The Filter portion of the Terrain Editor may help take the edge off of this visual illusion.

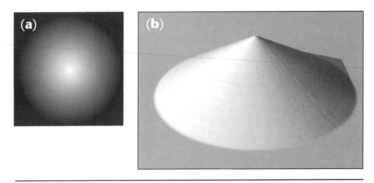

FIGURE 7–5 Cone or sphere? (**a**) G2H map appears to be a sphere; (**b**) when rendered, it is a cone.

Let's look at a series of terrains and their Filter adjustments. Figure 7–6 has three rows: The top row (a) shows G2H terrain maps, the middle row (b) shows the filters for the G2H maps, and the bottom row (c) shows the rendered terrains. The left G2H map has a black-to-white-to-black gradation. To help shift you away from seeing this as an illusion of a three-dimensional tube, notice how the Filter and the rendered terrain correspond to the G2H's linear transition from black to white. This is no tube; it's a straight diagonal wedge. This wedge terrain map is the starting place for every other G2H map in this figure. To create the other maps in the series, the Filter

FIGURE 7–6 Filters as cutaway views: Row (**a**) G2H maps shaped by the corresponding filter in row (**b**); rendered result in row (**c**).

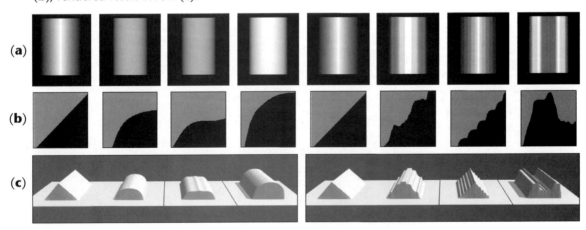

shapes in row (b) were first created. They were then applied to the wedge-shaped G2H map to result in the other G2H terrain maps in row (a). The rendered terrains in row (c) show the final result. Each filter in row (b) is a cutaway view of the corresponding rendered terrain in row (c).

Of course, a terrain won't precisely follow the Filter's shape, since terrains aren't conical in shape. Terrains go down in some places and up in others. (That's all a part of their charm!) They'll generally change depending on the Filter shape. But once you apply the Filter, the terrain itself changes. After any change, the new terrain shape acts as the straight diagonal wedge once again. If you continue to apply the same Filter over and over again to a terrain, you will get widely differing results (depending on the original image, the Filter, and the subsequent images).

Of course, you can use the Filter to completely flatten the terrain. Once the terrain is flattened, use the Gaussianize control to create a smoothed terrain. In Figure 7–7a, dragging the cursor across the top of the Filter results in a flat terrain. Clicking Gaussianize (see Fig. 7–7b) makes a gentle curve. Clicking Gaussianize again makes the terrain's edges completely flat (see Fig. 7–7c). Finally, changing the Filter changes the G2H map into a white circle (see Fig. 7–7d), thereby resulting in a perfectly round plateau.

FIGURE 7–7 Filtering and Gaussianize: (**a**) Filtering to flatten terrain; (**b**) clicking Gaussianize; (**c**) clicking Gaussianize again; (**d**) Filter for round plateau result.

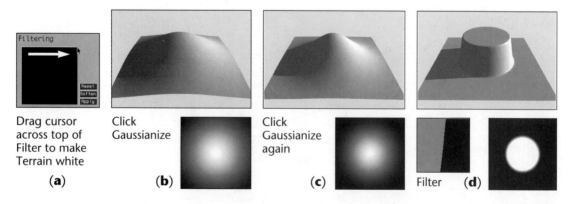

Merge PICT

Click the "Merge PICT" button in the Terrain Editor to open the
Merge PICT dialog box (see Fig. 7–8). There you can see that your
terrain (from the Terrain Editor) is in the left window (Fig. 7–8a)
and the middle window is blank. In the right window is your result.
There are two ways to bring in a second image to the middle window. You can paste a PICT from the clipboard, or you can open a
PICT image document that you have somewhere on disk.

Once you have pasted or opened a PICT, that image appears in the
middle window (see Fig. 7–8b), and a blend of the two shows in
the right window (Fig. 7–8c). Drag the slider all the way to the
right to see only the new terrain.

You can mix the terrains four different ways. The four radio buttons under the result window provide these options: a standard
Blend, Minimum, Subtract, and Add. To adjust the mix between
the two images, either drag the slider below or drag within the result window on the right. There's immediate feedback, so you can
see how each method will work out. As you move the slider, the
weight is shifted between the two images.

- *Blend.* Does a simple average combining of the two images.
- *Minimum.* Compares the two images and wherever it's darker,
  accepts that one.
- *Subtract.* Does a calculation between the two images where the
  value of one pixel is subtracted from the other. In grayscale, 0 =

(a)   **(b)**   **(c)**

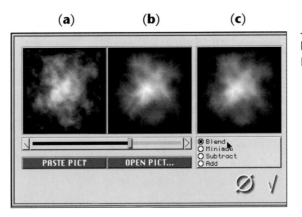

FIGURE 7–8 Merge
PICT dialog box.

black and 255 equals white. Subtract will tend to get lower (or even negative) numbers, so the image will get darker and move toward black. You end up with terrains that have more area that is "flat on the ground."

■ *Add.* Takes the values of individual pixels and finds their sum. The larger the number, the lighter the images. At 255 or more, the result is white. Add is a fine way to create high plateaus.

Zen and the Art of Terrain Shaping

Having shown you all of the controls in the Terrain Editor, I next discuss some methods for creating terrains. These are some of my favorite Terrain Editor working tips.

Resolution Fluency

When you are working in the Terrain Editor, your fluency in changing resolutions—depending on the task you are doing—will help you obtain certain types of terrain effects. The lower the resolution, the more powerful the erosive powers of the Add Erosion button. Figure 7–9 shows the process of the following series of steps. If you are working on a 256 terrain and want to do some serious eroding, then take your terrain down to 128. Several applications of the combination of Add Erosion and Smooth will cut more deeply into the terrain than if you just hold down the Add Erosion button all the time your terrain is at 256. Just before you take your terrain back up to 256, erode one last time. The image will be blurred ever so slightly by the change in size. Then click Add Erosion one last time for a finishing touch.

To get a terrain shape that is not your standard highest-in-the-middle/low-around-the-outside-edges, you will more likely get a quirky shape if you start with a very small terrain size, such as 32. Click the Fractalize button several times; each time, a new terrain is generated based on the information from the current G2H. When you're down to 32, add some erosion to take significant bites out of your land mass. Those bites can create valleys in your terrain.

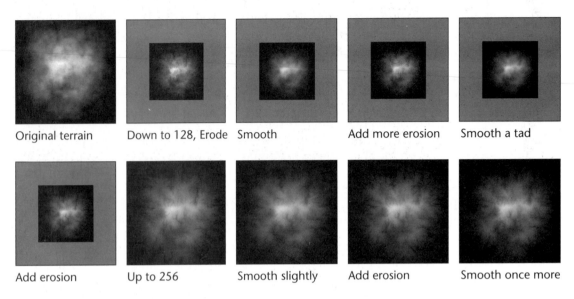

Original terrain Down to 128, Erode Smooth Add more erosion Smooth a tad

Add erosion Up to 256 Smooth slightly Add erosion Smooth once more

FIGURE 7–9 A series of manipulations that created a pleasantly eroded effect from a fractalized terrain.

Result

When you have your basic shape, enlarge the resolution and keep working it from there.

Plateaus

You can create plateaus by using the Filter. Two obvious filter moves for an extremely flat terrain are an abrupt horizontal line or making a certain portion of the terrain white (see Fig. 7–11b).

For a bit more natural effect, round off everything lower instead of taking everything to the highest white. The top part will be grayed. You then can make it higher by equalizing (see Fig. 7–11c). However, there may be some indentations and flat area left in the terrain. (Whoever heard of a terrain that was perfectly, absolutely flat on top?) This technique is good for making rounded mountains as well as plateaus.

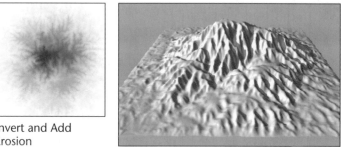

Invert and Add
Erosion

FIGURE 7–10 Inverting and then eroding for more
pronounced ridges.

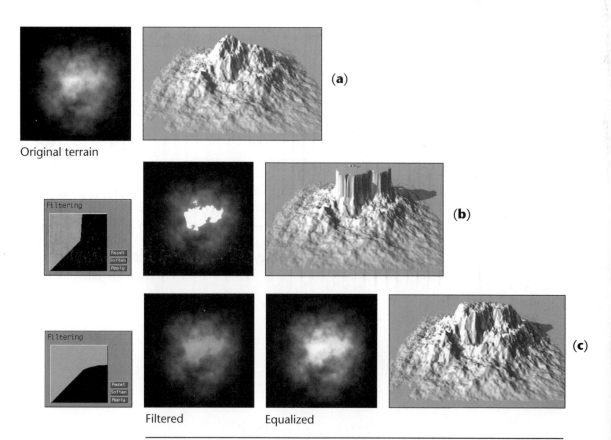

Original terrain

(a)

(b)

Filtering

Filtering

Filtered

Equalized

(c)

FIGURE 7–11 Plateau alternatives: Row (**a**) the original terrain; row (**b**)
dragging the Filter up to make a flat plateau; row (**c**) rounding the Filter and
then using Equalize to result in a rougher plateau.

Here are a couple more quick terrain ideas:

1. Create a terrain. Invert. Darken. Gaussianize. Equalize. Gaussianize again. Lighten to taste. You have a valley bowl. Figure 7–12 shows the steps given here.
2. A handy addition to the toolbag is the darken-terrain-at-very bottom trick. Figure 7–13 shows the process of carving the bottom edge of the Filter. Scrape away the bottom end of the wedge to flatten the terrain. A subtle scrape results in slight flattening, whereas a gouge in the Filter wedge will produce more vigorous flattening.

My Own Private Undo

When working in the Terrain Editor, you cannot undo the last little move you made. So if you add erosion, then add noise, invert, and add erosion, none of those single moves can be undone inside the Terrain Editor. If you have been working with a terrain for a while and then attempt some major tweak—such as a Filter apply—that

FIGURE 7–12 Creating a valley bowl.

Create a terrain

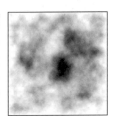
Invert

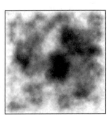
Darken

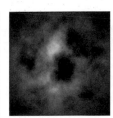
Gaussianize

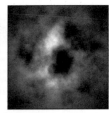
Equalize

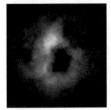
Gaussianize

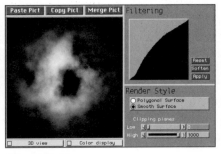
Filter to lighten

Result

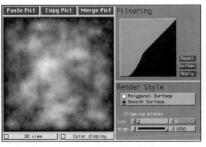

Before, with filter to be applied   After   Before   After

FIGURE 7–13 Darkening the bottom of a terrain.

is a miserable failure, you risk losing all of the little tweaks you made along the way. Here's how to avoid that.

There are two possible methods. I use 'em both. Both methods require a bit of action prior to the risky move. The first, of course, is to accept changes in the Terrain Editor. Then go back to the Terrain Editor and do your risky move. If you don't like the result, undo.

The other method gives you uninterrupted flow while working in the Terrain Editor. First, Copy PICT. Now you have your "undo" hanging out in the Macintosh clipboard. Do what you want to your terrain. If you don't like it, all you need to do is Paste PICT.

The corollary to this second method is a soft-undo. Say you try a risky move. If you "sorta" like what you did, then try Merge PICT. Your risky move is there to be blended with—of course!—the undo residing in the clipboard. Paste and blend to taste. If you still don't like the result, leave the Merge PICT dialog box and paste the PICT in the Terrain Editor itself.

Recipe for Copy-Merge-Paste-Blend

This recipe takes advantage of Bryce's powerful ability to copy, paste, and merge terrains. Hence you can work within the Terrain Editor to create variations on your terrain theme.

1. Start with a terrain that has fractal noise (just as Bryce created it). In the Terrain Editor, change the resolution to 256. Click Copy Terrain. Now the terrain is in the clipboard, and you can paste it as many times as you want.
2. With your terrain in the clipboard in reserve, change the terrain in the Terrain Editor to an eroded terrain. This generates a new terrain based on the information that is already there. You get the same basic shape, only it's eroded rather than fractal noise. Click the Erode button.
3. Now it's time to mix them! Click Merge Terrain. The eroded terrain is there in the left merge window. Click Paste PICT to bring the fractal noise terrain to the right merge window. Experiment with the blend modes and sliders to merge these two renditions together.

   The position of the slider changes the blend, giving relative strength to each terrain. To make the merged terrain have a rough, noisy mountaintop emerging from lower, eroded foothills, use the Minimum mode. Move the slider to adjust so that the eroded part is on the outer part of the terrain map, but the center part is noisy. Click OK.
4. Exit the Terrain Editor and render.

Figures 7–14 and 7–15 both show two images of different blends using the different merge options, with four resulting terrains.

Working with a Paint Program/Photoshop to Create Terrains

You probably don't have to work long in the Terrain Editor before you find yourself wishing for a brush tool in order to manually alter the terrain's shape. You've probably thought, "I'd like to put a river in right *there*!" Never fear. The wish for a painting tool in the Terrain Editor has been duly noted for future versions of Bryce.

Until then, however, you can use a paint program to make custom changes to your terrains. One approach is to take your terrain back and forth between Bryce and your paint program (I'll refer to

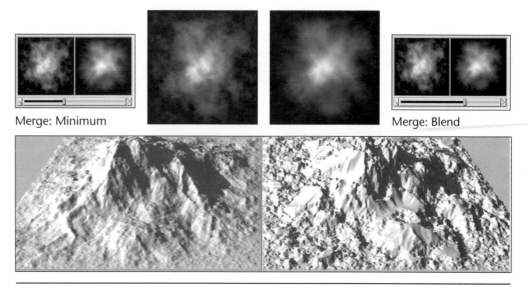

Merge: Minimum

Merge: Blend

FIGURE 7–14 Rendered terrains created by merging using the Minimum and Blend modes.

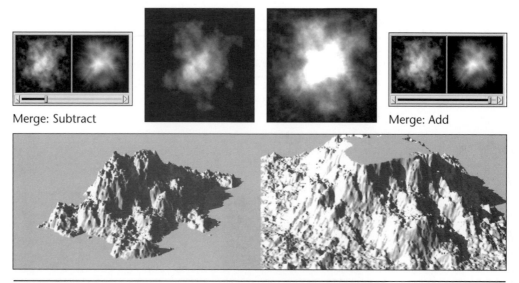

Merge: Subtract

Merge: Add

FIGURE 7–15 Rendered terrains created by merging using the Subtract and Add modes.

Photoshop here, though you may have a different application, such as Color It!).

Create the terrain in Bryce. Modify it in the Terrain Editor. Click the Copy PICT button to copy the image to the clipboard. Switch to Photoshop. Select a new document. (Photoshop sets up the attributes for a new document to match the contents of the clipboard.) Paste from clipboard. Now, alter the image as you will. When you are ready to try out your new terrain, copy it and take it back to Bryce.

When working with terrains that have already been created from the Terrain Editor, I use specialized brush modes. (I hardly ever paint with a straight Normal apply brush.) Sometimes I will use Lighten and Darken to fill in terrain masses up to a certain color level. Mostly I set the painting brushes to Multiply and Screen modes to darken and lighten my terrain in places. Multiply and Screen will proportionately lighten and darken, but the terrain detail that was there will still be there. Keep things subtle with partial applies and colors. For subtle lightening, set the painting color dark gray and use Screen. For subtle darkening, make your paint color light gray and use Multiply. Figure 7–16 shows a terrain with Screen, Multiply, Darken, and Lighten brush strokes next to the rendered terrain.

Note: This process is considerably more painful if your computer is limited in RAM (8 MB or less), as you need enough to keep both applications open simultaneously. Use something like RAM

FIGURE 7–16 Using Photoshop's specialized brush modes to raise or lower the terrain.

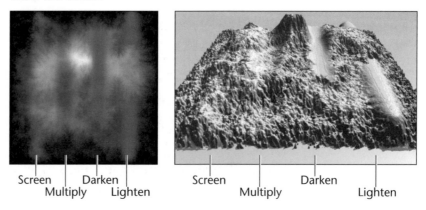

Doubler if you're in a pinch. As an alternative, you can create several variations on a theme in the paint application and save each one as PICTs. Unfortunately, you can't save a terrain image as a PICT straight from Bryce. You can, however, use a screen capture utility to do so. If you have limited RAM, a possible workaround is to create several variations on a theme of the one terrain in Photoshop and save each one as a PICT document. Then open the PICTs from the Merge PICT dialog box and select one or another or merge between the two.

More Terrain Merging in Photoshop!

The four blend modes from the Merge PICT dialog box do not constitute the entire realm of possibility for combining two images. If you want to explore further, take the two original terrains to Photoshop for more sophisticated combinations. They can be created from either Calculations or the multi-layering effects in Photoshop 3.0 (or both).

Alternative Terrain Forms

Everything discussed so far has pertained to standard mountainous terrain forms. It's nearly time to make a departure into the weird and fantastic and inorganic entities that also can be created using a G2H map. The best point of departure is clipping.

Clipped Terrains

Terrain clipping takes place using the two sliders in the lower right of the Terrain Editor. When the sliders are moved, portions of a terrain above or below a certain height disappear. This leaves holes in the terrain. In the Terrain Editor, when the preview is set to color, the portions that are red will be clipped. Once holes are cut in the terrain, the terrain is no longer square. It can be any shape. Let that implication percolate a bit, and the fantastic and unusual ideas begin to fly fast and furious.

Before I leave the organic world of natural mountainous terrains, however, the first top of terrain clipping will treat an organic form—the creation of limited bodies of water, or waterfall ponds. This is the technique used to create the waterfall on the book's cover.

RECIPE FOR A CUSTOM TERRAIN WATERFALL

To make a waterfall that spills over a rocky terrain, you create a second terrain. It will be flat except for the transitional places where water changes elevations, or falls. The information you need to create the waterfall terrain is contained in your first terrain. You'll modify a copy of the original terrain to create the second terrain. It requires some work in a paint program, but once mastered, it's one of the more rewarding things to do inside of Bryce. To do this technique, you must use an application that can edit grayscale images, such as Adobe Photoshop.

1. Transfer your terrain from Bryce to Photoshop. In the Terrain Editor, click the Copy PICT button. Open Photoshop. Select New file. Photoshop will assign characteristics to the new file to match the contents of the clipboard. Click OK. Paste. Now you have your working image file for creating the waterfall. The CD has waterfall files included.

2. The first thing to do is more clearly define on this terrain where the water will be. Use the paintbrush to create the water's path. Set the color to the same color as the lightest area of water. Change the brush mode to Multiply and the opacity to 20% or 30% or so. Using the brush, follow the best path from the highest area to the darkest color of the ground level. Save this file as a PICT and give it some name that you'll remember when you go to load it in to Bryce using the Merge PICT dialog box (see Fig. 7–17a). But don't close it on screen or leave Photoshop just yet; you're not through at all!

3. Now create a selection mask for this area. You will need to create a selection that encompasses a range of gray levels. There are several approaches for doing this. In Quick Mask, you can paint a selection. Or you can use the Arbitrary Map dialog box to isolate certain elevations. I chose a third approach that happens

(**a**) Original terrain

(**b**) Original selection

(**c**) Water terrain–Before

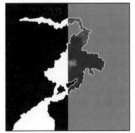

(**d**) Left: Grown selection; Right: Water Terrain

FIGURE 7–17
Creating a waterfall terrain.

to be the slowest and most painstaking of the three, but it works well for selecting only the limited "body of water" area. Double-click the Magic Wand tool and set the tolerance to 8. Make sure anti-aliasing is on. Select the area that's to be the waterfall and pond. Click to select and hold down the Shift key. Then continue selecting areas until you have it all. You will be adding portions of the same height level to the selection. Shift-clicking allows you to add different height levels. If you need to touch up your selection, use the Quick Mask feature and paint more selection in or out of the area.

Once you have created this selection for the "water area," save it. Select > Save Selection will put it in a channel all its own for you to come back to later (see Fig. 7–17b).

4. Next, use this selected area as a basis to create a terrain for the multi-tiered water surface. Load the selection into the Original Terrain channel. Copy selection. Create a third channel and paste the selection here in the exact position it was from the Original Terrain channel. (It needs to be perfectly aligned with the other terrain.) This will become a new terrain, your Water Terrain (see Fig. 7–17c). You'll work with the grayscale information of the first terrain to make flat water surfaces.

5. In order to make the water fit snugly in the rocky terrain area, you need to enlarge the water terrain area. Whatever isn't in the selection area will end up being clipped, and it's important to make sure that the water is large enough to "tuck" into the rocky terrain. To do that, you'll need to enlarge the size of the selection.

Photoshop's Grow command (under the Select menu) will do this. For this, select Grow several times. Save the grown selection to a new channel. Grow made the new selection partially gray. You don't want any aliasing in this selection at all; water is flat, and the terrain shouldn't curve up or down at the edges. Use Levels to make the mask white and black. Drag the white slider toward the left until the channel has either white or black in it. (As an alternative to using the Grow command, save the selection to the fourth channel, blur it, and adjust with Levels to make it grow. Take your pick.)

By now there should be four channels: the Original Waterfall Terrain, Original Selection, Water Terrain, and Grown Selection. Figure 7–17d shows the grown selection in the left half and the Water Terrain in the right half so that you can see the white edge where the selection has grown.

6. Now that you have a larger selection size for your Water Terrain, consider for a moment what you want to do next. You want to create a terrain that has spots of flat gray for the level pools, with transitional grays as the water falls from one pool down to the next one. Paint each area with flat color to do that. Since the intention is to make the terrain's surface flat, this is one time I make an exception to my "never paint a terrain with flat color" rule.

   Go to the Water Terrain channel. Load the Grown Selection. Now you'll brush in the flat color. Take the paint brush and Option-click within the flat color area to sample the color. Choose the predominant color for that area. Then paint the entire section out to the edges of the selection (for this, of course, opacity should be set to 100% and the mode should be Normal). Go to each of the different water sections and paint them the corresponding color for that level. See Figure 7–18a.

7. To paint the waterfall transitions, set the color to the lower (darker) pool and choose a fuzzy brush that is large enough to spread the darker gray into the higher (lighter) pool. Then select the lighter color and click in the higher area so that the color spreads "down" and the two blend. For sharper falling water, make the transition between the two colors more abrupt. Let the lighter color come "out" more into the darker color's area. After all, you want your water to be spilling *over* the edge of something, not cutting under the ground.

   If you're going to create water creases (for sheets of falling water), then use the brush set to multiply (to create darker ridges) and screen (to bring out highlights) with a gray color set at very light opacity (10%–15%). Subtle is as subtle does.

   All this time your waterfall area has been selected. Select the inverse and make everything else black. (My favorite method: Have the foreground color be black and Option-delete to fill

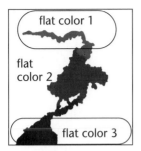

(**a**) Water terrain—after

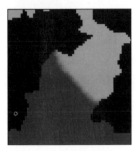

(**b**) Waterfall detail

FIGURE 7–18
Painting the waterfall terrain.

with black.) Figure 7–18b shows a detail of the waterfall transition. Duplicate your completed waterfall channel into a new file and save it as a PICT.

8. You're almost ready to go back to Bryce. But first, one last important alteration. As your grayscale levels are set at the moment, the water level is essentially the same as the terrain level. You want the terrain level to be *under* the water level. For that, you will need to darken the area where the water is. To do that, go back to the Original Terrain channel and load the second channel (Original Selection) into it. Using the Levels command, move the gray slider over slightly to darken the terrain. It doesn't have to darken by much.

   You can also go in and create rock structures that pop above the water's surface by painting them in with Photoshop's paintbrush (Screen mode). There are probably lighter places along the pool's bottom that won't require much convincing to make them emerge from the water. Use the brush to make them slightly lighter still.

   When you're through touching up your terrain, save it as a separate PICT image. You'll have three documents by the time you are through here—one composite multiple channel that has all the working steps in it, one PICT document of the altered terrain itself, and one PICT document of the waterfall.

9. Go back to Bryce. Create a terrain or select the one that's been there all along. Type ⌘-T to get to the Terrain Editor. Set the resolution to 256 and click Merge PICT. In the Merge PICT dialog box, open up your new terrain. Drag the slider all the way to the right to have only the new terrain. Click OK twice to accept the change. Back in your scene, duplicate the terrain right in place. ⌘-C copies the terrain; ⌘-V pastes it in the same place. Go back to the Terrain Editor and the Merge PICT dialog box. This time you'll bring in the waterfall. In the main Terrain Editor, switch on Colors display and drag the low clip slider until it reads somewhere between 30 and 75 or so. This will take out all but the waterfall itself. Click OK. Figure 7–19a shows both terrain wireframes from Top View. Select a camera position (see Fig. 7–19b). Then set your different material settings for each and render. See Figure 7–19c. See also Figure 9-29C in the color section.

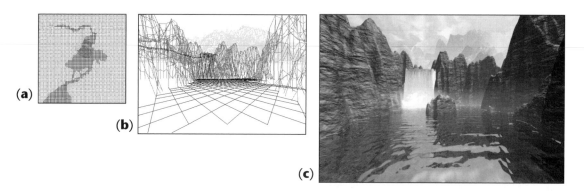

FIGURE 7–19 Terrain wireframes from (**a**) Top View and (**b**) Main View; (**c**) final render.

If you are going to do any moving or size changes or any manipulation of the terrains, make sure that you group them beforehand. Otherwise, they won't be aligned with one another. (If, for some reason, you get them misaligned, just select both, click the Unity button and click Align All. Then group and resize and move to taste.)

DUAL-TERRAIN THREE-DIMENSIONAL OBJECTS

Now it's time for a complete departure from organic mountain shapes. The waterfall is a clipped terrain tucked inside another one. The clipped terrains that follow are "freestanding," that is, two terrains are positioned back-to-back to create objects. For you to put two molded objects back-to-back, they need to mirror one another. There are two ways to do this. The first inverts the Grayscale Map inside the Terrain Editor. The second involves flipping a copy of the terrain from the Alignment menu.

The first method, inverting the actual terrain map, was used by Tony Smith in his scene called "Nautilus" (see Fig. 7–20a). He created submarine parts from terrains. In order to precisely align them back to back, he duplicated the terrain in place and inverted the terrain in the Terrain Editor. Figures 7–20b and 7–20c are the two terrains used to make the submarine hull. Since clipping is an integral part of the object's shape, the settings for clipping were inverted as well. For instance, the terrain that had Low Clipping set

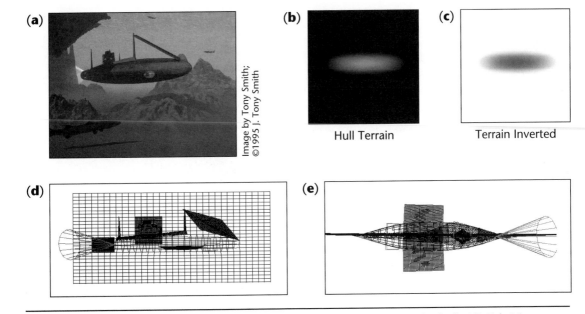

Image by Tony Smith;
©1995 J. Tony Smith

(a)

(b) Hull Terrain

(c) Terrain Inverted

(d)

(e)

FIGURE 7–20 "Nautilus": (**a**) Rendered image; (**b**) and (**c**) terrain parts for hull; (**d**) Side View wireframe; (**e**) Top View wireframe.

at 30 was inverted. He turned off Low Clipping and set High Clipping to the upper limit (1000) minus 30, or 970.

Incidentally, version 1.0.1 of Bryce clips the wireframe preview as well. However, this only works for Low Clip. When the Mesh shows for High Clip (or *any* clipped terrain in version 1.0), a direct click on that clipped portion of the object will not select it (because there's nothing there, you see). Figure 7–20d shows the Side View wireframe, where one terrain is clipped and the other isn't. The High-Clip wireframe preview should be corrected for any version of Bryce later than 1.0.1. Figure 7–20e shows the two terrains aligned from Top View.

The second method to put clipped terrains back-to-back was used by Jackson Ting and Robert Bailey of ArtEffect Design Studio in their "Truck & Trailer" scene. The terrains are identical for the sides of the trailer (see Fig. 7–21a). By selecting one of the Flip options in the Alignment menu on a duplicate terrain, they created the mirrored half of the trailer (see Fig. 7–21b). (Which way to flip, whether *x, y,* or *z,* depends on the object's orientation.)

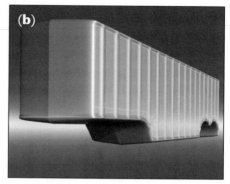

FIGURE 7–21 Using Flip to create a mirrored duplicate; (**a**) Terrain G2H map for both terrains; (**b**) trailer only; (**c**) rendered scene.

Image by Robert Bailey and Jackson Ting at ArtEffect Design Studio, California

In both of these cases, the terrains, once they are duplicated and inverted, need to be precisely aligned. Using the modifier keys to constrain movement is crucial to keep them in alignment. Move them first by "eyeballing" and then rendering a small test area using Distance Render from Top, Front, or Side View. Any gap between the two halves shows up by the anti-aliasing pass.

One potential drawback is that there's a seam where the two pieces join. You'll have to handle this one carefully. Placing the terrain so that the seam lies behind another object is one excellent solution.

ADOBE ILLUSTRATOR AND CLIPPED TERRAINS

Having departed from the world of nice, neat rectangular terrains, I next venture into the object-oriented world of PostScript, which will aid in the process of creating some clipped terrain shapes.

tip

When creating some object, use as many gray levels as you can. This will result in smoother transitions between levels. If the objects are generally flat with gradual bowing, then reduce the height (or width) of the terrain by using the Resize controls.

The transition from Adobe Illustrator to Adobe Photoshop to the Terrain Editor is smooth. Create your terrain shape in Illustrator, rasterize it in Photoshop, save it as a PICT, and then open it in Bryce through the Merge Terrain dialog box in the Terrain Editor.

The architectural details in the tower in Figure 7–22 were created using this method. The many parts of the truck and trailer also were created that way. Jackson Ting and Robert Bailey used Adobe Illustrator to create the blends and gradations that were used for their modeling "terrains." They made it into a science. First they created their black square background in order to define the object area and create the clip level. On top of that, they built their objects. They were able to create very precise blends this way, guiding the contours of the objects in Illustrator and creating gradations with just the right degree of blend from one gray to the next. When the object was completed, it was already set on a square background for importing into Bryce via Photoshop. The only remaining task was adjusting the clipping!

Using Gradients and Filters to Alter Terrain Shapes

Besides using an application like Illustrator to create terrain shapes, you can also do the same using anything that does image editing. This next set of examples are taken from Kai's Power Tools filters used inside of Photoshop.

FIGURE 7–22 Illustrator files that became PICT files in Photoshop and then became terrains in Bryce.

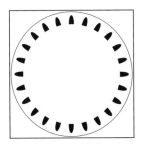
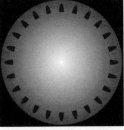
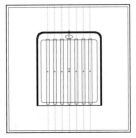

Tower Rivulets in Illustrator

Rasterized in Photoshop with additional gradient

Radiator—Illustrator onscreen preview

Radiator in Illustrator— PostScript printed file

Bryce's default method of creating terrains sets the highest point in the center of the terrain. If you have some PICT images with simple gradients—where the high point is not in the center—you can merge them to make other terrain shapes. Figure 7–23 shows a terrain altered this way. A diagonal gradient was merged with a terrain in the Add mode (see Fig. 7–23a). Then a semicircular gradient was merged using the Minimum mode (see Fig. 7–23b). The rendered terrain in Figure 7–23C is the result.

On the CD are a series of different "terrains" for you to use. They were created in Photoshop using the Gradation tool or Kai's Power Tools Gradient Designer. Have at 'em.

Another fun alternative uses image processing filters to change terrain shape. Figures 7–24 and 7–25 show two sets of terrains, all starting from the same original, that were altered using different filtering techniques with Kai's Power Tools and Photoshop filters.

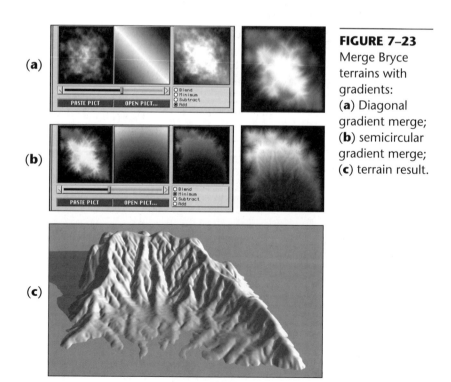

(a)

(b)

(c)

FIGURE 7–23
Merge Bryce terrains with gradients:
(**a**) Diagonal gradient merge;
(**b**) semicircular gradient merge;
(**c**) terrain result.

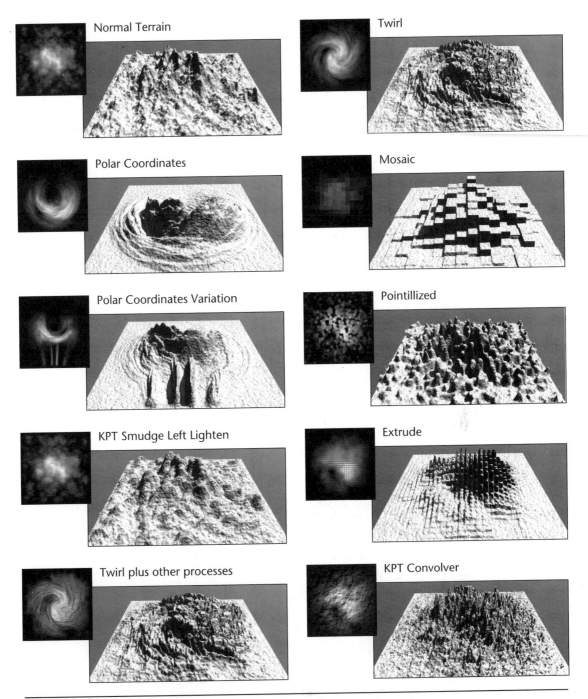

FIGURE 7–24 Using image processing filters to change terrain shape.

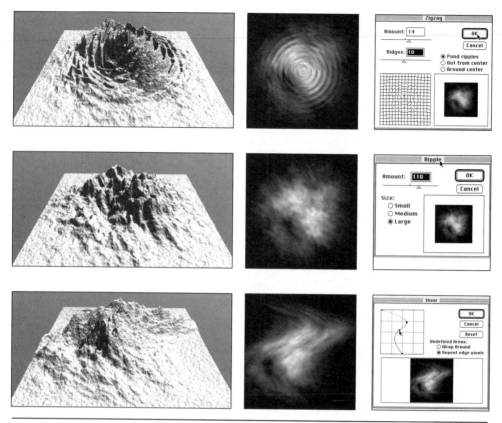

FIGURE 7–25 More Photoshop filters and terrains: Zigzag, Ripple, and Shear.

KPT and Terrains (Vortexing Tiles)

In the previous examples, gradients and filters altered basic mountain terrains. The same image-manipulation tools can be used to create fantastic terrains that resemble no earthly mountain. With Photoshop and Kai's Power Tools, you've a wealth of options for creating terrain forms. Since your work is mostly in grayscale, use the Gradient Designer presets, especially in the category "transparency masks," as your basis for gradients, fractals, and textures. There's a gold mine in there; you can do so much!

Here's an example of the use of Kai's Power Tools to create a terrain. The image, "Vortexing Tiles," started as an idea for a visual pun on the name KPT Vortex Tiling, one of the newer KPT filters. I

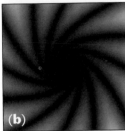

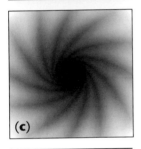

FIGURE 7–26
Making the Vortex Tiling terrain: (**a**) KPT Fractal Explorer; (**b**) applying gradient in Multiply Apply Mode; (**c**) applying gradient in Screen Apply Mode.

wanted to create tiles being sucked into a vortex. Tiles are easy: Create cubes and squish them down flat. But a vortex . . . well, that's a bit of a challenge.

First, I wanted a spiral. The Fractal Explorer has an option to create spiraling shapes. So I made one on the outside of a Mandelbrot set. I used the gradient preset "procedural blend me," which has light and dark gray tones, so that the spiral would have the illusion of waves. See Figure 7–26a.

However, this only created the spiral with a wavy surface. How could I create the effect of a vortex, where the center descends into the abyss? I needed to add dark to the inside and light to the outside. The Gradient Designer provided the solution. A simple grayscale gradient was applied in a circular sunburst algorithm. The gradient was applied two times. First it was applied in a Multiply Apply Mode to darken the center part of the terrain, thereby causing it to descend (see Fig. 7–26b). Likewise, it was applied again using the Screen Apply Mode, where it lightened the outside edges of the spiral (see Fig. 7–26c). A bit of judicious clipping in the Terrain Editor made it a circular surface. Vini Vidi Vortex! To finish the terrain, a water preset was assigned in the Materials Editor. Then the cubes were flattened and positioned as tiles, and 2D PICT image textures were applied. After adding a bit of fog and haze and then rendering, the image was finished—a watery vortex, one twisted person's whirlpool dream. See Figure 7–27C in the color section.

The Lost Continents of Text-land-is

You can create more than mere mountains out of terrains. Create illustrations from words that become a land formation. This section will explore the process used to create text terrains.

Use this with hand-lettering (my personal favorite), typography, and logos. If your logo is in an Adobe Illustrator format, you can rasterize it directly into Photoshop and take it to Bryce from there.

Text Terrain Recipe

1. Create the text itself as line art. In this case, I wrote out the words by hand with brush, ruling pen, and ink on paper, then vectorized it in Adobe Illustrator. You can follow this do-it-yourself method if you are handy with the pen, or you can use type or a logo as your starting place. Scan the words into Photoshop and save as PICT documents.

2. If you're starting with type, you'd start in Photoshop or Illustrator. If your logo is not in a format that you can rasterize into Photoshop, then use a scanner to create the PICT image of the logo. I prefer to have an original that has a resolution of 512. If it's smaller, you risk losing some detail in the actual letter forms. The terrain will be square. If your words do not fit into a square format (the likely case), you have two options for squaring up the situation. Pad your word/image document with empty white space to make the format square. Or wait until you've created your terrain and simply widen it by enlarging it on the x-axis.

   For a little flexibility in manipulating your image, create two more variations. Besides your original, create a slightly blurred and an extremely blurred version of your word or logo. Figure 7–28a shows three variations used for this text terrain.

3. Once you have all of your variations created as PICT files, open Bryce and create a terrain. ⌘-T takes you to the Terrain Editor. Click the Merge PICT button to go to the Merge Terrain dialog box. Click Open PICT and find your original text or logo image. When you have it there in your middle window, move the slider all the way to the right and click the check mark or press Enter. For this version, I first brought in one of the more blurred images.

   Now you're back in the Terrain Editor proper, ready to make the word more terrain-like. Notice that as a black-on-white image, it's in the inverted "valley" position. The next set of steps calls for work-then-invert, especially because the terrain will be merged with itself in order to maintain legibility. You'll go back to the original (or blurred version) of the image as many times as needed to refine the look. The end result should be a terrain that's flat at the top, with glorious rugged mountain descending below on all sides. The next series of steps will go into more detail about the working process.

4. Invert the image so that the text is white (higher)(see Fig. 7–28b). Click the Erode button. (Or click the Fractalize button.) Here, you're calling upon the Terrain Editor's create capability to generate mountainous terrain based on the word shape (see Fig. 7–28c). At this point, you can continue working with the terrain for a while or go straight back to Merge PICT. Do any and all of your favorite tricks with the Terrain Editor.

   Important Note: When you are ready to merge the PICT again, make sure that you re-invert the image so that the background is white (or light) and the text "image" is black. You can invert the terrain, but you cannot invert PICTs as you bring them in from the Merge PICT dialog box.

5. Click Merge PICT. In the Merge PICT dialog box, select your image variant. In this case, the image is a slightly blurred ver-

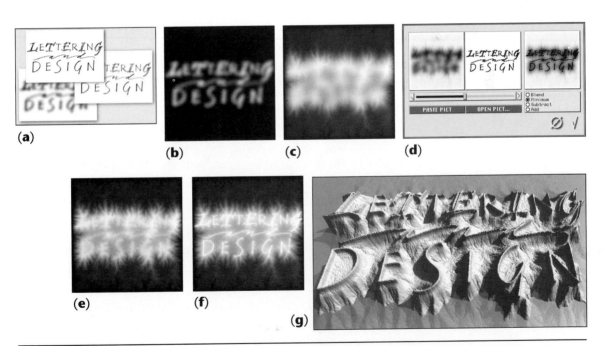

FIGURE 7–28 Creating text terrains: (**a**) Three blurred variations on text art; (**b**) inverted blurred version in Terrain Editor; (**c**) after clicking Erode; (**d**) merging eroded text with a fresh version; (**e**) additional terrain manipulations; (**f**) after last merge to make word legible; (**g**) final render.

sion of the original image. The merge will "beef up" the terrain heights just around the edges of the word.

Stop for a moment and think about what you have in the Merge PICT dialog box. The first terrain is on the left. The second (fresh) terrain is on the right. Both are black on white. (See Fig. 7–28d.)

In order to keep all the terrain processing you've done so far (left) and to keep the actual word shape itself (right), the Minimum mode is used. Minimize takes the *darkest value* of the two. Yep. The secret's out. Minimum keeps all the fun stuff you did in the Terrain Editor while restoring legibility from the fresh word image. However, Minimum works with dark values. That's why the image is inverted each time there's a merge. Click the Minimum button. Make sure the slider is smack dab in the middle (Bryce's default position). Click the check mark or press Enter.

6. Once back in the main Terrain Editor, continue working with the terrain. Erode the terrain when it's black-on-white. Then invert and erode some more. You'll create both ridges and gullies this way. Blur, add noise, change the shape of the terrain by using the filter . . . whatever you like. Figure 7–28e shows the terrain after erosion is added.

7. When you have completed the exploration process (please feel welcome to do intermediate merges, too!), invert your terrain one last time and click the Merge PICT button. Open the basic image PICT and click the Minimum button. Click the check mark to go back to the main Terrain Editor. Click Invert to reorient the terrain for a high mountain. Click Smooth for a nanosecond. (See Fig. 7–28f.)

Why this last step? It makes the word itself easily visible. Even when you have the word blurred or mostly light, any irregularities in tone will create elevation differences in the terrain that will make the word more difficult to read. Remember—for the umpteenth time—you're translating grayscale information to height. You may be able to "read" it fine in the Terrain Editor preview window, but it will be harder to "read" once you've rendered the terrain. After you've made the word the final flat top plateau surface, you can, of course, add a last touch of erosion for a more "natural"-looking word. The rendered result of this process is shown in Figure 7–28g.

Variation—Sloping Letters

These next variations don't make mountainous words so much as explore the interaction of gradations and text forms. Once you've played around with these, you can mix and match mountainous forms and gradations to your heart's content.

Use Photoshop to make text gradations. In Photoshop, make a document and fill it entirely with black. Create a text selection. Fill the text with a gradation. Try using gradations that run from left to right, as well as front to back. The two text gradients in Figure 7–29 (with their respective G2H maps) show both. Save your terrain as a PICT to import through the Merge PICT dialog box.

To have a background gradation in addition to the text gradation, invert the text selection in Photoshop and create a gradient for the background that runs in the other direction. If you make the gradations meet in the middle, then half of your text will descend into the background (see Fig. 7–30a). If you want all of your text to emerge from a sloping background, then make all of the background lighter than the darkest gradient level of the text. (See Fig. 7–30b.)

FIGURE 7–29 Two variations on text gradation: (**a**) and (**c**) G2H maps; (**b**) rendered words.

 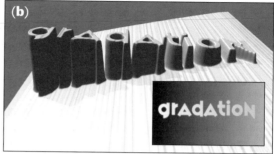

FIGURE 7–30 Text gradation and background gradation: (**a**) Gradations meet in the center; terrain descends below background; (**b**) text gradation is lighter (higher) than the background.

CIRCULAR LETTERS

When working with type terrains, you must take pains when using serif fonts. The font shown in Figure 7–31a (Bodoni Poster) has thick portions joined together by very delicate branches. Normally, when font like this is rasterized into Photoshop, the delicate joins show up as grayed aliased transitions. This presents no problem when the text is a flat two-dimensional image; the grays help convey the shape of the letter.

However, you aren't thinking two dimensional here when you're looking at the G2H map. (At the risk of bordering on the repetitive wheeze, "howmanytimesdoIhaftatellya?" you'll encounter time and again the ingrained manner in which you rely on two-dimensional image information to perform three-dimensional optical illusions. Only after a few nasty surprises when the terrain doesn't "behave" properly do you start to transition to seeing G2H maps for what they are.) In a G2H map, those delicate, slightly blurred branches between letter portions will end up at a different height. The joins *will* be there, but far below the level of the rest of the letter surface (see Fig. 7–31b). Compound this by the fact that you're going to make the letter surface a variable gradient, and you've got a tricky situation. You can't simply work exclusively in the world of sans-serif type, with its more uniform widths. (I can just see that client looking over your shoulder, saying, "But I want you to use that other typeface!") So, how do you navigate through *this* one?

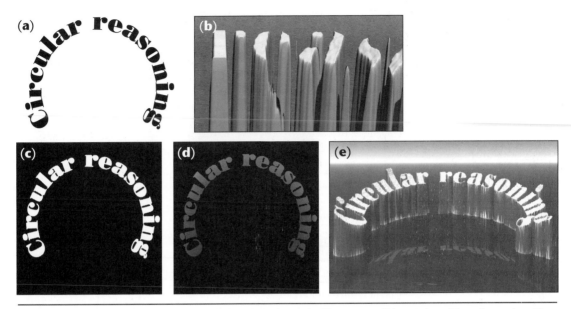

FIGURE 7–31 Beefing up serif text: (**a**) Original text in Illustrator; (**b**) terrain with collapsed serifs; (**c**) beefed up text; (**d**) additional gradients sculpt text levels; (**e**) final render.

First adjust the word so that it will live on the same level. In Photoshop, "beef up" the joins and serifs. To do that, you can brush them in (painstaking and prone to error). Or you can blur the entire image slightly and then use Levels to make the image darker. Or you can use the Burn tool to darken the portions that you want to darken (set it for shadows to darken only dark portions of the image). I prefer the latter two methods. Of course, you need to do the thickening before you add the gradation, while your word is still "flat."

This example uses a logo created in Adobe Illustrator, which allows you to create text upon a path. Then the Illustrator file was rasterized in Photoshop and "beefed up" using the Burn tool and levels (see Fig. 7–31c). Two circular gradients were applied using the KPT Gradient Designer to alter the letter shapes. The first one was set lower in the image to bend the letters so that the open ends of the "horseshoe" were lower than the top of the circle. A second gradient was applied to make the tops of the letters higher than at the baseline (see Fig. 7–31d). The text face is slightly curved as a result, and all the serifs are there (see Fig. 7–31e).

PICT Terrain Tricks

This next section won't take such a "literal" approach to terrain-making. Anything that can be saved in a PICT image file is game to become a terrain. Some of the more interesting (and, at times, horrifying) terrains are those created from an image source. Save the image as a PICT, go to the Merge Terrain dialog box, and Bryce will create the terrain based on the values of the image. This works well when the image is also mapped onto the terrain as the 2D PICT texture.

When you want to make the image recognizable, lower the terrain height overall in the Edit Palette. The Smooth button comes in handy here, as sharp transitions from light to dark take on a mellower, melted appearance.

Two sets of images in Figure 7–32 show examples of the process. The clock image is the basis for terrain shape. It illustrates the pleasing way that images create abstract forms. And Phil Clevenger's "Necrofelinia" sets the standard for Bryce's Terrain Editor making sinister Mr. Hyde transformations from sweet furry adorable Dr. Jekyll images. For more particulars on the way to use PICT images to inspire these transformations, see the sections on PICT textures in Chapter 8, "Material World," and the section of PICTerrain madness in Chapter 11, "Brycing Out of This World."

Working Tips: Side-by-Side Terrain Molding in Photoshop and Bryce

When you are working on a terrain in Bryce, there are times where it will be helpful to have Photoshop open. When there is sufficient RAM to devote to both applications so that they can be open simultaneously, you can go back and forth between the two. This is especially good for the times when you are creating intricate terrains that need to fit just so—shaving off a bit of land here, rendering there, and going back to adjust to get things done.

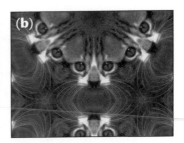

Photo courtesy of Digital Stock Corp.

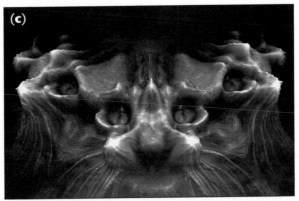

Image by Phil Clevenger, © 1994 Phil Clevenger

Image provided by PhotoDisk,
Inc., ©1995

FIGURE 7–32 Using a PICT to create a G2H map: (**a**) Original
kitty image for "Necrofelinia"; (**b**) G2H map; (**c**) rendered
"Necrofelinia"; (**d**) Clock Parts images for "GlockenFondue";
(**e**) rendered "GlockenFondue."

This is the time to work in Expert mode and toggle to Full Screen mode so that you have a window (⌘-F). If your monitor is large enough to allow for it, you'll be able to see both the rendered version in Bryce and the grayscale map in Photoshop for very precise manipulation.

You'll be working your Macintosh clipboard as you copy from Bryce's Terrain Editor and then Paste to your Photoshop document and then copy and paste going the other way.

In that intricate terrain-working situation, set up your views to have several perspectives on the same object. The trick to this lies in two things: First position your object in Top, Main, Side, and Front Views so that the object shows up in a different place in the active image area. Second, remember to marquee *only* the area that you want to render so that you'll be able to see all three renders-in-progress as you work.

tip

Remember the keyboard shortcuts for different views:

1 is Main View
2 is Top View
3 is Side View
4 is Front View
5–9 are your views in the "Add View As..." list

As you look at your scene from Top View, use the Hand Tool to scroll the 2D Projection plane so that the object is located in one corner of the active image area (see Fig. 7–33a). The other areas of your scene window are ready for additional views. For the Main View, use the Hand Tool to set your object into another corner. If you want to have a different Main View as well, save your first one in the Add View As... dialog box. Now you can create another Main View to look at your terrain from another angle. Scroll the second Main View to another corner and then add it to your Add Views As... list.

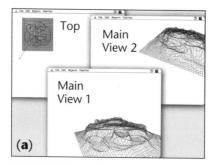 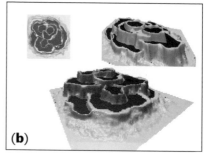

FIGURE 7–33 Simultaneous views of the scene: (**a**) Objects placed in different parts of the active image area for each perspective; (**b**) renders-in-progress for the three different views.

As you work with the terrain and other objects, toggle back and forth with the Escape (or Clear on keypad) key to switch to the render PICT mode and draw a marquee around only that area. Then render that portion.

Switch to another view, toggle to PICT mode, drag the marquee around the appropriate area, and render. After rendering it from different angles, it will be easier for you to see exactly what needs fixing. With each adjustment to your terrain, switch to the appropriate view, drag a marquee around the critical area, and render. Figure 7–33b shows a scene with three renders in progress from the three views of the scene.

Distance Render

Bryce's Distance Render is a good way to create a terrain from a render of objects from Top View. Create a new terrain based on objects that are already in your scene. This is especially good if you are trying to align several terrains in a mountain-valley formation. Alignment of the valley terrain with the mountain terrains can be tricky. This technique allows you to get the alignment "close" and then take a slightly different tack to get it "right." When in Distance Render mode, Bryce renders things according to this formula: "Whatever is closest to the camera is rendered as black. Whatever is farthest is rendered as white." When doing a Distance Render from Top View, the image is the opposite of a G2H map, which says that the highest point is white and the lowest point is black. All you need to do after creating a Distance Render is to invert the image in an image editing application or the Texture Editor. See also the Distance Render section of Chapter 12, "Render Unto Bryce."

Recipe: Using Distance Render to Create a Terrain

1. Set up a scene with multiple terrains. Make one terrain the rolling valley floor if you like.

tip

I find that using FILENAME with a DX suffix is good for a Distance Rendered file. It keeps the same name as the scene itself, but distinguishes the type of render. For that matter, you can do the same thing where a 360° file has a 360° suffix (for the Key Caps Curious, you get the degree symbol by typing Option-Shift-8) and a mask can have .MASK suffix.

2. From the Master Palette's Views popup menu, select Top View.

3. In the Render Palette, select Distance Render.

4. Render the scene.

5. Under the File menu, select "Save As..." and give this file a different name. You will open this up from Photoshop or an image editing application to set the proper size of the file.

6. In Photoshop, open up the file. Crop it into a square format. Crop out all the unnecessary image area.

7. Invert the image in Photoshop (⌘-I).

Digital Elevation Models

To create terrains based on already existing land forms, use what is called a Digital Elevation Model (DEM). DEM is the electronic file format used by the USGS for topographical information. The DEM file is a text file describing the elevation for each point on a mesh for a map. Imagine a grid laid over an area of land. At each point where there's a grid intersection, the question is asked, "What's the elevation here?" This is called a sample. Samples are taken for each point on the grid, resulting in a text description of the actual terrain. If you convert this DEM information to a grayscale image, where each point on the grid is represented by a pixel, you have a G2H map. The pixel color indicates the elevation, so you can build a terrain based on real data from the real world.

DEMs come in different types of resolution. If you adjust the grid so that more points are sampled in a fixed area, you have a higher resolution map with more detail. It's the exact same principle as changing your terrain resolution from 128 to 512. There is more information about the terrain contained in the 512 map than the 128.

DEM measurements are discussed in two ways: the amount of area covered and the amount of detail for an area. For the amount of land area covered, the measurements are conveyed in terms of Earth's basic measurements: latitude and longitude. Units of latitude and longitude are expressed in degrees, then minutes, then seconds. If you see reference to a two-degree map and a 15-minute map, the 15-minute map takes in a smaller area than does a two-degree map.

The other way of discussing DEM measurement, amount of detail, is referred to as meter samples. How many meters do you travel between one elevation sample and the next? A 100-meter sample is not as detailed as a 30-meter sample, since the 30-meter sample obtained just over three times the amount of data as a 100-meter sample did. There is a relationship between the amount of area in a DEM and the amount of detail in a DEM. For any number of data points in a DEM, the questions of scale and resolution ask, "Is this a highly detailed map of my four little acres?" or "Is this a moderately detailed map that spans four big counties?" The larger the area, the less detail. The smaller the area, the more detail.

So how do you get from DEM to Bryce? There is a freeware application on the CD that will convert USGS DEM data to grayscale PICT data. DEM View, created by Ken Badertscher, allows you to look at a DEM and save the entire thing as a PICT or select Bryce-sized terrain morsels to save as PICTs. Then all you need to do is use the PICTs to create terrains. There is a small sampling of DEM data on the CD as well, plus information about where you can go to download more by Anonymous FTP from Internet sites.

The ability to take real-world topographic data into Bryce has its scientific uses. Figure 7–34 shows some Bryce images created by USGS scientists to visualize geographical data over different time

John K. Nakata and Robert K. Mark, U.S. Geological Survey

FIGURE 7–34 Using USGS DEM data in Bryce: (**a**) Region in the past; (**b**) transitional stage; (**c**) region at present.

frames. Figure 7–34a shows an area in the past, when the region was under water. Figure 7–34b shows the transitional stage, as water subsided. Figure 7–34c shows that the same area today is completely dry—in fact, it's a desert.

Conclusion

This chapter went deep into the spine of Bryce—the Terrain Editor. From a description of the basic controls and what they do, I jumped off into Zen and the art of working in the Terrain Editor, the Merge dialog box, clipping, waterfalls, and freestanding terrain-based structures. Then I discussed text-based terrains and the unusual PICT-based terrains as well. I concluded with a discussion of Digital Elevation Models (DEMs) for creating Brycean terrains based on the real world.

FIGURE 1–1C
Bryce Canyon National Park at sunrise.

Photograph by Susan A. Kitchens

Two scenes by Eric Wenger based on a photograph of Yosemite National Park during winter.

Image by Eric Wenger

Image by Eric Wenger

FIGURE 6–20C Lightsource position affects sky and cloud color: These images show the sun at four different elevations ranging from overhead to horizon. These same elevations are repeated for three basic positions in the sky—behind, to the side, and in front of the camera.

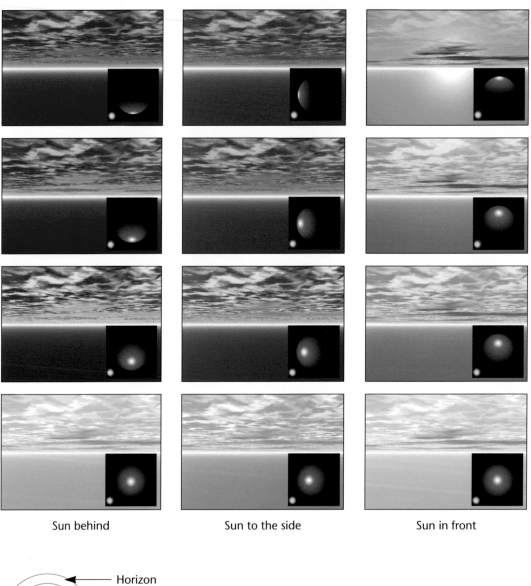

Sun behind   Sun to the side   Sun in front

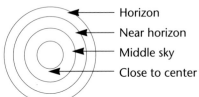

Horizon
Near horizon
Middle sky
Close to center

FIGURE 6–21C This set of images compares different settings for Sun color and Ambient color.

Sun in high position

  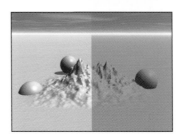

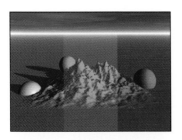  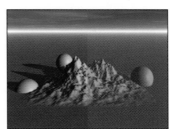

Sun in low position

 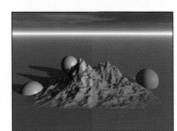 

Ambient Color	Sun Color	Both Ambient and Sun

Similar Colors	
Lighter Sun and Darker Ambient	Darker Sun and Lighter Ambient

Opposite Colors	
Lighter Sun and Darker Ambient	Darker Sun and Lighter Ambient

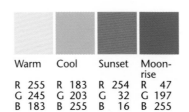

Warm	Cool	Sunset	Moon-rise
R 255	R 183	R 254	R 47
G 245	G 203	G 32	G 197
B 183	B 255	B 16	B 255

FIGURE 6–22C White and taupe haze shown at different amounts; taupe and black fog shown at different heights and amounts.

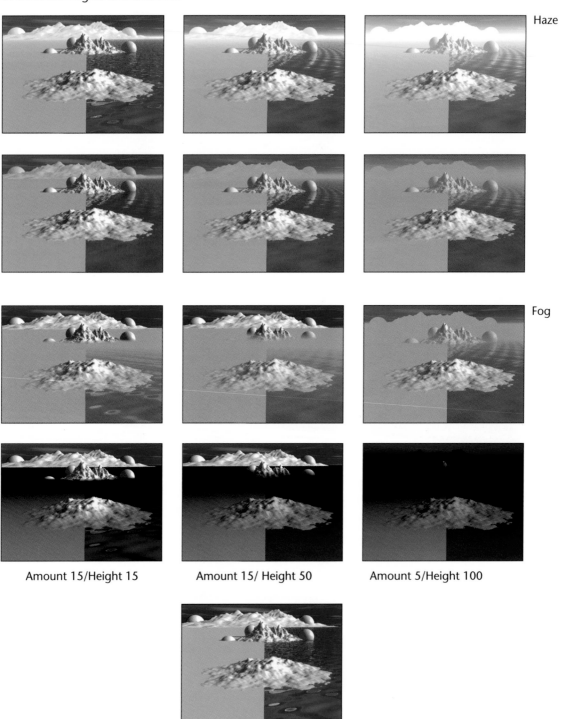

Haze

Fog

Amount 15/Height 15   Amount 15/ Height 50   Amount 5/Height 100

Original: no fog, no haze

FIGURE 6–23C The combination of different fog and haze colors; each combination is shown at three different times of day.

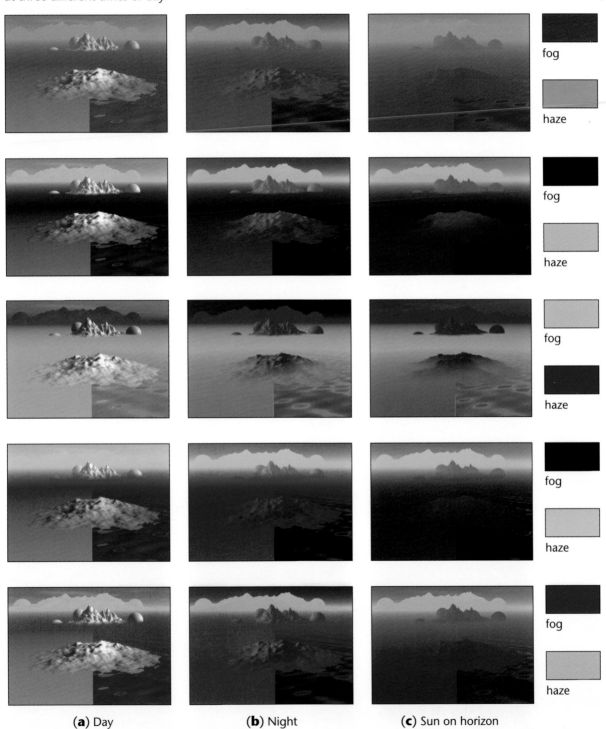

(**a**) Day   (**b**) Night   (**c**) Sun on horizon

FIGURE 6–24C Atmosphere *off*: (**a**) Scene by day; (**b**) scene by night; (**c**) Sky & Fog settings for both scenes (except Lightsource).

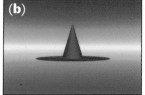

Render Palette Options: No Atmosphere

FIGURE 6–25C Using Atmosphere *off* to create a blue sky at sunset.

FIGURE 6–26C Adding a cloud infinite plane to get clouds in the "No Atmosphere" sky.

FIGURE 6–34C The sun dips below the smoke on the water. A glowing sphere is the sun. Cloud-spheres, haze, and fog create the smoke effect.

FIGURE 6–36C Result of sunset on water recipe.

FIGURE 7–27C "Vortexing Tiles."

FIGURE 6–32C Light bulbs created by placing one glowing object inside another; Ambient and Transmitivity settings vary.

FIGURE 8–7C The Hilites size and color interacts with Specular and Diffuse colors to create differing results.

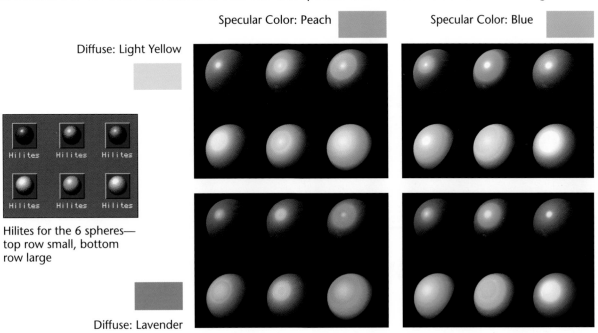

Specular Color: Peach

Specular Color: Blue

Diffuse: Light Yellow

Hilites for the 6 spheres—top row small, bottom row large

Diffuse: Lavender

FIGURE 8–26C Texture previews, shown with their colors, demonstrating that various combinations make the whole different from the sum of the parts.

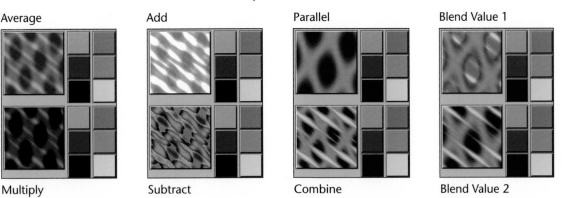

Average

Add

Parallel

Blend Value 1

Multiply

Subtract

Combine

Blend Value 2

FIGURE 8–13C These images show the same scene under different conditions; the Color Control switches between texture color and illumination color. The same texture is used throughout.

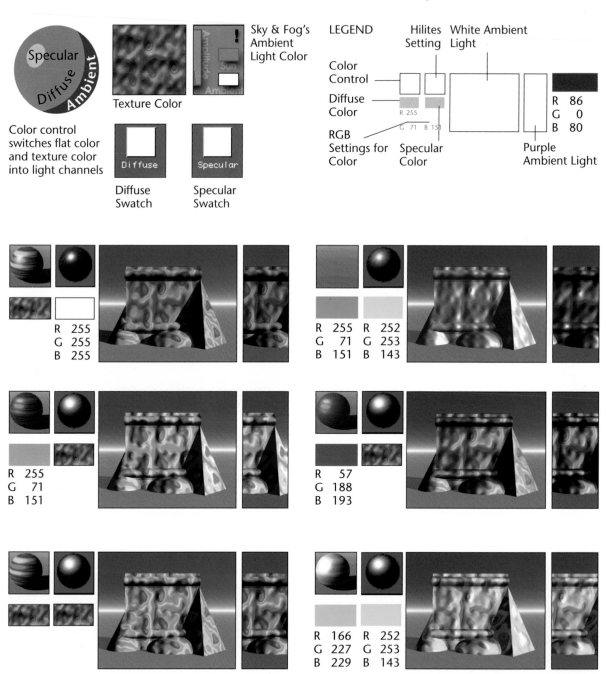

Specular
Diffuse
Ambient

Texture Color

Sky & Fog's Ambient Light Color

Amplitude
Sun
Ambient

Color control switches flat color and texture color into light channels

Diffuse

Specular

Diffuse Swatch

Specular Swatch

LEGEND

Hilites Setting

White Ambient Light

Color Control

Diffuse Color

R 255

G 71   B 151

RGB Settings for Color

Specular Color

Purple Ambient Light

R 86
G 0
B 80

R 255
G 255
B 255

R 255   R 252
G 71   G 253
B 151   B 143

R 255
G 71
B 151

R 57
G 188
B 193

R 166   R 252
G 227   G 253
B 229   B 143

FIGURE 8–40C A sample of each color mapping combination.

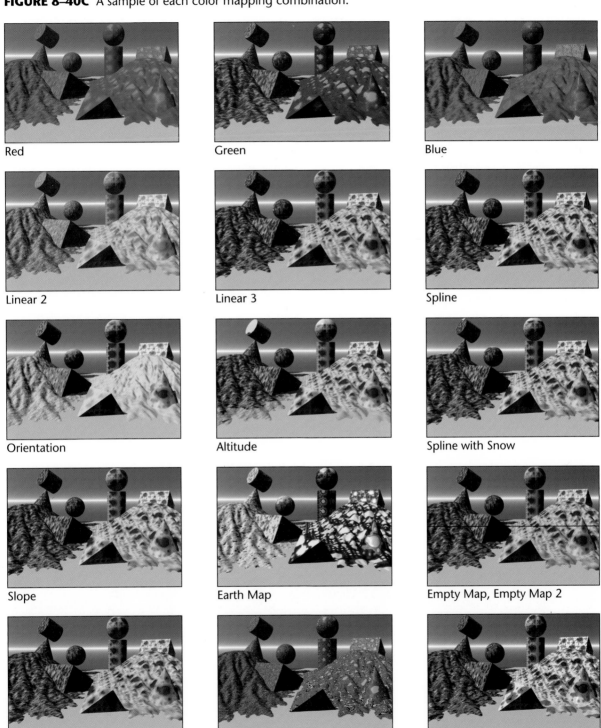

Red

Green

Blue

Linear 2

Linear 3

Spline

Orientation

Altitude

Spline with Snow

Slope

Earth Map

Empty Map, Empty Map 2

Randomized

Interferences

Interpolation + Interferences

FIGURE 8–41C Blend options in the Deep Texture Editor for combining texture components.

Add

Subtract

Average

Multiply   (Bump only)

Minimum   (Bump only)

Blend Minimum

Combine

Maximum   (Bump only)

Blend Maximum

Blend Value 1

Blend Value 2

Blend Random

Blend Altitude

Blend Slope

Fast Slope

FIGURE 8–41C (continued)

Component 1   (Value)

Component 2   (Value)

Component 3 (for Parallel)

Parallel

Blend Orientation

FIGURE 8–21C An excellent match of color and lighting makes the PICT image "belong" to the scene.

© 1995 Paul J. Kuehn

FIGURE 8–43C "Snowed Under," final result of a Deep Texture recipe.

FIGURE 8–47C "Puddlebumps," final result of a Deep Texture recipe.

Image by Eric Wenger

FIGURE 9–3C
Three nature scenes by Eric Wenger:
"Abisko Pine Trees" (top);
"Red Vulcans" (middle);
"Fjord A4" (bottom).

Image by Eric Wenger

FIGURE 9–29C Waterfall pond.

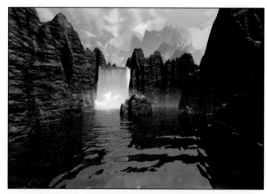

Image by Eric Wenger

Image by Susan A. Kitchens and Eric Wenger

FIGURE 9–24C Four sea scenes with different colors set in the Sky & Fog Palette.

Colors

	Fog	Haze	Clouds	Sun	Amb
R	16	85	255	235	255
G	16	123	255	254	255
B	16	175	255	15	255

	Fog:	Haze	Shad1	Clouds
Amt	88	93	0	Render: No
Ht	7.9			Atmosphere

Colors

	Fog	Haze	Clouds	Sun	Amb
R	138	63	238	226	253
G	108	93	37	112	41
B	86	134	0	125	7

	Fog:	Haze	Shad	Clouds
Amt	88	93	10	Render: No
Ht	7.9			Atmosphere

Colors

	Fog	Haze	Clouds	Sun	Amb
R	38	183	255	252	252
G	87	176	255	253	253
B	98	77	255	135	135

	Fog:	Haze	Shad	Clouds
Amt	17	80	0	Cover
Ht	10			Freq
				Ampl

Colors

	Fog	Haze	Clouds	Sun	Amb
R	156	63	238	235	255
G	168	93	37	254	255
B	100	134	0	15	255

	Fog:	Haze	Shad	Clouds	
Amt	88	93	10	Cover	62.332
Ht	7.9			Ampl	2.191
				Freq	0.4

FIGURE 10–17C
"Chromescape," a shining example of the types of effects achievable with spheres, cylinders, cones, terrains, a bit of time, and a unique vision.

Image by Brian Patrick Mucha, Graven Images

FIGURE 11–5C
"Necrofelinia."

© Phil Clevenger; original image courtesy Digital Stock

FIGURE 11–7C GlockenFondue series comparing two Opacity Map settings, Bump Gain and Alpha Reflection, on an object where terrain, PICT texture, and Opacity Map are all derived from the same image source.

Bump Gain, Reflection

No Bump Gain, Reflection

Bump Gain, No Reflection

No Bump Gain or Reflection

Image provided by ©1995 Photo Disc, Inc

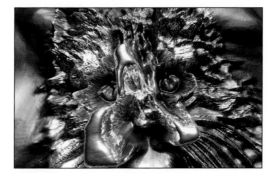

Original image courtesy Digital Stock

FIGURE 11–8C A dull metallic surface from an image that began with no metallic look.

FIGURE 11–10C "Remotely Cuboid."

Image by Dr. Robert L. Hurt

FIGURE 11–11C "Mirror Dot Polka": A combination of a simple 2D PICT texture and simple object elements to get a nice dramatic image.

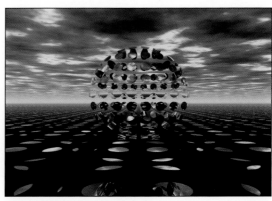

Image by Richard W. Vanderlippe

FIGURE 11–15C "Robots at Sunset" (left); "Impact Images" (right).

Images by Dave Teich, © 1994

"Serene Greece."

Image by Kai Krause

"Ethereal San Gabriel Morning."

Image by Susan A. Kitchens

CHAPTER 8

Material World

The lava, very porous in certain places, took the form of little round blisters. Crystals of opaque quartz, adorned with limpid drops of natural glass suspended to the roof like lustres, seemed to take fire as I passed beneath them. One would have fancied that the genii of romance were illuminating their underground palaces to receive the sons of men.

"Magnificent, glorious!" I cried, in a moment of involuntary enthusiasm; "what a spectacle, uncle! Do you not admire these variegated shades of lava, which run through a whole series of colors, from reddish brown to pale yellow,—by the most insensible degrees? And these crystals,—they appear like luminous globes."

"You are beginning to see the charms of travel, Master Harry," cried my uncle. "Wait a bit, until we advance farther. What we have as yet discovered is nothing—onward, my boy, onward!"

Jules Verne, *A Journey to the Centre of the Earth*

In This Chapter . . .

- The Materials Editor Interface and general organization of the Editor
- A deeper explanation of each part
- Discussion of some basic approaches to working in the Materials Editor
- 2D PICT Textures—description, how-to's, and pointers
- 3D Solid Textures and the two editors to work with them
- The Deep Texture Editor—what each thing does
- Building a couple of material settings from the ground up

This chapter introduces you to the heart of Bryce—the Materials Editor. All the surface appearance of objects in Bryceland are determined here. I will journey deep into the center of Bryceland, picking apart the details of each element along the way. Once I've reached rock bottom, I'll work my way up again by carefully examining a couple of textures—from the deep materials to their settings in the Materials Editor—to give you a feel for the entire material process.

Introduction to the Materials Editor

Before I discuss what the Materials Editor does, I'll first review our setup. There is an object in the scene. The renderer will shoot a ray (actually, many rays) into the scene that will intersect the object. What happens at that point? What information about the object is discovered? Where does the ray go after that? It will bounce off and go somewhere—to a light source or to other objects, eventually deriving a color for that pixel.

The Materials Editor is the place where you determine the surface properties of each object so that it has its own particular appearance. Settings in the Materials Editor determine the answers to these questions: How will the ray bounce? Will rays of certain colors be absorbed and others be reflected? Will the ray bounce directly, creating a specular highlight, or will it bounce from all directions, an indication of diffuse light? Is the object transparent, with some of the rays passing through the object to what is on the other side? Or is the object reflective, bouncing the ray to that other object over there, which is reflected on the surface of that primary object? Is it matte or shiny? What color is it? Are there patterns of colors? What are the shapes of those color patterns? Is the actual surface smooth or are there indentations?

The Materials Editor is the place to control the sum total of the object's surface properties—the way it absorbs, reflects, or transmits light, surface texture, color, and small indentations (bumps). More than a uniform means of coloring the object, the surface appearance may change depending on altitude, orientation, or slope (how level or upright the surface is), as well as incorporate all the additional information about lighting and surface qualities. The Materials Editor is the place to define *every aspect* of the object's surface as the renderer's rays hit it as they go forth from the virtual camera.

Materials Section by Section

I begin my tour through the Materials Editor with a bit of term clarification. When discussing how the surface of an object appears, it might be tempting to use the words "Materials" and "Texture" interchangeably. Don't. Each has a specific meaning; Materials and Texture aren't identical. Material is the *overall* appearance of the surface of an object. Texture is *a part of* the object's surface appearance. The organization of the Materials Editor dialog box demonstrates this. There is indeed a section called Textures, but there are other sections as well. In Figure 8–1a, the Materials Editor is divided into blocks for each segment that is a part of a material setting. Figure 8–1b breaks the Materials Editor down into the major sections: Textures and Illumination, with Color acting as a bridge between the two. But those aren't the only sections. I briefly consider each in turn.

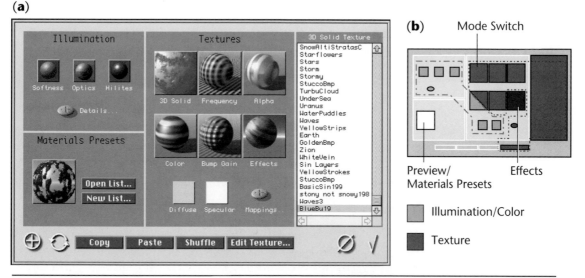

FIGURE 8–1 (**a**) The Materials Editor; (**b**) Materials Editor divided by sections.

- *Preset Preview/Render.* The lower left-hand corner is the business portion of the Materials Editor. Choose presets here or see a preview of your chosen material setting render as you make adjustments elsewhere. The buttons to the right, for saving and loading lists, allow you to create and access lists of saved presets. Scroll through the list by dragging in the Preview Window or click to either side of the window to move one preset at a time (see Fig. 8–2). This action works the same way on all controls in the Materials Editor.

- *Texture.* Six controls govern the properties of the surface texture. The primary control, Mode switch, is in the upper left of the Texture section. It toggles between *No Texture* (to create simple flat monocolor objects), *2D PICT* (to wrap a PICT image around the surface of the object for its appearance), and *3D Solid Textures* (to algorithmically create textures live in the three-dimensional World Space).

  Adjust the *Frequency* of the texture for more or less detail. Set *Alpha* to use information from the alpha channel to make portions of the texture either transparent or reflective. Adjust the *Bump Gain* to create the appearance of surface perturbances on the object. *Color* acts as a switch to determine where the texture's color information appears based on the Illumination settings and color swatches. *Mappings* takes you to a dialog box that gives you different choices for the way that your texture will be wrapped around the objects.

- *Effects.* Effects is a special control that determines how the object renders. Is the object solid or fuzzy? Is it additive (glowing)

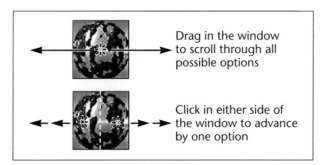

Drag in the window to scroll through all possible options

Click in either side of the window to advance by one option

FIGURE 8–2
Selecting presets or using other Materials Editor controls.

or not? This is the switch to use when you want to create diffuse clouds, glowing objects, planets, or regular land-based objects and terrains.

- *3D Texture List/2D PICT.* The area to the right changes depending on the type of texture selected by the Mode switch. When it's 3D Solid Textures, there is a list that shows all possible underlying textures that can be used for your material setting. For 2D PICTs, a small preview of the image is shown there so that you can see a small preview of the image that is being wrapped around the object.

- *Illumination and Details.* This portion of the Materials Editor enables you to select how the object will respond to light. *Softness* moves between three different types of lighting conditions. By how much will it be self-illuminating, that is, ambient? By how much will the light bounce off the surface with bright direct "hot spots," that is, specular light? And how matte will the object be, bouncing light off its surface in all directions to create diffuse light and shadow? The *Optics* settings control whether light passes through an object or whether its surface is reflective. The *Hilites* setting determines how large the specular hot spot is and whether there is an additional color in the specular highlight.

- *Color Swatches.* The two color swatches allow you to choose the color for the object. Diffuse sets the color of the object when struck by diffuse light. (Ambient too is affected by this color.) Specular determines the color that's reflected as specular highlights bounce straight from the object's surface to the camera. The color swatches work in concert with the Color control of the Texture section and the Illumination controls.

- *Edit Texture.* This button is a way to get to other things. It is a secret trap door that takes you to another room to work with the underlying textures, whether 2D PICT or 3D Solid. When working with the 3D Solid Texture, there are two levels of Texture Editor you can access. Click the Edit Texture... button to go to the Shallow Texture Editor; hold down the Option key while clicking this button to access the Deep Texture Editor. Like the mysterious room beyond a secret revolving bookshelf, the

Texture Editors behind the Edit Texture... button holds depth and fascination. Read further in the chapter to find many of the secrets and buried treasure (but no surprise cadavers, I hope!) contained in these secret spots. There is a second entrance into the mysterious room. The main menu has commands for accessing the Editors, which bypass the Materials Editor. Under the Object menu, there are commands. One is Last 3D Solid Texture... . No matter what object is selected, the command will access the most recent texture that was edited. Select this to get to the Texture Editor; hold down the Option key to get to the Deep Texture Editor. The other command, 2D PICT Texture..., allows you to directly edit the list of two-dimensional PICTs used in the scene. It's the same as clicking the Edit Texture... button when in the 2D PICT mode.

The Materials Editor in Depth

Now that I've given a general overview of all the options available for making that object's surface look just so, I'll take a more detailed look at each of the controls in the Materials Editor.

Illumination

The Illumination controls allow you to adjust the way light interacts with your object. Remember back to the idea of how the eye sees: Light bounces off of the object and hits your eye. Or, in the ray-tracing analogy, once the ray hits the object, it bounces from there to the light source. The Illumination controls determine how that ray will bounce and so how the object is lit.

You can drag the three preview controls to make your setting, but I prefer the Details dialog box for precise control. The Softness control is a three-way switch between the Illumination conditions on the left-hand side of the Details dialog box: Ambient, Specular, and Diffuse. Figure 8–3a shows the relationship between dragging direction in the Softness control and the corresponding Illuminations conditions.

Optics concerns itself with the right-hand side of the dialog box: Transmitivity and Reflection. There is a third parameter in the Details dialog box that you cannot adjust by using the sliders—the Refract Index (see Fig. 8–3b).

The Hilites control on the right has no parallel in the Details dialog box. Drag up for a small highlight; drag down for a large one. Dragging all the way left makes the highlight white (or the same color set in the Specular color swatch); dragging to the right takes you through different colors of the spectrum (see Fig. 8–3c).

Next I focus on the object's surface properties and light. Set these with the Softness control on the left-hand side of the Illumination control panel (or the left column of the Details dialog box). The three kinds of light controls are Ambient, Diffuse, and Specular. Since any object can be illuminated by any combination of these three types of light, Bryce has a separate channel for each. The amount of light and the color that is reflected from the object are controlled separately. First I'll discuss them in terms of light only in this description of the Illumination controls. Later in the chapter, I'll move on to color.

AMBIENT LIGHT

When an object has ambient light, it is self-illuminating. It resists shadows. The color for the self-illumination is set in the Ambient color swatch in the Sky & Fog Palette.

Ambient illumination resists shadows. Figure 8–4a shows a sphere at a maximum Ambient setting. Although the path from the light

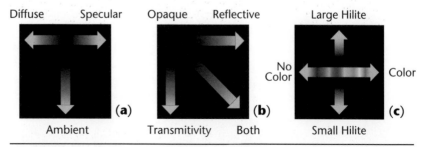

FIGURE 8–3 The directions in which you drag in the Optics controls and their corresponding settings or effects.

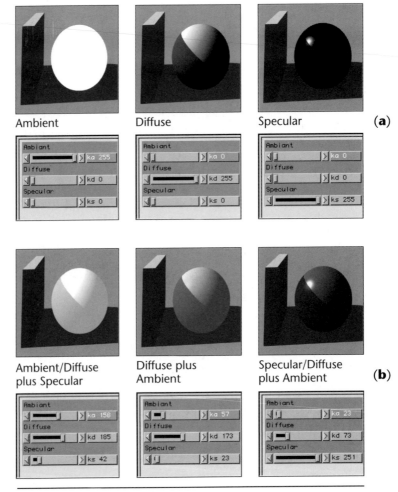

FIGURE 8–4 These spheres are in partial shadow, showing illumination in direct light and shadow. Row (**a**) shows a pure one from each category; row (**b**) is mixed.

tip

If you want no ambient lighting in your object, yet you do want some of the detail to show, you can always adjust the Shadow setting in the Sky & Fog Palette.

source is obstructed by another object, the sphere is not in shadow. When ambient is mixed with diffuse illumination, the shadows falling on the object will not be as dark and pronounced (see Fig. 8–4b). Most natural objects (terrains and such) have little to no ambient light. A low setting will allow you to see a bit of surface detail that is in shadow.

Important Note: It's important that the Ambient setting be consistent for most of the objects in your scene (stay tuned for exceptions). If you have one object that has a low Ambient setting placed next to an object with a high Ambient setting, they will not appear natural. The edge between the two objects will seem artificial, especially when the edge is in shadow.

In cases where you want an object to be especially bright, such as snow (atop a darker, rocky surface) or a glowing object, the Ambient setting should be different. Also, when you have an object whose surface is a 2D PICT and you want the details of that PICT image to be readily apparent, give the object a higher Ambient setting. Figure 8–5 shows an object with a 2D PICT texture at different Ambient settings. A shadow falls on the lower front surface of each cube.

Objects that are highly ambient are freestanding clouds, snow, and glowing objects (in conjunction with the additive Effects).

DIFFUSE LIGHT

When light strikes a rough surface, it doesn't bounce in a particular direction; it bounces away in all directions. Consequently, the surface appears matte. The object is in direct light or it is in shadow, but there is no hot highlight. Figure 8–4 shows a sphere with maximum Diffuse Illumination and mixed Diffuse and Ambient.

For many of the objects created in Bryce, especially ground and terrain surfaces, a high Diffuse setting is the norm. Much of the natural world has rough surfaces, and light bounces away from a matte surface in all directions.

The diagrams in Figure 8–6 compare how specular light and diffuse light bounce off of the surfaces of objects.

FIGURE 8–5 Different Ambient settings on 2D PICTS.

Ambient 50   Ambient 150   Ambient 230
Diffuse 255   Diffuse 200   Diffuse 200

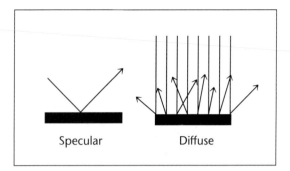

FIGURE 8–6 Specular light bounces directly off of a surface, creating a "hot spot"; diffuse light goes every which way.

SPECULAR LIGHT

When light hits a surface and bounces directly off of it, what is seen is a "hot spot," or specular highlight. Figure 8–4 shows a sphere with maximum Specular, as well as a sphere with some Diffuse and a tad of Ambient illumination. What is seen is not the color of the object but the color of the light (set with the Specular color swatch). An object with a high Specular setting appears very shiny, glossy, or wet. The size of the Specular hot spot is set using the Hilites control.

Although I said I would save the color discussion for later, I take a peek at Specular and Hilites and color here, since the Hilites control sets the color as well as the size of the hot spot. Specular light color and the Hilites color interact with one another when they make the hot spot. Drag the Hilites control all the way to the left and there is no additional highlight color. Drag to the right and you will go through the rainbow. The specular and highlight colors are combined, and, depending on the specific colors, one may augment, complement, or counteract the other. Diffuse color is also a part of the interaction. The basic color of the spheres in Figure 8–7C is set by Diffuse, so the Specular and Hilites colors interact with Diffuse as well. See Figure 8–7C in the color section for a sample of the range of color interaction.

tip

For chrome or other highly reflective surfaces with specular highlights, set two different specular colors—Specular and Hilites—for complex color interaction.

SETTINGS ON THE RIGHT SIDE

The right-hand side of the Illumination dialog box concerns additional properties: Reflectivity, Transmitivity, and Refraction. These are the settings that come into play if the object is not completely opaque. When there is Transmitivity, the ray will be split. Part will go through the object to what lies on the other side (and, further, if there is refraction; the ray will be bent as it bounces). Part will bounce until it reaches the light source. If there is Reflectivity, the ray will bounce off the object to other surrounding objects—and the light source—in the scene. Naturally, adding more complex factors to the situation means you'll have a longer render time, as there are more calculations that must be made in order to chase down those rays to their sources.

Reflectivity

Reflectivity determines how much the object reflects light. When rays of light bounce off of a reflective surface, they go elsewhere, to another surface. The other object is reflected. Water, mirrors, and metals are reflective. Adjust to taste. In the artificial world of a ray-tracer, light bounces off a reflective surface six times. Otherwise if you were to set up a scene in which light travels infinitely down a "hall of mirrors," then you'd never see that Macintosh watch cursor go away during your render! Figure 8–8 sets up an infinite hall of mirrors, as two reflective surfaces face one another. At the sixth reflection, the object turns black (it appears to be the third reflection, but count the reflections "behind" you).

Transmitivity

Does light pass through the object? This slider will make it so. Depending on the amount of transmitivity, a portion of the light

FIGURE 8–8 Bryce's six-reflection limit.

ray will bounce off of the object toward the ultimate light source and another portion will pass through the object to what lies on the other side. The higher the number, the more "transparent" the object will appear and the more of the object on the other side that will show through.

Of course, once the light passes "through" the object, the question arises: Do the light rays bend as they pass through? That's where the Refract Index comes in.

Refract Index

Refract Index determines how much light bends as it passes through an object. Adjusting this determines what the translucent object is composed of. In the real world, different types of physical matter refract light differently depending on their molecular structure and other physical and chemical properties. In this virtual 3D world that you're creating, you get to play molecular physicist by tweaking this little slider. Want air? Set it to 100. Want water? Set it over to 133. How about glass? Take it on up to 152. The higher the number, the more light bends. You'll reach a point where the world turns upside-down through your refracted object. (This is especially true of spheres.)

Changes in refraction can be quite dramatic taken in the small increments. This is a control to use with subtlety. Also, despite the Refract Index given for certain materials, there may be times when you want to "cheat" a little and have a lower refraction rate in the interest of allowing the viewer to see more easily through the object.

Figure 8–9 shows both a sphere and a square disk at different Refract Index settings. Starting at 100 (Air), each setting moves up by a factor of 5. After a bit, the world is upside-down as seen through the Refract Index. Each square in the bottom row has the same setting as the sphere directly above.

When the Refract Index goes below 100, there will be a halo around the edge of the object. Lower refraction, bigger halo. The light bends differently, like it does when passing through a concave lens. See Figure 8–10. Also see an animation on the CD, by Victor von Salza. It shows all of the Refract Index settings.

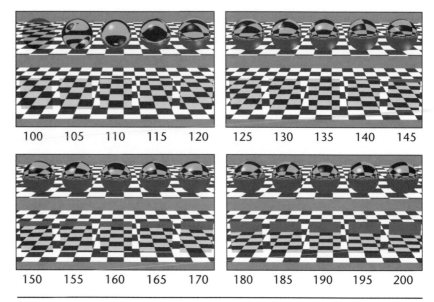

100	105	110	115	120	125	130	135	140	145

150	155	160	165	170	180	185	190	195	200

FIGURE 8–9 Refract Index.

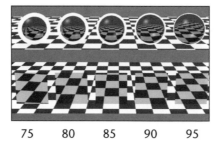

75	80	85	90	95

FIGURE 8–10
Refract Index
less than 100.

With judicious use of refraction, a couple of intrepid Bryce users have set up telescopes to take advantage of the laws of physics inside their worlds!

When you have a high degree of both transmitivity and reflectivity, the object will appear brighter, since more light reaches the object (see Fig. 8–11). When it reflects, the surrounding light bounces toward the camera. When it's transparent, light is passing through, so you see light from the other side and also light from everywhere else. If your object is a primitive with an enclosed shape, such as a sphere, there may be additional reflection as light bounces around

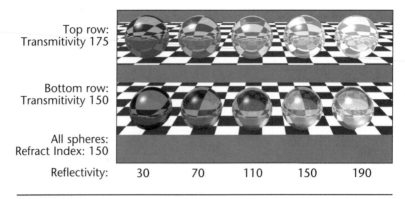

Top row:
Transmitivity 175

Bottom row:
Transmitivity 150

All spheres:
Refract Index: 150

Reflectivity: 30   70   110   150   190

FIGURE 8–11 Combining reflectivity and transmitivity makes the object brighter—more light comes from the object to the camera.

inside. To get the right appearance, you will have to noodle with your settings some.

Color

The Color control determines the manner in which the texture's color will be applied to the surface of your object. It operates in tandem with the separate lighting channels (Ambient, Diffuse, and Specular) to determine how the texture color or PICT color goes to which channel or channels.

The Color control acts as a filter between the actual color of the texture, whether 2D PICT or 3D Texture, the colors set for Diffuse and Specular underneath the control, and the Illumination controls.

When looking at the little control icons, look for the three different kinds of light on the object. These different controls determine how color is applied to the object (see Fig. 8–12).

It's sometimes confusing to think of this as general lighting. The default seems "natural" enough, and the others, especially the gray and white ones, seem "weird." Not so.

The Color control is a switch. It answers the question, "How does this object get its color?" It looks at the color of the texture and shunts it into one or two of the three Illumination Channels. If it

FIGURE 8–12
The Color control segmented into different lighting areas.

directs the color to one channel, then you can determine the color of the other two by using the color swatches. If the color control puts the texture into two channels, you can determine the color of the third.

For example, in the "default" the texture color is conveyed through ambient and diffuse light. The white "hot spot," the specular highlight, shows a direct bounce from light source to object to camera. You can choose the color for the specular highlight with the specular color swatch and the Hilites control. (The Hilites control determines the size of specular highlights. It also adds an additional color ring around the outside.)

When your texture color is coming through a particular light channel, the color swatch for that particular channel will not work. So, for the default Color control, where diffuse light strikes the object to show texture color, you cannot make any color changes by using the Diffuse color swatch.

Figure 8–13C (see the color section) shows examples of each Color control option. For each section, there is a series of smaller images. The legend at the top right identifies the smaller images. Each rendered image is shown under white ambient light and, in the smaller cutaway, under purple ambient light. To the left of the rendered images are the Color settings for that particular image. The Color control is shown, with the Hilites setting and the contents of the diffuse and specular channels. When the Color control switches the texture through a particular channel, the texture is shown. When the Color control switches the color swatch through that channel, then the flat color is shown and the RGB values given.

It's a bit complex, but after some study you will see that there is a wide range of possibilities for coloring your object using the Color control in conjunction with texture color and the color swatches.

Texture

This section of the Materials Editor gives you the options to adjust all the different parameters that affect your object's surface texture.

MODE

This is the main switch that answers the question, "Does Bryce use any additional source to determine the color and surface properties of the object?" There are three possible answers to that question: No Texture, 3D Texture, and 2D PICT Texture.

- *No Texture.* Bryce does not use any underlying information to create the object's surface color. When there is no texture, then all of the other options in the texture section are not available. (Effects, although grouped in this section, operates independently of texture controls. I don't count Effects as a member of the texture group.) Use this setting for monocolor objects and mirrors.
- *3D Solid Texture.* Bryce uses information generated by its 3D Solid Texture creator to provide color, bump, and Alpha information for an object. All of the texture options are available.
- *2D PICT Texture.* Bryce uses information from a flat two-dimensional image to give an object its color. If there is an Opacity Map with the PICT image, then there is additional information available for bump mapping and alpha manipulations.

FREQUENCY

Frequency determines the texture's size. Are there small details or large smooth areas? Frequency usually needs to be set higher for objects that are closer to the camera than for those that are far away.

With certain textures that have snow, the Frequency control will also determine the snow's altitude. The higher the frequency, the lower the snow level descends.

There are more places besides this control where you can adjust the texture's frequency.

Where You Can Adjust Frequency

Of course, for both the 2D PICT Texture and the 3D Solid Texture, you can adjust by dragging in the Frequency control. You can also adjust by numerical input in the Mappings... dialog box. At the

tip

If you need to fine-tune your frequency so that it falls somewhere between the options given by the Frequency control, then go to the Mappings... dialog box and adjust it numerically.

bottom is a slider labeled Texture Scale. The number and slider position correspond to the frequency.

If you are working with a 3D Solid Texture, these places for adjusting frequency in the Materials Editor aren't the only ones. There are several other frequency controls in the Deep Texture Editor. I discuss them later in this chapter in the Deep Texture Editor section.

ALPHA

Alpha takes information from the Opacity Map (2D PICT Texture) or the Value (3D Solid Texture) to "split" the object's surface in one of two ways: Transparent makes part of the object disappear, and Reflective makes portions reflect light.

When you use the Alpha setting to create portions of reflection on a surface, Bryce will automatically set a Reflectivity setting for you in the Details... dialog box. You can adjust Reflectivity to be higher or lower, if you want.

tip

Once you flip past that Alpha Reflective setting to Transparency or None, you'll need to change Reflectivity back to 0 in the Details... dialog box. Flipping past that Alpha setting is not a reflective reflex. Bryce will not automatically do it for you. You have to do it manually.

Whatever is white in the Opacity Map/Value will apply the Alpha effect. When you have Alpha Reflective, the white portion will reflect. When you have Alpha Transparent, the white area will be opaque. Figure 8–14 shows three objects with the different Alpha settings applied. The PICT image and the Opacity Map are identical so that you can see which part of the Opacity Map does what.

You can switch black and white in the PICT Opacity Map by clicking the button that says Invert Opacity Map (more on this later). Likewise, you can swap the Value areas in the 3D Textures by adjusting the Filter. (I'll walk through this technique at the end of this chapter after an in-depth discussion of the Deep Texture Editor.)

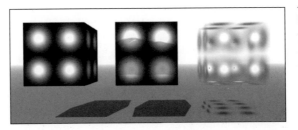

FIGURE 8–14 These three objects are created from the three Alpha settings. From left: None, Reflective, and Transparent.

Maximum bump

No bump

FIGURE 8–15
Bump Gain range.

BUMP GAIN

Bump Gain determines how much surface perturbances will be on your object. It relies on information from the Normale part of the 3D Solid Texture. For a 2D PICT Texture, it uses Opacity Map information. Whatever is lighter will be bumped higher; whatever is darker will be bumped lower.

The actual surface geometry of the object is not changed in bumping. Bryce takes the bump information and does a very smart "emboss" to the surface appearance to create the illusion of all those perturbances. Bump gain makes rendering costly, since information is used to tell Bryce to move a texture not only on the x- and z-axes but also on the y-axis. Additional calculations occur in order to create the appearance of displacement on the object's surface. (This is why in primitives that aren't terrains, you won't see little perturbances if you look closely at the edges of objects.)

Since this particular control has no numerical equivalent, it's all too easy when working with certain surface materials to think of all bump gain or none. Don't go to these extremes, however. There are 16 different settings for Bump Gain, so there is plenty of room for subtlety. Something that looks horrid at maximum bump will be pleasing and convincing at medium bump. Figure 8–15 shows the range of bump gain.

Mapping

You've already been introduced to one part of the Mapping dialog box in the discussion on Frequency. Besides having a numerical Frequency setting, Mapping answers the question, "How will this texture be applied to my object?"

For 3D Solid Textures, the default answer is World Space. The texture has an orientation in the world. Any object that uses the texture—no matter what its position, rotation, or elevation—will take on the texture for that place in the world. Move the object, and the object's texture will change to reflect what the texture is like in that other part of the world. This explains why Bryce provides seamless textural transitions between the ground plane and the terrain that rests on the ground. They both use the same texture in World Space.

2D PICT Texture's default answer to Mapping's question is Parametric Space. The PICT is applied to the object. If the object gets larger, the PICT Texture is scaled up as well. Figure 8–16 shows all of the different Mapping options applied to sets of objects. You can see how different options apply differently depending on the object's shape.

The Mapping dialog box also has a handy option: the Symmetric Tiling check box. When checked, Symmetric Tiling puts your PICT image back to back or front to front (see Fig. 8–17). If you've created a PICT image that's already tiled, then uncheck this box.

Effects

The Effects control allows you to choose from some basic rendering types for your object in order to create special, ahem, effects. There are four options, which are the possible combination of two different parameters: Additive Effects and Fuzzy Effects (see Fig. 8–18). Bryce's default is no special effect—no fuzzy blur and no additive lighting.

FUZZY OPTIONS

The Fuzzy options will give the edge of your object a diffuse edge for a soft look. Use those on any primitive object aside from terrains or the flat objects (disk and planes). Fuzzy is excellent to use on spheres that will be free-standing clouds, planetary atmosphere, or glowing light sources. The Fuzzy options are not available for use with terrains. Terrains are a slightly different animal from the rest of the primitives. The other primitives, being the product of a simple geometric equation, are not as complex as a wire-mesh whose shape is determined from grayscale data. Consider the default terrain at a resolution of 128. There are 16,384 individual points of data in that terrain. It gets worse when you go up to the 1024 resolution, which involves over a million individual points of data. It is far simpler to "fuzz" a sphere, which is expressed in one mathematical equation, than it is to "fuzz" a terrain, where anywhere from sixteen thousand to a million individual points of data must be brought into the calculation process. The terrain's irregular shape and the potential for changes in height makes it possible for the

FIGURE 8–16 How Bryce's Mapping options are applied to each object.

World Space

Object Space

Parametric

Parametric Scaled

Front Projection

Spherical Projection

Cylindrical Projection

Reflections Map

Random

FIGURE 8–17
PICT Symmetric Tiling: Box with 1s is not tiled; box with 2s is symmetrically tiled.

FIGURE 8–18
Effects control.

Default   Fuzzy

Additive   Fuzzy
Additive

camera's ray to pass over a dozen or more "ridges." Make each of those ridges fuzzy, and you're overburdening Bryce's renderer with an inordinate amount of calculation to determine that final pixel color. You *did* want the scene to render today, didn't you? Keep your Fuzzy settings to the other primitives and you'll get nicer results.

ADDITIVES

When this option is selected, Bryce uses a special process when rendering the object. The ray finds the object, say, a sphere, and determines its color and so forth. It then finds whatever is *behind* the object, whether an additional object or atmosphere. When it determines the final pixel color, it adds the two together—the object and what is behind the object. Essentially, adding things together makes them brighter. You have probably seen this if you've worked with Add in other image processing situations or by using the Add option in the Merge PICT dialog box. This brightening effect gives the object the appearance of glowing. (See Chapter 6, "Skies and Light," for more on creating glowing objects.) When this is combined with fuzziness, you can create glowing atmospheres and light bulbs. When it is not combined with fuzziness, you can create moons. Make sure only Diffuse is used in your Illumination Details. (See Chapter 11, "Brycing Out of This World," for more on planetary and lunar effects.)

Although Effects is visually grouped with the other controls for manipulating your texture (in the Texture section of the Materials Editor), I do not consider it to be part of Textures proper. The Effects control is a more independent materials creature. It acts as a bridge between the Illumination controls and special rendering techniques. It is not changed in any of the Shuffling processes. This may seem to be hair-splitting on my part, but I've found it helpful, especially when I render something that does not quite look right, wonder what's wrong, and go back to the Materials Editor to find that I had inadvertently set Effects to be something other than what I wanted.

Preset Practicalia

In this section, I consider some of the practicalities of working with Presets in the Materials Editor. First, you want to amass a precious hoard of them, and then, once you have them, you want to take good care of them. This section tells you how.

Building Healthy Collections of Materials Presets

The whole objective of working in the Materials Editor is to create splendid-looking surfaces for your Bryceland objects. But you needn't reinvent the wheel each time you work with a new object. There are ways to build collections of presets. You can't possibly collect 'em all, but you *can* trade 'em with your friends.

STEAL THEM FROM OTHER SCENES

To steal material settings from another scene, open up the Scene document. Select the object whose material setting you desire. ⌘-M takes you to the Materials Editor. Let the preset render. When it's completed rendering, click the encircled plus button to add the preset to your preset list. I used this method to compile a rather sizable preset list while roaming through the scenes on the KPT Bryce application CD. However, note that the Materials Preset renders with the Sky & Fog settings for that particular scene. The Sky & Fog settings aren't saved with the Materials Preset, but you get to look at them in the little preview.

Now that you have them, use them as your starting place for additional tweaking for your scene.

CREATE YOUR OWN SHUFFLE EXPLORER

There are three ways that you can let the Random Muse help you along in your search for the Holy Grail of Materials. All involve Shuffling.

1. *While in Wireframe View of Your Scene.* When one or more objects are selected, press the Control key and click on the Edit Materials control on the Edit Palette. Materials will be randomly shuffled in the same way as if you had clicked Shuffle (see next paragraph). If more than one object is selected, each one will be shuffled individually. This is handy for random materials shopping. Create a bunch of objects, select them all, Control-click the Edit Materials control, render, and refine each one from there.

2. *While in the Materials Editor Dialog Box.* When you click the Shuffle button, this will take the current Texture mode and alter it by applying different settings from the Materials Editor. If you have no texture, then you will get different combinations of illumination and colors. It will not change the Effects for you. You'll have to do that yourself.

    2D PICT shuffle will change the illumination and color swatches. Also frequency will be changed ever so slightly. (Check in the Mappings... dialog box for actual numbers. The range seems to be numbers under 1, such as .765, .38, and so on. It's probably negligible.) The texture will remain in its default mapping mode, Parametric.

If you start shuffling with the 3D Texture mode active, the Materials Editor will hop around to different base textures each time you click. Unlike the others, which limit the changes to illumination and color, this one shuffles all the different texture controls with the one exception of Effects, which remains in the default state (or whichever state was active when you began the shuffle). Also, the mapping stays in World Space, the default mode for 3D Solid Texture.

Use these parameters when you want to explore different kinds of sum-total materials settings. For random exploration of the underlying 3D Texture, cruise on over to the next place where you can practice random acts of beauty. Click Edit Texture... to bring you to the upper level of the Texture Editor.

3. *While in the Edit Texture... Dialog Box.* Click the Random button to cruise through a series of underlying textures. Different settings will be thrown into the random primordial texture soup. You can tell if a texture is an "expensive" one by how long it takes to render. Different noises, filters, apply blend modes, and color mappings will all be proposed for your acceptance. Keep clicking until you see something you like.

What happens when you click OK? That underlying texture will be changed for the duration of your Bryce session. So once you change a texture, for example "Graystone," it remains changed until you quit the application. When you relaunch Bryce, all 3D Textures revert to their normal state. If you create something along the way and like it, either save the scene (of course!) or create a preset for the entire material setting that uses this particular texture.

The Proper Care and Feeding of Your Materials Presets

The combined settings from all controls in the Materials Editor are saved in presets. Presets are the images seen in the window in the lower left-hand corner.

Presets can be stored in different sets of files. They are referred to as .SHD, or shader, files. Bryce's default set of presets are kept in a file called BASIC.SHD, a file that normally resides in the same folder as the Bryce application.

You can, however, create your own sets of .SHD files or load different Materials Presets from other .SHD files. This book's CD has sets of .SHD files for different kinds of materials: stratified terrains, snow, metals, and so on.

To create a new shader file, click the New List... button. You will be presented with dialog box that will prompt you to save your file name with a .SHD suffix (see Fig. 8–19a).

Once you have named the .SHD file, you can begin saving presets in it. Let the Materials Preset image render, then click the encircled plus button.

To open up a .SHD file that's already created (from the Bryce application CD or from this book's CD or from sources elsewhere), click the Open List... button. A dialog box will appear asking you to locate a .SHD file (see Fig. 8–19b). Locate one and click Open. This will take you back to the Materials Editor. The first thing that happens is the material setting that was previously active will render in the Preview Window. If, say, you wanted to add this particular preset to the shader list you just opened up, all you would need to do is let the preview complete its render, click the plus button, and gloat gleefully for a nanosecond. However, you're probably wanting to get at one or more of those presets that already exist in the .SHD file. Scroll to the other presets by dragging in the Preset Window.

 (a)
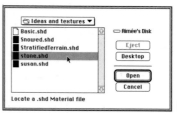 (b)

FIGURE 8–19 Dialog boxes for (**a**) creating and (**b**) opening a .SHD file.

If the .SHD file has only one preset in it, you'll be hard pressed to find it by scrolling. However, once you click, the preset is selected, even though you cannot see it in the Preset Window. (If you're unsure, scroll in the 3D Textures list on the right of the Materials Editor to see which one is active. The new one should be at the bottom with a number following it, for example, "Texture 013.") Click OK to accept your changes and then do a small test render.

WHAT IS STORED WHERE

Where is the shader information stored? For each scene, it's stored with the Scene document. You can open up any Scene document, select an object, access the Materials Editor, watch the preview render, and then click the plus button to add it to your own collection of marvelous materials.

In your Materials Preset files, it's stored in the current .SHD file. There is no way to tell which .SHD file is the current one, aside from recognizing that these presets belong to this .SHD file. Bryce's default is to open up the BASIC.SHD file when launching the application.

If you have a material assigned to a terrain or a ground and you save either as a preset in the Presets Thumbnails on the Master Palette, the .SHD information for that object will also be stored in the Preset file. The Preset file lives inside the same folder as the Bryce application.

Any time you click the encircled plus button to add a preset, you are adding data to the current .SHD file. Remember this when you back up your data.

2D PICT Textures

Bryce's 2D PICT options allows you to wrap images onto any object. Have a texture that repeats again and again or place a single photographic image into your scene as a separate object.

I'll briefly introduce the process with a recipe for the basic single photograph procedure and then dig in to discuss some deeper details.

A Basic Overview—How to Do Them in Bryce

To put a photograph into your scene, two image files are required: the object itself and a mask. The mask trims away extraneous image area so that your image retains its own shape inside the Bryce scene. The mask is referred to as Opacity Map in the Bryce PICT Scrapbook and acts according to the dictates of the Alpha control in the Materials Editor. There are other uses that Opacity Maps can be put to with the aid of the Materials Editor, but I first focus on the basic transparency model.

CASE STUDY: HOW TO CREATE A PHOTOGRAPHIC TWO-DIMENSIONAL IMAGE WITH ALPHA CHANNEL

1. In Photoshop or other image editing application, create an alpha channel for your selected image. If you can crop the image as a square, do so. Bryce will make your image into a square aspect ratio. If your image wasn't square to begin with, you'll have to resize the square plane primitive to put the image back to rights. Paul Kuehn solved this "square" problem by padding the image at the top to create a square in his "Sphinx" image (see Fig. 8–20a). See Figure 8–21C in the color section for the final image.
2. You may need to run the Minimum filter to make the alpha channel fit more snugly to the image. Do this if you find that your image has a minute "halo" where the background image information leaks into the image. (This is something you'll discover in Bryce while doing a test render.)
3. Save the image with the alpha channel as a PICT document.
4. In Bryce, create a square plane. While it is selected, go to the Materials Editor. Change the Mode to 2D PICT and click the Edit Texture... button or directly click the Bryce Image PICT. This takes you to Bryce's PICT Scrapbook.

 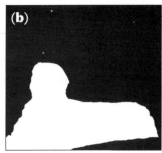 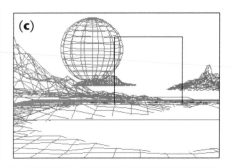

FIGURE 8–20 "Sphinx" series: (**a**) PICT image for "Sphinx"; (**b**) Opacity Map; (**c**) wireframe view of scene.

tip

For experimental images, try out the Opacity Map both ways, especially if you have a map that has more in-between grayscale tones.

5. Click the Open PICT button. Find your saved PICT image. Click OPEN.

6. Make sure the Opacity Map is "right-side out." The white part should be where the image is, and the black part should be where the extraneous surrounding area is (see Fig. 8–20b). Click Opacity Map to confirm. Click Invert Opacity Map if you need to switch it around. Figure 8–22 shows a different PICT image in the PICT Scrapbook with Opacity Map.

7. Adjust things in the Materials Editor proper (mostly your lighting and color controls). Change the Alpha control to Transparent. The default Mappings... setting is Parametric. When you change the mode to 2D PICT Texture, the Materials Editor changed the Mappings setting to Parametric. Go ahead and check if you're not sure.

8. Render.

FIGURE 8–22 PICT and opacity: (**a**) PICT image; (**b**) Opacity Map; (**c**) after inverting Opacity Map.

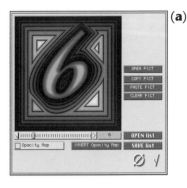  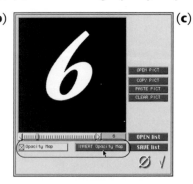

2D PICT Lists

Bryce keeps all of the images in a PICT Scrapbook. You see the Scrapbook when you click the Edit Texture... button or by clicking directly in the PICT image shown on the right side of the Materials Editor. You can also get to that Scrapbook directly (do not pass Go, collect $200) by advancing token to the Options menu and selecting 2D PICT Textures... . I will refer to the place as the Scrapbook and to its contents—the one or more PICT images stored there—as a "list." You can save the Scrapbook's contents into a list document for any scene you are working on. In fact, do so! Although the actual image is saved with the Scene document, there are times when you might put things in jeopardy. As a precaution, *save that list!* This discussion will explain a bit more why (with a touch of "how" thrown in).

The PICT list exists in two states. The first is a document list. This is the one that is opened and saved from the PICT Texture Editor (MYSCENE.LIST). Then there is the dynamic list, the entity that exists in RAM when Bryce is opened. When you save a list, you are saving the dynamic list to a document. When you open a list, you bring a list document into RAM where it can be changed. Each has particular behaviors.

LIST CAPACITY

There are 32 images that can be put in a list (dynamic and document combined). The first is numbered 0, after the manner of software programmers. Usually the 0 image is occupied by the default Bryce PICT image. If you continue adding images to the 32-capacity limit, Bryce will valiantly place the last one in the spot numbered 0 and, if it hasn't done so already, will give you a system beep and an alert that tells you there's not enough memory. Don't try this at home, kids.

PASTING PICTS

Paste PICT will put an image in the *current* spot in the Scrapbook's list. Make sure that if you are pasting a new image into the Scrapbook, you paste to an empty slot! Otherwise you'll be pasting over your previous image, sending it to file heaven. When pasting into a new slot, Bryce will insert the image at its own resolution. (Bryce will also change the aspect ratio to a square image.) If you are pasting into the Opacity Map, the Map's resolution will always match its accompanying image. Your just-pasted image will be resized accordingly.

CLEARING PICTS

When you click Clear PICT, the current image goes away and (assuming that there is more than one image in the list) the current slot is filled by the highest numbered image. It's better to clear PICTs from lower in the list than higher. Clearing the highest-numbered PICT will force the next highest one to jump into that place. Suppose you have a list with four images. If you clear from slot #4, the image that was in #3 will move to #4, leaving spot #3 blank. Once you scroll back down in the list, you're sunk. After that, when Bryce finds the blank #3 spot, it stops. "Ah! This is the end!" it says. You have, in effect, cleared both images 3 and 4. Lovely.

SAVING LISTS

Saving the list is the ultimate cover-your-you-know-what safeguard. Do it. Do it for each scene that has any PICT images in it. There are times when it's not necessary, when things are all right without the PICT list. Do it anyhow. You'll be able to come back to it, just in case there are any mishaps with your Scene document itself. If Bryce has a problem with the dynamic list and loses the PICTs that were in your scene, when you save the scene you risk losing the images. Keep a list and you can always restore things. The next topic will expand on this theme.

CUMULATIVE PICT COLLECTION (PART I)

During the course of a Bryce working session, when you open (or create) several scenes, each with its own PICT image (or set of images), Bryce will keep a cumulative tally of the images in its dynamic list. If, during a Bryce session, you open a Scene document, open another, and then come back to the first one, the set of images that are in the first Scene document will be brought into the

PICT Scrapbook's dynamic list *twice*. Obviously, you will have more stuff hogging up your precious RAM than you need. So, having carefully saved a list for that scene, you decide to open it. This clears out all the other images that aren't a part of that list document. It's a good way to strip away unwanted images.

OPEN LIST

When you click the Open List button, you get a dialog box by which you can navigate to your desired list document. Open the list document. Doing this will clear out any other images that were in the list.

CUMULATIVE PICT COLLECTION (PART II)

So, having opened up the list, you go to render. Only everything is all cattywompus. A bunch of images lost the PICTs altogether, and others have the wrong images assigned. Why? Bryce's manual tells you to save and open lists when you go back to a scene later. I just told you to do the same thing. Are we leading you down the path to destruction? No. Here's what happened.

Bryce keeps track of the images by assigning numbers to them. They're assigned by where they fall in the dynamic list. By the time you had opened that scene a second time, all the images in that scene were keyed to higher numbers in the list. Bryce, when it opened the scene, said, "Okay, this object is tied to that PICT. That other object is tied to this other PICT." When you opened the new list, you brought back your original images. But you also introduced what—by this point—is a new numbering sequence. Bryce is still tying the objects with the PICTs according to the old numbering system. So objects that lose a PICT become "blank" and other objects are assigned the wrong PICT altogether. How do you fix this? Close your Scene document (without saving) and then open it again. Everything should be right-side up again.

HOUSEKEEPING TIPS TO SAVE MEMORY

Here are some PICT Scrapbook maintenance tasks for you. The first has already been mentioned: Open a list. In fact, for this, create a "purge list" that has only the default Bryce PICT. When you want to clear out everything, simply open that list.

If you discover, to your dismay, that you've run out of memory and get that alert telling you there's a "Not enough memory, Revert to default format!" accompanied by two or more beeps and a disappearing scene, don't throw in the towel! You can do something very useful here. It's one of the few times that you have Bryce open without any document window. (I wish there were more!) You can open up the PICT Scrapbook this way: Objects > Edit 2D PICTs... . Then open a list or click Clear PICT to get rid of excess memory-hogging PICTs. Either of these methods will get you down to something manageable. Then open your Scene document and proceed along your merry way.

Resolution

The 2D PICT Scrapbook is not made for creating humongous high-resolution images for placement inside of Bryce. In fact, version 1.0's upper limit size was 512 × 512 pixels. Anything larger would be reduced to that size when opened or pasted into the PICT Scrapbook. Version 1.0.1 broke through the size barrier, thereby enabling you to import any PICT image regardless of its size. Your only limitation is RAM. There must be enough RAM allocated to Bryce to keep an image that size in memory while rendering. If you usually work with Bryce with a higher RAM allocation, then this won't be a problem for you.

Declaration of Resolution. But consider this. If the first version of Bryce was not meant to have PICTs above 512 × 512 pixels, then let this be a rule of thumb for optimized images brought into Bryce. They don't need to be outrageously huge! Rather than trying to see how large you can go, experiment to see how small you can make the images without sacrificing image quality.

Opacity Maps and PICT Textures

For each PICT in the list, Bryce can have an alpha channel or Opacity Map. If you open or paste an RGB PICT that has a fourth channel, Bryce automatically includes the fourth channel as the

Opacity Map. The PICT file format for PICT images allows for an alpha channel for RGB images, but not for a grayscale (one-channel) PICT image. Bryce has a solution for the grayscale situation, however. Name your grayscale alpha channel PICT with the suffix .MASK and Bryce will automatically place it. So your grayscale image called, say, GRAYIMAGE has an accompanying Opacity Map image called GRAYIMAGE.MASK.

That's what happens when opening files using Open PICT: Copying and pasting operates slightly differently. The aforementioned RGB + alpha PICT holds true for pasting (assuming you copied it as a 32-bit, four-channel PICT in the first place).

If there's a fourth channel, it's automatically placed in the Opacity Map. If there's not, you can paste to the Opacity Map specifically. Click the Opacity button to make the fourth channel the active area and click Paste to paste your image there.

If you're copying and pasting within the PICT Scrapbook's lists (say, to duplicate an image), be aware of these Brycean behaviors. When you click Copy PICT, both the PICT and the alpha channel are copied. This holds true even if you have activated Opacity Map by clicking the check box. You cannot copy *only* the Opacity Map within the Scrapbook.

Now that the Opacity Map is there, how can it be used with 2D PICT Textures? Besides transparency, which I already discussed, you can use the Opacity Map to create areas of reflection or bump gain (or both!). For reflection, just set the Alpha control to reflective. Those areas that are white in the image will be a reflective surface. (Adjust the amount of reflection in the Details dialog box.) For experimental and bizarre Bryce scenes, this is a good place to have Opacity Maps that are distinctly different from the primary image. Figure 8–23 shows a PICT image with a similar (but not identical) Opacity Map. Portions of the terrain appear to be reflective chrome.

tip
You'll get a more successful bump if the Opacity Map has smoothed gray shades.

The Opacity Map information is also used by the Bump Gain control to create the bump illusion in your image. The bump look may not be as successful when using a lower resolution image, since every pixel determines some bump gain information. Figure 8–23 shows the same image with bump applied as well.

2D PICT Texture

Opacity Map

FIGURE 8–23 (**a**) The PICT image and (**b**) Opacity Map are different; (**c**) Alpha set to Reflective for partial chrome; (**d**) a bumped version shows pixellated artifacts.

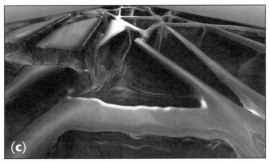

Opacity Map— Alpha for Reflective "Chrome"

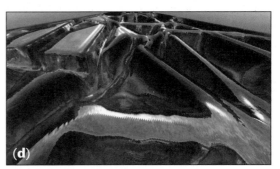

Opacity Map— Chrome and Bump Gain

3D Solid Textures—The Real Meaty Stuff

3D Solid Textures are what underlie all those natural-looking terrains and Brycean landscapes. This is where you can set textures that respond to altitude and slope and orientation. In this way, your Brycean landscape will differ depending on whether there's a sheer cliff face, a flat lowlands or highlands, or north-facing rocks that have lichen growth.

In the next sections, I take you through the Texture Editors—the places accessed from the Edit Texture... button in the Materials Editor—first the Shallow Texture Editor and then the Deep Texture Editor.

Edit Texture—Level I, or the Shallow Texture Editor

When you click the Edit Texture... button, you will arrive in the dialog box shown in Figure 8–24. Here you can do the following:

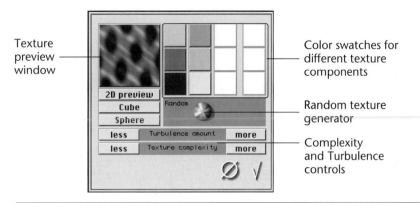

Texture preview window

Color swatches for different texture components

Random texture generator

Complexity and Turbulence controls

FIGURE 8–24 The Shallow Texture Editor.

- Look at the texture in one, two, or three dimensions with the different preview buttons, devoid of other material setting.
- Change the colors of the textures.
- Adjust the complexity for a texture.
- Adjust the turbulence for a texture.
- Randomly shuffle through different combinations to create a completely new texture.

I describe each of these options here. You will also be encountering information about the Deep Texture Editor later in this chapter. The Shallow Texture Editor and Deep Texture Editor are related and concepts will be described in a mutual frame of reference.

CHANGING COLOR

There are 12 possible colors you can use in a texture. When you take a peek here and see a texture that has one row of colors, it may mean either that there is only one component or that only one component has color and the others are assigned to other output methods. (More on components and output in the Deep Texture Editor section.)

Clicking on any color swatch accesses the KPT Color Picker, or, with the Option key held down, the numerical slider color pickers. This is good for selectively changing the colors of textures (see Fig. 8–25a). Change the one color and watch how the entire color scheme of the texture is changed.

tip

Create your own custom color palettes in a paint application. Place it in the background on your monitor so that you can drag directly to it with the color picker. Then let your little palette float there while you select the right color (see Fig. 8–25b). If RAM is a consideration, save the palette as a PICT document. Teach Text/ Simple Text can open a PICT image without hogging RAM.

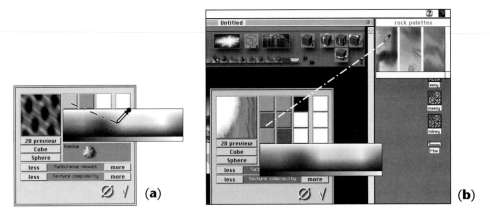

FIGURE 8–25 Selecting colors from the Shallow Texture Editor: (**a**) The popup color picker; (**b**) selecting from a custom color palette elsewhere on the monitor.

Sometimes the resulting color of the texture is not the direct result of the colors you see in the swatches. There are apply modes that determine how the final texture is mixed. The different sets of colors can be added, subtracted, and multiplied, as well as combined in other ways. To get to those apply modes, you'll need to go to the Deep Texture Editor. The fourth set of colors are for assigning color to the texture on a global basis. Figure 8–26C (see color section) shows the wide variety of color combinations resulting from the same sets of colors.

COMPLEXITY

When you click the Texture Complexity–More button, you are adding the same type of texture noise to itself in larger increments. It's the same thing as increasing the Octaves in the Deep Texture Editor. In fact, the word *octaves,* a musical term, is analogous. If you play both Middle C and the C above Middle C (an octave higher), you get the same "note tone" but with additional resonant frequencies. The sound is more complex. The same thing happens here with Texture Complexity—you generate additional octaves of the original texture noise. (More on this in the Deep Texture Editor.)

TURBULENCE

Turbulence introduces an additional texture noise to offset the original one. The more turbulence you set, the more vigorously the additional noise interferes with your original texture. In the Deep Texture Editor, this is introducing phase on a global level to all noises. The more turbulence you add, the greater the amplitude of this additional noise you're introducing (see phase later in this chapter for more explanation).

Adding more Turbulence and Complexity increases the cost of your render time, as you're asking Bryce to do more calculation to generate that texture.

RANDOM SHUFFLING

Clicking the Shuffle button generates entire textures randomly. Any combination can be generated. Just in case you were curious about the total number of possible combinations of 3D Solid Textures, the number is:

1,097,135,300,000,000,000,000,000,000,000,000,000,000,000,
000,000,000,000,000,000,000,000,000

(The calculator stopped filling in specific numbers after the first eight decimal places.)

Once you found something within one of those random combinations that interests you, you can adjust the colors, complexity, and turbulence in the Shallow Texture Editor. To carefully fine-tune a promising texture, however, you'll need to go to the Deep Texture Editor.

Deep Texture Editor

Access the Deep Texture Editor by pressing the Option key while clicking the Edit Texture... button. This editor is the heart of Bryce. It evolved over years of Bryce's development while Eric Wenger shaped the application. From time to time, he'd work on how to be able to create such-and-such an effect, devise a solution, write it up in some code, and put it in the Editor. Bit by bit, it has grown into what it is now.

It's a personal solution, much as your own method of keeping track of your files or how you organize your socks or kitchen utensils is a personal system for yourself. It's there. It works. All the complexities are self-evident to you, the creator. But it's not really meant for public attention or distribution.

When Eric Wenger's application was undergoing transformation into the software KPT Bryce, there was the question of what to do with the Deep Texture Editor. It was written for personal use and simultaneously was a central driving power of the application, so what was to be done? Should it be included in the commercial software? Should it operate deep inside Bryce, yet users would have no way to access it? The decision was to put it in but not to document it. In fact, in the next higher version of Bryce, the Deep Texture Editor interface will be revamped. That's why the *KPT Bryce Explorer's Guide* is sketchy about the details. The line was drawn in the sand, and its authors said, "Okay, let's put this out there as the first version. More will follow later." I offer you this section as the first step toward "more."

Overview

The Deep Texture Editor is analogous to a musical synthesizer. A synthesizer sends a tone through one or more filters to produce a new variation with unique qualities. Bryce's Deep Texture Editor does the same thing, only instead of synthesizing sound, it synthesizes visual noise. The result is visual texture.

The schematics in Figure 8–27 show the logical order of the Deep Texture editing process. Figure 8–28 shows the Deep Texture Editor's interface with sub-dialog boxes and menus. They're set up in a counterclockwise sweep to show the Deep Texture editing process.

Here you can start with either one, two, or three components. For each component, assign a noise. Then the noise goes through a

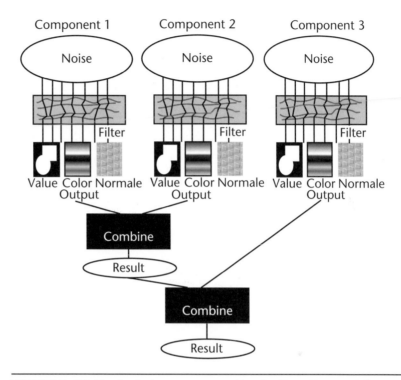

FIGURE 8–27 The logical sequence used by the Deep Texture Editor to create textures.

filter. At that point, there's a choice to be made between three output options. Will the component be output as Value (alpha channel), Color, or Normale (bump map)? Or will the output be some combination of the three? When there is more than one component, how are they combined? The first two components are combined together to form a new hybrid. If there are three components, the hybrid of the first two will be combined with the third component.

Finally, you can apply some global settings to the combined result of the component process. Overall frequency, a final color scheme, a final apply of global phase—and you're on your way back to the Materials Editor for fine-tuning and additional tweaking to create that perfect surface appearance for your object.

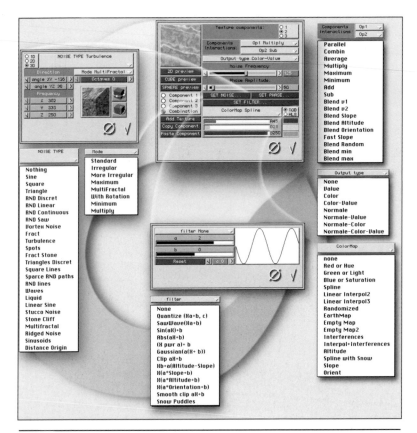

FIGURE 8–28 The scheme of the Deep Texture Editor Interface with sub-dialog boxes and menus.

This has been a quick take on the process; there are plenty of eddies and pools of complexity at each step along the way. I'll stop and explore them all as I go through the Deep Texture Editor part by part.

Noise

Noise is the source for textures in Bryce. Inside the Deep Texture Editor, clicking the Set Noise... button takes you to a dialog box, which I call the Noise Editor (see Fig. 8–29). There you'll find the following controls:

- Type of noise
- Number of dimensions

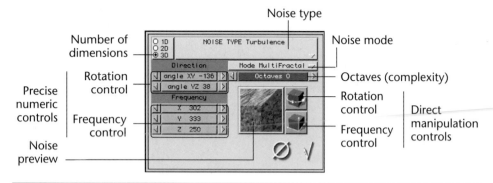

FIGURE 8–29 The Noise Editor.

- Frequency
- Spatial orientation
- Octaves
- Noise modulations

First, there's the type of noise that is generated. Choose from 25 types. Random (RND) Continuous is the default noise.

The Noise Editor renders the noise in two steps, first rough and then detailed.

The length of time it takes to render the preview gives you an indication of the processing time involved. Different noises will take different amounts of time to compute. RND Continuous does not take a long time to compute. The most expensive of the lot is Vortex noise, followed by Waves and Fractal Stone and Spots, and perhaps some others. Don't avoid the costly ones altogether; after all, they're there for a purpose. But if you're just experimenting around, don't use them cavalierly, unless you have all day—and then some.

NUMBER OF DIMENSIONS

Set the number of dimensions for your noise with the radio buttons. Noise that is 1D is a one-dimensional noise, 2D is two-dimensional, and 3D is three-dimensional. The number of dimensions for the noise is an integral part of the two controls described next, Frequency and Orientation.

Frequency

There are two ways to adjust the frequency of your noise to shape the look of your texture. The first, on the right of the Noise Preview, controls frequency proportionately. Drag to increase or decrease the frequency on all axes. The other method adjusts frequency on each dimension independently. The numeric tools on the left accomplish that. Click the arrows or type numbers directly. Although all three are constantly available for adjustment, you won't always need them. To determine which ones you'll need, check to see how many dimensions your noise has. One-dimensional texture is the *x*-axis. Two-dimensional adds the *y*-axis. Three-dimensional adds the *z*-axis. Don't try to fiddle with the *z* adjustment if you have a 2D Texture. If you do, the Noise Editor will take the time to recompute the noise, but nothing will change. When changing frequency on an individual axis basis, type the numbers in directly.

FIGURE 8–30 Three-dimensional noise with two-dimensional look to it.

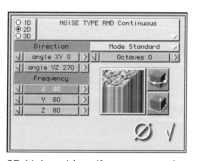 

2D Noise with uniform texture along the *y*-axis

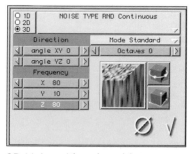 

3D Noise with reduced frequency on one dimension

Besides adjusting the noise frequency proportionately using the control to the right of the preview, you can use the Frequency slider in the Deep Texture Editor proper. The advantage to using the outer Frequency slider is that you can render a preview in the window and make an adjustment without having to go back and enter the separate dialog box.

When previewing the noise inside the Noise Editor, the part of the cube that faces front is the same as the two-dimensional preview in both the Deep and Shallow Texture Editors.

When you set the frequency of the noise, the x-, y-, and z-axes are established first. After that, you can rotate the noise in any general direction using the Rotation controls, which are discussed next.

ORIENTATION

Noise, whether it comes in one, two, or three dimensions, has a grain, or a fixed spatial orientation. In your scene, the direction in which that noise "points" will stay consistent no matter what the objects are or how they are oriented in space. The default mapping for 3D Solid Textures' World Space is based on this orientation. Here in the Noise Editor, you can change the orientation of the noise by rotating it so that the noise is oriented some other way. To rotate, use the control to the right of the noise preview. Drag to change direction. For precision (or to start over), use the numerical controls to the left.

Figure 8–31 shows one-, two-, and three-dimensional noise at Noise Editor settings 0 and 0. Settings at 0 and 0 favor the front. If you want to change the orientation to the top of your object, then you need to rotate so that the cross-hatches appear on the top.

OCTAVES

Octave in Bryce's Noise Editor is similar to musical scale octaves. The C an octave above Middle C is the same note, but higher. (Mathematically, it's double.) Adding an octave in Bryce is analogous to playing both Middle C and the C above it at the same time. The result is more complex than if you played only one "key." (In

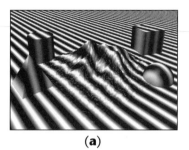
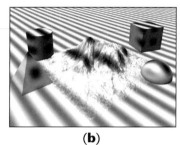
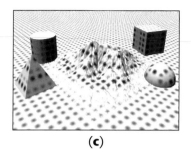

(a) **(b)** **(c)**

FIGURE 8–31 One-, two-, and three-dimensional noise oriented in space.

fact, in the Shallow Texture Editor, when you are adding *complexity,* you are increasing the Octave setting for the noise.)

Each time that you set the Octave to a higher number, you are introducing more processing time, as the noise has to be run through more frequencies for each octave that is computed.

When you add octaves to your noise, then you can modulate the noise in one of the several options available in the Mode popup menu.

NOISE MODULATIONS

When you add an octave, the noise is also generated at a lower frequency with longer wavelengths. Figure 8–32 shows a wave and its higher octave relative. So what happens when there are additional octaves? The Mode menu allows you to choose to tweak these in different ways. For instance, Maximum and Minimum will take the combined noises and select only the "top" and "bottom" values for the scale. This is analogous to lighten only and darken only.

Here are brief descriptions of each of the noise modulations. Figure 8–33 shows examples of octaves and modulations. Two different noise types, RND Continuous and Sine, are shown at four octave settings. RND Continuous noise is shown in each modulation option. To make modulations work, make sure you set Octave higher than 0. Remember, the higher the Octave setting, the longer the processing time, so set Octave judiciously.

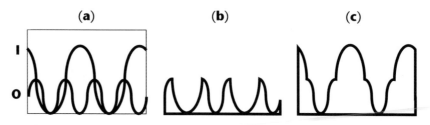

FIGURE 8–32 Octave and modulation: (**a**) A noise wave and its higher octave cousin; (**b**) Minimum modulation; (**c**) Maximum modulation.

- *Standard.* This default modulation adds the new octave at half the frequency and twice the amplitude (see Fig. 8–32a).
- *Irregular.* The same as Standard, but more weight is given to the higher frequency noise, resulting in a noise with more detail.
- *More Irregular.* Same as Irregular, only more so.
- *Maximum.* Analogous to Lighten Only, takes the highest (lightest) values together to produce the resulting noise.
- *Multi-fractal.* Lighter values mean more high-contrast noise.
- *With Rotation.* Puts a spin on the noise so that each additional octave is rotated in space. This is most easily seen in linear noises, such as a one-dimensional sine or in the RND linear.
- *Minimum.* Darken only. Selects the lowest (darkest) values of the combined noises.
- *Multiply.* Also a darker result. The different values are multiplied together.

In Your Phase

In the fast overview of the Deep Texture Editor, phase was briefly mentioned at the end of the process as something that can be globally applied to the entire combined texture. Phase is an added level of turbulence. (In the Shallow Texture Editor, you are calling on phase when you click the More Turbulence button.) However, you can apply phase to any one of your individual components or to the combined texture (or both!). When you are working with the Deep Texture Editor, you usually work for a while and then decide later that a bit of phase would do the trick. However, as Bryce's Deep Texture Editor processes things, it looks at phase first to see

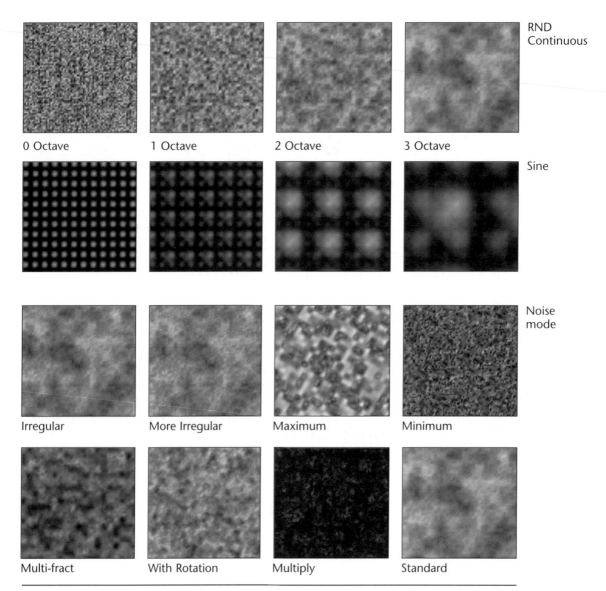

FIGURE 8–33 Two different noises—Sine and RND Continuous—at four octave settings; RND Continuous noise in all modulation options.

how the turbulence displaces everything else. So the first thing Bryce will look at is the global phase and then phase settings for individual components and then individual noises and so on through the loop.

So how does phase work? When you click the Set Phase... button, *surprise!* You go to the Edit Noise dialog box. All the particulars for editing noise apply to creating and editing phase as well, with two important distinctions:

1. The only place that you can set the phase frequency is in the Edit Phase... (Edit Noise) dialog box. The little slider on the face of the Deep Texture Editor allows you to adjust amplitude. This slider determines how much phase will interfere with the component's noise. I'll elaborate on this in a moment.

2. There is no such thing as filtering a phase. The filter applies to the noise. Once you have introduced phase into the equation, the combined phase-noise will be percolated together through the filtering process.

tip

This is a phase housekeeping tip. Check each component to see that phase isn't called upon unnecessarily. Even if your phase amplitude is set to 0, check the Edit Phase... dialog box for each component as well as the final combination to ensure the noise type is set to Nothing. If you have some noise type selected, even if there's no amplitude, you will still force Bryce to think about that noise type before it gets the "all clear" from the zeroed amplitude slider. When Bryce is forced to think about things needlessly, your render time increases.

Since my entire discussion of filtering follows this section, I'll let the filter matter rest here and take up again with this amplitude business.

The amplitude of the phase refers to the degree of phase's effect. The higher the amplitude, the more "offset" the original noise is. Figure 8–34 shows a sample of this. As amplitude is increased, there is more interference with the original noise. You don't need to set amplitude very high in order for phase to have a marked effect. In fact, restrain yourself to the lower parts of the amplitude scale until you've got a good grasp of what is happening.

Of course, by now you're starting to get a feel for the costliness of the process. Once you have introduced another element to offset all other elements, you're asking Bryce to process more, and so your rendering time will increase. Phase in your cost! Have a care when using phase. By all means, use it when the situation calls for it, but don't use it willy-nilly because you thought it would be cool to run into the Deep Texture Editor and tweak a few dials.

Filtering

This is an extremely powerful part of the Deep Texture Editor. When you refine a noise through a filter, you alter it to make it more contrasty, posterize, pull out details here and there, and make the noise occur only at certain altitudes or other spatial orientations.

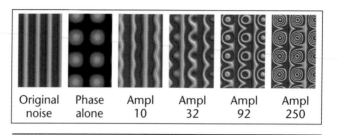

| Original noise | Phase alone | Ampl 10 | Ampl 32 | Ampl 92 | Ampl 250 |

FIGURE 8–34 Phase amplitude adjustment: Original noise is at left; phase is next to it; phase is applied with increasing amplitude settings.

FILTER DIALOG BOX—THE ABCS

Access the filter by clicking the Set Filter... button on the Deep Texture Editor. You will enter the Filter dialog box (see Fig. 8–35). Each filter has a Reset button. Clicking that changes the values and graph to show no effect, or the equivalent for None for that particular filter. When first exploring what these filters do, use Reset as a starting point.

The Filter dialog box has a graph and two sliders for adjusting *a* and *b*. Use the sliders to change the values. In a couple of filters, *c* is also an option for the equation. Generally the *a* control adjusts the intensity of whatever the effect is, while *b* adjusts the overall height. In some filters, *a* and *b* may stand for other things. Visualize the top part of the range as being white and the bottom part as black. Figure 8–36 shows the filter graph next to a gray ramp. Or think of

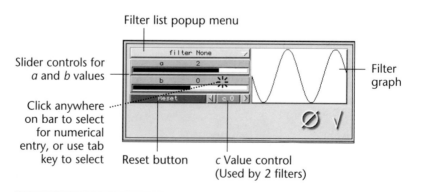

Filter list popup menu

Slider controls for *a* and *b* values

Filter graph

Click anywhere on bar to select for numerical entry, or use tab key to select

Reset button

c Value control (Used by 2 filters)

FIGURE 8–35 The Filter dialog box.

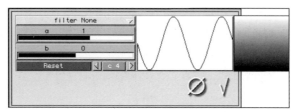

FIGURE 8–36 When looking at the graph, visualize white at the top, black at the bottom.

tip

When exploring in the Deep Texture Editor, set the output to value. Value has the fastest processing time, and you'll see everything in plain grayscale. Later you can change the output to one of the others, if need be.

the graph's range as a side view cutaway of a bump map. The deepest dents are at the bottom and heights are at the top.

There are two sets of number schemes in the filters. In the graph, which you should visualize as a continuum from black to white, the bottom (black) is 0 whereas the top (white) is 1. The graph will not go lower than 0 or higher than 1. The other set of numbers are for a and b (and c, in the couple of instances where c is used). They range all over the place.

Now let's get down to specifics. The following descriptions will show the relationship between the filter formula, the graph appearance, and the final noise result. The discussion will take them in a logical sequence, not necessarily the order they're listed in the popup menu. I'll begin with Clip aX + b because it is the most basic of the filters.

CLIP aX + b

The most often-used, ubiquitous contrast filter, Clip gets its name from portions of value being clipped at the upper and lower ends for higher contrast. When adjusting the sliders, a controls the contrast and b controls the overall brightness.

For a low-contrast effect, make the wave smaller. Decrease a to reduce the size of the wave and increase b to move the entire wave up. This one is a mid-gray. All the noise information will be output as expressions of middle grays for low-contrast noise. See Figure 8–37.

For a high-contrast effect, adjust so that the graph hits the top and bottom edges. When the wave hits the top, it clips at white; when it hits bottom, it clips at black. The wave actually ascends above and descends below the limits, but if the top represents white you can't get any whiter than white once you go "beyond" white. Give a a

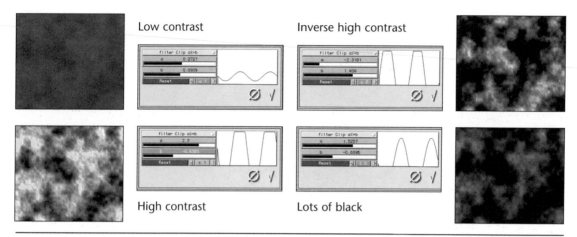

FIGURE 8–37 Four different Clip settings from the same texture demonstrate the range of possibilities.

large number for a higher range of wave motion; give *b* a negative number to move the entire curve down and then "center" it so that portions clip at top and bottom.

To invert the noise (white changes to black), make *a* negative and adjust *b* to the corresponding level.

Figure 8–38 shows examples of all filter types as they are applied to two types of noise—RND Continuous and Linear Sine.

SMOOTH CLIP aX + b

Smooth Clip is the same as Clip aX + b except that it smoothes out the hard transitions.

QUANTIZE

Quantize, analogous to Photoshop's Posterize, creates discontinuities as gray values stair-step from one level to the next. The setting for *c* determines the number of levels between black and white, and the settings for *a* and *b* determine overall contrast and height.

SAW WAVE

Saw Wave starts as a contrast filter (when there's a small curve in it). When the curve reaches the limits, instead of the top and bot-

(a)

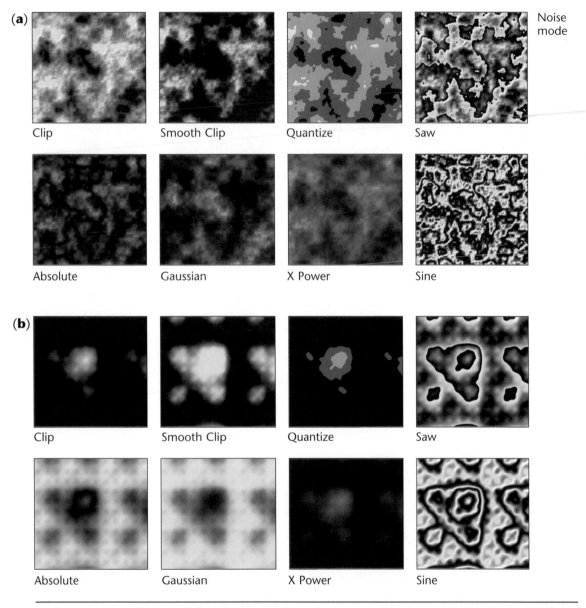

Noise mode

Clip   Smooth Clip   Quantize   Saw

Absolute   Gaussian   X Power   Sine

(b)

Clip   Smooth Clip   Quantize   Saw

Absolute   Gaussian   X Power   Sine

FIGURE 8–38 Noise filters: **(a)** RND Continuous; **(b)** Linear Sine.

tom being clipped, the curve is "bounced" back in the other direction. The result is high-contrast discontinuity (like a saw). Use this with color output to get portions of high-contrast alternating color. When you set *a* high, so that there are many waves bouncing top to bottom, you'll get areas where there is a lot of noise. Take care how high you set *a* when using this to filter noise for Normale bump output.

SINE WAVE—SIN(aX) + b

This filter gives you a high number of lines that follow the same path. Use it for creating things such as wood textures or perhaps desert sand. The number of lines is determined by *a*. This filter is continuous. As *a* increases, the curve maintains its curved shape as it bounces back down from the top. Higher numbers, say, 10 or 20, are better. You'll need to type these in by hand, as the slider will let you set numbers only up to 4. The value for *b*, as usual, adjusts the entire curve and will determine clipping at top or bottom.

ABSOLUTE—ABS(aX + b)

This filter, analogous to Photoshop's Difference calculation, takes the absolute value of the noise sine wave. So where the curve would otherwise clip at black, it ends up popping back up. This results in more light areas and additional complexity for bump maps, especially in those places where the bump would be flat (or 0). Absolute will clip at white if given the opportunity to do. To get twice the bump information, enter $a = 2$ and $b = -1$.

X POWER—(X pwr a) + b

X Power is similar to Gaussian. Both smooth out the darkest areas as they get to the bottom. However, X Power clips at white, whereas Gaussian "bounces" the curve back down. X Power's curve is offset halfway from Gaussian's, so what Gaussian clips is what X Power actually shows.

GAUSSIAN—(a(X + b))

Gaussian creates a bell curve and clips at 0. *a* determines how spiky or pinched the curve is; *b* determines the upness and downness of it (whether toward white or toward black). You get smooth areas near 0 and bump when the value is higher, toward white. When the value is up at white, Gaussian bounces it down, thereby resulting in noisier areas in the light range.

The next five filters adjust the noise and apply it depending on the object's orientation in the three-dimensional World Space. Their curves move in a diagonal direction. Figure 8–39 shows each filter applied to Sine and RND Continuous noise.

ALTITUDE—X(a•ALTITUDE + b)

The Altitude filter modulates the noise according to altitude. The setting for *a* determines how fast the noise is scaled by altitude. A lower number will result in a gradual transition, whereas a higher number will result in a sharper transition. For noise applied at high altitude, *a* is a positive number. The *b* setting determines the onset of the transition. The higher the onset of transition to noise, the lower the number. For noise applied at high altitude, *b* is usually a negative number. To apply the noise at low altitudes, reverse the settings so that *a* is negative and *b* is positive.

SLOPE—X(a•SLOPE + b)

Slope works the same way as the Altitude filter, except that it uses slope. It applies the noise according to the object's position, from flat and horizontal (no slope, or graph at 0) to sheer and upright

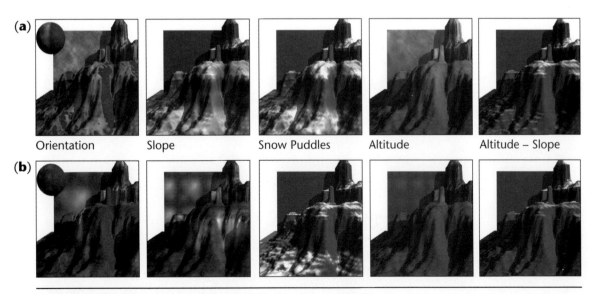

(a) Orientation · Slope · Snow Puddles · Altitude · Altitude – Slope

(b)

FIGURE 8–39 3D Noises applied: **(a)** RND Continuous; **(b)** Sine.

(high slope, or graph at 1). This is the filter to use to isolate textures to vertical cliff surfaces or flat surfaces.

When looking at 2D Preview of the texture, the left side represents no slope (or flat areas) and the right represents high slope (or upright areas). The best preview to look at, however, is the Spherical Preview, since you can see all of the transitions from flat to vertical.

The value for a determines the steepness of the noise; –4 is completely flat, while 4 is sheer upright. b adjusts the starting point of the transition and controls clipping at the sheer vertical or flat horizontal extremes. When the slope is 0 (as determined by the graph), only the setting for b acts on your noise. So if you want a little noise where there are flat places, set b slightly above 0 (0.1 or 0.075).

Noise on upright surface: $a = 4$ (or high 3's); $b = -2$ (or 2.5)

Noise on flat surface: $a = -4$ (or high –3's); $b = 1.5$ (or 2 or more)

ALTITUDE MINUS SLOPE—Xb+a (ALTITUDE–SLOPE)

Altitude Minus Slope puts the noise only at certain combinations of slope and altitude. When a is positive and b is negative, the result will be noise at high altitude and flat surfaces. When a is negative and b is positive, the result will be noise at low altitudes on upright surfaces. (Also, in the Materials Editor proper, the frequency of the texture determines where the snow level goes. A higher frequency lowers the snow level. But that is a slightly separate thing.)

ORIENTATION—X(a•ORIENTATION + b)

Orientation operates similarly to Altitude and Slope, only instead of change being oriented to degrees of height, it is oriented to degrees of "east" and "west."

SNOW PUDDLES

This filter turns noise into snow patches. a determines how much snow is affected by the noise. When $a = 0$, the noise doesn't apply at all, so the snow is uniform. When a is higher, the snow takes on the look of the noise. *b* shifts altitude, or the snow level. The Snow Puddles filter has a *c* value, too, which determines the slope. The higher the number, the flatter the surface needs to be for snow to stick to it.

Output Types

Now that the noise has been generated and filtered, it's time to determine the output type. The three options are Value, Normale, and Color. You can also combine them so that a component can have any one, two, or three output types. Value creates an alpha channel. It is further manipulated in the Materials Editor by the Alpha control. Normale creates a bump map. In the Materials Editor, the amount of bump is set by the Bump Gain control. Color output provides color for the texture. The texture color is controlled in the Materials Editor by the Color control.

If you activate one of the Materials Editor controls for an output type that is not a part of the texture, then Bryce will automatically readjust the texture to have one. A texture without a Normale setting will all of a sudden acquire a Normale output type when you adjust the bump using the Bump Gain control. The same is true for Value output and the Alpha control and for Color output and the Color control. This may come as a surprise, most notably with color. Bear this in mind if you get crazy color schemes and you don't know where they came from!

Value and Normale both take their information from the gray values of the noise. But if the output will be Color, then how will the colors be chosen? It should come as no surprise that Bryce provides plenty of options!

COLOR COMBINATIONS

Here is a description of each color combination option. Figure 8–40C (see color section) shows a sample of each. For all but the red/green/blue, the same set of colors was used. Also, there are two sets of textures for each image comparison: The objects on the left used a texture generated with Random Continuous noise; the objects on the right used a texture from Sine noise.

- *RGB/HLS.* The Red (Hue)/Green (Light)/Blue (Saturation) (RGB/HLS) options will set that one component to output for that one channel only. So you can have three components, each set differently for Color (or Color-Normale or Color-Value). Make one a Red Channel, another a Green Channel, and the last a Blue Channel. Click the radio button that changes the color model to HSV, and your noises are Hue, Saturation, and Light, respectively.
- *Linear Interpolation 2.* Creates a linear blend between the two colors chosen.
- *Linear Interpolation 3.* Creates a linear blend between the three selected colors.
- *Spline.* One of the more common color mapping options, it is similar to Linear Interpolation 3.
- *Spline with Snow.* Same as Spline, only it adds snow on top according to the altitude of the object.
- *Altitude.* Puts white snow level on your colors. Vary the snow level using the Material Editor's Frequency control. Anything below ground level is automatically colored blue.
- *Randomized.* Applies color using standard interpolation and randomized afterwards in RGB Space by means of a noise that Bryce generates internally.
- *Earth Map.* Generates color according to the bump map. Besides the colors you've selected, which are applied in the middle of the bump range, blue is applied at the lowest values. There are also white polar ice caps. Use this with Normale-Color on spheres in outer space for planets.
- *Empty Map.* It's simply that—empty.
- *Empty Map 2.* A second option that is—you guessed it—empty.
- *Interferences.* The individual red, green, and blue values for the *first* color create a repeating pattern around the contours of the noise. It's wild n' crazy.
- *Interpol+Interferences.* A combination of Linear Interpolation and Interferences.
- *Slope.* Gives an object a different color depending on its slope.
- *Orientation.* Assigns the colors to the object according to east-west orientation.

Combining Components—Blend Modes

By now you have generated noise, filtered it, assigned an output type of Value, Normale, or Color (or a combination of those), and assigned color maps for your color components. Assuming you have more than one component, now is the time for you to choose the parameters for the combined output and choose the way that the individual components interact with one another.

When you check the Combination radio button, you set parameters for the combined output. At this point, you can do several things with your combined output. The options should be familiar to you, since you could also do them working on the individual texture components:

- *Preview Combined Components.* When you look at a preview, you'll see the combined texture. (If you don't and it looks exactly like the first one, make sure you check 2 or 3 in the list of radio buttons in the upper right-hand corner of the Deep Texture Editor.)
- *Adjust Frequency.* This adjusts frequency on a global basis. Individual component frequencies are adjusted accordingly.
- *Assign Output Type.* Assign an output type for the Color, Value, Normale, or combinations of those.
- *Filter Combined Output.* Choose a filter and settings for the combined texture.
- *Add Global Phase to the Combined Texture.* This is the same as adding turbulence in the Shallow Texture Editor and similar to adding phase to any of the individual components.

If the final output type is something that is not matched by any of the individual components, those individual components will be converted to the final output type. So if you have one component that is Value and the final combined output is Color, Value will be converted to Color. (Parallel is an exception to this; see later in this chapter.) If you have a one-component texture and set the component's output type to Normale and then set the combined output type as Color, you'll get a scary color combination as your Normale information is converted to Color information. (This explains the strange behaviors you see when you are creating textures and it just doesn't look right.)

Conversely, if you have more individual output types in the individual components than you do in the combined, but at least one output type is shared between the combined and individual, the individual components won't be changed. Figure 8–41C (see color section) shows each of the different blend modes. Although Bryce calls them Components Interactions, I call them Blend Modes.

MAXIMUM/BLEND MAXIMUM

In Maximum, Bryce compares the two components and whichever is lighter is the final result. If you are familiar with channel operations or apply modes, this is the same as Lighten Only. Blend Maximum is the same as Maximum, except it creates blurring at points of harsh transition.

When you use Blend Maximum for normal bump mapping, the resulting bump map will generally have more high points and dip into low points only occasionally. When it's used with a Color output type, it's not the lightest color that determines the maximum result, but the value. Temporarily change the output type to Value to check. So you may have a result where a darker color is actually "lighter," since the dark color was assigned to an area of light value.

MINIMUM/BLEND MINIMUM

Minimum is the complement to Maximum. Instead of the lighter portions of noise prevailing, the darker ones do. It is analogous to "Darken Only" in two-dimensional imaging blends or channel calculations. Blend Minimum smoothes out any abrupt transitions between the two.

When creating Normale bump maps, use Minimum when you want areas that are generally lower with some points that are higher. The same situation about so-called darker and lighter colors holds true for Minimum as well as Maximum. These combination modes work better for components that use Normale as an output type.

PARALLEL

This is a nonblend mode. Use it when you have Normale in one component, Color in another, and Value in another. If you have one output type that is shared by components, such as Normale-*Color* and Value-*Color,* you won't get your desired result for color. The color will be taken from the first component only.

COMBINE

Combine (combin) is a blend mode for color only. For each component, you can assign three colors. I'll call the first of these Color A. Combine uses Component 2's Color A as an alpha channel. Wherever that color is located, you see Component 1 in the combined result. See Figures 8–41C and 8–27C (in the color section).

AVERAGE

Average is a normal blend between the two components, where all elements are mixed with equal weight. If one is black and the other is white, the result will be gray. This is a good, all-purpose output type for Bryce textures.

MULTIPLY

Multiply combines both components in such a way that they get darker. In the case of Value or Normale, where one is black, the result is black. Where one is white, the result is whatever the other one is. Where both are shades in between, they are proportionately darkened.

When using Multiply with Normale output type, the result will be a smaller bump map. Black is "flat" and, when multiplied, gets darker. However, use Multiply when one component has patches of black and white. The black will completely flatten the other map, and the white lets all the rest of the other stay as is. The Puddles recipe at the end of this chapter takes advantage of this handy feature.

ADD

Add combines colors so that they are dramatically lighter. However, it does not alter Normale information in the same dramatic way. Add uses a basic average for the bump information.

SUBTRACT

Subtract is a Blend mode that, in grayscale, tends to go toward black. In color, subtract results in brilliant and bizarre combinations that lean toward the complement of the original color. Be adventurous with color here and remember that the Normale information is averaged together in the same way as Add and Average.

BLEND V1; BLEND V2

Since you are never blending more than two components, you always choose between the first or the second. These modes blend the two components according to the Value of the first one (v1) or of the second one (v2). Essentially, these allow you to use one or another of your noises as an alpha channel for blending.

BLEND SLOPE/FAST SLOPE

These modes blend two different components according to slope. The first component is applied to areas that are flat; the second is applied to areas that are upright (or have high slope). Fast slope is a variation that blends in a more abrupt manner.

BLEND ALTITUDE

Blend Altitude blends the two different components—the first one at lower altitude and the second one at higher altitude.

BLEND ORIENTATION

This blend mode will put one component facing all directions and blend the other component on one direction only (used for such things as moss or something that grows only on north sides of trees and rocks).

BLEND RANDOM

Here's another alpha channel type of blend. A low-frequency random noise becomes the alpha channel. It chooses one component here and the other component there for the final version. Of course, since you're adding another layer of noise, it means you get that much more noise for your two or three components. But it's costlier, too.

3D Solid Texture Practicalia

FREQUENCY

There are several places where you can adjust texture frequency. Starting with the deepest Noise Editor and moving up to the Materials Editor, they are the following:

■ *Noise Editor, Frequency Control.* Control Frequency proportionately in the control to the right (identical to the Individual Component Frequency in the Deep Texture Editor) or set the frequency of the noise on each individual axis.

■ *Deep Texture Editor: Individual Component Frequency.* Adjust the frequency of the component noise. This slider works for both individual and combined components, depending on which is selected in the radio button to the left.

■ *Deep Texture Editor: Combination Frequency.* The slider will adjust the combined components. All individual frequencies will be increased or decreased proportionately.

■ *The Materials Editor: Frequency Control and Mappings... Dialog Box.* The Frequency control in the Materials Editor makes global adjustments to the texture frequency. It also alters the snow level of certain altitude-based textures.

ADD/COPY/PASTE TEXTURE

These three buttons in the lower left-hand corner of the Materials Editor are used for general housekeeping.

■ *Add Texture.* Add a texture to the list of 3D Solid Textures in the Materials Editor. Click the button, name your creation, and click OK. Your texture has joined the list *for as long as Bryce stays open.* When you quit Bryce, it will go away. You can save it permanently, though. Simply create a Materials Preset, and the base texture will be added to the preset with all the other material settings. Or, if you apply it to an object and save the scene, you will save the underlying texture. The texture will not, however, live in that list on its own.

- *Copy Component/Paste Component.* Use these buttons to copy one component (which one you copy depends on which radio button is checked in the list above) and paste it to another. (Change radio buttons first!) Do this within the same texture. Or, copy a component from one texture, close the Materials Editor, select another texture (or more likely an object you're working on), open up the Materials Editor for *that* one, and paste the component.

COMPONENT ORDER

The order in which the components are created sometimes makes a difference. How? In the way things are blended together. Depending on the output type, you may need to change them around. I'll talk about this type of situation when I talk about the "Snowed Under" material exercise at the end of this chapter.

NAMES IN THE 3D SOLID TEXTURE LIST

The initial release of KPT Bryce (1.0, for 68K Macintoshes only) had the textures placed in any old order. In version 1.0.1, the textures are in a certain order. The default ones are listed first and in alphabetical order. Then come any you have added to the list by using Add Texture. Next come all the ones that show up by virtue of the presets. Textures that are part of your open Scene document tag along at the bottom.

That first set of textures, the permanent ones that live inside Bryce, are yours to change while Bryce is open. Once you quit and re-launch, they go back to their original state. Likewise, any that you have added remain in that list only while Bryce is open.

If you save any presets in the Materials Preset Window, those textures are kept in the SHD. list (usually this is the file called BASIC.SHD). If you create or open up other .SHD files, then those names will be added to the list as well. Any materials assigned to objects in scenes will be stored with the actual Scene document and will show up in your list when that scene is open.

Warning: When you select a texture from the list, the first one you click on will be selected even if you drag up or down to another one before releasing your mouse. This is not standard Macintosh dialog box list behavior, so beware!

Anatomy of a Texture and Material

By now, I have poked into every nook and cranny of the Deep Texture Editor. But what does it mean? How do you use it? This Journey-to-the-Center-of-the-Earth has shown what everything is, but so far it hasn't provided a look at a real-live texture and how it was put together. That time has now arrived! To make sense of it all, I'll take a look at some specific textures and examine them in the Deep Texture Editor to discuss how they work. Then I'll cruise back out to the outer Materials Editor to talk about why they're set up the way they are for the particular scene they're in.

I'll bite off and chew three separate Deep Textures:

- Planet Rings: Variations on an existing Materials Preset
- Snowed Under: Snow atop a rock
- Bump and Reflections: Bumps with reflective puddles

Recipe for the Ringed Planet Material Adjustment

Chapter 11, which covers space scenes and other phenomena, contains a recipe for ringed planets. To create the planet rings, alter one of the existing presets from Bryce's BASIC.SHD Materials Preset list. The ringed planet recipe refers you back to here for the low-down on altering the preset. This first recipe is an example of how you might use an existing preset as a starting point to create some other effect. If you are following along from a cruise through the Deep Texture Editor section, create a scene with an enlarged flattened sphere. Set up your scene so that Atmosphere is *off*, there's no haze, and the cloud color is set to black.

1. Begin with the Materials Preset that has horizontal yellow rings, shown in Figure 8–42a. You'll be trying some successive attempts to get these to look like planet rings. First, in the

Materials Editor, try to make the rings fuzzy by changing the Effects control to fuzzy. It softens the outer perimeter of the ring. But the rings themselves are too even and too regular. How would you make them irregular? By changing the underlying noise!

2. Next, change the noise. Go to the Materials Editor. Hold down the Option key when you click the Edit Texture... button. This is a one-component noise. Click Component 1 and then click the Noise button. You will see that the noise is square and one-dimensional (see Fig. 8–42b). Are there other noises that would do as well? Let's try Random (RND) Linear. Just by changing that, you get many different shades of gray. Click OK to get back up to the main level of the Deep Texture Editor. Check out the preview in the 2D Preview Window.

3. Now click the Combination button to preview the full effect. Yikes! Now there are bright blue and yellow stripes in there! Change the colors of the rings. (Incidentally, with the color settings here, the black is in the places where the black/transparent areas are going to be. Bear that in mind as you make adjustments.) First, tone down the colors. The Deep Texture Editor is not blessed with a popup color picker, so you have to change colors using the sliders. If you don't like directly manipulating red, green, and blue, you can use the Shallow Texture Editor's color picker. Exit the Deep Texture Editor, go to the Materials Editor, and click the Edit Texture... button again to go to the Shallow Texture Editor. Using whichever way you prefer, change the colors to something softer. Click OK to exit the Materials Editor and do a little test render of your scene. (See Fig. 8–42c.)

4. Adjust the Mappings setting. Notice that the stripes are strange as they come around from behind the planet to the front. Perhaps the way the texture is mapped to the object could change a bit. Look at the Mappings control. Up to now, this one has been applied in Object Space. Other potential mapping candidates are: Parametric, Spherical, and Cylindrical. Try Cylindrical.

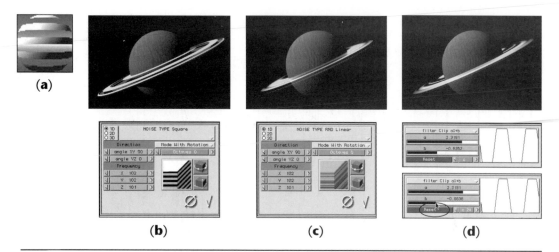

FIGURE 8–42 Adjusting an existing Materials Preset to create planet rings: (**a**) The starting preset; (**b**) square noise results in too-regular ring stripes; (**c**) changing noise to RND Linear for irregular rings; (**d**) adjusting the Clip filter to get more between-ring areas.

5. Go back and adjust the noise a little bit. Earlier, I mentioned that black was the transparent part. You'll need more of it, somehow, to create "in-between" areas of your ring stripes. So go get it back in the Deep Materials Editor. For a quick route there that bypasses the Materials Editor, press the Option key and then under the Object menu, select Last 3D Solid Texture... to go straight to the dialog box. Proceed directly to Component 1 and play with the filtering. Click Component 1 and then Set Filter... . The filter is the ubiquitous Clip. Where the curve reaches the top, it clips at white, and where it reaches the bottom, it clips at black. Fine. But you want more black. So, somehow, get the curve to be more "bottom-y." (No relation to a lobotomy!) The *b* value adjusts height. If you slide it to the left, you will be lowering the height of the curve. Do that a bit and then then click OK (see Fig. 8–42c). Click the 2D Preview in the Deep Texture Editor to see where the dark areas are now. There are more; that's good. Click OK to exit the Deep Texture Editor and then see how it looks when it renders.

Now you're getting somewhere! The stripes are fainter and there is more "in-between" area.

6. As a final noodle, try adjusting the frequency in the Materials Editor. And try again with those different mapping options. The one I was finally satisfied with was the Spherical mapping.

Snow Puddles Material

This next material description is not a walk-through so much as an analysis of a material setting that already exists. In examining all of what goes into it, you'll get a feel for how the controls in the Deep Texture Editor work together.

Here's a material that uses two components to create a snowy terrain. It is found on the CD in the Bryce file entitled SNOWED UNDER and in a shader file called SNOWED UNDER.SHD. See Fig. 8–43C (in the color section).

I'll begin by taking a look at the Deep Texture Editor to see what is there.

THE SNOW COMPONENT

The first component, snow, has its noise positioned in such a way that the grain is visible on the top as well as in "front" (see Fig. 8–44a). The significance of this will be apparent shortly.

Now, take a look at the filter (see Fig. 8–44b). It's Snow Puddles, the three-variable filter that makes snow occur at certain altitudes and slopes.

Remember that a determines how much the snow patches are influenced by the noise. The higher the number, the greater the noise's influence on the snow. Here, the number is 3.9922. Since the standard range is from 4 to –4, this is fairly high. (You can go higher than 4 by typing the number.) b shifts the altitude. The number is fairly close to 0, meaning the snow patches occur at pretty much any altitude.

The c value determines how much slope will influence whether the snow will appear. When c is 0, it does not matter whether the terrain is flat or upright; snow will "stick" to the terrain. The higher the number, the flatter the surface needs to be for snow to appear. Here c is 2, thereby requiring that the terrain be somewhat flat in

Component 1
Noise

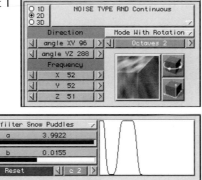

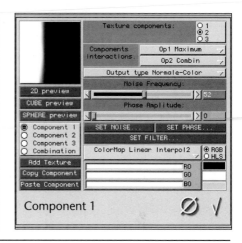

FIGURE 8–44 "Snowed Under"—Component 1.

order for the snow to stick to the ground. Snow won't stick to the upright surfaces, and the rocky portion of the texture will show through.

Now, look at the output type (see Fig. 8–44c). This component will output as Normale-Color. Normale is for the bump. Where the noise is white, the surface bump will be at its highest. This ensures the snow sits atop the terrain. Where there is no snow, the noise is black. The color for this is set as Linear Interpol2. This means that the color is linearly interpolated between two colors, black and white. The reason for the black will become apparent when I shortly discuss the interaction of the components. But first, take a look at your other component.

THE ROCKY MOUNTAIN COMPONENT

The second component (see Fig. 8–45b) is created from a three-dimensional noise, Random (RND) lines. Notice that the frequency for y is much less than that for x and z. This is a real-life example of how to make a three-dimensional noise have a vertical grain. It has a two-dimensional effect without the complete uniformity of a two-dimensional grain. Notice that there's no rotation to the noise and it's one octave with a More Irregular mode. So there's a bit of complexity to the noise and some random strains that aren't completely vertical or horizontal.

Go back to the Materials Editor and notice that the noise has the same output type as the first, that is, Normale-Color (see Fig. 8–45a). Normale is bump map, and Color, of course, provides the color for the object. Now take a look at the filter for this component (see Fig. 8–45c). The filter here is set to make the Normale just so. The standard contrast filter, Clip aX+b, is used. The *b* value (which controls the height of the graph) is negative, thereby making the range of output about half height. Think about this for a moment. If the graph went from the bottom to the top, you would have a bump that goes the full range from lowest to highest. But this rocky texture will be combined with snow, and the rocky surface had better jolly well be located *underneath* the snow. So the filtering curve that determines the rocky surface bump keeps it in the bottom- to mid-range of the bump. The lightest (highest) values of the combined output is reserved for the snow. (See, it all makes sense, doesn't it?) The actual shape of the curve is not changed much. It goes to about 60 percent of its height ($a = .5774$), and the bottom edge just dips below the bottom black part, thereby making for more pronounced bottom edges.

Look at the result of this filtering. (In Fig. 8–45d, I show it using Value for the moment, a handy little trick for seeing the component solely in terms of the gray values.) The values shown are all middle to dark gray.

FIGURE 8–45 Component 2's Noise Editor settings, filter, and output type.

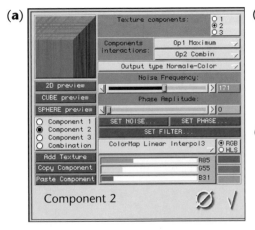

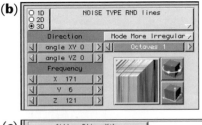

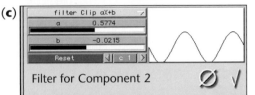

Component 2's output is Color-Normale. The Color Map is Spline. The three colors are generally closer to one another, not widely divergent.

COMBINING THE COMPONENTS

Now that I've looked at each component individually, I'll talk about how the two components are combined. Each individual component has its output type set to Normale-Color. Look for a moment only at the Normale (bump). The snow needs to be higher than other elements. Maximum (analogous to Photoshop's Lighten Only) compares the two and takes the lightest one as the result. See Figure 8–46a. Where it's white, there will be snow with a higher bump. Everything else will be the underlying rocky matter.

The output type is Color-Value. (The reason for including Value is that you can create an alpha channel and use Alpha Reflective to add an ever-so-slight bit of reflection to make the snow glow bright.) Although the first two components have Normale as their output type, the final output type does not. The Normale information is there, available for the Bump Gain control in the Materials Editor. Here's another important little fact about how the Deep Texture Editor works. It isn't necessary to set the final output with everything in it.

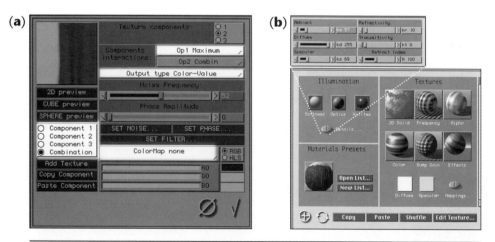

FIGURE 8–46 (a) Deep Texture Editor final combination and (b) the Materials Editor dialog box for "Snowed Under."

This is especially true if you are going to do any global filtering. In this case, there is a global filter, Quantize, that adds a bit of high contrast in a posterized fashion. This filter operates only on the Color and Value portions of the noise, not on Normale. In this case, it is rather subtle. I'll come back to filtering at the combination stage in the next material exercise. For now, just remember that you don't need always to assign all the output types in the final combination. If Normale is included in the individual components, the Materials Editor will find it and know what to do with it.

Render the snow. Notice that there are little indentations in the snow, as if there were animal tracks or tufts of grass peeking out through the layers. This effect is a result of the two-dimensional noise rotation that included the "top" as well as the "front" orientation.

Suppose you wanted to add a third component to the texture. The rocky substance is rather uniform and might be nice with something else to break it up. Perhaps some horizontal coloring of some sort. Think about this. If you add a third component, you'll want to change the order of the components, since you want the snow to come out on top. The snowy portions need to be highest, so Maximum is the blend setting. Any combination blend other than Maximum (Multiply, Add, Average) will result in funky snow.

If you don't believe me, try it out yourself. (You will anyway!) Make sure you switch the number of components to 3; otherwise you will wonder why nothing has changed. For Component 3, select some noise, give it some color, make the second blend (Op2) Average, and see what kind of madness ensues. To rectify the situation, copy your snow component and paste it to Component 3. Then create your rocky matter inconsistencies in the component where the snow used to be (in this case, Component 1). Set Op1 to be Average and Op2 to Maximum so that the snow in combination with the result of the first two components will have a "come-out-one-top" result.

SNOWED UNDER IN THE MATERIALS EDITOR

Now, how is this snow texture worked in the Materials Editor? Looking at the texture section of the Materials Editor, I first note the obvious: It's a 3D Solid Texture (see Fig. 8–46b). To create the full illusion of height for the snow, Bump Gain is set to Maximum (or close to that). The texture's frequency depends more on the amount of detail you want to see in the object and is adjusted interactively while you are working on the particular object in the scene. (For objects closer to the camera, the frequency will need to be set higher than for those far away.) The Color control conveys the texture's color to the Diffuse and Ambient Channels. When diffuse light falls on the object, you will see color. When the object is in shadow, some Color information will still be apparent, since there's a little bit of ambient lighting. In this case, the Alpha is set to Reflective, although in the Details... dialog box Reflective is not set very high at all. A tiny bit (less than 10) adds brightness to the snow, especially where it's directly lit by the sun. The specular color is determined by the color swatches. The Specular color swatch is a light blue, and there's an oh-so-tiny amount of blue color to the Hilites control as well. Also, the Ambient color (set in the Sky & Fog Palette) determines what the snow is like in shadow. For that, Ambient is set to a light blue. Incidentally, this color balancing is one of the trickier parts of Bryce. The colors all influence each other in little ways, and you'll have to do a bit of noodling to get your snowy rock to look just so. If you change the sun's color to a light blue or a light yellow, for instance, the look of the snow's surface will change dramatically.

Puddlebumps: Bump and Reflections

The other 3D Solid Texture that I will work with here is a variation on a theme. It has a bump and also (you guessed it!) reflection. (See Fig. 8–47C in the color section.) You've probably seen this before, since there's a Bryce Materials Preset that has a portion of rocky mass interspersed with flat reflective puddles.

DO THE BUMP

1. For Component 1, start by generating a noise. (If you need a starting texture, choose BasicSin(e).) The noise here is three-dimensional, Random (RND) Continuous, three Octaves, and Irregular (see Fig. 8–48). Set Frequency to 250. Filter it with

(a)

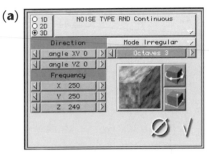

Component 1 Noise

(c)

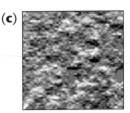

FIGURE 8–48
Component 1's
(**a**) Noise setting;
(**b**) filter setting;
(**c**) 2D preview.

(b)

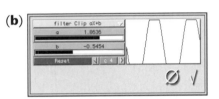

high-contrast Clip and set the output to Normale for a gray bumpy surface.

2. For Component 2, begin with the same type of noise as in step 1 (copy Component 1 and paste to Component 2) and then make adjustments. Adjust Component 2's noise to have a lower frequency setting. Bring the Octave setting down to 2. (See Fig. 8–49a.) Now, filter this with Clip. Adjust it to match the filter shown in Figure 8–49b. The filter is fairly steep, which makes for significant areas of black. Set Component 2's output type to Value. Why Value? The Value information is going to go straight to the Alpha control in the Materials Editor. There, a Reflective setting will provide areas that will be reflective for the puddle surface.

3. Next is the Blend mode. The first and second noises will be multiplied together. For the moment, make the final output type Value. The black portions of the Component 2's noise, when multiplied with the Component 1's bump map, will result in flat areas (no bump) in the combined final texture. This combination works on the Normale bump map, even though it's a Value component that's doing the "work." Now that you see where the large flat areas come from, you can see why the second noise was set to a smaller frequency than the first. Figure 8–50a compares a portion of the two components side by side

(a)
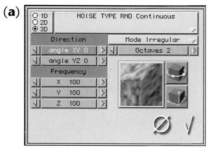

Component 2 Noise

(c)
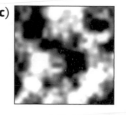

FIGURE 8–49
Component 2's
(a) Noise setting;
(b) filter setting;
(c) 2D preview.

(b)

with their multiplied result. You can see where the second noise is used to make flat areas.

4. In the Materials Editor, set the Alpha control to Reflective and the Bump Gain control for a moderate bump. Render. Take a quick peek at what's been created so far as it applies to the object's surface (see Fig. 8–50b). The resulting image has areas of flat and areas of bump height. When the Alpha control has been switched to Reflective, however, the reflection occurs in the high portions, not the low portions.

Why is the reflective area in the bumpy area? Component 2 is set for Value. Where Value is white, you'll get reflective areas from using the Alpha control. But where there's black, you're combining it with the Normale information in Noise 1 to flatten out the bump. You want portions that are flat and portions that are bumpy. You need the black to flatten the bump, but you also need to somehow swap the Value information so that the flat part is reflective.

You can't change anything in Components 1 or 2. You *can*, however, change the final output. If you set the final output to be Value and somehow invert it there, then you will end up reversing the Value information without touching the interaction of the two components to create bumpy and flat areas.

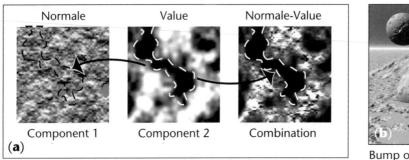

(a)

Normale Value Normale-Value

Component 1 Component 2 Combination

(b)

Bump only Reflection added

FIGURE 8–50 (a) Multiplying the two components to get flattened areas; (b) the result so far has flat areas interspersed with bump.

5. Adjust Combination's filter to invert the Value setting. When Component 2 is set to Value and Combination is set to Value, the textures look identical. So Component 2's filter settings can be the basis for Combination's filter. All you need to do is invert it. The filter is Clip aX+b, where a is 3.6 and b is −1.4. Now, before you invert it, a bit of background on Clip aX+b: The default values (no clipping) for this filter are $a = 1$, $b = 0$. A straight inversion is $a = -1$, $b = 1$. To invert *any* setting, change the value for a from positive to negative (or vice versa) and for b, change the number from negative to positive (or vice versa) and then add 1 to the number. So, in the filter for Combination, select Clip aX+b and provide the values of (roughly) $a = -3.6$, $b = 2.4$.

If you decide not to do the straight mathematical route, you'll need to switch back and forth between Component 2 and Combination to preview each. Make sure they're the inverse of one another. You'll need to play with this one a bit to make sure the white areas (reflection) are showing in the right place. If you make your white area grow a bit so that there's overlap, you'll have areas of reflectivity move up into the bump, thereby creating an illusion of wet land right where the two meet. See Figure 8–51.

If you leave the Deep Editor to do any test renders, select the menu item Objects > Last 3D Solid Texture... . You'll need to press the Option key before selecting it from the menu. For work that goes back and forth between scene and the Deep Texture Editor, it's a handy shortcut.

Component 2   Combination   Clip filter for Combination   "Overlap"

FIGURE 8–51 Changing the Value to make reflective area flat; (**a**) Component 2; (**b**) Combination after inverting; (**c**) filter settings for inversion; (**d**) overlap to create "wet" edges.

FIGURE 8–52 The result of swapping the Value in Combination's filter creates flat reflective surfaces.

Now that you've inverted the Value for your Combination, take stock of this texture.

6. The color for this texture, which is something of a land mass, goes to Component 2. Until now, the output type has been Value. Change the output type to Color-Value and set your colors for Component 2. In this example, the Color Map is Spline. For the final combination, make the color map to be None (since you already set it in Component 2). Now you're set. Figure 8–53 shows the color settings for Component 2 and for Combination.

Finally, adjust the contrast for the Combination filter to fine-tune the partially reflective wet edge around the puddle. Semi-reflective areas are gray in the final value, and they overlap very closely on the "shores" of the other bumpy areas.

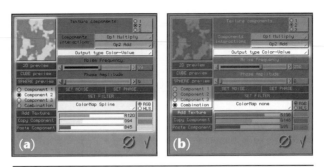

FIGURE 8–53 Color settings: (**a**) Component 2; (**b**) Combination.

Conclusion

The trip through this chapter on the Materials Editor has been no small journey! To help you gain an understanding of how Bryce creates surface appearances for its objects, I discussed the sections of the Materials Editor—the Illumination controls, Color controls, Texture controls, and Materials Presets. Then I descended deeper into texture realms, discussing the two kinds of textures that Bryce applies to objects, 2D PICT Textures, and 3D Solid Textures. For the 3D Solid Texture discussion, I first took you into the Shallow Texture Editor grotto and then into the caverns of the Deep Texture Editor. By the time I had poked into every nook and cranny, I had created what might seem to be a disheveled mess. But then I took three specific material settings and analyzed them for you so that you could see how all the controls work together in the Deep Texture Editor and Materials Editor. Obviously the trip through three material settings hasn't told you everything you need to know about *all* the possible combinations of textures, but you now have a basis for understanding other textures when you open up and explore them. The narrative of the working methods and thought processes will set you well on your way to creating your own perfect Brycean surfaces.

9

Superlative Nature Imagery

They are wonderful to behold, and therefore in the summer time strangers come here from all parts of the world to see them. They cross snow-covered mountains, and travel through the deep valleys, or ascend for hours, higher and still higher, the valleys appearing to sink lower and lower as they proceed, and become as small as if seen from an air balloon. Over the lofty summits of these mountains the clouds often hang like a dark veil; while beneath in the valley, where many brown, wooden houses are scattered about, the bright rays of the sun may be shining upon a little brilliant patch of green, making it appear almost transparent. The waters foam and dash along in the valleys beneath; the streams from above trickle and murmur as they fall down the rocky mountain's side, looking like glittering silver bands.

Hans Christian Andersen, "The Garden of Paradise,"
Fairy Tales of Hans Christian Andersen

In This Chapter . . .

- At the feet of the Master—Dissect some scenes by Eric Wenger, Bryce's creator
- Specific tips for certain nature effects
- Geology 101—how Earth formations occur and how to do them in Bryce
- Undersea worlds
- Rainy weather conditions

In this chapter, I jump back and forth from the natural world "out there" to the virtual world of Bryce "in here." Some of the time I talk about how land is formed in the real world and at other times about the way to reproduce those types of effects in Bryce. I also offer you a little Kodak moment as you consider some good rules of thumb for taking scenery shots. Those same photographic principles apply to the placement of the camera in Bryce.

Nature and Bryce—Reciprocal Observation

There is an interactive process of using Bryce and then being outdoors. The best way to make natural-looking Bryce images is to spend some time outdoors observing the lay of the land. After you've worked in Bryce, while you're outside you'll start noticing things about the environment—you'll observe geological structures, habitats, and atmospheric conditions. After inspecting the way things look in the natural world, you will apply your observations to your Brycean scenery. You'll set up your skies with haze and fog that's just so. Your terrains will benefit from all that careful scrutiny of the local land. Working in Bryce will give you a keener eye when you're in the out-of-doors. Analyzing that outdoor setting will develop your Bryce skills.

To give you a head start on the reciprocal observation process, this chapter discusses some of the common solutions for making convincing nature scenery. Not all natural possibilities can be explored in detail in this (or any!) book. I will, however, explore some common tricks. With the basic nature scene understanding and a few tricks as a foundation, you'll be able to continue on and more readily translate the outdoors to the inner workings of Bryce.

In the Master's Footsteps: Eric's Methods

The absolute master at creating nature scenes is Eric Wenger, creator of KPT Bryce. After all, he wrote the software to tickle his own funny bone long before Kai became involved to put together a version for public consumption. Eric knows it best. The best school of instruction for getting the natural-looking images is to study the methods of his Brycean madness. This section will do just that, exploring a few of his images and examining the characteristics common to superlative scenery. After reading this section, take a look at Eric's scenes on the Bryce application CD and on the CD in this book as well.

Here is a brief list of the principles that can be deduced from Eric's images. Each one is discussed in turn. If you want a master reference list of masterful techniques, then come back to this place.

- Create multiple terrains.
- Create a sense of relative distance from the camera with terrain size and resolution.
- Put all the detail right in front of the camera.
- Enlarge the terrains that go way off in the background.
- Create a sense of scale with Atmosphere and Materials settings.
- Pay attention to those Sky settings!

I explore these concepts by examining three scenes (see Figs. 9–1 and 9–2). They are shown in final rendered state and in wireframe from Top View. The final renders are also shown in Figure 9–3C in the color section. Figure 9–1a, "Fjord A4," is a scene that is on this book's CD. Figure 9–2 has two images, "Abisko Pine Trees" and "Red Vulcans." You can find the Scene document for "Red Vulcans" on the KPT Bryce CD. "Abisko Pine Trees" is on this book's CD.

Terrain Placement: Create for Depth

In this section, I analyze how Eric's terrain placement provides a sense of grand scale in his nature scenery. Multiple terrains are placed in the scene, and their resolutions and wireframe sizes vary depending on the distance from the camera.

WIREFRAME ANALYSIS FROM THE TOP DOWN

Figures 9–1b, 9–2b, and 9–2d are wireframe views. Notice how the camera is at one end and the small terrain sizes are closest to the camera. Farther away, the terrain sizes become gargantuan in comparison. In each of the figures, the ground is highlighted so that you can compare the relative sizes of the terrains. Nearly all of

FIGURE 9–1 "Fjord A4":
(**a**) The rendered image;
(**b**) Top View wireframe;
(**c**) Top View render.

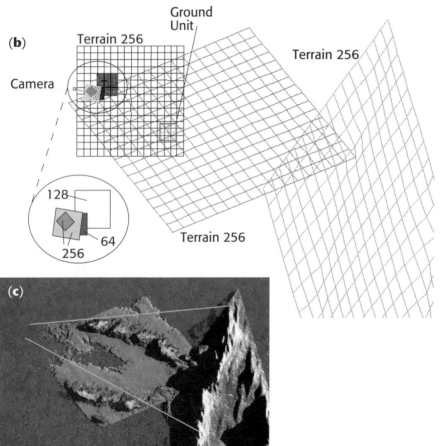

FIGURE 9–2
"Abisko Pine Trees":
(**a**) Rendered image;
(**b**) Top View wireframe.
"Red Vulcans":
(**c**) Rendered image;
(**d**) Top View wireframe.

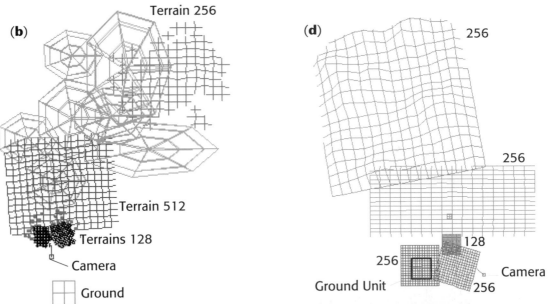

the terrains have been enlarged from their original sizes. The farther away from the camera, the larger the terrains are. This establishes a sense of scale.

The figures have numbers indicating the resolution in each of the terrains, as set in the Resolution popup menu in the Terrain Editor. Close to the camera, they are generally 256 or 512. But far away, the amount of resolution detail does not increase in proportion to the increase in wireframe size. The larger the terrain's resolution, the more RAM that is required to process your scene. When the terrain is far away from the camera, the detail is not required.

"Fjord A4" has high detail placed right in front of the camera. The four terrains in the foreground (shown in an enlargement) are mostly medium- to high-resolution. Their wireframe sizes have been *reduced*, creating even higher detail (see Fig. 9–1b).

Open up the Scene documents on the CD. Notice that the terrain maps for many of them are the same. You can also see this trend toward sameness in the Top View render of "Fjord A4" (see Fig. 9–1c) as well as the Scene document for "Red Vulcans." You don't need to create and painstakingly perfect a separate G2H map for every terrain. You can use the same one and change the terrain's orientation (rotate it around on the *y*-axis). Or make it a bit different by a slight tweak, if you must.

Having analyzed the scenes from the Top View, you may think that the general order of business is to create and place terrains from the Top View. A potential Top View formula would go like this:

Start in Top View. Create a terrain. Duplicate it and move it away from the camera. Enlarge it some. Stretch it out on one dimension. Duplicate the terrain again. Move it over and back a bit. Enlarge it. Rotate it around. Now create a ground. Give the terrains and ground a material setting. Add haze to taste. Go back to Main View. Sashay the camera back and forth to get the right perspective. Render. Violá! Instant natural scenery!

This will work, since it bows respectfully to the Major and Minor Deities of depth and scale. But the scenes shown here weren't created that way. Eric created them while in Main View, with forays into Top View to make adjustments. In the next section, I discuss camera perspective as part of the scene-building process.

CAMERA PERSPECTIVE

Each of these scenes was created for a one-camera perspective. They are not scenes created for a 360° panorama. In all of these, the camera's active image area determines the location of the terrains in the three-dimensional world. In the "Fjord A4" example, shown rendered in Top View, the lines roughly indicate the edge of the camera's field of view (see Fig. 9–1c). Like a movie set where all of the beams and frames can't be seen by the camera, so Bryce terrains end abruptly off-camera. This is a natural outcome of the process of working in Main View; as long as the object looks right through the camera, it doesn't matter how it appears elsewhere.

If you are going to create a scene for a 360° render or for animation, you'll have to work a bit differently. Smaller, detailed terrains are close to the camera, with larger terrains spread out along the perimeter. (More on 360° renders can be found in Chapter 12, "Render Unto Bryce.")

In each scene, the camera is located close to the ground. If you were to somehow take a "Fantastic Voyage" and actually enter BryceSpace, your eyes would be located—you guessed it—close to the ground. The mountains would be huge in comparison—hundreds of times taller than you are. Be sure to select the Ground Camera option from the Views popup menu to put you in your humble place. As a result, those massive terrains will look just that—massive.

Material Frequency Detail

The terrain placement and camera position are adjusted to give an overall sense of scale. Perpetrate this illusion of realism in the Materials Editor. In these scenes, the amount of surface detail is adjusted to ensure authenticity. The adjustments are most critical when an object is right in front of the camera. When the object looks blurry in the foreground, increase the frequency to add more detail. There are three ways to do so. In the Materials Editor, adjust the Frequency control. In the Edit Textures dialog box, accessed within the Materials Editor, click More for "Texture Complexity." Finally, in the Deep Texture Editor (Option-click the Edit Texture button) adjust the Frequency sliders for each of the different components or adjust the frequency of the noise itself. These detail-increasing controls are covered in greater detail in Chapter 8, "Material World."

MATERIAL SETTING: AMBIENT

For a sense of cohesion of all elements in these scenes, the objects' Illumination settings have been given identical Ambient amounts in the Materials Editor. If each of your object's Ambient settings differs, the scene won't look natural. The discrepancy between objects will be most apparent in their shaded areas. On occasion you can beautifully exploit different Ambient settings. If you have a terrain with dark rock and another with snow, the Ambient settings will differ. However, in most cases giving all your objects a consistent Ambient setting will make them live harmoniously in your Brycean habitat.

Sky Settings for Depth and Realism

How did Eric set up his skies in these scenes? The Sky settings contribute to the natural look. For my analysis of the three scenes, I focus on haze, sky colors, freestanding clouds, and the choice of atmosphere.

HAZE AND SKY SETTINGS

The Haze setting provides a feel of true depth and perspective. All the strategic placement and sizing of terrains does nothing without adequate haze to infuse distance into the scene. The objects close to the camera are clear; the distant mountains *are* far away. The presence of haze—in generous proportions—is common to these and most of Eric's landscape scenes.

What differs from scene to scene is haze and color. The haze colors for "Fjord A4" and "Abisko Pine Trees" are pale azures, whereas that for "Red Vulcans" is a murky mauve. In these instances, the haze color generally matches the overall color tone of the image. Don't take this as a strict rule, however.

If you *do* want to take a color observation as a rule of thumb for realism, I offer you this one: The color of ambient light should be in medium values on the cool side of the spectrum. In "Abisko Pine Trees," ambient color is a medium blue. In "Fjord A4," it is a middle gray—neither cool nor warm, but cooler when combined with a cool haze color. "Red Vulcans" has a warmer ambient color to match the warm overall coloring; however, the ambient color is much deeper.

Shadow color depends on three things: the Shadow setting in the Sky & Fog Palette (shadows need to be switched on in the Render Palette, too!), the haze color, and the ambient light color. In "Fjord A4," gray ambient and blue haze mix to create the overall shadow color. The Shadow setting is set to maximum. The Sky & Fog settings for that scene are shown in Figure 9–4. Of course, you can have one color or the other dominate. An increase in haze will always make that color dominate the shadow area.

TO ATMOSPHERE OR NOT TO ATMOSPHERE

Lest you think that realistic skies can be obtained only with Atmosphere switched *on* in the Render Palette, look at "Fjord A4" as a prime example of clear sky realism with Atmosphere switched *off.* There's not a cloud in the sky—that's the whole point. Rather than Clear Sky in the "!" dialog box being selected, Atmosphere was switched *off.* Doing this provided additional sky-creating license—

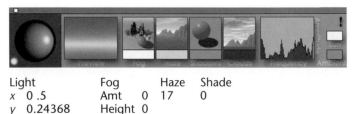

Render Palette Options:
No Atmosphere

Light		Fog		Haze	Shade
x	0 .5	Amt	0	17	0
y	0.24368	Height	0		
z	0.08				

	Colors			
	Haze	Clouds	Sun	Amb
R	181	13	247	94
G	193	0	247	94
B	201	94	247	94

FIGURE 9–4 All the settings for the sky in "Fjord A4."

Eric carefully selected the sky (Cloud) and haze color to produce a picture-perfect sky.

CLOUDS ARE HUGE

Freestanding clouds can add to a scene's sense of realism. Look at the Top View of the "Abisko Pine Trees" image. The spheres are the clouds. They are huge, especially when compared to the terrains in the scene's foreground. This is not merely a matter of creating a sphere, flattening it somewhat, and then applying a cloud material setting to it. No, these puppies are grandiose. Remember, this is a *world* you're creating, and clouds are large-scale objects. Creating and seeding clouds is not something you've had day-to-day practice in—until now. So think big!

Eric's Scenery Recap

Here's a summary of all of the tips I covered during my examination of Eric Wenger's scenes:

- *Number of Terrains.* There is more than one terrain in these scenes, ranging from 5–7.
- *Terrain Proportions.* Close to the camera, terrains are relatively small; father away, they are spread out and larger.
- *Terrain Size.* Both the terrains close up and the terrains far away use a size of 256 × 256. When the terrains are close to the camera, higher detail is needed. Far away, the same terrain resolution suffices even when the terrain wireframe is greatly enlarged.
- *Detail Right in Front of the Camera.* The greatest amount of detail is right in front of the camera.
- *Low Camera Position.* All of the camera views are close to the ground. Since the terrains far away are large, the low camera position tells you that you are in a big, big world.
- *Carefully Calculated Material Detail Frequency.* The material setting frequency is finessed to give the proper sense of scale. If repeating patterns or bump maps are too large, it makes the object seem too small.
- *Haze to Create Distance.* Haze provides a visual cue that the object is located far away.

- *Cool Ambient Colors.* Make your ambient color cool and medium-valued for realistic outdoor coloring.
- *Huge Clouds.* Spheres used for freestanding clouds are not small. Make 'em big!

Geology 101: Mountains and Valleys

Making landscapes in Bryce is not about creating things that you think up in your head (well, then again, yes it is!). But even a fantasy landscape looks impressive because it's based on some sort of reality, or at least a perception of reality. To aid your reality perception process, this section examines some basic matters of geology, or how Earth was formed. I'm not talking about the big plate tectonics stuff all the world over but rather what happens on a local level.

If you've ever been to a scenic spot, you may have wondered how Earth got to be the way it is. How were the canyons formed? Why do the mountains there look different from the mountains you're used to seeing at home?

Them Thar Objects

The natural world is made up of mountains and valleys. Your Bryce world is made up of terrains and grounds and other Primitives. How do you make mountains and valleys in your Bryce world?

The problem is, you can make a terrain that goes up into the air—a mountain. You can invert it so that it goes down into the ground—a descending abyss. But you can't take a ground plane and punch a hole in it into which you insert your descending abyss. Somehow you need to negotiate the height differences.

Following are some solutions to this problem. This list does not presume to be the final, ultimate list of ways to solve this problem, but it's a start.

- *Potential Solution #1.* One terrain solution: The terrain has both the mountain and valley. This is the "more valley for your money" solution. (See Fig. 9–5a and 9–5b.)

■ *Variation on Solution #1.* You can have the "ground level" be your valley floor with everything else rising from that point. (See Fig. 9–5c and 9–5d.)

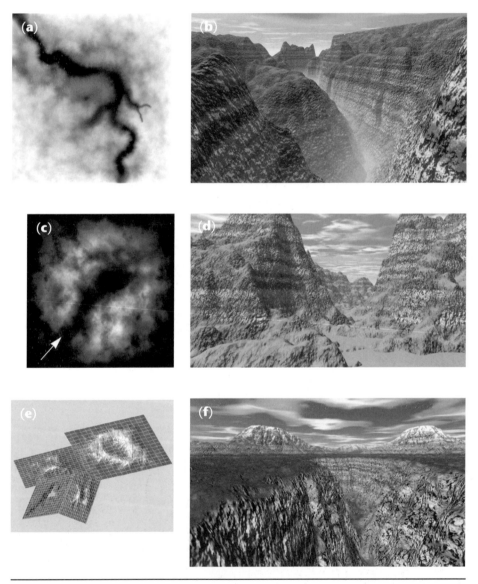

FIGURE 9–5 Mountains and valleys: (**a**) Terrain for (**b**) one terrain mountain and valley; (**c**) terrain and camera perspective for (**d**) one terrain with ground; (**e**) Top View of wireframes for (**f**) foreground crevasse with additional terrains.

- *Potential Solution #2.* Multiple terrains create both mountain and valley effects. Several terrains intersect. The lowest point of intersection is the valley floor.
- *Potential Solution #3.* Create a huge terrain with a deep crevasse in it. Place smaller terrains on top to create the mountains. (See Fig. 9–5e and 9–5f.)
- *Variation on Solution #3.* Create a flat plane for some "ground." Add terrains below and terrains above for different levels of elevation.

You don't need to have an infinite plane for your ground. There are plenty of scenes where a flat plane suffices; it stretches as far as Bryce's eye can see. Why not have more than one acting as a patchwork around your valley?

Make sure that with all of these, you have your camera angle set up to take advantage of the placement of the various terrain parts.

After a little discussion of the geological processes that take eons and eons, I'll dip into Bryce techniques that you can do in seconds to imitate those processes.

How New Mountains Are Created

New mountains are created in four basic ways:

1. *Volcanic Activity.* Magma from inside Earth forces its way to the surface. Lava spills onto the surface, thereby creating successive

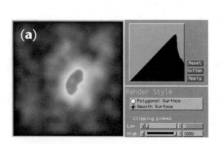

FIGURE 9–6 Volcano terrain map: (**a**) Filtering to collapse the terrain's center; (**b**) two rendered volcano terrains.

layers that build a mountain. Volcanoes are known for the central hole or crater from which lava emerges at the surface. Mt. St. Helen's in Washington State is one notorious example of such volcanic activity.

Volcanoes in Bryce. Use the Filtering control in the Terrain Editor to draw a downward line to make the top portion of the terrain descend (see Fig. 9–6a). Figure 9–6b shows two Bryce volcanic cones. One is level at the top; the other is jagged after an apply of Add Noise (located in the Terrain Editor).

2. *Compression.* Land masses are forced together. Where they collide, Earth's crust shortens and becomes thicker. What Earth's crust would call "thick" is what we call mountains. This process gives us folding and faulting and earth-shattering experiences. The Grand Tetons in Wyoming are mountains created by the compression of Earth's crust.

Compressed Land Masses in Bryce. There is no characteristic "look" to this type of mountain-making method. Just click the Terrain icon on the Create Palette and you'll be okay. However, bear this in mind: If land masses come together quickly, there will be a rapid rise with high relief faces where mountain-building vastly outpaces erosion. If the two land masses are compressed together more slowly, slopes won't be as steep and there will be more erosion.

3. *Extension.* Earth's crust is stretched apart. As it is stretched and thinned, cracks form, creating new faults. Some of the crustal blocks sag into the thinner crust along these faults (see Fig. 9–7). Those crustal blocks that don't sag become mountains by default (pun intended!). The Basin and Range Province of Arizona and Nevada was created by extension.

Extension Mountains in Bryce. Extension mountains create an alternating sequence of parallel mountain ranges and basins. Set up a ground terrain with multiple terrains for a basin-and-range effect.

4. *Broad Upwarping.* A large mass of crust bulges upward, creating broad mountains. The Black Hills of South Dakota were created by broad crustal upwarping.

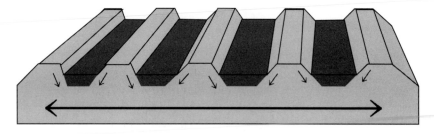

FIGURE 9–7 Extension: As Earth's crust is stretched apart, faults form and matter sags into the thinner crust along the faults.

> *Broad Upwarping in Bryce.* Enlarge your terrain with the Proportional Resize tool and then reduce it on the *y*-axis (height) for extremely broad rolling hills.

Then, on the other hand, there's the matter of valleys. Once the mountains are there, how are the valleys created?

Glaciers

Some landscapes have been formed by glacial erosion. During the ice age, massive ice sheets, drawn by gravity, crept downhill ever so slowly. In the battle between ice and land, these massive glaciers won. They carved a path for themselves, leaving behind huge sweeping U-shaped valleys as they retreated.

The "Abisko Pine Trees" scene in Figure 9–2 has a broad U-shaped valley. Although a peek at the terrain from Top View shows that the valley does not extend over a long distance (proper glacier-formed valleys do), it has the right shape.

Create a Brycean glacier by using the Brush Tool in Photoshop! To make U-shaped valleys, use a nice fat brush with the Multiply mode and cut a wide swath. Your brush is now the glacier. (How's that for being a virtual ice mass?) Figure 9–8a shows a normal terrain, which was taken into Photoshop. The terrain was then brushed with a large (150 pixel) brush in Photoshop using the Multiply mode (see Fig. 9–8b). The final rendered terrain has the characteristic U-shape (see Fig. 9–8c).

Faults

All the world over, Earth's crust has cracks, or faults. Add faults and diagonal roughness to your terrains by using the Merge Terrain dialog box, Photoshop, and the KPT Gradient Designer. (Check out this book's CD for some faulted terrains to merge with your own.)

When you run diagonal lines through your terrains, the land masses break up as though different layers of rock had shifted. It may be San Andreas running through your terrain, or it may be a little localized action.

In the Gradient Designer, you can create a series of linear gradients with a-b saw motions. Apply several gradients on top of another using the Multiply apply mode, and you'll have a fault image that will expose different stratographic regions of your terrain. Figures 9–9a and 9–9b are KPT Gradient Designer fault images: (a) shows two gradient applies and (b) shows the third apply.

Here are a few variations on a merge-fault-map-with-terrain theme:

- *Fault Map as Starting Place.* Open the fault map through the Terrain Editor's Merge Terrain dialog box. In the Terrain Editor, copy it and then click Fractalize. Click the Merge Terrain button. Paste the original and blend to taste. Add more effects back in the main Terrain Editor.
- *Begin with a Bryce Terrain.* Create a terrain. In the Terrain Editor, merge the terrain with the saw map (try Minimum or a straight Blend). Or invert the terrain before blending and then try Minimum.

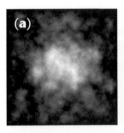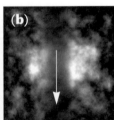

FIGURE 9–8 Brycean glacier making: (**a**) A normal terrain; (**b**) after brushing in Photoshop; (**c**) the rendered terrain.

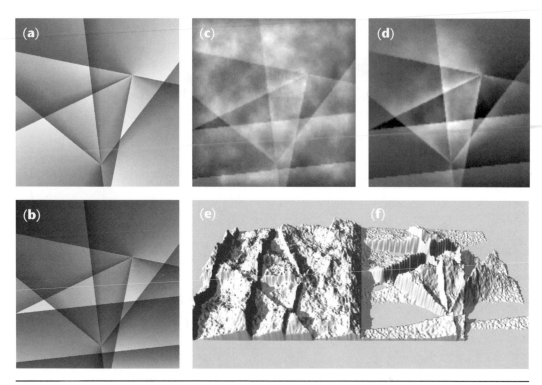

FIGURE 9–9 Faulted terrains from KPT Gradient Designer: (**a**) and (**b**) are two steps in the fault terrain process; (**c**) and (**d**) are terrain maps created from a fault terrain; (**e**) and (**f**) are the rendered terrains from the maps above.

- *Softer Sloping Jagged Terrain.* Start with the result of a previous variation. Copy the terrain, click Gaussianize, and then merge back with the pasted original to get a terrain that is higher in the middle than at the edges.
- *Rotate for Jagged Overhang.* Emphasize the jaggedness of the terrain by doing the rotating overhang trick. (I explain this later in the chapter in the "Angled Terrains" section.) Or set the terrain at an angle for the vertical rock face of a valley wall.

Obviously, a bit of experimentation is in order to exploit all the wonderful possibilities here. Figures 9–9c and 9–9d show two variations of merging faulted terrains. The rendered result of each is shown in Figures 9–9e and 9–9f.

Eroded Canyons

How are canyons created?

The Colorado Plateau, in the southwest United States, has over 30 wilderness areas set aside—either as national parks, national monuments, or national recreation areas—because of their scenic beauty. The Plateau is home to such wonders as Zion National Park, Bryce Canyon National Park, the Grand Canyon, and Canyonlands National Park. When it comes to erosion, this region's geology beckons a closer look.

Go to your library or bookstore and peruse any publications that have pictures of the American Southwest (*Arizona Highways Magazine, Islands in the Sky, Tony Hillerman Country,* Time-Life books, and so on). There are many places with fascinating land formations that are worth studying.

How did this type of land come into being? Once, the entire area was under water, depositing layer upon layer of sedimentary rock. Eventually, the water receded. That was the beginning—layers of rocks.

Then along came some source of erosion—water. Combine that with vast amounts of time, some wind, and Earth's gravity, and voilá! Layer cake geology!

How are canyons formed? At the base of the canyon is usually a river (or wash or arroyo). Depending on the hardness of the rock that the water cuts through, different types of canyons are formed. Figure 9–10 shows different types of valleys formed by erosion, depending on the hardness of rock. The darker substance is hard rock; the lighter substance is soft rock. Hard-rock valleys are narrow and V-shaped; soft-rock valleys are wide and V-shaped. Alternating layers of rock are called stair-step canyons.

SOFT ROCK

Water cutting through soft rock will make canyons that are shaped like a wide V. As the water washes away portions of the ground, higher rock breaks off and follows gravity's inexorable pull down to

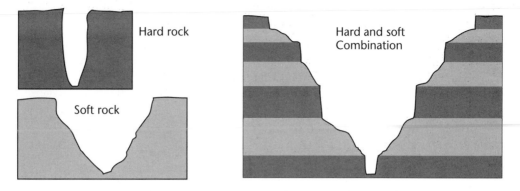

FIGURE 9–10 Three types of eroded valleys: narrow valleys from hard rock; wide valleys from soft rock; stair-step valleys from alternating layers of rock.

the water source, where it is washed away. The process continues, deepening and widening the V-shaped valley.

Making Soft-Rock Valleys in Bryce

To make Bryce have soft-rock canyons, you don't have to do much to change the default terrains. Make the canyon walls the shape that you want them using the Terrain Editor's Filtering tool. That little diagonal line is like a cutaway side view of the shape of the mountain or valley (see Chapter 7, "Terrains, Terrains, Terrains," for more details on this). Since it's already V-shaped (well, half of a V-shape), you don't have to do much else to shape it that way. To make the valley broader, stretch out the terrain using the Resize controls on the Edit Palette. The terrain from Figure 9–5b was widened to create Figure 9–11.

FIGURE 9–11 The terrain from Figure 9–5b was widened to create a soft-rock canyon.

HARD ROCK

Over time, water acts like a saw, digging a deep gulch into the rock. Canyons formed in hard rock will be deep, narrow, and V-shaped. Water cuts through just the one section of rock, but the newly exposed rock is more resistant to erosion. See Figure 9–10 for a side view diagram of this type of hard-rock valleys.

Set up your Bryce images two ways. You can try to get all of these effects with one terrain. But there will probably not be enough terrain detail once you put your camera in there. So try the second alternative. Set up multiple terrains, where each terrain is a portion of the deep gorge walls. Four terrains, two on each side, is a good start. You may want to have more if your scene calls for it.

The scene in Figure 9–12 was created to resemble that kind of canyon. The terrains are all set up sideways to represent the canyon walls. From the camera angle, you're not even able to see the canyon's rims, so no terrains are placed there.

VERTICAL CLIFFS

Vertical cliffs are formed in rock that is generally hard but has softer areas. As water cuts through an area where the softer rock is under some hard rock, the softer rock is worn away, undercutting the harder layer of rock above. The weight of the rock causes the overhanging rock to break off, thereby forming a sheer vertical surface.

Making Vertical Cliffs in Bryce

Form vertical cliffs using the Filtering tool. You can also create cliffs by putting in a vertical drop-off in the Filter. Drag the cursor so that there's a vertical drop off.

You can also exaggerate vertical cliff faces by enlarging the terrain on the *y*-axis.

STAIR-STEP CANYONS: MIX AND MATCH ROCKS

In the formation of sedimentary rock, multiple layers of different types of rock were deposited at different times under different conditions. When water cuts through more than one layer of rock,

FIGURE 9–12
Hard-rock canyon.

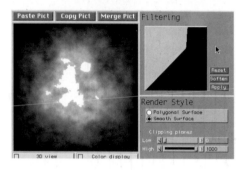

FIGURE 9–13
Forming sheer
cliffs by using
Filter in the
Terrain Editor.

each layer erodes in its own way. Where hard rock alternates with soft rock, the manner of erosion alternates as well. Hard rock erodes to form vertical cliff formations. Soft rock erodes in gentle sloping formations. The resulting series of straight cliffs interspersed with gentler slopes form a type of canyon called a "stair-step" canyon. See Figure 9–10 for a side view diagram. The most famous example of a stair-step canyon is the Grand Canyon.

To make stair-stepped terrain, use the Filtering tool in the Terrain Editor.

Figure 9–14 shows the process of creating a stair-stepped canyon. The canyon begins with a meandering river (see Fig. 9–14a). The Terrain Editor coaxed it into a broader terrain by a click on the Erode button (see Fig. 9–14b). After the basic shape was created, the terrain was inverted. Then the terrain was stair-stepped by an apply on the Filtering control (see Fig. 9–14c) to result in the terrain map shown in Figure 9–14d. With materials and haze, Figure 9–14e is the rendered result.

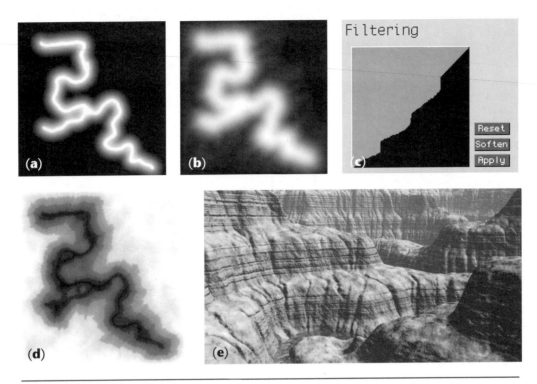

FIGURE 9–14 Creating a stair-step canyon: (**a**) Beginning with a meandering river; (**b**) using Erode to broaden terrain using the Terrain Editor; (**c**) stair-step Filtering on the inverted terrain; (**d**) resulting terrain map; (**e**) final rendered canyon.

VOLCANOES

Earlier, I discussed volcanoes as one way new mountains are born. That was the beginning of the mountain's life. Later, after time and erosion have worn down the volcanic combination of hard and soft rock, a different type of volcanic terrain develops. The hard and soft rock are a result of the volcanic birth. The volcano erupts, spewing material everywhere. The channel through which lava passes is called a root, or throat. Molten magma that subsided back into the throat, never erupting, is harder than the surrounding pile of volcanic debris. Over time the surrounding apron of debris from the outer volcano erodes away, leaving the now-solid core of harder rock that remained in the neck. That becomes a cylindrical high plateau or spire.

Shiprock in Arizona and other dramatic vertical rocks of the American Southwest are ancient volcano plugs. Make your own by using the Darken button and the Filtering tool in the Terrain Editor. Figure 9–15a shows a volcanic plug scene and 9–15b, the darkened, filtered terrain that created it.

Multiple Terrains

The earlier discussion of multiple terrains focused on the use of several different-sized terrains placed in different locations in order to create a sense of depth and scale in the scene. But there is also a way to use multiple terrains in close proximity with one another for a different natural effect. Portions of one terrain protrude from another to create realistic image detail. Stones scattered over a landscape, high-relief cliff faces emerging from a gradually sloping valley, rock formations that jut at an angle—all can be created by popping one terrain out of another. The element common to all is one terrain emerging from another. There are peculiarities with each, the lurid details of which I divulge in these pages.

Stones 'n Water

This first technique allows you to scatter stones across a landscape or plop them in shallow waters. The foreground of the "Fjord A4" image was created this way. Different rock elements protrude from

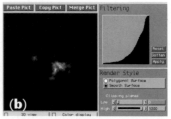

FIGURE 9–15 Volcanic plugs: (**a**) The rendered scene; (**b**) darkened, filtered terrain.

FIGURE 9–16 Side view diagram of a stone terrain poking through the main terrain.

the water. The stones are in a separate terrain positioned under the main water plane or the main terrain. (Spain has nothing to do with it, 'enry 'iggins!) The stone terrain varies in height. It is lower in most places, except, of course, where the stones pop through the top. Figure 9–16 is a side view diagram of two terrains. The stone terrain pokes through the main one.

TERRAIN STONE SHAPING

There are two things necessary to create nice boulder-like stones: The stones should have a pleasing rounded shape, and they should be distinct from one another. To create the rounded shape, your terrain map should have diffused blotches of gray. If your G2H map has points of light, you will create pointy rocks, which won't be as convincing. So, to make stones that *are* convincing, let's take one of those Bryce-to-Photoshop-and-back trips.

1. Create a terrain. In the Terrain Editor, enlarge it to at least 256, and then click Copy PICT.
2. In Photoshop, create a new document and then paste the PICT into it.

For different stony treatments, the goal is patches of flattish areas. There are some filters that are excellent for this.

3. Try Median with a setting of 5–7. Next, apply Diffuse with a Lighten apply mode. Do this a few times until you can see the diffusion action. Figure 9–17a is the result of this basic technique. More applies of the Diffuse filter results in rounder stones. Figure 9–17b shows more applies and fewer applies from left to right.

Variations on a stone theme:

■ Try other filters, such as Facet followed by Diffuse. Also, try KPT PixelBreeze (hold down the 1 and 2 keys to minimize the effect).

FIGURE 9–17 Stony median diffuse: (**a**) Basic apply of Diffuse filter; (**b**) different amounts of Diffuse filter (most, some, least).

- Use the Diffuse filter alone. Apply it repeatedly (again, using the Lighten apply mode) to get squared boulders.
- Another trick for working with an excessively noisy terrain is to use KPT Gaussian Glow to smooth it out. Gaussian Glow will retain the darker parts, that is, crevasses and canyon formations, while smoothing out the lighter parts of the terrain.

This last variation begins to address the other necessity for realistic stones—make them distinct from one another. To do that you need to introduce darker outlines around the edges of each stone. "Edge" is the operative word, as this technique uses the Find Edges (or KPT Find Edges and Invert) filter to create dark crevasses that separate each boulder.

1. Make a copy of your stony grayscale terrain and bring it into Photoshop (see Fig. 9–18a).
2. Select Filter > Stylize > Find Edges (or KPT Find Edges and Invert). The filter will darken places between elevation levels, leaving the rest white. You'll need to tweak it a bit more. Select Image > Adjust > Levels. Click the Auto button or slide the black slider over until you see more definition (see Fig. 9–18b).
3. Then apply the Blur filter (see Fig. 9–18c). You have your stone edges now.
4. Copy that and paste it over your original stony terrain image. While the pasted selection is still floating, change the mode to Multiply and the Opacity to about 40% (see Fig. 9–18d).

The areas in between stones are darker, thereby making each one "freestanding." The rendered result of this process is in Figure 9–18e.

Of course, another way to create stones is to take that ole paint-brush and put a dollop of light gray or white pixels on each place that you desire a rock to be. For the squarish boulder-like effect, pass your rocks through a Diffuse filter with a Lighten mode.

Obviously there is more than one way to create stone boulders. Consider this a starting point and don't ignore the little leanings that strike you along the way.

Angled Terrains

Not all rock formations are conveniently oriented vertically. Some rocks jut from the ground at an angle. If you rotate the terrain so

FIGURE 9–18 Using Find Edges to make stones appear "freestanding": (**a**) Original terrain; (**b**) after Find Edges; (**c**) blurred slightly; (**d**) multiplied over original terrain; (**e**) rendered result.

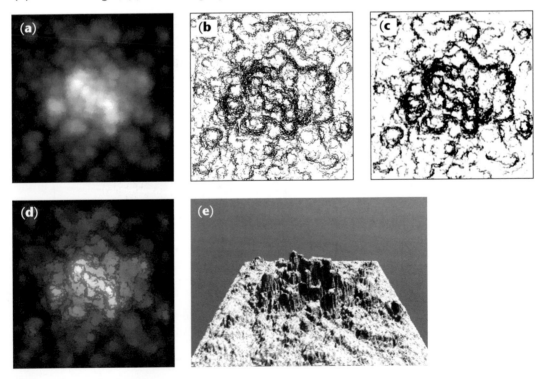

that it is at an angle, you'll get the very unreal result of the higher edge poking out from the ground. Not cute. Here's a method to get around that high edge: Create the elusive angled terrain *with overhangs*. The secret to making terrains with angled orientations is in the Edit Palette.

RECIPE FOR A TERRAIN OVERHANG

1. Create a terrain. (See Fig. 9–19a.)
2. In the Edit Palette, rotate along the z-axis so that the terrain is tilted diagonally as you look at it from the front. (See Fig. 9–19b.)
3. Then, shorten or heighten the terrain along the y-axis. (See Fig. 9–19c.)
4. Rotate back on the z-axis so that the bottom of the terrain is level again. Notice that the peaks of your mountain are all drooping toward the one side. Instant overhang! Shortening and heightening cause the terrain to lean in opposite directions. (See Fig. 9–19d.)

FIGURE 9–19 Creating an overhang: (**a**) Beginning terrain; (**b**) rotated; (**c**) shortened or heightened; (**d**) rotated back to level.

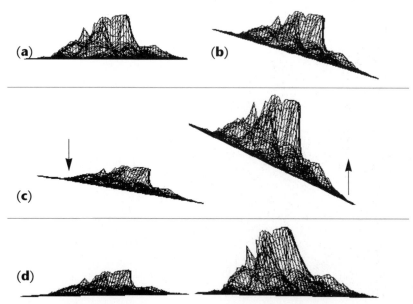

The more you rotate the terrain before changing it along the *y*-axis, the more extreme the terrain's angle will be (see Fig. 9–20). The parts of the figure are marked a, b, c, and d to match the steps from the previous recipe.

Look at angled terrains from another angle, all you Photoshop fans. Take a terrain map into Photoshop and apply the Wind filter. The resulting terrain map is lighter on one side than another (see Fig. 9–21a). This creates a leaning geological formation of another sort (see Fig. 9–21b).

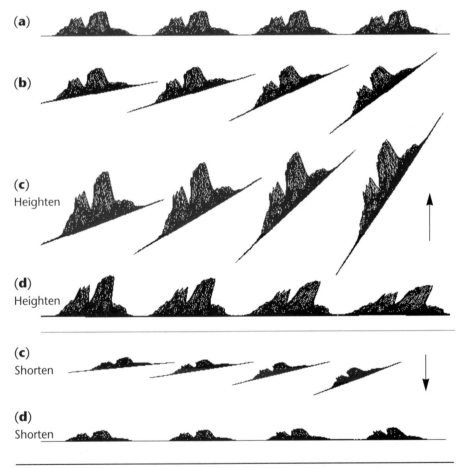

(a)

(b)

(c)
Heighten

(d)
Heighten

(c)
Shorten

(d)
Shorten

FIGURE 9–20 The more extreme the rotation, the more extreme the resulting overhang.

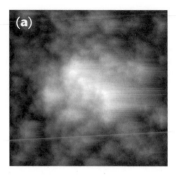

FIGURE 9–21 (**a**) Photoshop's Wind filter applied to a terrain, resulting in (**b**) an angled effect.

For the terrain's surface appearance, give the 3D Solid Texture an angled setting. Rotate the noise in the Deep Texture's Set Noise... dialog box to shift the grain to an angle.

Finally, take any of these terrains and plop them under a regular terrain for those jutting rock protrusions. See Figure 9–22.

Double Terrains for Snow and One Thing Protruding from Another

What if you want high-relief rock faces to emerge from a more gently sweeping valley below? Create this effect by using two terrains. Make each terrain distinct using your Materials setting, where sheer vertical faces have one type of treatment and gentle sloping surfaces have a different one.

FIGURE 9–22 Jutting rocks: an angled terrain placed below another terrain.

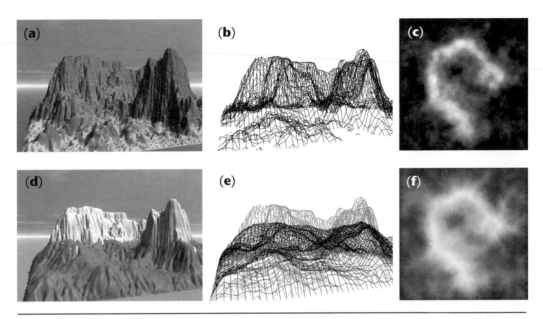

FIGURE 9–23 Sheer cliff emerging from gently sloping valley: Original terrain (**a**) rendered; (**b**) wireframe; (**c**) G2H map. Both original and smoothed terrain (**d**) rendered; (**e**) wireframe; (**f**) G2H map of smoothed terrain.

RECIPE FOR ONE MOUNTAIN SURFACE POPPING OUT OF ANOTHER

1. Create the sheer cliff terrain. Noodle with it to taste. Figure 9–23 shows the rendered terrain (a), its wireframe (b), and the G2H map (c).

2. When you are finished with that terrain, copy it and paste in place. The second terrain will become lower and more gradually sloped.

3. In the Terrain Editor, copy PICT. Then click the Erode button. If you feel the need to, merge the PICT and blend it together with the original that you so conveniently copied moments ago. Smooth and Lighten are two other processes that help make the new version better for a smoother, lower terrain. Figure 9–23f shows the altered G2H map for the second terrain.

4. Reduce the height of the second terrain along the x-axis, to taste. Figure 9–23d shows the rendered terrains. Their wireframes are shown in Figure 9–23e.

Assign the same Materials setting where Slope determines the surface. The different slopes of the different terrains result in two contrasting types of surfaces. Or choose a different setting altogether, such a snowy surface for the lower one and a rocky surface for the higher one.

Undersea Worlds

One of the disadvantages of being creatures with lungs is that we don't have the same opportunities to observe undersea landscapes as we do basic mammal-inhabiting landscapes. But don't let this stop the Jacques Cousteau fans among you from creating undersea scenes. Here are a few things to bear in mind while you create exotic waterlogged vistas.

The undersea world has two limits: the sea floor below and the water's surface above. When creating undersea worlds using Bryce, use these two objects to provide the limits of your watery world: the ground primitive becomes the sea floor, and an infinite plane becomes the surface water above. Add terrains to taste. Terrains that go above the surface of the infinite plane are all the more convincing.

Sky & Fog settings make your sea look as realistic as possible. Set them to make your undersea world cool and murky. Besides water, there are plankton, minerals, and nutrients suspended in this liquid soup! You won't give that impression if you have a crystal-clear "sky." A high Haze setting (70 or more) will give everything its briny appearance. On a clear day, you can never see forever underwater. Haze color is the predominant Sky & Fog setting that gives your sea its color. Keep your colors on the cool side: blues, greens, olives, drab browns, purples. Crank back the saturation so that they aren't so vivid, unless, of course, you're in a tropical undersea world.

Combine the haze with a complementary fog color. Fog will cling to the sea floor, so you can create a second localized murk color. Give fog a high amount and low height. You needn't keep the color aqua-cool. Sandy colors and drab olives as well as deep ultramarines will give you some intriguing sea effects.

Figure 9–24C (see the color section) shows the same sea scene using different colors. The haze and fog amounts are constant; only the colors change. Some scenes have Atmosphere turned off, so the sky—the *real* one above the water's surface—takes the cloud color.

And, just so that you don't get a case of the bends underwater in Bryce, put in some air bubbles. Give tiny spheres a highly reflective setting. (See the default Mirror material preset in the beginning of the BASIC.SHD list. If this sentence is Greek to you, then hop on over to Chapter 8, "Material World," for more information.) Stack them atop one another to run from ocean floor to surface. Realism tip: They're smaller the lower they are. The pressure of all that water diminishes as they rise toward the surface.

Creating Underwater Plant Life

To create underwater plant life for your scene, you will have to coax Bryce to grow seaweed. Use primitives and wrap plant forms around them. In Eric's "Sea Eggs" scene on the KPT Bryce CD, plants are wrapped around a cylinder. You can create a plant form by using multiple primitives, too.

Figure 9–25 shows a series of undersea plant studies. A cone was inverted and a 3D Texture applied to it with the Alpha set to Transparent so that the "plant" is mostly transparent. The underlying 3D Texture was created from cliff noise, which has "strings" going this way and that. The trick is to set the frequency and rotation so that the strings are oriented mostly vertically.

FIGURE 9–25 Underwater plant life studies: inverted cones with stringy texture and transparency.

Caves

Making caves in Bryce involves the use of two or more terrains. One is turned upside down (Flip Y) and set atop the other one.

To make a stacked terrain, create a V- or U-shaped light portion of terrain.

1. Create a terrain. In the Terrain Editor, copy it and then go to Photoshop and paste your G2H map into a new document window.
2. Use the brush in Screen mode to create a light portion, either a U-shape or a V-shape. The light portion is where the top and bottom terrains meet to enclose the open cavity.
3. Copy the altered terrain map and go back to Bryce. Open the Terrain Editor. Paste. Exit the Terrain Editor.
4. Now that you have a bottom half, make the top half of your cave. Copy the terrain and paste it in place again. Then from the Alignment menu in the Edit Palette, select Flip Z. Move the terrain up until it rests flush with the bottom half.

There it is, a cave!

After rendering it a bit, you might notice that the seam where the two terrains meet is too obvious (see Fig. 9–26a). If the terrain map has gradual slope from the point where the cave parts meet, that seam will be more noticeable (see Fig. 9–26b). Figure 9–26c shows a side view diagram of two terrains stacked atop one another. Notice the angle where they meet. It is not perpendicular. The other rendered cave, shown in Figure 9–26d, has a more abrupt drop off (see Fig. 9–26e and 9–26f). Where the two terrains meet, the seam isn't quite so contrived.

After creating the basic shell, make adjustments to your cave. One or the other terrain can be heightened or shortened (make sure that you have Center Scaling off in the Edit "!" dialog box). Take one of the terrains into Photoshop and noodle with it some so that your cave is not completely symmetrical. Create an additional terrain that will poke through the bottom (or top) for additional rocky matter. In the Terrain Editor, apply Sharpen a couple of times to

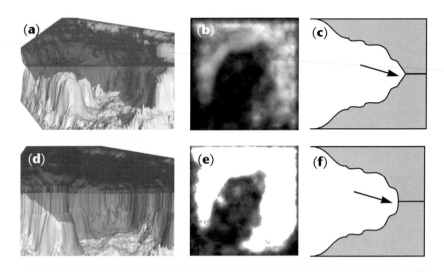

FIGURE 9–26 G2H cave series: (**a**) Cave with shallow angle; (**b**) terrain map; (**c**) side view diagram; (**d**) cave with abrupt angle; (**e**) terrain map; (**f**) side view diagram.

make a whole series of spiny protuberances. Figure 9–27 is a view out of the cave to the valley below and the mountains in the distance.

A River Runs Through It

To make a meandering river, create a terrain that is fairly flat. Copy it to the clipboard and open up Photoshop. Using the brush tool, paint a meandering path through the terrain. Remember, water doesn't usually travel in a straight line. It can, at times, but it usually meanders.

Figure 9–28a shows an image created from a Julia Set in the KPT Fractal Explorer. The wireframe is shown in Figure 9–28b and the Julia Set river source in Figure 9–28c. A Julia Set has the right S-shapes of a river. After a bit of cleanup, it was made into a terrain, where a river ran through it!

FIGURE 9–27
Looking out from
inside the cave.

FIGURE 9–28 River created from Julia Set: (**a**) Rendered image; (**b**) Top View wireframe; (**c**) Julia Set source.

For the riverbed terrain, the darker part is the river. Create a plane in the scene. Stretch it out to fill the same area as the riverbed. The plane becomes the river surface. Lower it into the river terrain.

If you've got a waterfall in your scene, then this method won't work. For a river that turns into a waterfall, you'll have to create the water surface from a terrain. A copy of the land terrain is a good place to start, as it will follow the contours of that particular area. Here's a very quick description of the waterfall terrain. A thorough recipe can be found in Chapter 7, "Terrains, Terrains, Terrains."

Make your waterfall terrain have two flat levels. The higher level is the water surface before the fall, and the lower level is the pool or river below. To fit the waterfall or a limited body of water snugly in your terrain, you'll need to clip off the unused portions of the terrain. See Figure 9–29C in the color section.

Rainy Weather

To create sheets of rain that fall from your clouds, create a plane (not an infinite plane!). Give it a material setting with a 2D PICT texture. Some of them are supplied on the CD. A nice, smudgy rain-falling image is good for that. This scene by Eric Wenger (see Fig. 9–30) uses grayscale PICT images to create rain smudges.

The PICT texture is used again as its own Opacity Map. With Alpha Transparency to cut away the excess, you have a rain smudge. This image, shown from Top View (Fig. 9–30a), shows the placement of the weather-smudge rain sheets amidst the clouds.

Save those material settings for a rainy day. On the CD is a .SHD file with the clouds, two rain smudges, and rain splatters for you to create your own storm-drenched skies.

USGS Maps G2H Information

If you want to create superlative nature imagery, how about recreating real places? Render real terrains from real places on Earth! The USGS has created DEMs (Digital Elevation Models) for the United States. They can be converted to grayscale information in order to make terrains. See Chapter 7 (which deals with terrains) and this book's CD for more information.

The Greening of Bryce

Why don't "real" trees work easily with high-quality renders? You may have noticed by now that Bryce does not have an icon for a tree in the Create Palette. For natural landscape imaging software, this seems to be an oversight. Not so. To create trees that have as

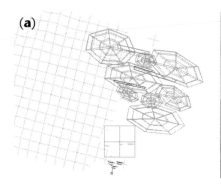

Image by Eric Wenger

FIGURE 9–30 "Rainy Day": (**a**) Top View wireframe; (**b**) rendered scene.

much depth and detail as the rest of Bryce requires the ability to model all of the different surfaces of foliage. For a tree with thousands of leaves, that is a lot of computation.

The makers of Bryce do not want to settle for some in-between method that cuts on quality. Their philosophy: Give us the best or none at all. While you may see "the best" in future versions of Bryce, for this 1.0.1 version, it's "none at all." Don't despair. There are some other ways to create trees. Here are a few methods:

- *Terrain Forest.* If you're looking at a scene faraway, you can create a terrain that has many pointy spires to emulate a forest of trees. Use the Terrain Editor's Sharpen feature. Have it poke out through the surface of another terrain for large patches of forest. The terrain map in Figure 9–31a resulted in the rendered forest shown in Figure 9–31b.

- *PICT Trees.* You can take a picture of a tree and put it on a plane and stick it in your image. Of course, you will need to be facing in the direction of the tree. Or, take the same plane and create several copies that all rotate around the common center. Figure 9–32a is a set of wireframe planes, also shown in Top View (b). The material settings show how the extraneous "nontree" is cut away using Alpha Transparency (see Fig. 9–32c) to result in a final rendered tree image (see Fig. 9–32d). Eric's "Abisko Pine Trees" uses this method.

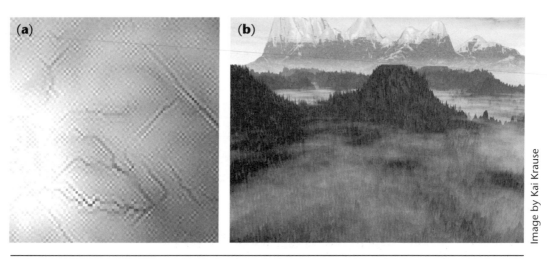

FIGURE 9–31 Forest: (**a**) Terrain map for trees; (**b**) rendered image: Four Aest.

Image by Kai Krause

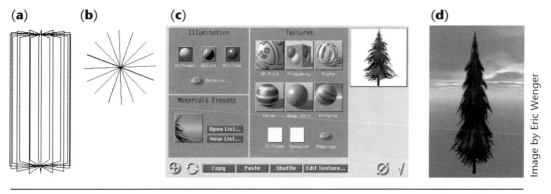

FIGURE 9–32 "Abisko Pine Trees": (**a**) and (**b**) wireframe; (**c**) material settings; (**d**) rendered tree.

Image by Eric Wenger

Other ideas for foliage—make tree trunks from terrains (with clipping) and then use planes or terrains to create foliage. For a closely grouped forest, an infinite plane could be used to create layers of branches and leaves. Or use discs or planes for individual tree branches. After you've created one, duplicate like mad to populate your scene.

The scene shown in Figure 9–33 takes a slight departure from this. It uses clipped terrains for the foliage as well. Foliage has been cre-

Image by Paul Ware

FIGURE 9–33 "Tee Time": (**a**) Terrain for leaves; (**b**) terrain for trunk; (**c**) two terrains superimposed; (**d**) final rendered image.

ated with the Terrain Editor and special PICT methods. In Paul Ware's "Tee Time," KPT PixelStorm applied to a selection has created enough of a noisy area to emulate tree foliage.

Figure 9–33a shows the terrain map for the leaves. Noise was created with KPT PixelStorm. The dark background is clipped in the Terrain Editor. Figure 9–33b shows the terrain map for the trunk. Figure 9–33c superimposes the two. Ware painted the image file in Photoshop, working in two layers that were in register with one another. Then he saved each layer as an individual PICT for importing into Bryce. Figure 9–33d shows the final rendered scene. Recognize the tree in the foreground?

Conclusion

Obviously I haven't reproduced the entire world in this chapter. What I have done, though, is to take a look at some marvelous nature scenes and analyze the manner in which they were put together. I did a bit of Geology 101 to discuss ways that land is formed in the real world and discussed particular ways in Bryce to reproduce those kinds of effects. Finally, I offered a case study of other natural phenomena that lend themselves particularly well to Brycing.

10

Multiple Object Construction

F lappity, Floppity, Flip!
The Mouse on the Möbius Strip.
The Strip Revolved,
The Mouse dissolved
In a chronodimensional skip.

Orientable planes,
Their stresses and strains—
And my story is well on its way;
An erudite thesis
On Psychokinesis—
And that will be all for today.

Frederick Winsor, two selections from *The Space Child's Mother Goose*

In This Chapter . . .

- Simple ways to make complex shapes and nonnature objects using multiple primitives and multiple terrains
- Architectural objects: castles and towers
- Circular objects, such as spiral staircases, gears, and waterwheels
- Merging scenes

Although the original purpose of Bryce was to be a landscape modeler, there is potential for far more complexity when different objects are constructed together. This chapter introduces you to some working methods for creating sophisticated models using multiple objects in Bryce.

Building Blocks

First, some term clarifications: When I talk about the creation of an object made from multiple objects, I use the term *conglomerate object.* I refrain from using the term *group,* since that term has its own meaning in Bryce. A conglomerate object can be grouped or ungrouped.

A conglomerate object is a bigger something that is created from a lot of littler somethings (a "lot" means more than one something). Each something is a building block that helps construct the greater whole.

Using Primitive Objects to Create Conglomerates

You can use Brycean primitives as building blocks to create a *conglomerate* object. There are many things in the real world that work this way, also; not all objects come prefabricated fresh from a mold.

This method is good for creating architectural objects—buildings of an unearthly or earthly sort. For example, a building is made of cube-shaped components. A tower is made of cylindrical-shaped components.

Build a Little, Duplicate a Lot

You have your simple primitive elements. Put them together so that they stack or intersect with one another. If you want a pillar, you can put a cylinder in your scene and stretch it up high. If you want something that is somewhat realistic, you can do some work at the base and the tops so that there are architecturally finished details. In Figure 10–1, the pillar's base is comprised of two spheres, a cone, and a cylinder. Figure 10–1b is the wireframe view of the conglomerate base.

Don't reinvent the wheel. Once you have built a conglomerate element, duplicate it and place it elsewhere as needed. So now that the column base is constructed, type ⌘-G-C-V (group, copy, paste).

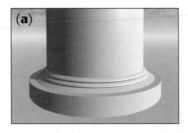 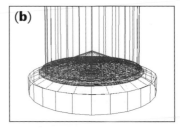

FIGURE 10-1 The base of the column: (**a**) rendered; (**b**) wire-frame, showing two spheres, a cone, and a cylinder.

Then select Flip Y from the Alignment menu on the Edit Palette to flip it upside-down. Move it to the top of the column.

Now you have one column. Group the entire column so that it acts as one unit. Duplicate that column unit to create a row of columns.

When on your duplicitous duplication spree, remember the Brycean universe grid and units of measure (Chapter 5). They're indispensable to the process of painlessly putting together a conglomerate object. Make sure to use the rotation options, nudging, center scaling, and noncenter scaling to their full advantage.

Now that you've built the set of columns, why not build an entire building around them? Figure 10–2 shows a conglomerate object comprised mainly of cubes that are flattened considerably and stacked atop one another. A flat plane makes the water surface for the little water pool. The triangular shapes that are part of the temple's face are created with the pyramid, stretched very, very wide.

FIGURE 10–2
Temple conglomerate object.

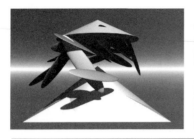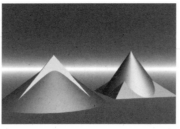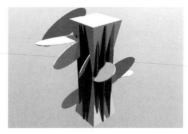

FIGURE 10–3 Abstract shapes created with different primitives.

Depending on the way primitive objects intersect, you can create objects that have a look of realism or you can create abstract sculpture-shapes (see Fig. 10–3). Create your own Brycean Sculpture Garden consisting of primitives put together in this fashion.

(Not So) Vicious Circles

Creating a spiral staircase (or anything that has multiple objects arranged in circular fashion) is very easy in Bryce, once you get the hang of it.

RECIPE FOR A SPIRAL STAIRCASE

Follow these steps to create a spiral staircase. Figure 10–4 shows the results of steps 1–3.

1. Create your initial object. In this case, make a spiral staircase that has flattened cylinders for stairsteps (see Fig. 10–4a). Make that one object the size and shape you want; once you get started, there's no going back to readjust the basic shape. (I talk about exceptions to this and ways to exploit it later in the chapter.)

2. Go to Top View. Duplicate a copy of the object and place it "above" the first one on your screen. Group them (see Fig. 10–4b).

3. Now these objects, being grouped, will move around a common center when you rotate them. Here's what to do. Copy and

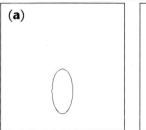
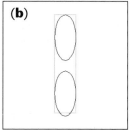
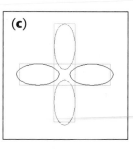

FIGURE 10–4 Stairstep-making process (Top View): **(a)** Original stairstep; **(b)** duplicated and grouped; **(c)** copied, pasted, and rotated.

paste. Then rotate. To get evenly spaced stairsteps, rotate 90° (see Fig. 10–4c).

4. Keep copying, pasting, and rotating until you have filled up the circle. Go back and add the first set of stairsteps to the selection and duplicate all four (see Fig. 10–5a). Keep pasting and then rotating until your circle is completed (see Fig. 10–5b).

5. When you have all of your stairsteps in place (it looks like a primitive flower petal image, doesn't it?), select all groups of objects and ungroup. After ungrouping, all of your individual objects should remain selected.

6. Now it's time to place each stairstep on a different elevation. Press the Shift key and click one of the stairsteps to deselect it (see Fig. 10–6a). Then press the page up key to move the rest of the stairsteps up. Press the Shift key and click the next stairstep. Press page up again. Keep doing this, deselecting a stairstep and then moving up the rest of the stairsteps. See Figure 10–6b.

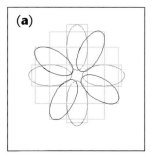
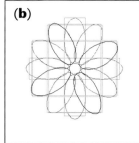

FIGURE 10–5 Completing the circle (Top View): **(a)** Placing the next four stairsteps; **(b)** placing the final four stairsteps.

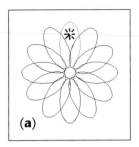

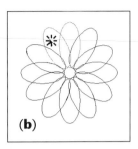

FIGURE 10–6
Different elevations:
(**a**) Deselecting a stairstep and moving the rest of the stairsteps up; (**b**) deselecting the next stairstep.

(**a**)

(**b**)

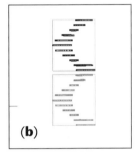

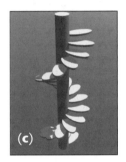

(**a**)

(**b**)

(**c**)

FIGURE 10–7 Final steps: (**a**) Each stairstep at a different elevation; (**b**) set of stairsteps duplicated and moved up; (**c**) final render.

7. Each stairstep is now on its own elevation (see Fig. 10–7a). Group the stairsteps again so that you can move them as a unit. If you need more, simply duplicate the whole group and move them up. Repeated use of the page up key will ensure the stairsteps are spaced precisely. See Figure 10–7b. Add a cylinder as a center column and render. See Figure 10–7c.

8. If you need more (or less) height to the stairsteps, you can adjust their heights while they're grouped. The height of the individual stairsteps will also be affected. To adjust individual stairstep height, ungroup and use the Resize Y control.

GEAR VARIATION ON SPIRAL STAIRSTEPS

Here's a variation on spiral stairsteps. Make gears! Instead of flat stair objects, make these uprights. Cubes are good for this.

The "create, copy-paste-move, group, copy-paste-rotate" process is the same. Of course, you don't elevate each gear to a different level. (Or do you? I leave that to your discretion!)

This alternative theme of gears uses the Rotate controls in the Edit Palette:

1. Create a set of gears. Ungroup them. Copy and paste. Move the new set up using the page up key (you will be trying some variations, so you need to start from the same starting place for each variation). If you want, when you do the duplication, change each group to a different color (Object Options dialog box, ⌘-K) for easy selection later. Create three sets of gears (see Fig. 10–8a).

2. When you ungroup a set of gears, each individual gear can be moved on its center. Select one set of ungrouped gears. Switch to Top View. Rotate along the *y*-axis. This causes the gears to be set at an angle (see Fig. 10–8b). This uniform rotation works only on the *y*-axis.

3. For more fun, try the *x*- and *z*-axes rotation. Select another set of gears, making sure the objects aren't grouped. Now Rotate X. You get a result that looks like some strange möbius strip or a series of monoliths from 2001. Figure 10–8c shows rendered sets of gears rotated on the *x*-, *y*-, and *z*-axes.

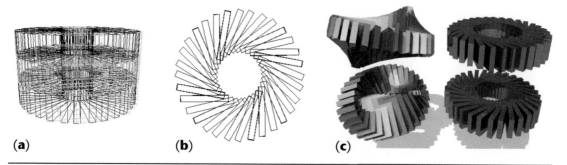

(a)   **(b)**   **(c)**

FIGURE 10–8 Gear rotation: (**a**) Wireframe view of three sets of gears; (**b**) Top View of gear set rotated on the *y*-axis; (**c**) set of rendered gears that have been rotated on the *x*-, *y*-, and *z*-axes.

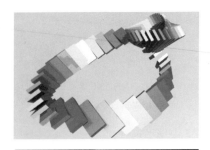

FIGURE 10–9 Group-enlarge-ungroup-reduce to make a conglomerate object occupy a larger area of space.

FIGURE 10–10 A well built by duplication.

GROUP-CHANGE-UNGROUP-CHANGE

The group-change-ungroup-change sequence is very powerful for certain manipulations in Bryce. At any time, you can have the same formation occupy a larger area. You don't necessarily have to enlarge the individual objects. First, group the objects. Enlarge *the group* uniformly. Ungroup and then reduce *each object* uniformly. Enlarging as a group expands the overall area; reducing brings each object back down to size. Simple, isn't it? Figure 10–9 shows the result. The larger set started at the size of the smaller set. It was grouped and then enlarged; ungrouped and then reduced.

START WITH SMALL PRIMITIVES AND BUILD UP FROM THERE

If you have something with repeating elements, you have to painstakingly build only one set of them. From there, you can duplicate. Figure 10–10 shows a well made from a circle of bricks. It won't hold water in its current state, but it does illustrate another multiple-object construction principle. After the first circle of bricks was made, they were copied, pasted, and moved up. At that point, the group of bricks was rotated slightly on the *y*-axis in order to stagger the bricks. Once the two sets were created, both were copied, pasted, and moved up as a unit to build the well.

Model Management

When you are working on a conglomerate object scene, there are a couple of ways you can keep track of the model as you build it. The first is to save documents progressively. For the temple, say, you could save first the pillar file and then, after the temple is built, the temple file, which incorporates the pillars as well. The pillar scene can be part of a library of resources to use in other scenes.

Another approach to model management is to create different scenes for each conglomerate object and then merge the scenes later. This is a variation on the previous method. It is geared more toward conglomerate objects that don't depend on one another as a temple depends on pillars. Some specific examples of this follow later in the chapter.

If you plan to merge your conglomerate objects with other conglomerate objects into one master scene that has all the objects, don't build any extra objects into the individual Scene documents. When you merge scenes, all objects (including grounds) will be imported into the new scene. You don't need several grounds or other extraneous objects in your final scene.

Castle Building

Figure 10–11 shows a sample scene that has many individual elements. The castle was constructed of several primitives. For square building parts, cubes were used, with a pyramid for a roof of a large square tower. For the walls, cubes again were used. One is stretched long and thin for the courtyard walls, with a series of small cubes atop the main wall for the checkerboard thingies.

For the towers, cylinders with cone roofs were used. The castle has two types of towers—those that originate from the ground and those that originate from the side of a larger building. The latter have spheres at their bases, with a tiny cylinder to finish off the building edge. The sloped roofs are also cubes, rotated and enlarged on the y-axis.

(a) 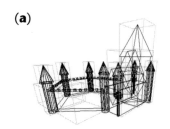 **(b)** 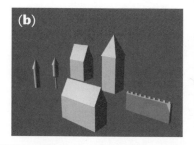 **(c)**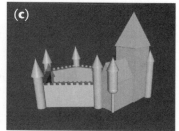

FIGURE 10–11 A castle constructed entirely from primitives: (**a**) The wireframe view; (**b**) different segments of the castle; (**c**) a render of the constructed castle.

Terrain Moldings

If you want to get fancier with the construction of your model, include terrains as a part of your conglomerate object. The terrain does not function as a mountainous surface but as a component for a conglomerate object. A grayscale-to-height map, combined with terrain clipping, gives you two powerful features for creating unusually shaped objects.

Figure 10–12a shows two towers created using the standard primitives. One tower uses an inverted cone to make the transition between the two cylinders. The other tower uses a terrain. The terrain wireframe is more complex than the inverted cone (see Fig. 10–12b). The terrain adds some additional detail to create architectural interest.

The terrain cone began as an Adobe Illustrator document. In Illustrator, the black cutouts were constructed in a circular shape. The PostScript document was subsequently rasterized in Photoshop and a gradient applied so that the terrain would be shaped as a cone. Figure 10–12c shows the terrain map. The area outside the circle was clipped, so it does not show in the scene. (For more information on how to create this and other wild and crazy terrains, see Chapter 7, where I discuss the Terrain Editor.) The terrain was placed carefully in between the two cylinders.

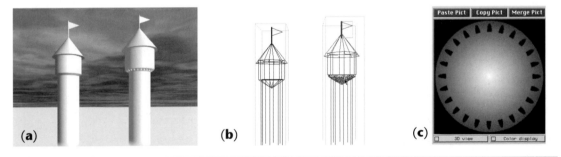

FIGURE 10–12 Two tower versions: (**a**) Rendered towers; (**b**) tower wireframes; (**c**) the grayscale-to-height map of the terrain used in the one tower.

More Terrain Multiplicity

The truck in Figure 10–13 was created in Bryce and is an outstanding example of what can be done with grayscale-to-height maps. The figure includes several wireframe views of the scene if only to convince you that this was indeed generated using terrains. Notice the enormous amount of detail in this model. There are a mere 174 objects and a paltry 94 terrains. (It's safe to say that this was not created on a Macintosh with 8 MB RAM!) Many of the different elements were created in Adobe Illustrator and imported into Bryce via Photoshop.

Merging Scenes

So, you've created this splendid conglomerate object. It's in this document over here. And over there, in another document, is another exquisite conglomerate. You want to put them together. For extremely simple objects, you can copy an object (or several objects) from one scene and then open another scene and paste those objects. But Bryce gives you another option—merge scenes.

Art by Jackson Ting and Robert Bailey, ArtEffect

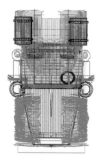

FIGURE 10–13 Tractor-trailer truck constructed in Bryce from terrains and primitives: 174 objects total and 94 terrains.

Merging in Theory

What happens when you merge scenes? Here's the theory behind merging. You already have a scene open. This is the host scene, as it will invite another scene (the guest) within. The invitation is extended via the Merge Scene... command. All objects from the guest scene are brought into the host scene in the same position they previously occupied. For example, a terrain at world center scene in the guest scene comes into the host scene at world center. However, sky, camera, and render settings of the guest scene stay behind; those of the host scene prevail.

Merging in Practice

What happens when you merge scenes in practice? By this, I do not mean to imply practice deviates from theory, as in "do as I say, not as I do." But here is the sequence of events you'll discover when merging:

1. To bring one or more scenes together, use the Merge Scene... command in the File menu. If your current (host) scene has not been saved after you have manipulated some objects, Bryce asks you if you want to save your scene. If you do save, you are presented with a dialog box in which to change the name of the scene, if you want. Click OK to save the scene.

2. You are immediately presented with what seems to be the same dialog box as in step 1. It's not. It's an OPEN dialog box. Bryce is asking you which document to open, that is, which guest is being invited into the merge. Select the guest scene and click OK.

3. Bryce merges the scenes. All objects from the guest scene come in selected (red wireframes). You may want to group objects if they are not already grouped. You may want to deselect or move them. You may want to change all items to one color. But host and guest are both together now in one scene.

eMERGEncies

Sometimes when you are merging scenes, strange things happen. After merging one or more times, you may notice that when you click an object, it won't be selected. Or, you may select all and then click away from any object to deselect all, but some wayward object stays selected. This is a minor eMERGEncy in Bryce. The uncooperative object probably came in as a grouped object. To select and fix the object, do this:

1. Select all, then individually deselect all other objects by shift-clicking. (Yes, I know, this is a pain, but it will save that precious scene!) The one remaining selected is your wayward group.

2. Ungroup (⌘-U). Group again.

Now it should work.

If it is *really* stubborn, then select the object, ungroup, cut, and then paste again. It will come back in right where it was before. Pasting fixes this. In fact, this is the "method of last resort" to fix *any* object that is acting strangely. At times objects disappear—that is, they won't render. Cutting and pasting will bring them back into the land of the living again.

This merge problem is in KPT Bryce versions 1.0 and 1.0.1. It should be fixed in later versions.

Other Strange and Fanciful Examples

In this section, I present three images that were created from conglomerate objects: "Water Works" (featured in Fig. 10–16); "ChromeScape," by Brian Patrick Mucha (shown in Fig. 10–17C); and a space station by Eric Wenger, creator of Bryce (see Fig. 10–18).

"Water Works"

"Water Works" consists of two different composite images: a log cabin and a water wheel. Next I explain how these two were constructed.

LOG CABIN

The log cabin was created primarily from cylinders. First a cylinder was created and reduced proportionally to one-fourth size. Then

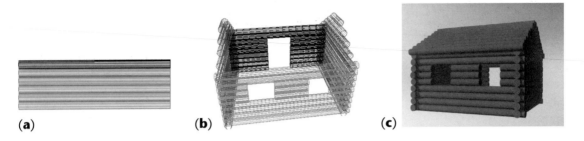

(a)   **(b)**   **(c)**

FIGURE 10–14 (a) A log cabin created from elongated cylinders stacked on top of one another; **(b)** wireframe view of the cabin prior to the roof-raising party; **(c)** the rendered image.

it was enlarged on the *y*-axis and rotated so that the long part was on the ground and it could conceivably roll away.

Since the width was that magic nudge size, a series of copy-paste-nudges stacked a set of logs atop one another (see Fig. 10–14a).

When there were enough logs to form a wall, they were all selected and duplicated. The duplicate wall was moved over to form the opposite side. Then, to form a perpendicular wall, the wall was duplicated again. This new wall was shortened by reducing along the proper axis. Then it was rotated 90°. Finally it was duplicated one last time to create the last wall. Where the walls joined at each corner, they overlapped slightly. To take off the edge of perfection, individual logs were option-nudged slightly in different directions.

The cabin had four walls. To create a doorway, one set of logs was shortened, duplicated, and then dragged to the other end of the wall. For windows, the shorten-duplicate-move process was used to make three sets of logs with two sets of gaps. See Figure 10–14b.

The original log cabin had a log roof (see Fig. 10–14c). But later, for the Water Works image, the roof was traded in for one of those fancy corrugated models, courtesy of the Terrain Editor. (The new roof was a bargain. Plus it's lighter and more water resistant.)

THE WATER WHEEL

The water wheel is a variation of the spiral staircase/gears motif. With the exception of the rod around which it rotates, the water wheel is constructed entirely from cubes.

To create the spoke, the first cube was stretched high, copied, and nudged three or four steps over to form the other side. Then another copy was reshaped to be the wide paddle portion and positioned between the two long "spokes." That set of three cubes was grouped, moved up to the opposite side of the wheel, and then flipped on the y-axis (see Fig. 10–15a).

The top and bottom spoke-and-paddle assembly was grouped, and then the process of copy-paste-rotate completed the circle of paddles.

Next a brace was added toward the outside edge of the wheel and duplicated to the opposite side. The two braces were grouped and then copy-paste-rotated several times to add braces all around the wheel. Finally, a little adjustment ensured that they fit snug and the wheel was structurally sound. See Figures 10–15b and 10–15c.

To create the final scene, the two images were merged. A cylinder was created to act as the wheel's axle, and terrains created to complete the scene. See Figure 10–16.

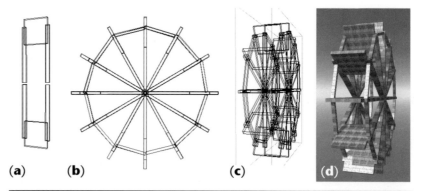

(a)   (b)   (c)   (d)

FIGURE 10–15 **(a)** The first set of spokes for the water wheel paddle; **(b)** and **(c)** cross braces added to complete the basic wheel model, shown in Side View **(b)** and oblique view **(c)**; **(d)** the rendered wheel.

FIGURE 10–16 The final image, with cabin and wheel merged and placed in a natural setting.

"ChromeScape"

"ChromeScape," by Brian Patrick Mucha, is a masterpiece of conglomerate object construction. (See Fig. 10–17C in the color section.) It is a smart combination of primitives and terrains that results in a surprising image.

The series of trees on a long flat metal dock is another example of the power of the process of creating a conglomerate object and duplicating it many times. If you haven't gotten the idea yet, this image underscores it yet again. Create one small section, group it, and then duplicate it to your heart's content. The trees are composed of cones, spheres, and cylinders. Notice the finishing details of the cones used at the very base of the tree's trunk, as well as the sphere connecting piece for the low branches.

In Figure 10–18, the detailed Side View study of the dragonfly shows how it too is created from the same primitives: cones,

FIGURE 10–18 Side View detail of the dragonfly.

spheres, and cylinders. Slight rotation of each segment of the dragonfly's body gives a subtle curve overall.

Terrains are also used in this scene, although not in their typical rough-mountain fashion. The stylized lily pads are created from terrains. The other two large vertical structures also are terrains.

Eric's Space Station

This space station by Eric Wenger also demonstrates the use of spheres, cones, and cylinders to create a fanciful image. Figure 10–19a highlights the cylinders, and Figure 10–19b highlights the cones used to create the space station. It is another example of the ingenious manner of putting primitives together so that the whole is greater than the sum of its parts.

Be sure to take a look at the Scene documents for this chapter on the CD. Also, wander through the gallery of work done by others. There are plenty more examples of conglomerate object constuction in Bryce.

Original model by Eric Wenger

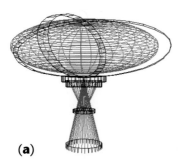
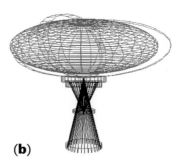

(a) **(b)** **(c)**

FIGURE 10–19 A space station composed of spheres, cylinders, and cones: (**a**) Cylinder objects highlighted; (**b**) cone objects highlighted; (**c**) the final rendered image.

Conclusion

In this chapter, I took you through the process of using primitives as "building blocks" to create conglomerate objects. Duplication and precise movement are possible in square or circular shapes. A small cluster of objects can be grouped and duplicated to be part of a larger group of objects. Terrains can be used to create shapes that are part of the conglomerate objects.

11

Brycing Out of This World

A Follower of Goddard
And a rising Astrogator
Were agreed that superthermics
Was a spatial hot pertater.

They reached a Super-Nova
On a bicycle named Beta
And I'd tell you more about it
But they fused with all the data.

Frederick Winsor, *The Space Child's Mother Goose*

In This Chapter . . .

- Outer space images—planetary and ringed planets
- Lunar spheres in Brycean skies
- Abstract Brycean images
- More suggestions for using 2D PICT textures
- Using Bryce with other 3D applications

In this chapter, I offer a sampler of other things to do in Bryce besides your basic normal, Brycean landscape. It's for the out-of-this-world landscape. It's for abstract images and other cool effects that don't fit into the "nature imagery" category.

Bryce Star Galactica

Although Bryce's original purpose was to make outdoor scenery, with a click here on the Render Palette and a drag there on the Sky & Fog Palette, you can have instant outer space for out-of-this-world Brycescapes.

Recipe for Space Scenes

In this recipe, I walk you through creating space scenes. You'll make a multi-sphere planet world and a planet with rings.

For space scenes to be convincing, your planets must live inside a hostile environment, one that's devoid of atmosphere. That's easy enough to arrange, as follows:

1. In the Render Palette, click the Atmosphere option to uncheck it. Return to the Sky & Fog Palette and set your space color in the Clouds color swatch. Black or extremely deep colors are good.
2. For Fog & Haze, you have a few options. Switch them off for "deep space." Or use them judiciously to create some additional color. If you do include haze, you will need to position your objects and camera angle so that you miss the horizon. Aim the camera up somewhat. Then choose a nice dark, rich color for haze, just to add a sense of mystery. Likewise, with fog, take the *height* all the way to maximum and make the *amount* rather small. Choose a deep color for the fog and watch it mix with the haze.

Create your planets with sphere primitives. Your planet system can be as easy as *one-two-three:*

One is a solitary sphere, the planet itself, devoid of atmosphere.

Two is a planet with rings, where the second sphere is larger, yet squooshed to be nearly flat.

Three is a planet with atmospheric conditions—the planet sphere, the cloud layer sphere, and the diffuse atmosphere layer sphere.

SOLITARY SPHERE

I'll talk first about the settings for the planets and then discuss the two- and three-sphere systems.

Start with your initial sphere, your planet. Now, "make it so!" via the Materials Editor, as follows:

- Effects: Set to either default or the Additive/Blur.
- Alpha: Off (unless you have a watery reflective world, in which case, make it reflective).
- Illumination Details: Ambient off. Lots of Diffuse and some Specular. Your planet is not self-illuminating; it is lit by the major stellar light source. Reflectivity and Transmitivity off (if your planet has water on it that is somewhat reflective and your Alpha is set for reflection, then set Reflection low for greater realism).
- Bump Gain: By all means, put a bit of bump gain in there! Keep it subtle, though, because by the time you get into outer space, the elevation difference between Death Valley and Mount Everest appears negligible.
- Color: Default.

TWO-SPHERE PLANET—SATURN RINGS

Now that you have your first sphere, your planet, duplicate it (or create another sphere) to make your rings. Enlarge it using Proportional Resize so that it extends considerably beyond the planet itself. Then reduce it along the *y* axis to flatten it. Rotate it to a jaunty angle. Next, you need to create some type of ring pattern on it. Parts will be transparent and other parts will be "ring-y." For this, you need an alpha channel arrangement of some sort in order to create transparency. There are two ways to use Alpha Transparency in the Materials Editor: with a 2D PICT and with a 3D Solid Texture.

2D PICT Texture

To create an alpha channel, you need to make a mask for transparency. You can create a color layer to color the rings—or not—but you definitely need an Opacity Mask. Use the KPT Gradient Designer to make this.

To make a 2D PICT and mask is doable. However, you'll find that there's too much going back and forth—from the application you use to create the mask, to Bryce, to the object, back for more refinements of the image, and so on. You'll also need to set your PICT resolution high enough so that the rings aren't affected by anti-aliasing at the curved edges.

However, I prefer using the second method—3D Solid Texture—because you can perfect your planet rings without ever leaving Bryce.

3D Solid Texture

Scroll through the presets to find the one with the stripey yellow lines (Fig. 11–1a). (Or, on the CD, find the shader file called SATURN RING SERIES.SHD.) Figure 11–1b shows an example of using this preset.

This preset is a good starting place to get you where you want to go because it already has stripes and Alpha Transparency to cut out the other half of the stripes. When applied to the flattened sphere, it makes a good start for rings. With a few adjustments and some noodling, you'll have your rings. I won't go into the specifics of the noodling here because it is one of the tutorial examples for modifying an existing preset that is presented as one of the last recipes in Chapter 8, "Material World."

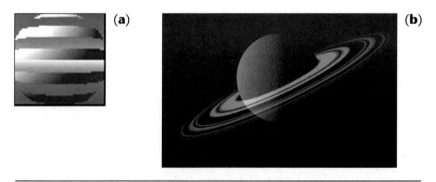

(a) (b)

FIGURE 11–1 Planet rings: (**a**) Stripey yellow Materials Preset; (**b**) planet rings created from that preset.

THREE-SPHERE PLANET—PLANET CLOUDS AND ATMOSPHERE

This planet and atmosphere world comprises three spheres, one set inside the other: the planet proper, a cloud layer atop the planet, and a fuzzy atmospheric layer. To ensure the spheres are in alignment as you create them, have Center Scaling (Edit Palette's "!" dialog box) *on*. Then do the following:

1. Starting with your basic planet, copy once and paste twice. You now have three spheres (even though it appears that you have one).
2. Using the Tab key or the arrow on the Edit Palette, select only one sphere and make it slightly smaller using Proportional Resize. Hold down the Option key for greater precision. This sphere will be the planet's surface. So that you can tell easily which sphere is which, give this innermost sphere its own wireframe color.
3. Select another sphere and enlarge it using Proportional Resize. Give it a unique wireframe color. This sphere will be your atmosphere layer.

Figure 11–2 shows (a) wireframes and (b) resulting render of a three-sphere planet.

You now have three spheres. The first, whose color and size you did not change, is your cloud layer. Inside that is your actual planet.

(a) 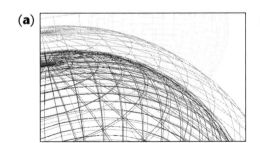   **(b)**

Image by Eric Wenger

FIGURE 11–2 Three-sphere planet world: (**a**) Wireframes for the planet, cloud layer, and atmosphere layer; (**b**) rendered image.

Outside both of those is your outer atmospheric sphere. (If you forgot to put Center Scaling *on*, you can switch it on later, select all three spheres, and in the Alignment menu, choose Align All.)

Now, what about the material settings for each? All of your spheres have a planet Materials setting (assuming you created one following the previous steps). Now you need to change the settings for the outer two spheres to cloud and fuzzy atmosphere, respectively.

Clouds

The cloud layer sits just outside of the planet's edges. The 3D Solid Texture called Atmosphere (in the textures list on the right side of the Materials Editor) is a good one for providing clouds. So are any of the other cloudy ones (Sirrus, Cumulus, Low Smogg, Turbo-Cloud).

- Effects: Default.
- Alpha: Transparent. Look at the planet underneath the cloud layer.
- Color: None. Specular and Diffuse colors to white (or another color if you want to have your clouds be a strange alien world color).
- Illumination: Diffuse lots, Specular some, and Ambient none (clouds don't show up when you're in shadow).

Atmosphere

This is the little extra glowing part, where the atmosphere extends beyond the planet's surface.

- Effects: Fuzzy Additive (the edge of the atmosphere is not crisply defined and the atmosphere glows).
- Texture: None.
- Color: Choose a color for your atmosphere.
- Illumination: High Diffuse, low Ambient, Specular to taste.
- Transmitivity: Some, depending on how strong an atmosphere you want.

Add some space effects in one or more infinite planes for stars and intergalactic phenomena. Then render.

"Clair De Lune"

If you don't want to be in outer space, then you can put a little "luna-tic" fringe in your scene and have partial or multiple moons. In this section, I discuss lunar (and planetary, if you desire) phenomena in Brycean skies when viewed through an atmosphere. Bryce's own moon is always directly opposite the sun. But if you put a moon or other planet somewhere else, it will reflect the sun's light, even as Earth's own moon does when it's in other phases.

MATERIALS SETTINGS AND THE "MOON LIGHTING"

A partial moon in Bryce is made from a combination of Effects and Illumination settings in the Materials Editor. Forget any notion about what revolves around what or what rotates and what doesn't. In Bryce, it doesn't matter. What does matter is the relationship between the location of the light source and the location of the lunar object, as well as the lunar object's material settings.

- Effects: Additive/No Blur. The only part of the sphere that is visible is the part that is directly lit. (This depends, in part, on Illumination, discussed next.) If your sphere is "in front" of another object (say, a terrain), the shaded part of the sphere will cut through that other object and all you'll see is the sky behind.
- Illumination: Diffuse only; no Ambient, no Specular. (Any Ambient light will add a slight glow to the shadowed part of the sphere. If you use it, do so sparingly.) Adjust the strength of Diffuse light depending on the circumstances. The higher the setting, the stronger the appearance of the lunar surface in the sky. Stay away from specular light, too, since it will create a central hot spot on the lunar surface. Figure 11–3 shows a series of moons that have different Diffuse light settings.
- Texture: 3D Solid Texture for bump mapping and overall patterning.
- Color: To make your moon a uniform color, set the Color control to None. Then choose the color from the Diffuse color swatch. If you want to see lunar surface details, then set the color filter to Diffuse-Ambient (the default). Light and dark variations will appear.

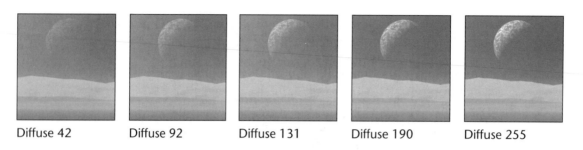

| Diffuse 42 | Diffuse 92 | Diffuse 131 | Diffuse 190 | Diffuse 255 |

FIGURE 11–3 Lunar surfaces with different Diffuse settings.

■ Bump Gain: Put a little dent in your moon. You don't need much to get the feeling for lunar dimension. Too much will make it look as though the moon is too small and too close.

Your partial moon can be in Bryce's sky during day or night (as set by the Illumination control on the Sky & Fog Palette). When viewing the moon by night, keep in mind the following: If you are going to have Bryce's moon light up your sphere-moon, then remember that the illumination position is opposite at night. You will need a higher Diffuse setting.

When you are in "night" mode and turn Atmosphere off, you will not be able to light the lunar surface from Bryce's "moon" light source. You'll get a fainter projection from the sun on the opposite side of the Bryce sky dome.

Ring Around the Moon

When you look at Earth's moon through high hazy moisture, there's a ring around it. The fuzzy outer atmosphere from the three-sphere planet works to create this effect. Make the sphere significantly larger than the moon. Be careful with the Haze settings for this kind of scene. Moderate haze will show more of the shaded surface and the atmosphere, resulting in a too-artificial effect. See Figure 11–4.

Making a Full Moon Elsewhere at Night

To create a moon that is large, imposing, and glowing, one that dominates your scene, use a separate sphere. Do all that has been

FIGURE 11–4
A ring around the moon made with an atmosphere sphere and a slight haze.

mentioned here previously but crank up Ambient to make the moon self-illuminating.

Strange Terrain-Based Images

In the terrain chapter (Chapter 7), I discussed how to set up a scene for an image-as-terrain. The possibilities here are endless.

Now I give a few examples and talk about the integrated approach to doing this. Using the Opacity Map as a means for creating a bump map, you can give different looks to your terrain image.

"Necrofelinia"

The image in Figure 11–5C (see color section), by Phil Clevenger, is a prime example of how strange PICT terrains can be. The original cat image was filtered with Xaos Terrazzo to get the kaleidoscope effect. It was then brought into the Terrain Editor, where it was blurred, then inverted, and eroded a bit. The inverted erosion created the veiny bumps and ridges. It was then inverted back. In the Materials Editor, the color image was applied to the terrain, with Illumination settings being high Diffuse, medium Ambient, and low Specular.

The camera angle swoops down from above. There is no atmosphere and the "cloud" color is black. A generous layer of black fog is the final touch to make this the killer kitty with the macabre meow.

PICT Terrain Chrome

What can be done with the Materials Editor's Alpha control using the Opacity Map of the PICT terrain? For your run-of-the-mill "slap a PICT on a square and cut out the background using an Opacity Map," you'll have a high-contrast Opacity Map that has black and white. However, when using an Opacity Map that has gray values (see Fig. 11–6a), the outcome is not quite so simple. When it contains grays, you run the risk of generating mesh patterns and other artifacts (see Fig. 11–6c). When you have the same image in the Opacity Map as in the PICT image, Alpha Transparency is probably not your best bet. However, the Materials Editor's other Alpha control, Alpha Reflection, is very powerful when used with PICT terrains. Where the Opacity Map is white, the texture is reflective. To make this highly polished chrome, Reflectivity was adjusted to maximum (see Fig. 11–6d). (When Bryce sets the Alpha control to Reflective, the Reflectivity setting in the Illumination Details dialog box is automatically adjusted to a half-way point. You can increase or decrease this as you see fit and it will affect *only* the area that is masked by the Opacity Map.) As the Opacity Map adjusts from black to white, the texture makes a transition from a titanium-looking metal to chrome.

(a) Opacity Map

(b) Alpha: "None"   **(c)** Alpha: Translucency   **(d)** Alpha: Reflectivity

FIGURE 11–6 PICT terrain created using a fractal image: **(a)** The Opacity Map is a variation of the terrain gray map; **(b)** no Alpha effect; **(c)** Alpha set to Transparent; **(d)** Alpha set to Reflective.

GlockenFondue

The GlockenFondue series in Figure 11–7C (see color insert) shows some additional ways to manipulate a PICT terrain using the Opacity Map. There are two sets of variations. The Alpha Reflective effect is changed further by adjusting the Illumination and Color controls. Also, the Opacity Map information can be used to determine the bump gain on the object's texture. Modifying these different controls will result in a variety of metallic looks.

The original image of the clock parts, courtesy of PhotoDisc, is the basis of the terrain, 2D PICT texture and Opacity Map. It is the photograph of the clock's metal gears and so it has metallic colors. The image works well as a terrain when it is smoothed slightly. In the first set of variations, the Opacity Map uses the fine-engraved detail to emphasize the object's shape when applied as bump gain. Figure 11–7C shows two sets of the same image with and without bump gain so that you can see the type of effect it has. Make sure to experiment with bump gain for your PICT terrains.

The other Opacity Map variation is Alpha Reflection. One set of images has Reflectivity adjusted near maximum, the other set has none. In this case, Alpha Reflection is interacting with another couple of settings in the Materials Editor— Color and Illumination. The GlockenFondue images all have a dulled appearance although Specular illumination is set to maximum. Instead of the usual bright hot spot that comes from Bryce's default Color setting, the dulled appearance results from the Color control begin set to Specular Diffuse. When the Color control is set this way, Specular light conveys the texture color—the color of the image—as it bounces off the object. So the metallic appearance is softened. In the two images with Alpha Reflection, portions of the object reflect in a subdued manner. A sheen is added to the object, but it's a muted sheen. Rather than a brash chrome reflection, the result is subtle.

For an object that began with metallic coloring, these treatments result in an unusual metallic appearance. The CD has additional

GlockenFondue images which explore the result of different settings in the Materials Editor.

In other PICT terrain images where the image itself has no metallic elements, the same technique will make a pleasing pewtery look. Again, there is Alpha Reflection without any specular hot spots in this alternative treatment of the original kitty image (the same source used in Phil Clevenger's "Necrofelinia"). (See Fig. 11–8C in the color insert.) The kitty image is used for the terrain, as well as the PICT Texture and the Opacity Map. The Bump Gain is set for maximum, thereby resulting in additional surface texture details. The Color control is set to show color in the Diffuse and Specular lighting channels. At the same time, the Alpha control is set to Reflective, and Illumination's reflectivity is set high. So there are reflective areas, but instead of being shiny, the specular area shows only color. In this case, it's white. The result is a soft, pewter-like, brushed metal surface.

Quick 'n Dirty Opacity Map Editing

When you need to work on your Opacity Map, and you're feeling lazy—you don't want to leave Bryce to go to a different application —try a copy-paste shuffle between the Materials Editor and the Terrain Editor. The Terrain Editor is, after all, a very specialized image editing tool.

1. Copy from the Opacity Map in the PICT list. Exit PICT Editor/Materials Editor.
2. Open up Terrain Editor. Paste PICT. Do your stuff. (I like to use the filter for quick blurring and to change the contrast of my Opacity Map.)
3. Copy PICT. Cancel (yes, *cancel!*) out of the Terrain Editor to leave your terrain unchanged. Now you have what you need in the clipboard!
4. Hop back to the PICT Editor (you can do this through Objects > 2D PICT Textures...), get to your Opacity Map, and paste your newly edited Opacity Map.

The lovely chrome edge strip in Figure 11–6c is the result of combining Zero Edges with a subsequent blur in the Texture Editor.

For that matter, when you want only an Opacity Map, you need *something* in the picture area as a placeholder. The Terrain Editor is perfect for this. Use the filter to make all values white (drag along the entire top of the filter), copy the "terrain," and paste it in the PICT Editor's *image* area. Then go back and create whatever Opacity Map you'd like and paste it behind the white image.

Abstracts

You can create abstract images with Bryce. Start from scratch to make something that is neither landscape nor object model, but merely interesting shape and lighting and surface. Or you may be working with some scene and may decide that you'd like to render just this one area over here.

The Zoom to Selection command is good for this. In Render mode, drag a marquee around the area that interests you. Select Zoom to Selection from the View pop-up menu. Begin rendering again to create that abstract image. Figure 11–9 shows a couple of abstract images. Reflectoglobemania uses an abstract KPT Gradient Designer-generated terrain and Jell-O is a study in cylinders and Illumination settings. There are plenty more samples on the CD.

(a)

(b)

FIGURE 11–9 (a) Reflectoglobemania and (b) Jell-O.

Sci-Fi

Bryce lends itself well to the creation of science-fiction worlds. Figure 11–10C, "Remotely Cuboid" by Robert Hurt, is an excellent example (see color section). (Many more examples of Brycean sci-fi are on the CD.)

2D PICT Image Textures

2D PICT image textures for Bryce objects can be used in a variety of ways. Of course, the most startling application is the insertion of a PICT image so that you can place photographic elements inside your Bryce world. The same thing applies to images created in 3D applications. I discuss other 3D applications and Bryce in a bit. First, though, I discuss some nice abstract and experimental uses for 2D PICT textures and the types of images that can be created with them.

Use simple shapes for 2D PICT textures. The images in Figures 11–11C through 11–13, by Richard Vanderlippe, demonstrate the powerful use of simple 2D PICT shapes in Bryce imagery. "Mirror Dot Polka" (Fig. 11–11C, color section) uses a simple circle. Alpha Translucency creates freestanding dots and overall Reflectivity changes them into mirrors. This next scene, which was adapted from one of Vanderlippe's scenes, has interlocking rings. Spheres are placed together so that they overlap and then are alternately rotated (see Fig. 11–12a). The interlocking rings (see Fig. 11–12b) are created with a PICT Texture of a simple horizontal bar (see Fig. 11–12c).

Finally, Figure 11–13 shows one more application of PICT texture that I find particularly charming. A basic spiral (same PICT and opacity, see Fig. 11–13a) is applied to a sphere using the Mapping option of Front Projection. The spheres were elongated and then rotated so that what was facing front is now facing up. Setting Alpha in the Materials Editor to Transparency cut away the extraneous image. Maximum ambient and diffuse illumination made these spirals glow. (See Fig. 11–13b.)

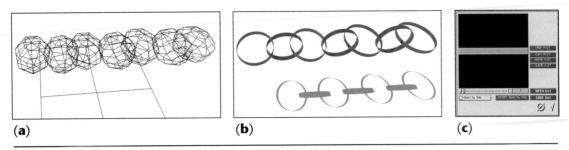

(a) **(b)** **(c)**

FIGURE 11–12 Interlocking rings: (**a**) Overlapping spheres; (**b**) rendered rings; (**c**) PICT texture with horizontal bar.

Image by Richard W. Vanderlippe

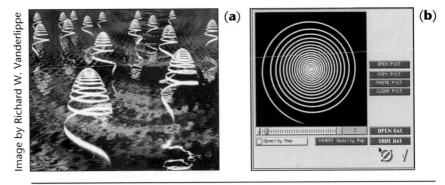

(a) **(b)**

FIGURE 11–13 Spirals: (**a**) The spiral PICT texture; (**b**) rendered image.

2D PICT Texture Hints

The object you are importing into Bryce through the 2D PICT Texture can be a photograph or an image created with a 3D rendering application. When working with importing PICTs for image elements, be aware of the following:

■ *Lighting.* The lighting in Bryce needs to match the lighting in your photograph. In the Paul Kuehn Sphinx image (see Fig. 8–21C in the color section), the lighting conditions were created based on the Sphinx photograph. Colors were taken from the imported image and assigned to the texture of the Bryce terrains in the scene. Of course, if you are working with objects modeled and rendered in another 3D application, then you can make the lighting in the 3D application match Bryce's.

Image by Michael Pilla

FIGURE 11–14 Scene in which the photograph's windowpanes are replaced with Bryce windowpanes so that the floating pencils reflect in the window.

- *Shadows.* Your PICT object will cast shadows, which, of course, helps to maintain the illusion that it's a three-dimensional entity. However, beware of the shadows from other elements in your scene that might fall on the object. If they do, they will betray the fact that the object is flat, thereby ruining your beautiful illusion of full, three-dimensional depth.
- *Reflection.* If you want to create realistic reflections, you may need to mix Bryce elements with PICT elements. The image in Figure 11–14, by Michael Pilla, has a PICT image of French doors with Brycean "glass panes." Pilla used an Opacity Map to remove the photograph's glass panes. He then created his own glass in Bryce using Square primitives so that *all* objects in the scene would reflect from the glass surface.

Bryce and Three-Dimensional Models

Just like photographic elements that have been composited, models generated by other 3D applications can be brought into Bryce. There are three options for bringing the images together:

1. Render the model in the 3D application, then import the image as a 2D PICT Texture to render within Bryce.
2. Render the Bryce scene and the third-dimensional scene separately and use an image editing application to composite them.

All currently available 3D applications will render masks along with the model, for ease in selecting and compositing.

3. Render the Bryce scene and bring it into another 3D application.

My discussion of photographic PICT importing covered the basics of the first option. The second is demonstrated in Figure 11–15C (see color insert). The two images there, by Dave Teich, are Bryce renders and three-dimensional models composited together in Photoshop.

For "Robots at Sunset" (Fig. 11–15C, part a), Teich created the backdrop for the scene in Bryce. He then modeled the robots in Form·Z and rendered them in ElectricImage. He placed peach and lavender light sources on either side of his models to match the sky's color in the Bryce image and also positioned a white parallel spotlight directly in front of the robots. ElectricImage rendered them as one image with masks. Due to the large file size of the ElectricImage render, he composited the two in Photoshop, adding an air-brushed shadow. ("Robots at Sunset" was done back in the 1.0 days with the 512×512 PICT size limitation.)

"Impact Images," commissioned by a service bureau, was developed according to the same general technique (see Fig. 11–15C, part b). Teich created a Bryce scene, with a sphere moon, fog, and an infinite plane for wispy fog effects. The three-dimensional models, the airbrushing eye, printer, and camera were modeled in Form·Z and rendered in ElectricImage. Unlike the robots image, each one was modeled and rendered individually. The text was rendered in perspective with the scene. Everything was composited together in Photoshop. To place the text behind the terrain, Teich rendered the terrain as a mask.

The third option is a flip side to importing images of three-dimensional renders into Bryce: exporting Bryce landscape renders to other three-dimensional applications. Bryce makes environments; those other applications can import images as an environmental map.

Michael Murdock of Pixar used a 360° panorama Bryce image (see Fig. 11–16a) to create a reflection map that was placed inside a scene generated by Pixar Showplace (see Fig. 11–16b). Pixar RenderMan, the rendering engine, is not a ray-tracer; therefore it renders much

Images by Michael E. Murdock, Pixar 1995

FIGURE 11–16 (**a**) Bryce 360° image used as a reflection map inside (**b**) Pixar RenderMan image.

faster. However, for objects to have reflections, those reflections must be created in reflection maps. The reflection picture is mapped spherically in a latitude-longitude map. All of the spheres reflect the Bryce 360° render, but they do not reflect one another.

Animations

Bryce 1.0/1.0.1 was never meant to be an instrument for animation. However, where there's a will, there's a way. Set a few zealous souls loose, and they'll devise the means to generate movies from Bryce images. It's an arduous, painstaking adventure, where each animation is composed of many scenes. The camera position changes incrementally frame by frame, er, um, scene by scene. Rodney L'Ongnion, Victor vonSalza, and Ben Day have made great strides in animation, complete with ingenious ways of using spreadsheet applications to calculate all the in-between camera positions. They have generously volunteered tips and sample movies, which you can see on the CD. So if you've got a hankering to follow the Animation Muse, check it out.

Rest assured, the high-end version of Bryce is slated to include a far easier way to animate Bryce. None of this frame-by-frame stuff; SuperBryce will have a highly intuitive method to fly through BryceLand.

Conclusion

In this chapter, I roamed all about the place, starting way out in outer space to discuss how to make different kinds of planets. Drawing closer to the home world, I discussed lunar phenomena. I then followed with a brief overview of a series of abstract images mixed with a tad of science fiction. A deeper look at PICT terrains came next in order to see more of what can be done with fanciful terrains. Next I turned to other PICT-uresque images, ranging from Bryce and photos to Bryce and 3D applications. Finally, I mentioned animation, oh, so briefly.

12

Render Unto Bryce

As the conductor waved his arms, he molded the air like handfuls of soft clay, and the musicians carefully followed his every direction.

"What are they playing?" asked Tock, looking up inquisitively at Alec.

"The sunset, of course. They play it every evening, about this time."

. . . The conductor let his arms fall limply at this sides and stood quite still as darkness claimed the forest.

"That was a very beautiful sunset," said Milo, walking to the podium.

"It should be," was the reply; "we've been practicing since the world began." And, reaching down, the speaker picked Milo off the ground and set him on the music stand. "I am Chroma the Great," he continued, gesturing broadly with his hands, "conductor of color, maestro of pigment, and director of the entire spectrum."

"Do you play all day long?" asked Milo when he had introduced himself.

"Ah yes, all day, every day. . . . I rest only at night, and even then *they* play on."

"What would happen if you stopped?" asked Milo, who didn't quite believe that color happened that way.

"See for yourself," roared Chroma, and he raised both hands high over his head. Immediately the instruments that were playing stopped, and at once all color vanished. The world looked like an enormous coloring book that had never been used. Everything appeared in simple black outlines, and it looked as if someone with a set of paints the size of a house and a brush as wide could stay happily occupied for years. Then Chroma lowered his arms. The instruments began again and the color returned.

Norton Juster, *The Phantom Tollbooth*

Everything I've talked about in earlier chapters—objects, terrains, materials, and sky and fog—culminates in rendering, the creation of a two-dimensional PICT image of the scene. Here, I take a deeper look at what goes on during rendering.

The Basic Rendering Model

First, I'll review ray-tracing. After all, when an image is rendering, what's actually taking place is ray-tracing. Then I delve deeper into some of the mechanics of and techniques for rendering. For an image to render, Bryce shoots a ray into the scene for each pixel. What is rendered depends on what is or isn't struck by the ray. When the ray doesn't intersect an object, it renders sky. When it does intersect an object, it bounces off of the object. Then, depending on the surface features of the object, it bounces elsewhere until it finds the light source(s) that contribute to that object's color. From that it determines one final color for the pixel. Of course, the area that Bryce considers a "pixel" changes with each progressive rendering pass. Recall that in the first pass, Bryce determines a color for an area that is actually 32×32 pixels. The second pass covers a 16×16 area, the third pass an 8×8, and so on until every single pixel has been rendered. The final anti-aliasing pass shoots nine rays to determine a color for one pixel (in those areas of high contrast), averaging together all the information to come up with a color for that one pixel.

If there are 16 objects in a scene, then Bryce must test for 16 objects for each ray that goes out in your Bryce world. Each ray "knows" how many objects are out there. It will "ask," "Did I hit 1? Did I hit 2? Did I hit 3? Did I hit 4?" and so on. The more objects in your scene, the more "tests" it performs to see if it struck any of them. The more tests, the slower the render. This happens for each ray that is shot out. The same 16 questions are asked each time. There are no shortcuts.

But what if there were some way to reduce the number of objects that Bryce has to test for at any one time? You could speed up your render time. Well, there is! You can do this by grouping objects.

Grouping Objects to Save Render Time

Consider a ray that is shot out into the scene that has 16 objects. However, objects 1, 2, 3, and 4 are in one group (group A) and objects 7, 8, 9, and 10 are in another group (group B). The ray then will "ask" its questions like this: "Well, objects 1, 2, 3, and 4 are a group, group A. Did I hit that group? Did I hit 5? 6? 7? . . . well, 7, 8, 9 and 10 form group B, so did I hit group B? Did I hit 11? 12?" and so on.

You can see that here Bryce must ask fewer questions for each ray that is shot into the scene. When it asks, "Did I hit (anything in) group A?" the answer is either no or maybe. A maybe answer results if it struck the bounding cube for the group. At that point, it will ask, "Did I hit 1? 2? 3? 4?"

If the area of the bounding rectangle is limited, then the ray must ask only the additional level of questions a few times in comparison to all the times it would ask about 1, 2, 3, and 4 for the rest of the rays shot into the scene. Although you may lose a bit of speed when the ray must ask about the specifics of the group, you gain speed by its not having to ask about the specifics of that group everywhere else.

This process also works in deeper levels. Instead of a ray's hitting a group of 10 objects and asking, "Did I hit 1? 2? 3? 4? 5? 6? 7? 8? 9? 10?" you can form groups of the group of 10. In this case, the ray would ask, "Did I hit sub-group A? Sub-group B? Sub-group C?"

Here, 10 objects are segmented into three questions. The specifics are asked only when a ray hits a group that has the specific objects. Fewer questions are asked overall, and so the scene renders faster.

When objects are grouped and groups are grouped (nested groups), Bryce is asking after only a few objects at a time. Rather than a scene with, say, 80 objects, Bryce is confronted with a choice about 8 objects or fewer.

SETTING UP GROUPS FOR BETTER RENDERING

There are three points to keep in mind when grouping objects for efficient rendering: group objects that are close to each other, make each group distinct from its neighbors, and create nested groups. All three of these strategies depend on the camera position.

Group Close Objects

Make sure the objects you group are close to one another. A grouped box that stretches clear from one side of the scene to another has more "in-between" area than it has actual objects. In this case, Bryce won't gain in render time because any time a ray hits the group (including all that in-between area), the ray must ask whether it hit any of the objects that are part of the group. The more between area, the more wasted render time, since so many of those additional queries are for naught. When objects are close to one another, you have more object area than in-between area. The more object area, the more efficient the render. The additional queries about the group elicit more positive responses. Of course, what is object area and what is in-between area will change depending on the camera angle. If you change the camera angle, you may need to ungroup and regroup to keep objects close.

Make Groups Distinct

By making each group distinct from its neighbors, you will gain in render time. When two groups overlap, Bryce asks about all of the contents of both groups. If the two groups overlap in "thin air," then all that extra query was for nothing. Overlapping groups is unavoidable in some cases, but be aware of this point so that you can keep overlapping groups to a minimum. Again, camera angle determines what overlaps and what doesn't.

Group (Nest) Groups

Nesting groups within other groups increases efficiency. Avoiding overlap in the grouped groups is even better. Figure 12–1a shows a rendered scene of 20 objects. In Figure 12–1b, those objects are shown in their groups. When the ray tracer first looks at the scene, it asks if it hit any of the five objects or grouped sets of objects (see Fig. 12–1c). When the ray strikes group A in Figure 12–1d, it asks if it hit the two subgroups. When it finds that it has struck one of the subgroups, it then asks if it has hit the specific contents (see Fig. 12–1e). Instead of asking about all 20 objects at a time, it first asks about five and then two somethings and then the three specific

FIGURE 12–1 Rendering group strategy: (**a**) The rendered scene; (**b**) objects in groups; (**c**) what the ray first sees; (**d**) group of two subgroups; (**e**) objects in one of the subgroups; (**f**) where the groups overlap.

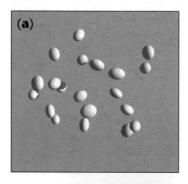
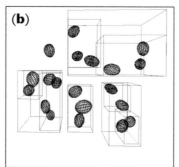
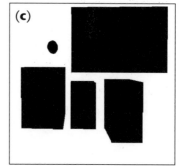
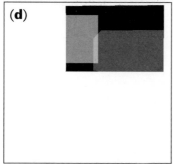
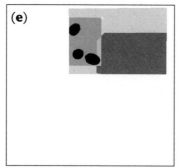
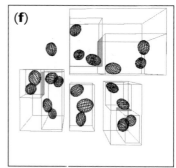

objects. Where the groups overlap (see Fig. 12–1f), there is ineffi-
ciency, since Bryce tests for all of the objects of both groups without any constructive result. But in comparison to the overall time
savings, the inefficiencies are negligible. A change in camera angle
will probably change whether there is overlap.

Grouped Objects and Rendering—Clipping

An additional note about groups: When objects are grouped, Bryce
treats the group as one object. A group is now an object whose
edges *are* the bounding box. Incidentally, this is why you will select
the group when you click anywhere inside the group's bounding
box. Contrast a group's behavior to that of selecting a single object
that is displayed as a box: If you click in the box where the box *is*
but the object *is not*, the object won't be selected.

Once a set of objects is grouped, Bryce treats them as a whole when
rendering. Sure, it renders each individual item, but there's something about those rays intersecting that bounding box that changes
the nature of the objects within. There's a potential drawback here,
however. If a tiny portion of an item happens to fall outside the
limits of the box, as viewed from a certain angle, it gets clipped off.
Figure 12–2 shows how this works. The ray strikes just outside the
box. It asks, "Did I hit anything in this group?" It is not asking
about *that object*; it is asking about the group. The answer, since it

---

FIGURE 12–2 (a) Wireframe view; **(b)** rendered view showing
part of a sphere cut off because it is outside of the bounding box.

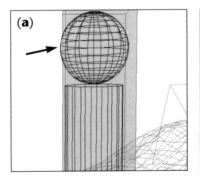
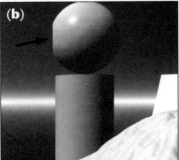

didn't strike the group's bounding cube, is no ("I didn't hit the box"). It gets around to asking about the individual object only when it does strike the group. So when those little portions of an object poke outside the confines of the bounding box, they are not rendered. They're part of a group but not entirely inside the group. Those tiny innocent little portions go to Ray-Trace Limbo.

This happens most often with a rounded object, such as a disc, cone, or sphere, when the edges of the bounding box are nearly aligned with the camera's line of sight. See Figure 12–2. A tiny portion of the round object pokes out of the bounds of the box. It happens more often when your wireframe resolution is lower. Bryce developers are aware of this problem, and it should be fixed in KPT Bryce versions later than 1.0.1. In the meantime, you can get around it by ungrouping that set of objects and rendering. Or you can set your wireframe to a higher static resolution before grouping.

"While You Are Working" Rendering

Of course, in Bryce you don't simply build a scene, place objects hither and thither, and assign Materials and Sky settings without also doing many intermediate, "am I on the right track," renders along the way. Here are a couple of global tips for those intermediate renders while your scene creation is "in progress."

RENDERING "IN PROGRESS"—EARLIER STAGES

To get a better sense of overall image detail, zoom out while in PICT mode (click the Minus Sphere or type ⌘-minus) and then begin rendering your scene. Those first few passes will give you a general sense of the image. Reducing the image's size onscreen increases the apparent resolution, so you can get a better idea after one or two passes how the image is developing.

RENDERING "IN PROGRESS"—LATER STAGES

This render technique is good for the later stages of scene building, when you're doing some serious fine-tuning. You have done at least one initial render and you come back to the scene the next day or after your lunch hour or . . . .

Suppose you have a scene and PICT saved. From a previous working session, you open up the image and decide it needs further tinkering. After tweaking it here and there and doing little test renders for each tweak, what do you have? Many subtle changes displayed in a fine mess of coarse pixels. What if you want to get a quick look at the changes—against a completely rendered background—before you leave your computer to complete its rendering work in peace?

Use the "Open PICT..." command to go back to your original PICT. Think of this move as a partial revert to saved. With it, you revert to the saved PICT image but retain all the intermediate changes you made to your Scene document when you were having that fruitful dialog with the Bryce Muse. (Of course, if you saved your Scene document along the way, it might not be as dramatic when you go to re-render over the old PICT image.) After you open your original PICT image, simply drag a marquee around the area you want to render and then select Clear and Render. The rest of the image stays. You can clearly see the changes you made. Your Scene document underneath keeps the changes.

You can render on top of *any* PICT, even if it's not an image created with Bryce. If you're looking for a new experimental medium for creating rendered abstractions, open any PICT file, drag a marquee around an area, and render. The Abstract Muse will tell you what to do next.

When you save the scene (and your Preferences are set to open and save PICT with scene), Bryce will write the new PICT over the old PICT. Say you have open a Scene document called ORIGINAL SCENE. The accompanying PICT document is called ORIGINAL SCENE.P. Then you open a PICT from a variation on this scene that is named SECOND SCENE.P. Opening a subsequent PICT closes the first one. You render over portions of the new PICT to see changes made since you worked in SECOND SCENE and SECOND SCENE.P. When you save the scene (⌘-S), then this new rendered PICT will be renamed ORIGINAL SCENE.P. The Scene document that is open takes precedence in the writing and naming of the accompanying PICT document.

This technique of opening older PICTs is good for seeing changes in a scene's placement, size, materials, position, and sky. It is not as successful for seeing changes in camera position, since everything in your scene will have changed.

"When You Are Finished" Rendering

You have finished working with your scene. Now it's time for the final render.

For your final render, ensure you start from scratch. On the Render Palette, click Render Scene (see Fig. 12–3). Or, when you are in PICT mode, select all and then select Clear & Render. You can select Clear and Render from the Edit menu by clicking the Clear and Render button on the Render Palette or by using the keyboard shortcut, ⌘-H.

Why do either of these? In all likelihood, you made minor changes since the first tentative pixels were rendered at the beginning of your session. Perhaps you moved the camera slightly or changed the orientation of the 2D Projection plane. If you just click Resume Render (or type ⌘-R), you will not completely overwrite the older rendered portion. In fact, the finished render will have ghosts of the old render.

It all comes down to what's in that fourth channel of the PICT. Figure 12–4a shows a progressive render, and Figure 12–4b shows the fourth channel, where Bryce keeps track of the render's progress. The fourth channel has different patterns for each stage of the render. A scene that has not been rendered is black, and a scene rendered through six passes is white. So when Bryce looks at the

FIGURE 12–3 The Render Palette.

(**a**)

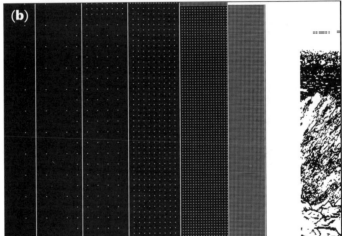

(**b**)

fourth channel, it might say, "Yes, well, but that's been done already" and so overlook an area for the next couple of passes. That portion that's been "done already" may not be the most recent revision of the scene. The PICT's fourth channel remembers where the render left off, but it doesn't check to make sure that what it calls "rendered already" is, in fact, the *latest* version of the scene. That's for *you* to do. And it's easy enough to do by clicking that big Render Scene button on the Render Palette.

If you do not start a render from scratch, when things come down to the last 1 × 1 pixel pass and the anti-aliasing pass, there will be

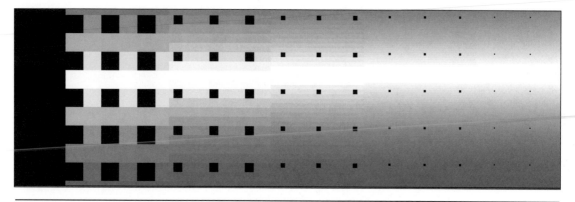

FIGURE 12–5 Rendering over an old image. As the render progresses, the old black sky never completely disappears.

tiny rows of pixels in an orderly formation, but they won't fit in with the remainder of your image. Not cute. Figure 12–5 is an image that has been rendered over an old image. The original image had a black sky (see left edge of image). The new sky, with haze and horizon, was rendered on top of the black sky in progressive steps. With each subsequent pass, more of the new sky shows, but even after the final anti-alias (see right edge of image), the old black sky is faintly visible.

Rendering on Both Platforms

If you happen to have computers of both persuasions—68K Macintosh and Power Macintosh—keep your rendering on one platform or the other. KPT Bryce version 1.0.1 is fat binary, so you *can* take scenes created on one platform to the other for rendering. However, although both the 68K and the Power Mac start up with that familiar little "happy Mac" icon and Apple has done its best to make the transition from one to the other as smooth as possible, the little processor beastie inside the Power Mac is a different species altogether from that inside the 68K. Bryce happens to be an application that accentuates the differences. As a result, you'll experience hiccups and differences in haze and atmosphere between platforms. So, for best results keep your scenes on one machine or the other.

While writing this book and rendering hundreds of test images, I began on a 68K Mac and later brought a Power Mac into the process. I had plenty of opportunity to transfer images back and forth. As a result, I discovered several cross-platform gremlins, listed next. They all show up in the render stage, which is why I include discussion of them in this chapter.

■ Altitude and haze will give you problems (these are more fully discussed in Chapter 6, "Skies and Light"). Most of these will be fixed in KPT Bryce versions later than 1.0.1.

■ A 68K-created pyramid primitive renders on the Power Mac as an extremely extended, flattened cube. If you are going to move the scene permanently from 68K to Power Mac, then do this:

  1. Create a Power Mac pyramid and position it on top of the 68K pyramid.
  2. Select the 68K pyramid and copy the material setting in the Materials Editor.
  3. Select the Power Mac pyramid and paste the material setting.
  4. Ditch the 68K pyramid and then render.

  If your scene has many many pyramids in it, I extend to you my deepest sympathies and encourage you to leave your 68K machine in peace during the time it will take for it to render that scene.

■ A scene created on a 68K with 1.0.1, brought over to the Power Mac for rendering, and enlarged in size will sometimes lose the bump information in the higher-resolution rendering. (Keep that slower Mac busy doing the larger render. You'll get all the information you designed into the scene—eventually.)

■ A scene with only a sky in it (no objects) will not save properly on a Power Mac. (The PICT will, however.) You'll get an out-of-memory message. Create an object and tuck it out of sight; you'll magically have enough memory. Go figure. This one too should be fixed in KPT Bryce versions after 1.0.1.

Batch Rendering

One of the joys of Bryce is its ability to do batch rendering. It works through the Macintosh Finder's Drag and Drop feature. Drag the Scene icons (*not* the PICT icons) and drop them onto the KPT Bryce Application icon. You can also use aliases to do this. I keep a KPT Bryce application alias on the desktop and drag all of my Scene icons onto it.

Of course, batch rendering, like other complete renders, should be started from scratch to ensure there are no weird anomalies left over from previous work sessions. Before you save your scenes for the last time prior to rendering, hit the Render Scene button and let 'er go for a couple of passes. Then include the scene as part of your batch.

If you're on a 68K, you don't need to do anything particular in the Preferences dialog box (⌘-P) for batch render. The Power Mac, however, is more finicky. Here you want to set Preferences with Expert mode *on* and Launch Preferences set to New Document. On both platforms, you can begin a batch render either by launching Bryce or after it is already running.

When batch rendering, Bryce opens a scene, renders it, saves it, and then moves on to the next one on the list. Of the selected scenes that are dropped onto the Bryce Application icon, how do you know which one will render first? That depends on how the scenes are listed in the Finder. If you select View by Date, then the most recent scene will render first, followed by the next most recent scene, and so on. If you select View by Size, the largest scene file will render first, followed by the next largest, and so on. View by Name scenes will render in alphabetical order, as will View by Kind scenes, in the latter case because all Scene documents are the same kind. Scenes that are labeled (such as Essential or Hot) will render according to the label pecking order. So if you want to ensure one scene renders before another (just in case you need to interrupt the render mid-batch), arrange the labels accordingly so that the high-priority scene is labeled "Essential," while the other ones are "Project 2" or "None."

Beyond the Basic Rendering Model

Everything I've discussed so far fits into the category of basic rendering—how Bryce operates during rendering and how you can make your trips to RenderLand more pleasant. In this section, I depart from the basic. First, I discuss rendering large images. Then I consider each of the other render options available on the Render Palette: 360° Panorama and rendering for post-processing using Distance Render and Mask Render.

Rendering Large Images

How large can you make your Bryce images? In non-Expert mode, you are limited in size to the number of pixels on your monitor or the largest default size (Photo: 768 × 512), whichever is larger. Bryce senses the number of pixels you have on your display and doesn't allow you to set the size any higher. But the size differs from monitor to monitor. A Macintosh with an Apple 13-inch monitor can set your Bryce image resolution up to 640 × 480 pixels. A Macintosh with a 17-inch monitor can go up to 832 × 624 pixels. And one with a 20- or 21-inch monitor can go up to 1024 × 768 or 1152 × 870 in the non-Expert mode. When you change to Expert Mode, the maximum size you can render is limited by available memory.

There are two ways to enlarge the size beyond the standard sizes. In the User Custom... dialog box, you can set a custom size that is bigger. Or in the "!" dialog box on the Render Palette, you can proportionately enlarge an existing size to one of the available ratios: 1:1.5, 1:2, or 1:3. You can combine both these, too. If you want to take your image up to 1:4, then see what the number of pixels are if you enlarge the image to 1:2. Take those numbers and enter them into the User Custom... dialog box. Double them again by increasing the resolution to 1:2. (If you run into any memory ceilings, you will be told along the way that Bryce won't participate to your liking.) Larger renders, however, require Expert mode.

Here are some image resolution and memory considerations to keep in mind. Bryce will limit your maximum image size according to the amount of memory available. If you have chosen a size larger than what Bryce will be able to accommodate, you will get the alert "Not enough memory, revert to default format!" Your custom size image will then be reduced to one of those listed in the Render Size popup menu. Changing the resolution will, in turn, change your 2D Projection plane, as Bryce does its "best guess" at fitting everything to the new size. So your old image may be shot. Therefore do as the wise and cautious do: Before making a drastic change in size, save your scene. If all "not-enough-memory-revert-to-default" hell breaks loose, you can simply revert to saved and then try again using a less ambitious image size.

If your scene is wider than 2047 pixels, Bryce may freeze during renders or, when you go to save, will refuse to save the PICT. To fix this, change your scene to a vertical format and rotate the camera by 90°. So if your old scene has 2100 × 1387 pixels, swap the dimensions so that 2100 is the height. Double-click on either of the Camera Crosses or the Trackball. Change the setting for z to 900°. Render. (When you take the image to an image editing application, you can rotate it back.)

When you're rendering large format scenes (ones that take 12 to 24 or more hours to render), saving the scene from time to time is a good precaution. Then if a thunderstorm winks your electricity off and sends that big beautiful render to file heaven, you'll at least have the rendered image data from the last time you saved the render.

Now that I've told you to take the precaution of stopping your render periodically to save your scene, I need to add a further admonition. Interrupting a large render to save wreaks havoc with Bryce's memory allocation. Simply resuming rendering may result in a Type 11 system error. When you interrupt to save your scene, quit Bryce and then relaunch it.

360° Rendering

To render the entire panorama encircled by the camera position, select 360° render. Whatever your current image size is, the 360°

---

tip

A large-render troubleshooting tip: Even while taking these precautions, you may get a Type 11 error. If this happens during the anti-aliasing pass and the render hangs in the same spot, perform a bit of alpha channel surgery. Using Photoshop, delete the bottom few rows of black pixels from the fourth channel. If there was something there that caused the render to hang, it's gone now. This technique was used to complete the anti-aliasing pass on this book's cover image.

(a)

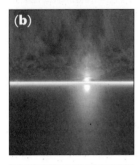

(b)

FIGURE 12–6
(a) Wide and
(b) squished pano-
ramas.

panorama will be squished into that space. And "squished" is an accurate word, especially if your image format is nearly square. See Figure 12–6. A 360° panorama is better for very wide images.

Another critical point is to ensure your camera is level. An unlevel camera causes your horizon to undulate like a sine wave, as shown in Figure 12–7.

Ensure your horizon is level by double-clicking the View crosses on the Main Palette to access the Camera dialog box. There, the Camera Angle value of x and z should be 0. (Remember, there are 3600 units in a complete circle, so multiply whatever angle setting you want by 10, that is, 90° is 900, 180° is 1800, and so on.) For a 360° panorama that takes in what's below and above as well as both horizons, enter 900 for either the x or the z-axis.

To have convincing image detail close to the camera and larger ter-rains far off (see Fig. 12–8a), set up a whole series of small terrains very close to the camera. In fact, make sure that a terrain is placed *under* the camera. It needs, of course, to be a higher-resolution terrain. Figure 12–8b shows the Top View of the scene with terrains on all sides of the camera.

Because you are creating a panorama that goes in a complete circle, you need to look at your scene from different perspectives as you set it up. Do that with the Add View As... pop-up menu. Add dif-

FIGURE 12–7 A wavy horizon resulting from an unlevel camera.

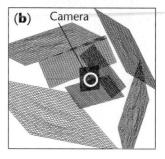

FIGURE 12–8 A 360° render where land surrounds the camera: (**a**) 360° render; (**b**) Top View of wireframe.

ferent perspective views so that you can move back and forth between them. Or go to Top View and move the camera position (the needle end, not the box "base" of the camera!). Then switch back to Main View and save.

Or enter the numbers in the Camera dialog box. Note that if you want to position your camera at world center, then set the offsets for x and z to 0 (y refers to how far off the ground the camera is. A negative value sets the camera above ground. The Camera Angle y points your camera to the four directions: 900, 1800, 2700, and 0 (or 3600). Enter those numbers and save a view for each. You can work with developing your scene that way. In the end, you panorama will incorporate those views.

Here's another way to preview the placement of objects in a panorama: Use the Perspective Trackball. Press the Control key and then drag the Trackball. The camera will be constrained along the x-axis and rotate in a circle. You can check for object positioning in wireframe view.

The Zoom and Focale controls have no bearing on 360° rendered scenes. Your placement of the camera in the 2D Projection plane, however, does affect the way the final render appears.

Rendering Post-Processing

Besides Basic Perspective and 360° Panorama, the Render Palette offers two other options: Distance Render and Mask Render. These are useful for creating post-processing effects after the initial render. With them, you're not making an either/or choice: either do a Basic Perspective render *or* a Mask Render. Rather you can do both. First, do the Basic Perspective render. Then go back and render an additional image, a mask to use for special post-processing. The same is true for Distance Render. Since Mask and Distance Renders are both much faster than are a Basic Perspective render, you can render them "live" and then save the PICT only.

DISTANCE RENDER

Distance Render creates a grayscale image based on the distance of the object from the camera. The closer the object is, the darker the value that is rendered; the further away the object is, the lighter the value. Sky far away is white.

Distance Render is handy for creating selection masks that vary depending on distance for such things as motion blurs, depth-of-field focus, and so on. In the ray-tracing render model, all objects are rendered "in focus." To create a realistic unfocus, use Distance Render.

Distance Render is also good for intermediate renders while you are working on a scene. If you're working with a difficult perspective and want to know if something is showing, do a Distance Render to see what is showing and what is not. It's faster than a Basic Perspective render, since Bryce needs to think only about "how far do I go before I hit something?" If you are running on a slower machine, this is helpful since you're not dealing with the usual material settings or any other factors that slow things down. The Distance Render doesn't help in all cases. But in matters such as a narrow ravine, where there is definitely something far and something close, it comes in handy. See Figure 12–9.

If you have an object that has a Transmitivity setting above 0 (in the Illumination Details of the Materials Editor dialog box), it will

FIGURE 12–9 A Distance Render in a narrow area helps with camera aiming.

not render at all. So for an object that is transparent, such as water, change the Illuminations settings for the Distance Render.

Here's another "intermediate render" situation in which in you can use Distance Render. Suppose you need to take a look at a terrain's shape in the context of the scene. Your terrain is in place, resized, and rotated, and you don't want to touch its orientation. You do, however, want to shave off or augment a ridge for aesthetic balance. In order to know which part of the terrain to darken, you need to understand how the terrain is oriented. A Distance Render from Top View (see Fig. 12–10a) will give you an inverse image of the grayscale terrain you see in the Terrain Editor (see Fig. 12–10b), enough to recognize key features and to see how it's oriented.

FIGURE 12–10 Distance Render for terrain context: (**a**) A Top View render of the terrain in position, next to the (**b**) G2H map of that same terrain; (**c**) Top View render shown inverted for easier reference.

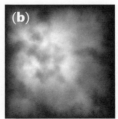

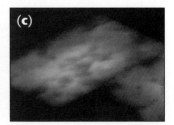

Go to Top View. Locate the terrain, go to PICT view, and draw a marquee around the area to be rendered. In the Render Palette, change to Distance Render and then click Clear and Render. After a few passes, you will see the orientation of your terrain.

You can also use Distance Render to create a larger terrain comprised of smaller ones. When creating mountains and valleys, do a Distance Render from Top View. The render will become the image used to create the larger terrain that incorporates transitions between smaller terrains (see Fig. 12–11).

In this scene, Distance Render was used to solve the problem of creating a smooth transition from mountain to valley (see "Superlative Nature Imagery," Chapter 9). Rather than the scene's having four separate terrains, (three as mountains and one as valley; see Fig. 12–11a and 12–11c), the entire area was rendered from the top as a Distance Render in order to incorporate both mountain and valley.

1. To create a new terrain map, the scene was rendered from Top View using Distance Render. See Figure 12–11d.
2. Then, the rendered image was captured with a screen capture utility, which copied it to the clipboard.
3. The old terrain that had been the valley was selected and then the Terrain Editor was accessed. A paste brought the Distance Render into the Terrain Editor, where it was inverted to get the correct G2H orientation. (You can see the camera showing from the Top View, too). See Figure 12–11e.
4. Finally, the terrain was spread out over the area covered by the Distance Render screen capture. See Figure 12–11f.

I have been describing methods for using Distance Render as a temporary part of the scene creation process. The render is used to check something or to create something, but no Scene or PICT document is saved as a Distance Render.

In this next section, I explore the post-processing use for Distance Render. Using Distance Render to create a selection mask requires that the entire scene be rendered and the PICT saved. The naming convention I use is a .DX suffix; resource documents on the CD with that suffix are Distance Renders.

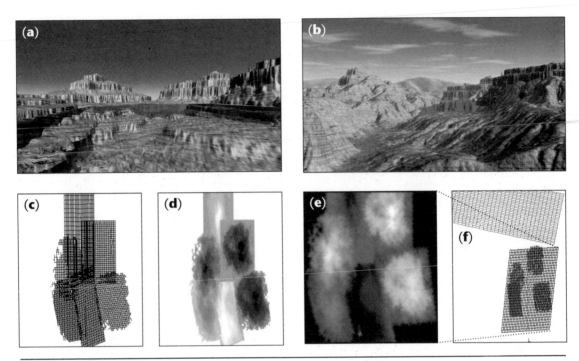

FIGURE 12–11 (**a**) The old scene; (**b**) the new scene; (**c**) Top View wireframe of old scene; (**d**) the Distance Render; (**e**) the new terrain G2H based on the Distance Render (note camera, too!); (**f**) wireframe for the new scene.

Creating Blur Effects with Distance Render

Although you see a grayscale image, the Distance Render is still an RGB PICT with four channels. In Photoshop, load one channel as a selection for the Basic Perspective image (see Fig. 12–12a). If you invert the selection, the blur will take place in the foreground (see Fig. 12–12b). If you leave the selection as is, the blurring will occur in the distance.

I find that several applies of the Blur More filter (see Fig. 12–12c) are better than a single apply of Gaussian Blur (see Fig. 12–12d). In Gaussian Blur, the edges of the mask will prohibit the blur from being applied to the masked-off area. However, it will not prohibit the blur from picking up information from behind that mask to mix with the neighboring pixels. The result is a strange, unnatural glow. See the close-up of the two types of blurs in Figure 12–12e. Blur More is on the left, and Gaussian Blur is on the right.

FIGURE 12–12 Distance Render blurring: (**a**) Distance Render mask; (**b**) foreground blur; (**c**) distance blur using Blur More; (**d**) distance blur using Gaussian Blur; (**e**) detail comparison of Blur More and Gaussian Blur.

Another approach to blurring is to change the selection mask to create a depth-of-field blur. The blur is applied to the foreground and background, with the area "in the middle" staying in focus. To do this, you need to use Photoshop's Curves. The grayscale information in the selection mask is based on distance. So if you change the gray values to make portions lighter or darker, you will enable something to affect only that one area.

Figure 12–13a shows a grayscale image. In the middle ground is a cabin and waterwheel. Those objects need to be changed to black (or very dark gray) so that the image will be in focus and any blurring applied won't affect them. Change it using the Curves dialog box in Photoshop (see Fig. 12–13b). Adjust the curves so that the darkest colors, up close, are lighter. Darken the tones where depth-of-field sharpness is important. The resulting blur is applied to the foreground and in the distance. See Figure 12–13c.

MASK RENDERING

Mask Rendering takes a selected object or objects and renders a mask. The selected object(s) (see Fig. 12–14a) will be black and all

Distance render

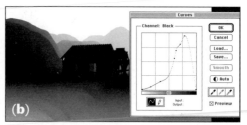

Adjust using Photoshop's Curves

Blur in foreground and distance

FIGURE 12–13 Adjusting a Distance Render mask to create depth-of-field: (**a**) The original mask; (**b**) mask adjusted with Photoshop's Curves; (**c**) resulting blur.

else will be white (see Fig. 12–14b). If the object is behind another object, then only the portion that is visible to the camera will render. If nothing (or everything) is selected (see Fig. 12–14c), then all objects in the scene will be rendered as a mask. The sky will be white and everything else will be black. See Figure 12–14d.

The object will *not* render as a mask if any of the following settings are activated in the Materials Editor:

- Any Effect other than Normal (Fuzzy, Fuzzy Additive, Additive)
- Alpha Channel Transparency
- A Transmitivity setting other than 0 (opaque)

So, if you need to see if an object is showing or do a quick test, make a note of your Transmitivity setting. Change Transmitivity to 0, render your mask, and then go back and change your Transmitivity setting when you're through.

Mask Rendering for Work in Progress

Use a Mask Render while you work in progress to see if a particular object is showing and if so, how much of it is showing from a particular camera angle or from the object's placement. Mask Render

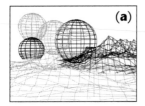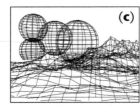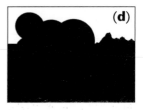

FIGURE 12–14 (**a**) Objects selected and so (**b**) are rendered as a mask; (**c**) all or no objects selected and so (**d**) all are rendered as a mask.

helps you fine-tune the object's and the camera's position. Like Distance Render, Mask Render requires much simpler computation on the part of Bryce's renderer. Figure 12–15a shows Mask Render used to verify that the "waterfall" shows from the indicated camera position (see Fig. 12–15b).

Mask Render is good to use in the case where one terrain (rocks) is poking out of another terrain. When the scene is viewed as a wireframe, you can see what part of an object is above ground level. But when both objects are above ground level, you can't easily see if one object pokes out beyond another object. Select the one underneath and use Mask Render.

Because Mask Render allows you to specify which object or objects will render, you can test certain things by selecting the objects and rendering. Suppose there's a scene with many objects that appear

FIGURE 12–15 Mask Render used in progress: (**a**) Mask Render; (**b**) final render.

onscreen as a confusing jumble. You want to know whether object A has the same wireframe color as the others (you want to assign the same material setting to the whole set, and you want to ensure all are included.) Select by wireframe color and then render as a mask. If you can see object A in silhouette, you'll have your answer. If the jumble of objects is sufficiently confusing, using this method may be faster than tabbing through the lot until the one is selected.

Mask Render for Finished Rendering

Of course, Mask Render also creates a mask for selections to use in post-processing. Select all elements in your scene to render a mask that will have only your sky showing. If you need to do any post-processing of just the sky, then you can easily select just that one part of the scene with the mask.

MASK RENDER, ANTI-ALIASING, AND COMPOSITING

What if you want anti-aliasing only on the edges of objects? Doing this involves a bit of extra work, but for the right scene, it's worth it. The scene in Figure 12–16, "Deep Undulating Canyon," has a lovely texture when seen in the last render pass. It's rough, and you can just sense the sandpapery texture of the rock face by the way the render looks. Once it's anti-aliased, the rock will have been metamorphosed into some other thing that, well, might be plastic (see Fig. 12–16a). Needless to say, the un–anti-aliased is better (see Fig. 12–16b). However, the edges of objects are a bit too rough.

FIGURE 12–16 Scene shown rendered (**a**) with and (**b**) without anti-aliasing.

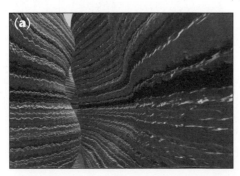

Those are the areas that need to be anti-aliased. How to do it? Combine Mask Render in Bryce with some Photoshop manipulation to create masks for the edges and then happily marry the two render versions, anti-aliased and rough.

CASE STUDY: ANTI-ALIASED EDGES IN A ROUGH RENDERED WORLD

To begin in KPT Bryce, follow these steps:

1. Use Mask Render to create masks of each individual object (see Fig. 12–17a). This generally happens pretty quickly, so you can use the one Scene document and save the PICTs, giving each PICT a different name.
2. Change your render option to Basic Perspective. Then save the scene with a suffix that includes something meaningful, such as .NO AA. In the "!" dialog box, uncheck the Anti-Aliasing option so that this first render will not have anti-aliasing. When the scene is finished rendering, save it again.
3. Immediately save the Scene document as a different name, changing the suffix to .YES AA. Change the Render "!" option so that Anti-Aliasing is *on* and then click Resume Render or type ⌘-R. (Don't start from scratch; you've already done the first six passes!) When the anti-aliasing pass is completed, save the scene/PICT combination again.

Continue in Photoshop or other image editing application with these steps:

4. Open up each of the mask PICT images and change them to grayscale. Blur each one slightly and then apply the Find Edges filter (see Fig. 12–17c).
5. Create a combined edges mask. Use Calculations and the Darken mode to combine them (see Fig. 12–17d). (In this case, the area at the bottom where the water is located was added to the mask using a painting tool.)

  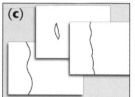 

FIGURE 12–17 Creating a mask for compositing: (**a**) Selecting one wireframe; (**b**) mask for each object; (**c**) Blurred and Find Edges; (**d**) combined edges mask.

FIGURE 12–18
Anti-aliased edges
and non–anti-aliased
everywhere else.

6. Open up both color PICT renders of the scene. Invert and load the combined mask as a selection into the non–anti-aliased version. The selected area should be the edges. In QuickView, check that the mask area has taken in sufficient border area and if necessary adjust using Levels.
7. Change back to the selection. Copy all of the anti-aliased version and paste it inside the selection. Adjust the opacity; this sample (see Fig. 12–18) had the anti-aliased edges at 70% strength.

There you go! You have your beautiful, rough, rocky surfaces and smooth transitions from edge to edge.

Conclusion

In this chapter, I took you through some of the dynamics of ray-tracing so that you could understand how to set up your scenes to make your renders even more efficient. Then I discussed some tips for working in render-in-progress mode and render-when-complete mode and for batch rendering and large image renders. Next I launched into the other render options offered by Bryce—360° panoramas and the two types that are good for post-processing techniques: Distance Render and Mask Render. I finished with an example of how to use Mask Render to make a composite mask in order to put anti-aliased edges on an otherwise un–anti-aliased terrain surface.

13

Printing Bryce Images

Still, somehow, the thing got finished at last, without much
loss of temper.

Kenneth Grahame, *The Wind in the Willows*

In This Chapter . . .

- All about resolution and printing
- Different categories of printers
- A strategy for working in Bryce and image resolution
- Conversion from RGB to CMYK
- Strategies for Bryce (grayscale)
- Strategies for Bryce (color)

How do you get that beautiful image from your computer's monitor onto paper of some sort? You'll want to print your images
sometime. It's inevitable. Given the type of images Bryce creates,
and the plummeting costs of desktop color printers, it's only a matter of time.

Whether you want to print one copy of your Bryce image so that
you can give it to your sweetheart or tack it up on your bulletin
board, or whether you're going to take the image to four-color
process offset printing, you'll have to wade through some
additional issues besides the best place to position your sun or terrain or whatever.

If you haven't done any printing of images, then this chapter is for
you. Here, I introduce the basic concepts of printing so that you get

a feel for what you will have just gotten yourself into once you say to yourself, "I want to print that image I just created!"

If you're an old hand at taking RGB (Red/Green/Blue) PICT images and converting them for printed output, then you probably aren't reading this chapter anyhow. (You've got your nose stuck in the section that talks about the Deep Texture Editor, don't you?) Still, you'll find one section useful: Bryce Images and CMYK Printing.

The Basic Situation

Bryce is not an application for printing; ⌘-P brings you the Preferences dialog box, not the Print dialog box. There is no way to print images directly from Bryce. You create scenes and render them and save the rendered images as PICT documents. To print your images, you need to use a different application, any that can open and print PICT documents or convert PICTs to other types of image documents (TIFF and EPS).

But what if the scene is not to be printed, such as in multimedia or still images on screen? In this case, you won't undertake such a far journey—your onscreen image will be converted into another form of onscreen image. Some good tools for converting color palettes for multimedia are Photoshop and DeBabelizer (sample copies of both are on the enclosed CD). This chapter, however, concerns itself more with the physical printing process.

An Output Device Primer

When you print an image, you will be choosing from among a plentiful array of printers, or output devices. (I use the term "output device" because a computer monitor fits into this category—yet it does not print.) Each output device has its own optimal setup and preferred image resolution.

Each type of output device has its own setting for the degree of detail it can print. The device's own detail capacity is expressed in dots per inch (dpi), that is, how many single points of detail can the device fit into an inch? The dpi is a fixed number; it's derived from the physical specifications of the output device. Physically, any output device can do so many *somethings* in an inch. What the somethings are varies from device to device. A monitor projects electron beams, various printers use laser beams, and ink jet printers eject individual spurts of ink.

The physical specifications also concern the particular media involved. The output device is doing *something* to *something else.* You can shoot a higher number of individual laser beams onto a smoother, harder surface (film or resin-coated photo-sensitive paper) than you can onto a softer, more porous surface (paper). Therefore devices that output to film generally have significantly higher dpi settings than those that output to paper.

So that's dpi. There's a relation between the output's dpi and the individual image resolution, or pixels per inch (ppi). In the document itself is a header that says (more or less), "This is the total number of pixels in this document. Smoosh them in such a way that *N* many pixels fit into one inch." The default setting of 72 ppi matches the setting of the monitor's, which is 72 dpi.

Let's look at this relation between the output device's dpi and the image's ppi. A good start is to examine the first few render passes of a Bryce scene. The image has large, square chunky pixels. Why do those large pixels seem odd to us? Because the image itself does not have the level of detail that the monitor (output device) is able to display. This is why for the first few render passes, clicking the zoom out (Minus Sphere) button enables you to see a more detailed version of the render. You are changing the resolution of the image in order to see as much of the image's detail as can be seen for that output device. Otherwise the image looks too chunky, or pixellated.

This works fine for the first few passes. After a point, though, the render reaches a threshold where there are more individual points of information in the image than you can see at that output device's resolution. (Remember: The monitor has a fixed dpi; it can show only 72 distinct pixels in an inch.)

This last example discussed the situation common to all output devices. They are capable of output at a higher dpi resolution than 72 dpi, the default image size. Therefore they need more information going *in*. The image itself needs to be bigger. It needs more pixels so that more of them can be packed into a square inch. For any given device, you'll need to have a corresponding setting for image resolution (ppi).

If this "somethings per inch" is not confusing enough, there is yet another level of confusion for certain types of printers—lines per inch (lpi), or linescreen. (Are you *sure* you really want to print that Bryce image? After a moment of staring at it longingly, you'll probably conclude that you do in fact want to press on with these matters of your own private printing press. Take two or three deep breaths, then let's continue.)

Most printers are not capable of laying down pigment color in all shades of the rainbow. If you're using a grayscale printer, you have a choice between two colors—black and white. So to create all those shades of gray, the printer distributes little black dots of certain sizes. For dark gray, the dots are either fatter or more numerous. For light gray, the dots are either tinier and more sparsely distributed. This is referred to as a halftone, that is, there are tones generated from bits of color that are either black or white. When the eye takes in the image, the dots are blended in with the neighboring area, thereby creating the illusion of all the tones of gray that are in between black and white.

Color printing does the same thing, only it uses four primary colors: cyan, magenta, yellow, and black (CMYK). So where does linescreen come in? The number of lpi is set independently of the printer's physical dpi capability or the ppi image resolution. Linescreen is dependent on the printed paper's ability to accept ink and hold image detail. It is also dependent on the printer's overall dpi.

Newsprint is a porous paper. It can hold only a 65–80 linescreen (65–80 lines of halftone dots per inch). If the linescreen is any higher, the ink bleeds together and the image becomes dark and fuzzy. On the other hand, glossy coated paper can hold 150 or 175 linescreen, even 200. The higher the linescreen, the greater the detail you are able to display. The greater the detail you are putting *out*, the greater the amount of detail you need to have going *in*. So the higher the linescreen, the higher the image resolution.

To review the three different "somethings per inch" just discussed:

- *ppi, or pixels per inch.* The image document's resolution, or how much pixel detail is in an inch.
- *dpi, or dots per inch.* The output device's capability for detail.
- *lpi, or lines per inch, or linescreen.* In half-tone printing, the measurement of the density of the dot pattern.

The dpi of the device determines how much detail you can see. For linescreen halftone, the possible number of lpi is far below the total dpi capability of the printer. In other words, the printer can use many more dots to print a solid line than it uses halftone dots to create an illusion of continuous color tones. The image resolution, or image's ppi, is dependent on the output device's capacity. Where the image will end up being printed using halftone dots, the image resolution (ppi) is determined by the number of lpi.

So here it is, one of the hazards of printing images. The size you make your Bryce image depends on the requirements of the output device. Different devices have different requirements. So the image that has a set number of pixels can be output to a film imagesetter to create a full color 8- × 10-inch CMYK image or output to a slide recorder to create a piece of 35mm color transparency film. The physical size of the actual printed entity is very different, but the amount of information that went into it is not, since each printing device handles information of different densities.

Next I talk about the different categories of printers.

Different Kinds of Printers

So far I've discussed printers as "output devices," noting that different ones have different physical capabilities and requirements. Now I take a look at the major categories of printers. This is a general introduction. For more-detailed information about what each type of printer requires, consult the manufacturer's specifications or a service bureau.

Many of these printers are for one-off printing. The (one) print is the end, not the means to a mass-produced end. With these, you can create individual prints of your image for that sweetheart, bulletin board, or gallery show.

Laser printers and ink jet printers generally can output at 300–600 dpi. This means the printer can output 300 or 600 distinct points of information in an inch.

- *Desktop ink jets* (Apple, Hewlett-Packard, Epson, Tektronix). These printers lay down different colors of ink on your page. Individual cartridges hold the ink. The printers come in one-color (black) or multi-color (CMYK) varieties. The patterns created by each color are blended together by the human eye, thereby creating the optical illusion of continuous-tone color.

- *Large ink jets* (Iris, Laser Master). The larger ink jets come in two basic types. The first, electrostatic, lays stippled dots of color on the paper (maximum paper size is approximately 36 × 48 inches). The printer head assembly moves back and forth over the surface of the paper as the paper advances through the printer. The second type of large ink jet, the Iris, has the paper set on a rotating drum. The ink heads stay stationary relative to the "left and right" parts of the page. They move, however, in the sense that they advance "down" the page. This type of setup results in a much higher precision. Printers range in sizes, with the maximum able to print on 30 × 47-inch paper. The Iris will print on a variety of papers, including watercolor paper for a "fine art" digital print. Some service bureaus specialize in fine art printing. They work with different types of inks and treatments to make the print far more stable than it would be otherwise.

- *Dye Sublimation* (3M Rainbow, SuperMac, Kodak XL Series, Tektronix). These printers take ink dyes and fuse the dyes to the surface layers of a specially prepared paper. The dye is vaporized as it is forced onto the paper's surface, resulting in an unusually smooth image that appears to be a continuous tone print. This is a CMYK color process.

- *Color Laser* (Canon, Xerox, Tektronix). This is a combination of computer and color photocopy technology, similar to the way the black-and-white laser printer is a further development on photocopy technology. In the photocopy analogy, the image is exposed to light and the rays captured. (See? More ray-tracing of a different variety! It's all over the place!) Areas that are dark create a static charge on the toner drum surface. Toner adheres to the areas that are charged. The toner then is transferred to the paper surface and fused there by heat to produce the copy. A laser print operates in the same way. Instead of using a photographic process to determine which area receives an electrostatic charge, the image is computer processed and to tell a laser beam to etch the areas that will receive toner. For a color image, several passes are taken to produce the color layers. These color laser printers can print on paper of up to 11 × 17 inches.

- *Thermal Wax Printer* (Tektronix, QMS). This type of printer does CMYK printing. A thin layer of waxy substance is on a mylar sheet. During printing, it is transferred to the special printing paper. The image has a rather noticeable halftone dot, which makes it less desirable for one-off printing than are most of the others I mention here.

- *Film recorder* (Solitaire, LVT). This type of printer takes the information from your image file and exposes film transparency to create a color "slide." Different sizes of film can be used, from 35mm to 2¼ inch, to 4- × 5-inch and 8- × 10-inch film. It's better to think of "total number of pixels" for a film recorder than to think of "image resolution." When printing to a film recorder, you aren't talking about variable sizes (say, like an image that takes up 5×7 inches on your $8\frac{1}{2} \times 11$-inch piece of paper). To generate 35mm film, your image should be w pixels $\times$ h pixels. That's your final number. End of story.

- *Photographic Process* (FujiX Pictography). A relatively new process generates a photochemical print. The process is similar to how the color laser printer is an adaptation of a related image reproduction process, where the light exposure is replaced by computer image processing to determine what does or does not print for the final output. It's the same general process as exposing a color negative to special photographic paper. Instead of a darkroom enlarger and negative being involved, however, the printer is fed information from an image document. It creates a "donor" plate that transfers the photochemicals to the paper that is subsequently developed to result in a final print. Because this is a photographic process, it works in RGB.

- *Film Imagesetter.* This type of printer is used for reproduction more than one-off printing. It is more precise; it can produce from 1200 to 3000 dpi. It can output only one color at a time and is used to create film that will be used for offset printing, whether for one-color (black) or four-color process film. Whether one piece of film or four, the actual film can be either black (opaque) or white (transparent). Any shade in between is composed of small dots (halftone).

Interpolating Images

Suppose you want to create a poster-sized image (22×30 or so). It would be sheer madness (sheer "RAMdess" actually) to render at the full size at a high enough image density for that size. It's time consuming to render images at extreme sizes in Bryce. You can render an image to a fairly large size and then use an image editing application such as Photoshop to enlarge the image even further. When you enlarge, you create new pixels. The means of determining which color those new pixels will be is called *interpolation*.

Bryce's anti-aliasing pass, which checks the surrounding area to determine the final color of each pixel, is a friend of image interpolation. The oversampling to determine the pixel colors also helps when resolution is increased. When those new pixels come into being, they do so based on the pixels that are there, and where anti-aliasing has taken place, it's based on an oversampling of the surrounding area of that one point. As a result, Bryce images interpolate to larger sizes rather smoothly. Photoshop's bicubic interpolation method is an excellent choice for doing this. If you have Live Picture, use it to resize the image. Live Picture's interpolation routine is even better. Don't do it all in one fell swoop, however, especially if you are doing it in Photoshop. Interpolate to one size. Then do it again. You will probably need to do a bit of custom touch-up at the end.

When you set up your Bryce scene, figure out what your target resolution is going to be for the final-final-final image size. Then set your Bryce resolution to render your image to a size that's comparable, say one half or one fourth. Make it the same ratio, but smaller.

Color Models

One of the fascinating and troublesome things about printing Bryce images (or any computer generated image, for that matter) is the inevitable switch from one type of color model to another. When you are creating your scenes, you are working with colors that are created in RGB color space. This is called *additive color* because when you add the colors together, they form white. Red, green, and blue are the primary colors when you are using anything that projects light—computer monitor, video, cinema, and transparency film.

If you are going to be printing in a four-color process, CMYK, you are working in what is called a subtractive color space. The combination of all colors results in black, not white. White is the absence of color. Most color printers and the entire established color printing industry are based on this standard, where actual pigments are placed on paper and light bounces off of them, reflecting back certain colors as it reaches the eye.

There are certain problems inherent in transferring an image from one type of color space to another. The gamut of possible colors is larger in the RGB color space than it is in CMYK color space. Brilliant electric blues and hot reds, highly saturated colors, and hot purples don't make the transfer from RGB to CMYK.

It's far beyond the scope of this chapter to discuss all the whys and wherefores of color. Entire books have been written on the subject. A new system of color printing, Hi Fi color, has even been developed in response to the problem of different color gamuts. Hi Fi color takes advantage of six- and seven-color presses to add back in some of the colors that are lost during the conversion to CMYK. It would be ludicrous to attempt to sum up in a paragraph or two what the entire computer, color imaging, and printing industry has come up with over the last eight or nine years' worth of hard work on the issue of color. The best that can be done here is to put up a signpost that says "caution" and to point you to resources that are more thorough. I leave you with the experts here. These include books about desktop color, color separation houses, and service bureaus, as well as user groups and various discussion groups on online services and the Internet. (An especially good one is in America Online's Photoshop SIG, under the topic "CMYK Separation." When on America Online, use keyword "Photoshop" to get there.)

Not all of the color output devices are CMYK, though. The photographic printer mentioned earlier works in the RGB color space, and film recorders take in RGB images and then output them the same way. One good, creditable way to create a color separation for offset print is to print your image as a color transparency (from RGB to RGB) and then have it traditionally separated.

Bryce Images and Black and White Printing

Okay, so maybe I'm not the *only* one out there who has set out to create many Bryce images that are eventually printed in black and white. I'll pass on to you what I learned in the process of creating all of the grayscale illustrations in this book.

When you are setting up your scene for optimum color, a straight conversion to grayscale probably won't get you a desirable image with accompanying contrast. For just about every scene I created that was converted to black and white, I had to do some custom tweaking. I'll tell you my favorite method. Yes, it's in Photoshop (where else?). It involves using the Hue Saturation dialog box (⌘-U), where you can choose to alter colors or alter the entire image.

I select Master, which globally affects the file, and pull saturation all the way to the left (or nearly all the way to the left, in case I wanted to tell what my original colors were). This drains the image of color and provides an onscreen preview of the image in grayscale, but I'm still working in the RGB color space. At this point, I can see where I need to add contrast and adjust lightness color by color. There's immediate feedback. After using Photoshop's Hue/Saturation dialog, I adjust further with curves or levels if necessary to provide overall contrast.

Bryce Images and CMYK Printing

Now that I've discussed the concepts of converting from RGB to CMYK in general, I'll talk about a couple of situations and Bryce.

Smooth Gradations and Banding

When you convert Bryce images from RGB to CMYK, the images tend to have marked banding, especially in the sky area. Two things are happening to cause banding. First, there's a change to a smaller color space in CMYK (especially where blues are concerned).

Second, the sky area can be a gradation with a limited number of steps between the two end colors (from, say, medium blue to light-medium blue). The best solution here is to add a very slight amount of noise while the image is still in RGB color space. I like to use KPT Hue Protected Minimum and press the 1 key down for a very light application. In most cases, changing from RGB to CMYK after that either eliminates or drastically reduces the banding.

To apply a noise to only one area of the scene (the sky), do a mask render with all objects selected. The only thing that will be left over is the sky. Load that mask as a selection and then apply the noise. You will have only applied it to the one area and not necessarily globally to the image.

Saturation

If your images have that natural look, you probably adjusted the saturation in the colors you choose for the textures and in the introduction of a lot of haze. Your image won't be that saturated to begin with. However, there are other situations, and other times of day (those spectacular sunsets, for example) when this will not be the case and you'll need to adjust saturation.

Depending on the color scheme of your image, your colors may be more saturated than the CMYK color space allows for. Lower the saturation a bit before converting from RGB to CMYK. To do a test, I open up the trusty Hue Saturation dialog box, as well as the Info window, in Photoshop. While in the dialog box, I drag the cursor around the image. There's a simultaneous numeric readout in the Info window. When the CMYK values are followed by an exclamation point (!), then I know I'm out of gamut. I adjust saturation, either overall or in certain colors (blues especially). Then I cruise over the image again with the cursor. The information is shown in two readouts separated by a slash for before/after. When the occurrence of the exclamation points is significantly reduced, the image will convert to CMYK more smoothly.

This is but one method used in one software application. There are plenty of other methods and other software packages available for converting from RGB to CMYK. As I said before, this is not a chapter about the details of color, but an introduction to the overall concepts.

Conclusion

This chapter provided an introduction to printing Bryce images. When printing an image, care must be taken to ensure there is sufficient image detail (ppi) for a given printer's physical ability to print (dpi). In cases when the image has a halftone dot pattern, then the lpi comes into play as well. For most color output, the image will need to be converted from the RGB color space to CMYK color space. If the image will be printed in black and white, then it needs to undergo some adjustments to provide sufficient contrast, Finally, to reduce banding—especially in Bryce skies—an extremely light application of KPT Hue Protected Noise will do the trick.

What's Wrong with This Picture?

Humpty Dumpty sat on a wall.
At three o'clock he had his great fall.
The King set the Time Machine back to two.
Now Humpty's unscrambled and good as new.

Frederick Winsor, *The Space Child's Mother Goose*

In This Chapter . . .

- How to tell that terrain resolution is okay
- How to tell when to adjust the noise rotation for your scene
- How to get rid of "grids" in your materials
- How to fix a scene by establishing a credible sense of scale
- How to fix Ambient problems
- When to reduce a too-bumped bump gain

This chapter is a troubleshooting guide. No, it's not about troubleshooting the software—the technical support variety. It's about some common pitfalls in Bryce scene-making and how to handle them. If you've worked with a scene and said, "I know something here isn't quite right," but you can't tell what is wrong, then take a look here. I show before and after images, analyze what went wrong, and how to fix it. So let's dig right in.

Terrain Resolution

There's your beautiful scene. But you look at your terrain, especially that one in the foreground, and notice it has very odd, angular pock marks. See Figure 14–1 (Before). The pock marks are a sign that you don't have enough terrain resolution. To rectify this situation, select the terrain, go to the Terrain Editor, and increase the resolution. Edit the Terrain Editor and then test an area to see if this fix worked! Figure 14–14 (After) shows the outcome of increasing terrain resolution.

Other methods for solving this problem:

- Click the Smooth button, especially if you have added a lot of erosion to your terrain.

Terrain at 256

Before: Terrain has geometric artifacts

FIGURE 14–1
Increasing terrain resolution to get rid of geometric artifacts.

Terrain enlarged to 512

After: Terrain with smoother surface

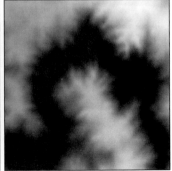

Terrain (512) plus smoothing

- If you have one terrain spread out in a large area, then consider making multiple terrains do the job your one big terrain is doing now.
- Augment the large terrain with additional terrains, making them either smaller in size as a result of resizing in the Edit Palette or making their resolutions higher.

Ground with Horizontal Streaky Lines

Figure 14–2 shows an image with a ground that has horrible streaky lines. The same material setting is used for the terrain as for the ground. Why does it work successfully on the terrain but not on the ground? Noise from the underlying 3D Solid Texture has only one or two dimensions to it. In addition, the noise is oriented to face "front" at the expense of facing "up." When seen as a two-dimensional preview, the combination and the individual component noises are either one- or two-dimensional. See how the top edge of the cube just has stripes? So your flat ground has stripes as well.

To fix this, rotate the noise so that it faces a different direction, thereby cutting through both the top and front surfaces.

Another method for solving the problem:

- Change the noise from one- or two-dimensional to two- or three-dimensional noise.

Grid Lock

You look at your object and you see something resembling a grid (see Fig. 14–3). First, check in the Terrain Editor to ensure the terrain is smooth and not polygonal. (As an example, try out Terrain #4 in the KPT Bryce presets. Select one of the terrains and change it from polygonal to smooth and then render.)

Reason: Texture is oriented toward the "front," and there is no noise detail along the top flat surface plane.

Before: Ground plane has horrible stripes.

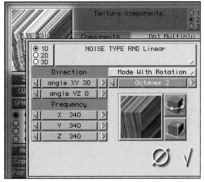

Component 1: One-dimensional Noise

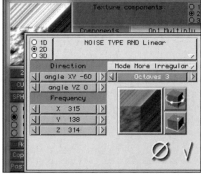

Component 2: Two-dimensional Noise

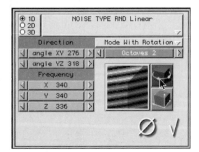

Solution: Rotate noise

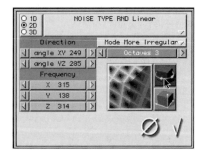

Solution: Rotate noise

After: Texture is now oriented to both "top" and "front" directions.

FIGURE 14–2 Getting rid of streaky lines in ground plane by rotating noise.

 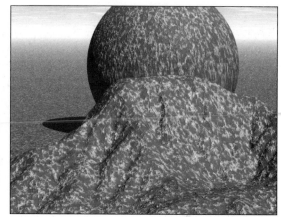

Before: Object's textures have a visible grid.   After: Increase frequency in the Materials Editor.

FIGURE 14–3 Fixing a grid by increasing the texture's frequency.

However, in Figure 14–3, the same grid appears on a sphere and a terrain, so the problem cannot be only with the terrain. Here, the noise Frequency setting in the Materials Editor is set too low, in this case, at its lowest setting. There are more opportunities for the grid to show up at lower frequencies than at higher ones. So increase the Frequency settings.

Other methods for solving the problem:

- In the Noise Editor of the Deep Texture Editor, change the mode to "with rotation" and increase the octaves setting.
- Change the noise to a three-dimensional noise.
- Add another texture component to interact with this gridded one.

Frequency for a Sense of Scale

When you have different elements that don't seem to fit together, the problem may be one of scale. In Figure 14–4, the water does not "fit" the scale of the rest of the scene. The large waves belie the scale of the terrains, the bridge (made from terrains), and the distant mountains. The solution to this is simple: Increase the Frequency setting in the Materials Editor. A bit of reduction in bump gain helps, too.

Solution: Increase the frequency of the water material and slightly reduce the bump gain.

Before: Water waves are too large, thereby throwing off the entire scale of the scene.

FIGURE 14–4 Adjusting the water so it fits the rest of the scene's scale.

After: Higher frequency "waves" and lower bump give the image a sense of scale.

Ambient Conflict

In Fig. 14–5, the rock that juts out of the ground doesn't look like it belongs there, for some reason. Look in the shadow areas where the two terrains meet. The protruding rock, although darker overall, is not darker in the shadow areas. This indicates the Ambient setting for each object is different. The two Illuminations Details dialog boxes confirm this. A higher Ambient setting "resists" shadows. Once you make the settings identical, the two objects "belong" together in a way they didn't before.

Before: Rock object doesn't "fit" with ground

After: Rock object and ground with identical Ambient settings (Ground Ambient setting)

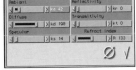

Rock Ambient setting   Ground Ambient setting

Reason: Rock object and ground have different Ambient settings. This is most obvious in shadow, when the darker object is as light as the lighter object's shadow.

FIGURE 14–5 Adjusting Ambient settings to make the scene appear cohesive.

This problem is important to watch for, especially when you are stealing textures from another scene or when you are shopping for presets in .SHD lists. The Ambient setting for that preset is left over from its previous life, when it was created for a previous scene. Make sure Ambient settings are all cohesive in the scene you are working on *right now*.

Excessive Bump

When a texture has small black lines that overpower the rest of the texture, there is too much bump gain (see Fig. 14–6). When you assign bump gain to an object, you are not "physically" changing it. Rather, you're calling on Bryce to perform a custom "emboss" that creates shadows in the texture based on the light source and surface properties of the object, as well as on the information from the

Before: Black lines from maximum bump gain.   After: Reduced bump gain.

FIGURE 14–6 Reducing the bump gain setting to get rid of black lines.

Normale part of the 3D Solid Texture. When you have those black lines, you've asked Bryce to emboss too much. The solution is easy: Reduce the bump gain setting. (You may also want to reduce the Shadow setting in the Sky & Fog Palette.)

Conclusion

In this chapter, I took you through some of the most common problems in Bryce and showed you how to fix them to create a more realistic scene. Aside from making sure that the terrain resolution is okay, the rest of the common problems occur in the Materials Editor or in the Deep Texture Editor—Ambient, Frequency, Bump, Noise Rotation, and Gridded Texture. All of these scenes are on the CD, so you can open them up and try the solutions out for yourself.

Keyboard Shortcuts

View/Master Palette

⌘ 1	Master Palette
⌘ 2	Create Palette
⌘ 3	Edit Palette
⌘ 4	Sky & Fog Palette
⌘ 5	Render Palette
⌘ Tab	Disappearing palettes toggle
⌘ F	Full screen (in expert mode)
⌘ P	Preferences Dialog Box
1	Main View
2	Top View
3	Side View
4	Front View
5	Other views in the list (becomes new Main View)
6	Other views in list
7	Other views in list
8	Other views in list
9	Other views in list
+ (Keypad)	Zoom in
Shift +	Zoom in
⌘ –	Zoom out

Option key plus Views popup menu	Delete view preset from list
Escape key/clear (on keypad)	Toggle between PICT and Wireframe View

Edit

STANDARDS

⌘ C   Copy
⌘ V   Paste
⌘ X   Cut
⌘ Z   Undo (Edit functions only!)

OTHERS

⌘ T   Edit Terrain
⌘ M   Edit Materials
Double-click
  object   Edit Materials
⌘ K   Object Options
⌘ D   Duplicate object
⌘ A (**wireframe**)   Select all objects
⌘ A (**PICT**)   Select entire image (make all active for
                             rendering)
= key   Unity

Control key, click on Materials   Shuffle materials for selected
  Edit Control icon   objects

RESIZE

* (**multiply**)   Enlarge to twice the size
/ (**divide**)   Reduce to half size

SELECTION

Tab   Cycles through objects in scene
Enter   Cycles through objects in scene
Shift key held down
  while clicking objects   Multiple object selection/deselection

MODIFIER/CONSTRAIN KEYS

Option-resize keys   Smoother motion resize, not so jerky

MOVING OBJECTS

Right arrow, left arrow	Nudge along x axis
Up arrow, down arrow	Nudge along z axis
Page up/page down	Nudge along y axis
Option key plus nudge key	Minute incremental nudges

MODIFIER KEYS WHILE MOVING OBJECTS

Control key	Constrains on x axis
Option key	Constrains on y axis
⌘ key	Constrains on z axis

WHEN TWO OR MORE OBJECTS ARE SELECTED

⌘ G	Group objects
⌘ U	Ungroup object

DISPLAY OBJECT

⌘ L	Show object(s)/group(s) as mesh
⌘ B	Show object(s)/group(s) as box

Render

⌘ R	Render
⌘ H	Clear and render
⌘ A	Select all PICT area (to make all active for rendering)

APPENDIX B

Vendors

Following are the addresses of companies whose products are mentioned in the book.

HARDWARE ACCELERATION

Daystar Digital
5556 Atlanta Highway
Flowery Branch, Georgia 30542
phone: 404/967-2077;
fax: 404/967-3018

Digital Eclipse Software, Inc.
5515 Doyle Street, No. 1
Emeryville, CA 94608
phone: 510/547-6101;
fax: 510/547-6104

Newer Technology
7803 E. Osie Street, Suite 105
Wichita, KS 62707
phone: 800/678-3726,
316/685-4904;
fax: 316/685-9368

SOFTWARE COMPANIES

Adobe Systems Incorporated
1585 Charleston Road
Mountain View, CA 94039
415/961-4400

Connectix (RAM Doubler)
2655 Campus Drive
San Mateo, CA 94403
phone: 415/571-5100;
fax: 415/571-5195

Equilibrium
475 Gate Five Road, Suite 225
Sausalito, CA 94965
phone: 415/332-4343;
fax: 415/332-4433

HSC Software
6303 Carpinteria Avenue
Carpinteria, CA 93013
phone: 805/566-6200;
fax: 805/566-6385

PHOTO RESOURCES

Digital Stock Incorporated
400 South Sierra Avenue
Suite 100
Solana Beach, CA 92075
phone: 619/794-4040;
fax: 619/794-4041

PhotoDisc
2013 Fourth Avenue
Seattle, WA 98121
phone: 800/528-3472,
206/441-9355
fax: 206/441-9379

IRIS PRINT SERVICE BUREAUS

Cone Editions Press
P.O. Box 51
East Topsham, VT 05076
phone: 802/439-5751;
fax: 802/439-6501

Digital Pond
50 Minna Street
San Francisco, CA 94105
phone: 415/495-7663;
fax: 415/495-3109

Nash Editions
P.O. Box 637
Manhattan Beach, CA 90266
phone: 310/545-4352;
fax: 310/545-8565

Paris Photo Lab
1961 S. La Cienega Blvd
Los Angeles, CA 90034
phone: 310/204-0500;
fax: 310/837-7017

Index

D

E

ADOBE SYSTEMS INCORPORATED
MINIMUM TERMS OF END USER AGREEMENTS

(1) Licensor grants Licensee a non-exclusive sublicense to use the Adobe software ("Software") and the related written materials ("Documentation") provided by Adobe Systems Incorporated ("Adobe") to Licensor as set forth below. Licensee may install and use the Software on one computer.

(2) The Software is owned by Adobe and its suppliers and its structure, organization and code are the valuable trade secrets of Adobe and its suppliers. Licensee agrees not to modify, adapt, translate, reverse engineer decompile, disassemble or otherwise attempt to discover the source code of the Software. Licensee agrees not to attempt to increase the functionality of the Software in any manner. Licensee agrees that any permitted copies of the Software shall contain the same copyright and other proprietary notices which appear on and in the Software.

(3) Except as stated above, this Agreement does not grant Licensee any right (whether by license, ownership or otherwise) in or to the intellectual property with respect to the Software.

(4) Licensee will not export or re-export the Software Programs without the appropriate United States or foreign government licenses.

(5) Trademarks, if used by Licensee shall be used in accordance with accepted trademark practice, including identification of the trademarks owner's name. Trademarks can only be used to identify printed output produced by the Software. The use of any trademark as herein authorized does not give Licensee rights of ownership in that trademark.

(6) LICENSEE ACKNOWLEDGES THAT THE SOFTWARE IS A "TRY-OUT" VERSION OF AN ADOBE PRODUCT, CONTAINING LIMITED FUNCTIONALITY. ADOBE IS LICENSING THE SOFTWARE ON AN "AS-IS" BASIS, AND ADOBE AND ITS SUPPLIERS MAKE NO WARRANTIES EXPRESS OR IMPLIED, INCLUDING, WITHOUT LIMITATION, AS TO NONINFRINGEMENT OF THIRD PARTY RIGHTS, MERCHANTABILITY, OR FITNESS FOR ANY PARTICULAR PURPOSE. IN NO EVENT WILL ADOBE OR ITS SUPPLIERS BE LIABLE TO LICENSEE FOR ANY CONSEQUENTIAL, INCIDENTAL OR SPECIAL DAMAGES, INCLUDING ANY LOST PROFITS OR LOST SAVINGS, EVEN IF REPRESENTATIVES OF SUCH PARTIES HAVE BEEN ADVISED OF THE POSSIBILITY OF SUCH DAMAGES, OR FOR ANY CLAIM BY ANY THIRD PARTY.

IF A SHRINKWRAP LICENSEE IS USED [Some states or jurisdictions do not allow the exclusion or limitation of incidental, consequential or special damages, so the above limitation or exclusion may not apply to Licensee. Also some states or jurisdictions do not allow the exclusion of implied warranties or limitations on how long an implied warranty may last, so the above limitations may not apply to Licensee. To the extent permissible, any implied warranties are limited to ninety (90) days. This warranty gives Licensee specific legal rights. Licensee may have other rights which vary from state to state or jurisdiction to jurisdiction.]

(7) Notice to Government End Users: If this product is acquired under the terms of a: <u>GSA contract</u>: Use, reproduction or disclosure is subject to the restrictions set forth in the applicable ADP Schedule contract. <u>DoD contract</u>: Use, duplication or disclosure by the Government is subject to restrictions as set forth in subparagraph (c) (1) (ii) of 252.227-7013. <u>Civilian agency contract</u>: Use, reproduction, or disclosure is subject to 52.227-19 (a) through (d) and restrictions set forth in the accompanying end user agreement. Unpublished-rights reserved under the copyright laws of the United States.

(8) Licensee is hereby notified that Adobe Systems Incorporated, a California corporation located at 1585 Charleston Road, Mountain View, California 94039-7900 ("Adobe") is a third party beneficiary to this Agreement to the extent that this Agreement contains provisions which relate to Licensee's use of the Software, the Documentation and the trademarks licenses hereby. Such provisions are made expressly for the benefit of Adobe and are enforceable by Adobe in addition to Licensor.

Adobe is a trademark of Adobe Systems Incorporated which may be registered in certain jurisdictions.

APPLE SOFTWARE LICENSE

1. License. The application, demonstration, system and other software accompanying this License, whether on disk, in read-only memory, or on any other media (the "Software"), and the related documentation and fonts are licensed to you by Addison-Wesley Publishing Company. You own the disk on which the Software and fonts are recorded but Addison-Wesley Publishing Company and/or Addison-Wesley Publishing Company's Licensors retain title to the Software, related documentation and fonts. This License allows you to use the Software and fonts on a single Apple computer and make one copy of the Software and fonts in machine-readable form for backup purposes only. You must reproduce on such copy the Addison-Wesley Publishing Company copyright notice and any other proprietary legends that were on the original copy of the Software and fonts. You may also transfer all your license rights in the Software and fonts, the backup copy of the Software and fonts, the related documentation and a copy of this License to another party, provided the other party reads and agrees to accept the terms and conditions of this License.

2. Restrictions. The Software contains copyrighted material, trade secrets and other proprietary material. In order to protect them, and except as permitted by applicable legislation, you may not decompile, reverse engineer, disassemble or otherwise reduce the Software to a human-perceivable form. You may not modify, network, rent, lease, loan, distribute or create derivative works based upon the Software in whole or in part. You may not electronically transmit the Software from one computer to another or over a network.

3. Termination. This License is effective until terminated. You may terminate this License at any time by destroying the Software, related documentation and fonts and all copies thereof. This License will terminate immediately without notice from Addison-Wesley Publishing Company if you fail to comply with any provision of this License. Upon termination you must destroy the Software, related documentation and fonts and all copies thereof.

4. Export Law Assurances. You agree and certify that neither the Software nor any other technical data received from Addison-Wesley Publishing Company, nor the direct product thereof, will be exported outside the United States except as authorized and as permitted by the laws and regulations of the United States. If the Software has been rightfully obtained by you outside of the United States, you agree that you will not re-export the Software nor any other technical data received from Addison-Wesley Publishing Company, nor the direct product thereof, except as permitted by the laws and regulations of the United States and the laws and regulations of the jurisdiction in which you obtained the Software.

5. Government End Users. If you are acquiring the Software and fonts on behalf of any unit or agency of the United States Government, the following provisions apply. The Government agrees:

(i) if the Software and fonts are supplied to the Department of Defense (DoD), the Software and fonts are classified as "Commercial Computer Software" and the Government is acquiring only "restricted rights" in the Software, its documentation and fonts as that term is defined in Clause 252.227-7013(c)(1) of the DFARS; and

(ii) if the Software and fonts are supplied to any unit or agency of the United States Government other than DoD, the Government's rights in the Software, its documentation and fonts will be as defined in Clause 52.227-19(c)(2) of the FAR or, in the case of NASA, in Clause 18-52.227-86(d) of the NASA Supplement to the FAR.

6. Limited Warranty on Media. Addison-Wesley Publishing Company warrants the diskettes and/or compact disc on which the Software and fonts are recorded to be free from defects in materials and workmanship under normal use for a period of ninety (90) days from the date of purchase as evidenced by a copy of the receipt. Addison-Wesley Publishing Company's entire liability and your exclusive remedy will be replacement of the diskettes and/or compact disc not meeting Addison-Wesley Publishing Company's limited warranty and which is returned to Addison-Wesley Publishing Company or an Addison-Wesley Publishing Company authorized representative with a copy of the receipt. Addison-Wesley Publishing Company will have no responsibility to replace a disk/disc damaged by accident, abuse or misapplication. ANY IMPLIED WARRANTIES ON THE DISKETTES AND/OR COMPACT DISC, INCLUDING THE IMPLIED WARRANTIES OF MERCHANTABILITY AND FITNESS FOR A PARTICULAR PURPOSE, ARE LIMITED IN DURATION TO NINETY (90) DAYS FROM THE DATE OF DELIVERY. THIS WARRANTY GIVES YOU SPECIFIC LEGAL RIGHTS, AND YOU MAY ALSO HAVE OTHER RIGHTS WHICH VARY BY JURISDICTION.

7. Disclaimer of Warranty on Apple Software. You expressly acknowledge and agree that use of the Software and fonts is at your sole risk. The Software, related documentation and fonts are provided "AS IS" and without warranty of any kind, and Addison-Wesley Publishing Company and Addison-Wesley Publishing Company's Licensor(s) (for the purposes of provisions 7 and 8, Addison-Wesley Publishing Company and Addison-Wesley Publishing Company's Licensor(s) shall be collectively referred to as "Addison-Wesley Publishing Company") EXPRESSLY DISCLAIM ALL WARRANTIES, EXPRESS OR IMPLIED, INCLUDING, BUT NOT LIMITED TO, THE IMPLIED WARRANTIES OF MERCHANTABILITY AND FITNESS FOR A PARTICULAR PURPOSE. ADDISON-WESLEY PUBLISHING COMPANY DOES NOT WARRANT THAT THE FUNCTIONS CONTAINED IN THE SOFTWARE WILL MEET YOUR REQUIREMENTS, OR THAT THE OPERATION OF THE SOFTWARE WILL BE UNINTERRUPTED OR ERROR-FREE, OR THAT DEFECTS IN THE SOFTWARE AND THE FONTS WILL BE CORRECTED. FURTHERMORE, ADDISON-WESLEY PUBLISHING COMPANY DOES NOT WARRANT OR MAKE ANY REPRESENTATIONS REGARDING THE USE OR THE RESULTS OF THE USE OF THE SOFTWARE AND FONTS OR RELATED DOCUMENTATION IN TERMS OF THEIR CORRECTNESS, ACCURACY, RELIABILITY, OR OTHERWISE. NO ORAL OR WRITTEN INFORMATION OR ADVICE GIVEN BY ADDISON-WESLEY PUBLISHING COMPANY OR AN ADDISON-WESLEY PUBLISHING COMPANY AUTHORIZED REPRESENTATIVE SHALL CREATE A WARRANTY OR IN ANY WAY INCREASE THE SCOPE OF THIS WARRANTY. SHOULD THE SOFTWARE PROVE DEFECTIVE, YOU (AND NOT ADDISON-WESLEY PUBLISHING COMPANY OR AN ADDISON-WESLEY PUBLISHING COMPANY AUTHORIZED REPRESENTATIVE) AS-SUME THE ENTIRE COST OF ALL NECESSARY SERVICING, REPAIR OR CORRECTION, SOME JURISDICTIONS DO NOT ALLOW THE EXCLUSION OF IMPLIED WARRANTIES, SO THE ABOVE EXCLUSION MAY NOT APPLY TO YOU.

8. Limitation of Liability. UNDER NO CIRCUMSTANCES INCLUDING NEGLIGENCE, SHALL ADDISON-WESLEY PUBLISHING COMPANY BE LIABLE FOR ANY INCIDENTAL, SPECIAL OR CONSEQUENTIAL DAMAGES THAT RESULT FROM THE USE OR INABILITY TO USE THE SOFTWARE OR RELATED DOCUMENTATION, EVEN IF ADDISON-WESLEY PUBLISHING COMPANY OR AN ADDISON-WESLEY PUBLISHING COMPANY AUTHORIZED REPRESENTATIVE HAS BEEN ADVISED OF THE POSSIBILITY OF SUCH DAMAGES. SOME JURISDICTIONS DO NOT ALLOW THE LIMITATION OR EXCLUSION OF LIABILITY FOR INCIDENTAL OR CONSEQUENTIAL DAMAGES SO THE ABOVE LIMITATION OR EXCLUSION MAY NOT APPLY TO YOU.
In no event shall Addison-Wesley Publishing Company's total liability to you for all damages, losses, and causes of action (whether in contract, tort (including negligence) or otherwise) exceed the amount paid by you for the Software and fonts.

9. Controlling Law and Severability. This License shall be governed by and construed in accordance with the laws of the United States and the State of California, as applied to agreements entered into and to be performed entirely within California between California residents. If for any reason a court of competent jurisdiction finds any provision of this License, or portion thereof, to be unenforceable, that provision of the License shall be enforced to the maximum extent permissible so as to effect the intent of the parties, and the remainder of this License shall continue in full force and effect.

10. Complete Agreement. This License constitutes the entire agreement between the parties with respect to the use of the Software, the related documentation and fonts, and supersedes all prior or contemporaneous understandings or agreements, written or oral, regarding such subject matter. No amendment to or modification of this License will be binding unless in writing and signed by a duly authorized representative of Addison-Wesley Publishing Company.